PMBeck

To Bob, with all good wishes.

ALEXANDER POPE

Byron: The Years of Fame
Byron in Italy
Caroline of England
Four Portraits
John Ruskin: The Portrait of a Prophet
Hogarth's Progress
The Sign of the Fish
Shakespeare: The Poet and his Background
The Singular Preference (*essays*)

Alexander Pope and his dog Bounce; portrait by Jonathan Richardson, about 1718.

ALEXANDER POPE

THE EDUCATION OF GENIUS, 1688–1728

PETER QUENNELL

WEIDENFELD AND NICOLSON
5 WINSLEY STREET LONDON W1

SBN 297 76490 X

Printed in Great Britain by
C. Tinling & Co. Ltd.,
Liverpool, London and Prescot

To Alexander Quennell

b: 23 June 1967

Note

Source notes are collected at the end of the book, starting on page 261

Illustrations

Acknowledgments

Grateful acknowledgment is made for permission to reproduce the following pictures: frontispiece, by permission of the Viscount Cobham; 1, by courtesy of Mrs Browne-Swinburne; 2 and 3, by permission of the Lord Petre; 4, by permission of the Curators of the Bodleian Library; 5, by permission of the Marquess of Bute; 6 and 17, by permission of the National Portrait Gallery; 7, by permission of the Earl of Harrowby; 8 and 14, by courtesy of Mr Edward Malins; 9 and 13 by permission of Mrs Sonia Quennell; 10, 15 and 16, from the Devonshire Collection, Chatsworth, reproduced by permission of the Trustees of the Chatsworth Settlement; 12, by courtesy of the Earl Bathurst; 18, by courtesy of Hubert Bennet, FRIBA, Architect, Greater London Council; 19, by permission of the Rev. N. D. Gill; 20, by permission of the Board of Trinity College, Dublin; 22, by permission of the British Museum; 23, by permission of Dr Dallas Pratt.

Foreword

At the outset, this biography was intended to cover the whole extent of Pope's life. But, as time went on and my material accumulated, I was obliged to adopt a less ambitious plan; and the present study concludes with the year 1728 – a climacteric period in the poet's existence, when he reached his fortieth birthday and declared open war against the literary underworld by publishing his first *Dunciad*.

I have many debts to acknowledge. Like every modern student of Pope's life and work, I have received invaluable assistance from the late Professor George Sherburn's excellent volume, *The Early Career of Alexander Pope*, and from the editors of the splendid Twickenham Edition of Pope's poetic writings. It is their text I have employed throughout. Prose quotations, however, have been modernized, both in spelling and in punctuation, for the convenience of twentieth-century readers.

I am also deeply indebted to Dr Robert Halsband, who consented to read through and criticize the section devoted to Lady Mary Wortley Montagu; Mr James Lees-Milne, who kindly gave his imprimatur to my account of Lord Burlington; to Mr James Laver for advice about tye-wigs; and to Professor Bonamy Dobrée for friendly encouragement and the loan of an important book.

At the same time, I must thank Lord and Lady Bathurst, who welcomed me to Cirencester Park, which Pope, as the adviser of Lord Bathurst's ancestor, the 1st Earl, did so much to beautify; and Lord Harcourt, who entertained me at Stanton Harcourt, where, in 1718, Pope completed the fifth volume of his translation of the *Iliad*.

For permission to reproduce pictures I am grateful to the Earl Bathurst; Mr Hubert Bennet, Architect to the Greater London Council; the Curators of the Bodleian Library, Oxford; the Trustees of the British Museum; Mrs Browne-Swinburne; the Marquess of Bute; the Trustees of the Chatsworth Settlement; the Viscount Cobham; the Rev. N. D. Gill, of

St Mary's Parish Church, Battersea; the Earl of Harrowby; Mr Edward Malins; the Directors of the National Portrait Gallery; the Lord Petre; Dr Dallas Pratt; Mrs Sonia Quennell; the Board of Trinity College, Dublin.

Finally, I must express my gratitude to Miss Jacqueline Needham, Mrs de Mariassy, Mrs Hutchison and Mrs McAdam, who have patiently typed out my manuscript.

I

On 20 April 1706, Jacob Tonson, an important and distinguished figure in the London book-world, purchaser and publisher of *Paradise Lost*, an old associate of John Dryden, with whose help he had launched the famous series of *Miscellanies*, addressed from his shop at Gray's-Inn-Gate a letter to Alexander Pope at his father's house near Windsor.

The text was brief, but its message flattering. 'Sir,' wrote Tonson, 'I have lately seen a pastoral of yours in Mr Walsh's and Mr Congreve's hands, which is extremely fine and is generally approved of by the best judges in poetry. I remember I have formerly seen you at my shop, and am sorry I did not improve my acquaintance with you.' If the author intended his poem for the press, nobody should 'be more careful in the printing of it' than himself; 'nor no one can give greater encouragement to it. . . .' Though Pope's answering letter has now vanished, and his contributions to Tonson's *Poetical Miscellanies* – pastoral verses, a fragment translated from Homer and a modernized rendering of a Chaucerian tale – did not appear until three years later, on 2 May 1709, he must have responded with polite alacrity. When he received this agreeable overture he was only eighteen; and, despite the reputation that he had already acquired, both at home and in London literary circles, as an uncommonly gifted and precocious youth, none of his manuscripts had yet been published. He had begun to compose, however, while he was still a child, and had grown up under the shadow of a bookish father who, notwithstanding his keen taste for theological controversy, allowed the poetic art its proper due. Mr Pope would set his son to producing English verses; but, reported his widow, 'he was pretty difficult in being pleased'. 'These are not good rhymes', he would often remark severely, and send the boy away to turn them better.

Otherwise Alexander Pope the elder has left behind him few records. Born in April 1646, he was the offspring of an Anglican clergyman, also named Alexander Pope, rector of Thruxton in Hampshire,* whose gran-d son sometimes claimed that he was related to Lord Downe, a member of the Irish peerage. But the poet's father had earned his modest fortune as a London linen-merchant; his commercial apprenticeship is reputed to have taken him to Lisbon; and it was there possibly that he renounced the Anglican faith and made his submission to the Roman Catholic Church. Little is known of the merchant's first marriage, except that his wife Magdalen bore him a daughter who became the wife of Charles Rackett; but for his second wife he chose Editha Turner, the descendant of a worthy Yorkshire family, a sober gentlewoman four years older than her husband. Their son was born, in Lombard Street, presumably above his father's counting house, on 21 May 1688. That winter, on 5 November, the Prince of Orange, with an army of some fourteen thousand men, disembarked at Torbay. During the night of 11 December, James II fled from Whitehall, abandoning his throne and government; and by 28 December his future successor had arrived in London.

Meanwhile, during this prodigious 'Convulsion of State', a wave of terror and violence had struck the capital. Once their Stuart sovereign had withdrawn, a fierce Protestant mob poured into the centre of the city; Catholic chapels were attacked and burnt; Catholic embassies and legations were besieged and plundered. On 12 December a rumour circulated that a horde of bloodthirsty Irish Papists, cutting throats as it went, was advancing from the western suburbs; the chief thoroughfares were barricaded, and the London Trained Bands stood to arms. '. . . This shaking,' wrote John Evelyn to his fellow diarist Samuel Pepys, who had already suffered so acutely in the period of the so-called Popish Plot, 'menaces every corner, and the most philosophic breast cannot but be sensible of the motion.' It must certainly have shaken the courage of a Catholic linen-draper in Lombard Street. Nor, when the arrival of the Prince of Orange restored tranquillity and public order, can he have looked forward in a very hopeful spirit to the coronation of the new sovereigns. Under a staunchly Protestant government, the existing restrictions on the freedom of English Catholics would be revived and even reinforced. His fears were well-founded. Early in the reign of William and Mary, an act was passed 'for amoving papists and reputed papists from the cities of London and Westminster, and ten miles distance

* His father, Richard Pope, had kept the Angel Inn at Andover, where he ranked as an important citizen. Alexander was a protégé of the Paulett family, and married the daughter of another country clergyman. See George Sherburn, *The Early Career of Alexander Pope*, 1934.

from the same'. The elder Pope then decided to sell his business; and, having first taken a house at Hammersmith, a pleasantly secluded riverside village, between 1698 and 1700 he transferred his family to the neighbourhood of Windsor, where they occupied Whitehill House at Binfield, a small manor house with some fourteen acres of land. His son-in-law Charles Rackett, through whom he had effected the purchase,* lived at Hall Grove, Bagshot. Binfield Manor was the property of a Catholic squire, John Dancastle; and other Catholic families, including the Englefields of Whitenights, were established near by.

Thus Binfield, a scattered hamlet, and the adjacent forest-lands, rolling off northwards to Windsor and its castle, became the beloved background of the poet's youth. Here he developed into a gay and attractive child; at the age of ten, his face is said to have been 'round, plump and pretty, and of a fresh complexion';† and we are told that he was afterwards called 'the little nightingale' in tribute to his sweet voice. Naturally, he was educated as a Catholic; but his early education, he informed his admirer Joseph Spence, was exceedingly 'loose and disconcerted'. From the Popes' family priest named Banister, alias Taverner, he acquired the rudiments of Greek and Latin; and 'if it had not been for that', he added, 'I should never have got any language: for I never learned anything at the little schools I was at afterwards; and never should have followed anything that I could not follow with pleasure'. Among those useless schools was one at Twyford, near Winchester, where he 'wrote a satire on some Faults of his master' and was consequently 'whipped and ill-used'. Next he was despatched to London and joined 'Mr Deane's ‡ seminary at Marylebone', which presently moved to Hyde Park Corner. 'With the two latter masters' he 'lost what I had gained under the first. About twelve years old, I went with my father into the Forest, and there learned for a few months, under a fourth priest. This was all the teaching I ever had, and, God knows, it extended a very little way.'

Pope, in fact, like many gifted children, was principally self-instructed. Having 'learnt to read of an old aunt', Elizabeth Turner, he taught himself to write 'by copying from printed books'; and, once he had plunged into

* As a Catholic, Alexander Pope was legally debarred from holding land.

† Joseph Spence, *Observations, Anecdotes and Characters of Books and Men*, edited by James M. Osborn. Here Spence quotes both the poet's mother and Father William Mannock, the Racketts' family priest, who said that, as a boy, Pope had a 'great deal of sweetness in his look'. See Appendix A.

‡ 'Mr Deane . . . was depriv'd of his Fellowship of University-College in Oxford, soon after the Revolution; he having declared himself a Papist in the reign of King James. . . .' William Ayre, *Memoirs of the Life and Writings of Alexander Pope, Esq.*, 1745.

the study of Greek and Latin, 'I did not follow the grammar; but rather hunted in the authors for a syntax of my own: and then began translating any parts that pleased me particularly, in the best Greek and Latin poets: and by that means formed my taste; which, I think, verily, about sixteen, was very near as good as it is now'. Similarly, 'when I had done with my priests, I took to reading by myself, for which I had a very great eagerness and enthusiasm, especially for poetry. In a few years I had dipped into a great number of the English, French, Italian, Latin and Greek poets. This I did without any design but that of pleasing myself, and got the languages by hunting after the stories in the several poets I read ... I followed everywhere as my fancy led me ... like a boy gathering flowers in the fields and woods ...'* Ovid and Statius, the protégé of Domitian, author of a *Thebaid* and an *Achilleid*, were Latin poets, for whom he had a special fondness. Among the English poets, 'Waller, Spenser, and Dryden, were Mr Pope's great favourites in the order they are named. ...'

Here the writer's existence as a child bears some resemblance to that of John Ruskin, who, incidentally, when he began to use a quill, modelled the script he used on printed letters. Pope, too, was the son of middle-aged parents, and, under their devoted guardianship, must have lived just such a 'small, perky, contented, conceited, Cock-Robinson-Crusoe sort of life' as Ruskin has described in his unfinished autobiography. But Whitehill House was evidently a far happier place than the Victorian sherry-merchant's solemn villa. In this story of an Augustan childhood there is no mention of parental discipline; Pope was never beaten for interrupting his father's and mother's evening conferences, or thoughtlessly and selfishly tumbling downstairs. Mr Pope might criticize his son's verses. In other respects he allowed him to go his way, conduct his education as he pleased, and read the books that most amused him. Yet, although gentle, his parents' influence was strong; and the first piece of juvenile versification that Pope preserved among his adult poems – true, he was a diligent editor of his private memorials and, at a later period, he carefully touched it up – appears to be a poetic reflection of his father's point of view. Now he had severed his link with the metropolis and retreated to a Berkshire village, the retired merchant, who 'took great delight in husbandry and gardens', must frequently have talked of the advantages of a quiet country life, and explained how much he preferred his rustic solitude to the fret and hubbub of a vast commercial city. His son seems

---

* Spence, op. cit. Spence owned the manuscript of an early translation of the Ovidian story of Acis and Galatea: 'the title-page ... is so like print, that it requires a good eye ... to distinguish it'.

to have adopted the hint. The poem that resulted was far from original – his theme, the blessings that an unambitious recluse enjoys, is nearly as old as European literature; but the effect it produces is delightfully fluent and easy, and its simple, neatly turned stanzas have a beguiling, unaffected rhythm:

> Happy the man, whose wish and care
> A few paternal acres bound,
> Content to breathe his native air
> In his own ground . . .
>
> Blest! who can unconcern'dly find
> Hours, days, and years, slide soft away,
> In health of body, peace of mind,
> Quiet by day,
>
> Sound sleep by night; study and ease
> Together mix'd; sweet recreation,
> And innocence, which most does please,
> With meditation.
>
> Thus let me live, unseen, unknown;
> Thus unlamented let me dye;
> Steal from the world, and not a stone,
> Tell where I lye.

These lines, according to Pope's early biographer William Ayre,* were composed, and, one assumes, approved by his father, 'in the year 1700', when their author 'wanted a few days of twelve years of age'. So far Pope's development, both physical and intellectual, had been extra-ordinarily smooth and fortunate; and the worst mishap that had yet befallen him occurred while he was 'a child in coats', playing amid the Binfield pastures and heaping stones into a little barrow. 'A wild cow that was driven by the place where he was at play, struck him with her horns', tore off the feathered hat tied under his chin, 'wounded him in the throat, beat him down, and trampled over him'.† In Pope's existence cows were dangerous animals; for, when he was twelve, he suddenly succumbed to a malignant and disfiguring illness, which his guardians attributed to his

* William Ayre, op. cit. An early version of these lines appears in a letter from Pope to Henry Cromwell, dated 11 July 1709, where he describes it as a 'short Ode on Solitude . . . written when I was not yet twelve years old' and discovered 'yesterday by great accident'.

† Spence, op. cit. Spence's authority was Pope's half-sister, Mrs Rackett, who 'was by when it happened'.

sedentary habits – 'his perpetual application (after he had set to study of himself)' – but which has since been diagnosed as Pott's Disease, a tuberculous affection of the spine that causes the collapse of a vertebra, saps the strength of the vertebral column and at length deforms the whole body. The disease is transmitted through infected milk; somewhere near Whitehill House a tuberculous milch cow was tethered beneath the roof of an insanitary byre. Its presence determined Pope's destiny and may well have supplied an important factor in the evolution of his adult genius. The plump, good-looking, fresh-faced child was to become a hopeless and, as time went by, an almost helpless invalid.

For the moment he seems to have recovered; but before long he once again collapsed; and none of the physicians his parents called in could produce an efficacious remedy, until a well-known London practitioner, Dr Radcliffe, consulted by the good Abbé Southcote, recommended the benefits of air and exercise, and suggested he should go out riding. On these daily rides through the Forest that lay at his door the companion Pope chose was a sexagenarian diplomatist. Sir William Trumbull, a Protestant neighbour at Easthamsted, had served Charles II and James II as envoy and envoy extraordinary to the courts of Turin, Florence, France and to the Sublime Porte, and under King William had been appointed Lord of the Treasury and afterwards Secretary of State. But in 1697 he had resigned the latter office and was enjoying a life of literary seclusion, often visiting the family at Binfield, from whose garden he received presents of delicious 'hartichokes'.* It is an agreeable picture – Pope, mounted on the cob or pony that would have suited his tender years and fragile health; Sir William, jack-booted, plumed and periwigged, with velvet coat and jewelled order, bestriding one of the huge and heavy horses – possibly a rampant stallion – that in English stables had not yet been replaced by the lighter Middle-Eastern breeds. Both riders were passionately addicted to poetry; they conversed as fellow enthusiasts and as fellow men of the world. 'We used,' Pope recollected, 'to take a ride out together three or four days in the week, and at last almost every day.'

'From this gentleman's acquaintance,' remarks William Ayre, 'we may date Mr Pope's first entrance into the polite world', the society of fashionable persons and men of wit and learning; and Sir William, we are further

---

* 'I wish also I could learn some more skill in gardening from your father (to whom, with your good mother, all our services are presented, with thanks for the hartichokes). . . .' Sir William Trumbull to Pope, 15 June 1705. George Sherburn, *The Correspondence of Alexander Pope*, 1956.

informed, gave him 'leave to call him patron'. But new patrons very soon emerged; the *cognoscenti* were pleased to examine and criticize his early works. Besides a praiseworthy, if somewhat conventional, rendering of the *Thebaid* of Statius, he was engaged on an ambitious epic, 'which I begun a little after I was twelve', and which occupied his attention until the age of fifteen. In that production he had 'endeavoured . . . to collect all the beauties of the great epic writers . . . there was Milton's style in one part and Cowley's in another; here the style of Spenser imitated and there of Statius; here Homer and Virgil, and there Ovid and Claudian'. The hero was Alcander, Prince of Rhodes; 'there was an underwater scene in the first book . . . I wrote four books toward it, of about a thousand verses each. . . .' A slightly earlier effort was 'a kind of play, which I got to be acted by my school-fellows. It was a number of speeches from the *Iliad*, tacked together with verses of my own'. For some time Pope preserved a copy of the epic, but finally burned it in 1723 at the prudent suggestion of his friend the Bishop of Rochester.

At this stage, Pope's precocious facility of expression now and then alarmed his intimates. 'For you know, to speak plain with you', admitted Mrs Rackett, 'my brother had a maddish way with him'; and a literary acquaintance, Edmund or 'Rag' Smith, 'after being in Mr Pope's company when about fourteen', declared that 'that young fellow will either be a madman or make a very great poet'. The adolescent's restless, enquiring spirit was ridiculously ill-suited to his fragile body; as his intelligence expanded, his physical organism lagged behind. Soon its development was completely arrested. Meanwhile the disease that had begun to deform his back brought with it sleeplessness and agonizing headaches; and he experienced long spells of pain and lassitude, accompanied by profound depression. Even as an adolescent he sometimes despaired; and before he was sixteen (he assured Spence) he had at one moment 'resolved to give way to his distemper, and sat down calmly, in a full expectation of death . . . to take a last farewell of some of his more particular friends. . . .' But again he rallied. On Pope's side were both intense natural vitality and a resolute, ambitious character; already he was laying his plans – not haphazard, vaguely and fancifully, as most ambitious adolescents do, but with an exact appreciation of the task that he had set himself. He possessed, moreover, a keen historic sense; and, if he cultivated the friendship of older men – we never hear of Pope as a boy showing any particular regard for masculine companions of his own age – it was because they provided an imaginative link between the present and the past.

He had been 'about twelve', Pope believed, when he had first ventured into Will's Coffee House – he may have come straight from 'Mr Deane's seminary' – to pay his silent homage to the greatest of living poets, who sat enthroned there amid his courtiers and companions, in winter months next to the hearth, and on a balcony above the street in summer. Dryden was almost a septuagenarian; within a year he would be gone. Pope 'observed him very particularly'; he never forgot that memorable face. It was rounded and rosy, noted the boy; but the ageing poet had a downcast look, and appeared 'not very conversible'. Nor was he 'very genteel'; he had lived too much among literary people; and Pope was learning to admire the free-and-easy air of men of fashion. Yet a master-poet he undoubtedly was; like some high-arched Roman bridge, Dryden's work had carried on the Elizabethan genius across from the Giant Age 'before the Flood'* into the later seventeenth century. Now the eighteenth century had dawned; and he had bidden the old world good-bye in his poignant *Secular Masque*. He typified genius, integrity, fame, breadth of accomplishment and strength of purpose – all the attributes that, as a man and an artist, the adult Pope would most value.

During the course of the next two or three years, largely spent on the verge of Windsor Forest, writing, drawing – he had become a proficient amateur draughtsman – or jogging with Trumbull along the forest-paths, he cannot often have returned to Will's. But in 1705 he revisited the upper-storey room, which overlooked Russell Street, at the end of Bow Street, Covent Garden, where the young wits, who otherwise kept their distance, had formerly esteemed it a special privilege to take a pinch from Dryden's snuff-box; and he was then conducted by a young Catholic acquaintance, the Chevalier Charles Wogan.† He had had the honour, Wogan subsequently told Swift, of bringing Pope up to London, dressing him 'à la mode' and introducing him to the assembled company. Englishmen of the Age of Anne were no less gregarious, no less devoted to convivial gatherings and public debate, than their Elizabethan ancestors. Every clique, fashionable, political or literary, had some appointed meeting-place, customarily a chocolate house or coffee house. Rich young gamblers frequented White's, Tory politicians the Cocoa Tree, their Whiggish adversaries the St James's; and Will's was the home of the intelligentsia, poets, journalists and dilettante critics. Will's was presently to give way to Button's when Addison moved his 'little senate' across the street to a house kept by an old servant whom he had recently set up in business. At the

* 'Theirs was the Giant Race, before the Flood . . .' Dryden: 'To my Dear Friend Mr Congreve', 1694.

† Wogan was a devoted Jacobite, afterwards associated with the Old Pretender.

beginning of the century, however, it was still the haunt of Dryden's circle. Congreve, for example, was to be seen there, accompanied by his fellow-dramatist William Wycherley, the vigorously talkative relic of a vanished social period.

Wycherley, as it happened, Pope had met a year earlier, probably through Sir William Trumbull; and an odd friendship was springing up between the innocent, precocious novice and the jaded literary veteran. Like Dryden on a considerably higher level, Wycherley had a strong historic interest; the reign of Charles II now seemed as remote as the legendary epoch of the Civil Wars. Almost twenty years had gone by since the King's death: some thirty-three since the author of *Love in a Wood* had enjoyed a particularly gratifying triumph. Just after that comedy appeared, 'as Mr Wycherley was going thro' Pall Mall . . . in his chariot', he had passed another chariot occupied by the Duchess of Cleveland, Charles II's ruling favourite, with whose proud inaccessible beauty Pepys had once been glad to 'fill his eyes', and whose smocks and petticoats, hung up to air in the Privy Garden, had, he related, done him good to look upon. 'Thrusting half her body' out of the window, 'You, Wycherley, you are the son of a whore,' she cried, 'at the same time laughing aloud and heartily'.* Wycherley, we learn, was 'very much surprised'; until it occurred to him that she was merely making a civil reference to a lyric from his new comedy;† at which he ordered his coachman to drive back and overtake her chariot, exchanged some further complimentary badinage and added a bold suggestion that they should meet that evening in the playhouse. Naturally, he became the favourite's lover, and, while he prosecuted his career as a modern dramatist, was soon playing a decorative rôle among the good-natured King's attendants. Wycherley's masterpiece, *The Country Wife*, was published in 1675: *The Plain Dealer* in 1676. But then a single disastrous mis-step – his clandestine marriage to the widowed Lady Drogheda, whom he had met in a Tunbridge Wells bookshop where he heard her enquiring for his latest play – had ruined all his worldly chances. The King, though he had had thoughts of appoint-

* John Dennis: *Familiar Letters*, 1721.

    † When parents are slaves,
      Their brats cannot be any other;
      Great wits and great braves
      Have always a punk to their mother.
        Love in a Wood: or St James's Park, Act I, Scene II.

By the time Wycherley met the Duchess, probably in 1671, she seems to have been already past her prime; for Pepys writes on 11 October 1664: 'My wife tells me the sad news of Lady Castlemayne's being now so decayed, that one would not know her, which I am sorry for.' Lady Castlemaine was created Duchess of Cleveland in August 1670.

ing Wycherley guardian to his illegitimate son, the Duke of Richmond, immediately withdrew his favour; and Lady Drogheda herself proved to be a jealous scold. She died young, leaving an ample fortune; but her family disputed the will and involved him in a costly law-suit. Broken and bankrupt, Wycherley was consigned to the Fleet, and there vegetated four miserable years.

It was Charles's hapless brother and successor who eventually rescued him from prison. Having been persuaded to attend a revival of *The Plain Dealer* and informed about the author's sufferings, James had agreed to discharge his most urgent debts and grant him an annual pension of two hundred pounds; which, with the meagre remains of his family property, allowed him a fairly comfortable existence. Such was Pope's new friend – according to Father William Mannock, a member of the Rackett household, the 'first poet-friend' he ever made. Sixty-four in the year 1704, ageing but incorrigibly ribald, superannuated yet still ambitious, Wycherley was also, Pope discovered, astonishingly absent-minded. He had a 'nobleman look', and was 'not unvain of his face'; but, as he contemplated the engraving of a portrait for which he had sat before the age of thirty – the sleek, arrogant, large-nosed mask of a practised *homme à bonnes fortunes* – he used sometimes to repeat, 'with a melancholy emphasis', the words, '*Quantum mutatus ab illo*', that he had had inscribed beneath the likeness. Pope owned another portrait of him, 'drawn when he was very old'. The artist, Sir Godfrey Kneller, had volunteered to produce 'a very fine head without a wig'; and 'it was drawn at first with his little straggling grey hair'. The venerable beau 'could not bear it when done', and Sir Godfrey was obliged to add a wig – an ornament that, framing the cheeks and the brow, cast a grateful shade on age-worn features.

As a dramatist, Wycherley had long been mute; but the vanity of a once-triumphant writer somehow never quite expires; and in 1704 he had decided to publish a collection of *Miscellany Poems*, the carelessly thrown-off 'madrigals' with which from time to time he had amused his leisure moments. Their reception was not completely satisfying; and he was inclined to suspect that, for all their wit, verve and gentlemanly devil-may-care abandon, his rhymes might lack a certain literary elegance. In this mood, he welcomed a young disciple; and it must have occurred to him that a sympathetic admirer would one day make an extremely serviceable aide. His reception of Pope was condescending and encouraging. Towards the end of the year 1704, the sixteen-year-old boy was invited to call upon him at his London rooms, and duly arrived, a shy and quiet visitor, not yet dressed 'à la mode', but wearing his own short-cut locks. Charles Gildon, a critic who had good cause to dislike Pope, afterwards described how, at that time, he himself had had occasion to visit Wycherley, and found in the dramatist's chamber a diminutive, rough-headed and round-shouldered youth, a 'little *Aesopic* sort of an animal in his own cropt hair, and dress agreeable to the Forest he came from. I confess the gentleman was very silent all my stay there, and scarce uttered three words on any subject we talked of. . . . I thought indeed he might be some tenant's son of his, who might make his court for continuance in his lease on the decease of his rustic parent, but was sufficiently surprised when Mr Wycherley afterwards told me he was poetically inclined, and writ tolerably smooth verses.' When Pope retired to Whitehill House, he wrote his 'poetic friend' a carefully phrased epistle:

It was certainly a great satisfaction to me to see and converse with a man, whom in his writings I had so long known with pleasure. But it was a high addition to it, to hear you, at our very first meeting, doing justice to your dead friend Mr Dryden. I was not so happy as to know him; *Virgilium tantum vidi* – Had I been born early enough, I must have known and lov'd him: for I have been assur'd, not only by yourself, but by Mr Congreve and Sir William Trumbull, that his personal qualities were as amiable as his poetical. . . .

Pope's letter is dated 26 December 1704; and the correspondence thus launched was to continue until 2 May 1710.* Like other correspondences of the day, the letters exchanged by Pope and Wycherley seem today decidedly formal, even somewhat prosy and affected. Each correspondent seizes the opportunity to parade his literary airs and graces, and to interpose sententious maxims. '. . . Critics,' observes Pope, 'as they are birds of prey, have ever a natural inclination to carrion. And though such poor writers as I are but beggars, however no beggar is so poor but he can keep a cur, and no author is so beggarly but he can keep a critic.' On 25 January, Wycherley replied by apologizing for having 'omitted to return you an answer to your most ingenious letter. So scribblers to the public, like bankers to the public, are profuse in their voluntary loans to it, whilst they forget to pay their more private and particular, as more just debts, to their best and nearest friends. However, I hope, you who have as much good nature as good sense, (since they generally are companions) will have patience with a debtor, who . . . has an inclination to pay you his obligations, if he had wherewithal ready about him. . . .'

Wycherley also excused his dilatoriness by alleging that he had recently been much occupied 'in correcting and transcribing some of my madrigals

---

* Pope afterwards reprinted these letters, with various additions and improvements.

for a great man or two who desir'd to see them. . . .' But he did not immediately suggest that Pope should assist him in his editorial work; and it is only after the lapse of a year, on 5 February 1706, when many ceremonious missives had passed to and fro between Whitehill House and Wycherley's rooms in Bow Street, that we find a mention of a 'paper to Mr Dryden' that the young poet had been good enough to correct and cut down. Wycherley was grateful, but at the same time slightly nettled. Of course, the poem had gained much by losing so many superfluous lines: 'I own you have made more of it by making it less, as the Dutch are said to burn half the spices they bring home to enhance the price of the remainder, so to be greater gainers by their loss, (which is indeed my case now). Well, you have prun'd my fading laurels of some superfluous, sapless, and dead branches, to make the remainder live the longer. . . .' Yet, although Wycherley was not altogether pleased to watch his poetic branches falling, evidently he had decided that he must not flinch. Next month he returned to the subject: 'Now after all, I must lay a penance on you, which is to desire you to look over that damned miscellany of madrigals of mine, to pick out (if possible) some that may be so altered that they may yet appear in print again, I hope with better success. . . .' Pope replied by enquiring just how thoroughly he was expected to perform his office – 'whether it was to pick out the best of those verses . . . to make the method and numbers exact, and avoid repetitions . . . or if you mean to improve the worst pieces, which are such as, to render them very good, would require a great addition, and almost the entire new writing of them? Or, lastly, if you mean the middle sort? . . . For these will need only to be shortened . . . the words remaining very little different from what they were before.'

The full comedy of the situation may perhaps escape a reader who has not himself at some time been a writer. Literary nerves are always overstrained; a poet's feelings are unconscionably sensitive. Whatever his secret doubts and forebodings, a professional author is bound to be deeply disturbed by any violation of his own text; and the critic Wycherley had called in was young enough to be his grandson. Still, the older man courageously persisted, and the younger bravely persevered, always civil yet always resolute and firm, never hesitating to cut or re-word a passage where he felt that he could improve its style or meaning. Pope had accepted a remarkably delicate commission; for, although Wycherley had once been a masterly playwright with an abrasive sense of fun and a splendid flow of tart colloquial dialogue, he was at his best a coarse and clumsy versifier, whose awkward attempts to revive the libertine mood of his heyday produce a singularly lugubrious impression. Those sad trifles Pope edited and recast. Three poems, on 'solitude', 'a middle life' and 'a life of business',* received particularly strenuous attention; certainly they are less inept than most of the surrounding pieces. And then, the old dramatist had lost his memory, as the result of a fever he had contracted a quarter of a century earlier; 'the same chain of thought would return into his mind at the distance of two or three years, without his remembering that it had been there before'. Pope would point out these recurrent ideas; and Wycherley would ruefully acknowledge that his friend was in the right, exclaiming 'Gads-so, so 'tis! I thank you very much – pray blot it out'.

Just as tiresome was his habit of unconscious plagiarism. Having read himself to sleep with one of his favourite books, Montaigne, La Roche-foucauld, or Seneca, he awoke next morning cheered by the delightful belief that the sentences and images that ran in his head had originated from his own intelligence. Again Pope would patiently point out the error; and the sleeper awakened would meekly, if reluctantly, agree. But nothing could satisfy the perfectionist critic: not content with removing and inserting lines, he persuaded his victim to demolish some of his poetic edifices and, since Wycherley's mind had an epigrammatic turn, re-assemble the fragments in a sheaf of sagacious prose reflections. Wycherley, admitted Pope to Spence, 'was really angry with me for correcting his verses so much. I was extremely plagued, up and down, for almost two years. . . .' But, at the outset, he certainly enjoyed their meetings; while Wycherley became genuinely devoted to his 'great little friend', in whose character, as it emerged from the crysalis of childhood, experience and innocence, wisdom and naïvety, combined to form so rare a pattern. Like Sir William Trumbull, he treated his young companion as an adult *homme du monde*, moreover as a fellow rake, complaining, for example, of the 'damned battered jades' with whom he had just been 'jumbling' in a public coach, or reminding him of an anecdote – one that he believed he might have told already – about the Spanish Lady who 'said to her poor poetical gallant, that a queen, if she lay with a groom, would expect a mark of his kindness from him, though it were but his curry-comb'.

Pope's next 'poet-friend' was William Walsh, a versifying Member of Parliament, author of *Letters and Poems Amorous and Gallant*, whose own works merit little notice, but whom Dryden had acclaimed as 'without flattery . . . the best critic of our nation'. Correctitude was Walsh's forte;

* I have assumed these poems to be 'For Solitude and Retirement', 'For the Various Mix'd Life' and 'For the Publick Active Life'.

'he encouraged me much', remembered Pope, 'and used to tell me that there was one way left of excelling, for though we had several great poets, we never had any one great poet that was correct – and he desired me to make that my study and aim'. In 1707,* Pope, who had already begun his life-long round of pleasant country houses, was to spend 'a good part of the summer' at Walsh's seat, Abberley in Worcestershire; and Walsh corrected Pope's translation of Statius and criticized some of his more original products. A 'knowing' gentleman, who held a minor position at Court and 'loved to be well dressed', in literature he distrusted conceits and 'glaring thoughts' of the kind that had been popularized by poets of the previous age, doubted whether Petrarch, unlike Catullus, Tibullus, Propertius and Ovid, had had a genuine human affection for the mistress whom he served, and exalted a classical simplicity based upon a strict fidelity to Nature. At the same time, he warned Pope that 'a man may correct his verses till he takes away the true spirit of them, especially if he submits to the correction of some who pass for great critics', and slavishly adopted their 'mechanical rules', which disregarded a poet's native genius. He found Pope's *Pastorals*, he observed to Wycherley on 20 April 1705, 'very tender and easy', and their preface 'very judicious and very learned'; and in June 1706, having received a letter from the poet – presumably they had been introduced at Will's – he wrote earnestly soliciting the 'continuance of a correspondence' through which he felt he would be 'so great a gainer'.

A more lasting influence was that of Dr Samuel Garth, renowned physician and celebrated author of a mock-heroic poem *The Dispensary*. Pope believed that they had met in 1703; and, although his recollections perhaps have erred – he was always fond of emphasizing his own precocity – there is no doubt that he must have encountered Garth soon after he came up to London. Everybody esteemed the poetic physician, whom Mr Townley, a cultivated Lancashire squire, called the 'most agreeable companion I ever knew', and Pope, 'one of the best-natured men in the world'. Garth was an avowed sceptic; but, 'if ever there was a good Christian', declared the poet, 'without knowing himself to be so, it was Dr Garth'. No physician, added Spence, knew his art as thoroughly, 'nor his trade less'. When he lay dying in 1719 and discovered that his case was desperate, he first endeavoured to make a philosophic end, by ordering that he should be bled, tearing off the surgeon's bandages and lying back quietly until his life had drained away, then declined to 'use any remedies'

* In conversation with Spence, Pope gave the date as 1705, but Sherburn, op. cit., thinks that the actual date was probably 1707. See letter from Trumbull to Bridges, quoted p. 22.

and 'let his distemper take its course'. Some three years before he expired, Garth, we are told, ceased talking in his usual 'libertine manner'. He was 'rather doubtful, and fearful, than religious'; but he was accustomed to say that, 'if there was any such thing as religion 'twas among the Roman Catholics'; and Pope was convinced that, like Wycherley, in his last hours he had received the Catholic sacraments. Meanwhile, he was still a delightful talker and an agreeably accomplished writer. *The Dispensary*, published in 1699 and often reprinted throughout the eighteenth century, is not a very good poem. Yet it has a certain individual charm, and can show a number of attractive lines, for example the triplet on death, a subject in which, both as a man of science and as an epicurean philosopher, the poet felt a special interest:

> To Die, is Landing on some silent Shoar,
> Where Billows never break, nor Tempests roar:
> Ere well we feel the friendly Stroke, 'tis o'er.

– a series of pretty botanical passages:

> At the sad Tale you tell, the Poppies weep,
> And mourn their vegetable Souls asleep.
> The unctuous *Larix*, and the healing *Pine*,
> Lament your fate in Tears of Turpentine.

– and amusing flights of mythological fancy:

> So when the Pigmies, marshall'd on the Plains,
> Wage puny War against th' invading Cranes;
> The Poppets to their Bodkin Spears repair,
> And scatter'd Feathers flutter in the Air:
> But when the bold imperial Bird of *Jove*
> Stoops on his sounding Pinions from above,
> Among the Brakes the Fairy Nation crowds,
> And the *Strimonian* Squadron seeks the Clouds.

Otherwise the going is apt to be heavy. Garth gives us a mock-heroic picture of the battle between London's physicians and apothecaries (whom some recreant physicians had decided to support) over the proposed establishment of a dispensary 'for the relief of the sick poor', which was to provide free or inexpensive drugs. 'The description of the battle (according to the author's preface) is grounded upon a feud that happened in the dispensary . . .' Syringes, pestles, chamber-pots and close-stool pans are the weapons that the antagonists employ; and among a series of literary personifications – Night, Death, Envy, Sloth, Disease, Health, Discontent,

Faction and Hypocrisy – we find savage satirical portraits of fellow-practitioners whom Garth particularly disliked, abortionists, fashionable quacks and purblind academic drones. But Pope's admirer, if he troubles to study the poem, is often haunted by a vague suspicion that he has met a line or couplet elsewhere, in a very different, much more spacious context; and it soon occurs to him that, although Pope may not have borrowed from Garth – as he would borrow and adapt a beautiful isolated phrase from Lady Winchilsea – his old friend's poem may have lingered in the background of his mind, and that, while he was imagining and writing, he was also unconsciously remembering. An image or simile would float to the surface, which he seized upon and gave a novel form. Thus Garth's pensive dew-drenched floweret –

> Tell me, dear Shade, from whence such anxious Care,
> Your Looks disorder'd, and your Bosom bare?
> Why thus you languish like a drooping Flow'r,
> Crush'd by the Weight of some relentless Show'r?

– receives a sharp satiric twist, and the image is applied to a noble poetaster-patron who, hearing himself lauded by a parsonic client, affects a languorous air of false modesty:

> Narcissus, prais'd with all a Parson's pow'r,
> Look'd a white lilly, sunk beneath a show'r.*

The creative artist possesses an unequalled gift not only of inventing, but of recollecting and assimilating. From all his early friends – Trumbull, Wycherley, Walsh and Garth – Pope took something that his genius needed; but Garth's contribution, both as a writer and a man, would seem, on the whole, to have had most lasting value.

Simultaneously, he was gathering fashionable acquaintances, even more distinguished than a one-time ambassador or a Member of Parliament with a place at Court. George Granville, created Lord Lansdowne in 1712, was a leading Tory magnate. But politics did not monopolize his attention; he enjoyed literary pursuits and the company of writers; and about 1705 or 1706 he wrote to a friend called 'Harry', offering to introduce him to Wycherley and, at the same time, to a young author of pastoral poems who had already shown extraordinary talent. Granville's London lodging was the place appointed:

I can give you no Falernum that has out-lived twenty consulships, but I can promise you a bottle of good old claret that has seen two reigns. . . . He shall

* The Dunciad, Book IV, 1742. Both poets, of course, were indebted to famous passages in the Iliad and the Aeneid.

bring with him, if you will, a young poet, newly inspired, in the neighbourhood of Cooper's Hill, whom he and Walsh have taken under their wing;
his name is Pope; he is not above seventeen or eighteen years of age, and
promises miracles. If he goes on as he has begun, in the Pastoral way, as Virgil
first tried his strength, we may hope to see English poetry vie with the Roman,
and this Swan of Windsor sing as sweetly as the Mantuan.*

Granville was not by any means Pope's only admirer in the world of high
politics; many other important gentlemen passed around his early verses,
often discovering faults and raising various 'objections' that he did his best
to satisfy. In a note on the manuscript of his pastorals, having first acknowledged his indebtedness to Walsh, Congreve, Garth and Sir William
Trumbull, he records opposite the first page, written in his minutely
delicate typographical script, that this copy had passed through the hands
of 'Ld. Halifax, Ld. Wharton, Marq. of Dorchester, D. of Bucks, &c....
The alterations from this copy were upon the objections of some of these,
or my own.' Pope, during his literary apprenticeship, was singularly
responsive to the criticism of well-meaning amateurs. His juvenile poems
were intended for 'the polite world', and would be more eagerly read if
the arbiters of that world felt that they themselves had had some share in
administering a final polish.

Years later, as he reviewed his literary progress, Pope again drew up an
impressive list of his poetic benefactors. Fame, he implies, had been thrust
upon him. He had 'lisped in numbers'; and these infantile numbers had
at once received a kindly hearing. With such an audience could he have
failed to continue?

> *Granville* the polite
> And knowing *Walsh*, would tell me I could write;
> Well-natur'd *Garth* inflam'd with early praise,
> And *Congreve* lov'd, and *Swift* endur'd my lays;
> The Courtly *Talbot, Somers, Sheffield* read,
> Ev'n mitred *Rochester* would nod the head,
> And *St John*'s self (great *Dryden*'s friends before)
> With open arms receiv'd one Poet more.

Here we remark that he has omitted Wycherley and Trumbull – the old
dramatist aroused irritating memories; while Sir William's solid British
surname would have been difficult to fit into heroic verse – but has
included Lords Talbot, Somers (Queen Anne's Lord President of the

* Lansdowne: *Works*, 1732. *Cooper's Hill* is, of course, the title of Sir John Denham's
famous historical-topographical poem, published in 1642, one of the first English poems of
its kind, and much beloved by eighteenth-century critics.

17

Council), Sheffield (otherwise the Duke of Buckingham), and the Jacobite Bishop of Rochester, Dr Francis Atterbury, none of whom, despite their link with Dryden, can have afforded any real assistance. Swift and St John, on the other hand, were invaluable allies and beloved members of his private circle. They cannot be said, however, to have protected his youth and seconded his early efforts, since neither of them seems to have made his acquaintance before 1711 or 1712, when his work had appeared in print and his reputation was already flourishing.

Meanwhile he was still involved with the pastorals that would soon come to Jacob Tonson's notice. He had undertaken them as a means of poetic exercise; and it is as exercises that we should judge their merit. Whereas the modern poet often begins his career with a period of wild experiment, Pope adopted the forms that lay ready to hand and did his best to refine on a poetic convention established by his predecessors. This convention was exceedingly artificial, and had had a highly artificial origin. Theocritus had been born in Syracuse, and Doric was his native tongue; but he spent most of his life in the huge cosmopolitan city of Alexandria at the oriental court of Ptolemy Philadelphus and his sister-queen Arsinoë, and in the classrooms and courtyards of the Museum, the greatest repository of literary tradition that the ancient world could show. His shepherds probably bear as little resemblance to any countryman encountered in real life as A. E. Housman's Shropshire yokels; and his Sicily, like Housman's Shropshire, is largely the creation of nostalgic feeling. Later pastoral poets, from Virgil to Tasso and Spenser – though Spenser had made an enterprising attempt to accommodate his personages to an English country landscape – had followed much the same road; and by the end of the seventeenth century pastoral versification had become an elaborate literary pastime, with strict rules governing the poet's choice of subject, the language his shepherd and shepherdesses spoke, and the mellifluous sentiments they expressed in song.* Virgil and Spenser, it was felt, had now and then gone astray by introducing 'allegorical' themes beyond a simple rustic's comprehension; for, as Pope announced in the 'Discourse on Pastoral Poetry',† the true object of pastoral literature was

* The two recent authorities most often quoted were the mid-seventeenth-century René Rapin and his successor Bernard de Fontenelle. Rapin deduced his rules from the ancients; while Fontenelle invoked the aid of modern Reason. But 'it is possible to imagine pastorals written according to the premises of the one being very much like pastorals written according to the premises of the other'. *Pastoral Poetry and An Essay on Criticism*, edited by E. Audra and Aubrey Williams, Introduction. Twickenham Edition.

† This essay remained unpublished until 1717, when it appeared among Pope's collected *Works*.

to recreate the Golden Age, and to produce a 'perfect image of that happy time; which, by giving us an esteem for the virtues of a former age, might recommend them to the present. And since the life of shepherds was attended with more tranquillity than any other rural employment, the poets chose to introduce their persons. . . . A pastoral is an imitation of the action of a shepherd; the form . . . is dramatic, or narrative, or mixed of both; the fable simple, the manners not too polite nor too rustic. . . .' An 'air of piety to the Gods should shine through the poem. . . . As for the numbers themselves . . . they should be the smoothest, the most easy and flowing imaginable.'

Such was the poet's own view of the difficult form that he was handling. 'Simplicity, brevity and delicacy', a blend of realism and nostalgic emotion, were the qualities he sought to cultivate; and they are not qualities we can today distinguish in the limpid, but somewhat colourless *Pastorals*. During later years, Pope himself was inclined to question their poetic interest, and compared them to the work of a courtly rhymer whom, at the moment, he particularly detested and despised:

> Soft were my Numbers, who could take offence
> While pure Description held the place of Sense?
> Like gentle *Fanny's* was my flowery Theme,
> A painted Mistress, or a purling Stream.*

'Spring', 'Summer', 'Autumn',† 'Winter', all merge into one slow-moving pageant, only differentiated by some conventional touches to mark the progress of the year and the change of season. The verse flows smoothly; but it has the silken smoothness of a stone-paved garden-rill. His shepherds and their bevy of shepherdesses are presented as indistinguishable puppets. When his *Pastorals* appeared in Tonson's collection, they were printed alongside those of Ambrose Philips; and there seems little to choose between Pope's provocative Delia –

> Me gentle *Delia* beckons from the Plain,
> Then hid in Shades, eludes her eager Swain;
> But feigns a Laugh, to see me search around,
> And by that Laugh the willing Fair is found.

and Philips' no less teasing Lydia –

* 'An Epistle to Dr Arbuthnot'. It has often been suggested that Pope is referring here to *The Rape of the Lock;* but that was a poem of which he never felt ashamed.

† Pope himself claimed that his third eclogue had been written last. In September 1706 Walsh reminds the poet that he has not yet seen it.

> As I to cool me bath'd one sultry day,
> Fond *Lydia* lurking in the sedges lay.
> The wanton laugh'd, and seem'd in haste to fly;
> Yet often stopp'd, and often turned her eye.

The music of the verse, which delighted contemporaries – and has won praise from a modern poet, who speaks of the 'delicate sense of texture which was, in later years, to produce . . . a thousand variations in speed, a thousand differences in texture, height and depth' – now strikes us as strangely weak and thin; it is a melodious, monotonous rivulet, seldom increasing either its volume or its pace. Yet even now Pope reveals his ·mastery of the couplet, the art he was presently to develop of welding two lines of heroic verse into a separate melodic entity:

> The moving Mountains hear the pow'rful Call,
> And headlong Streams hang list'ning in their Fall!

He shows, too, that, although still a voluntary prisoner of the numerous restrictions that his form imposed, and never reluctant to equip a noun with its customary poetic epithet – shades are 'cool'; sprays, 'blooming'; groves, 'shady'; showers, 'vernal' – he had already a devoted regard for his medium and was beginning rapidly to extend his control over the vast resources of the English language.*

Pope must have completed the bulk of his eclogues by the spring of 1705, when Wycherley passed them on to Walsh, and Walsh delivered an approving judgement; but it was not until April 1706 that Tonson's letter arrived at Whitehill House. This professional accolade was doubly welcome from the man who had been Dryden's publisher, who had purchased the copyright of *Paradise Lost*† (which he sold more success- fully than any other volume), and whose brother Richard, a close associate, had issued Otway's *Don Carlos*. Neither in his character nor in his appear- ance was Jacob Tonson an entirely pleasing personage – mean and sharp, so Dryden complained, red-haired, singularly awkward, ill-washed and malodorous:

> With leering looks, bull-faced, and freckled fair;
> With two left legs, and Judas-coloured hair,
> And frowsy pores, that taint the ambient air.

* 'To charge these *Pastorals* with want of invention [wrote Johnson] is to require what never was intended. . . . It is surely sufficient for an author of sixteen . . . to have obtained sufficient power of language and skill in metre to exhibit a series of versification, which had in English poetry no precedent, nor has since had an imitation.' *Lives of the English Poets*, 1779–81.

† Tonson bought a half share from Barbazon Ailmer in 1683, the remaining rights in 1690. It proved an immensely profitable transaction.

Despite these drawbacks, however, in 1700 he had been appointed honorary secretary of the fashionable Kit Cat Club; and Wycherley describes him as 'long ... gentleman usher to the Muses'; which again suggests that he had some social aptitude. No doubt he was a keen commercialist, and drove his needy employees hard; but he was also the kind of talented middleman who possesses an instinctive taste for value; and to flair he added the useful knack of quietly picking other men's brains. At his Gray's Inn shop, whither he had moved, towards the end of the last century, from the sign of the Judge's Head near Fleet Street, he daily entertained modern writers and critics, and gleaned the latest literary gossip. On hearing his visitors talk of Pope, and having been allowed to read a manuscript copy of one of the young poet's pastorals, which both Congreve and Walsh assured him were 'extremely fine', he determined that they must appear in the next *Miscellany*, and framed his brief, judicious letter.

2

Pope was not easily dazzled, even as a young man; and Tonson's letter seems to have had no immediate effect, either on the poet himself or on his quiet, pious family. Most of his time he continued to spend at home, cared for by his devoted mother and his old nurse, Mary Beach.* But since his boyhood, he afterwards told Spence, he had always felt a keen desire to travel – had his health been less precarious, he would certainly have made the Grand Tour; and now, whenever an opportunity occurred, he would slip away from Windsor Forest. Thus, early in the summer of 1707, he decided to undertake a particularly adventurous expedition. Naturally, his well-wishers were much alarmed. 'Our little poet,' reported the kind Sir William Trumbull to his nephew, the Reverend Ralph Bridges, 'is gone a dreadful long journey into Worcestershire, to Mr Walsh, from whence I never expect to see the poor creature return. He looked, and really was no more than a shadow.' But, 'if I ever see him again', added Sir William, who was possibly a trifle jealous of his latest patron's tutelary influence, 'he will come full-freighted with new criticisms'. Sir William's solicitude was wasted: Pope triumphantly survived his ordeal. He gained Abberley on its bosky hill-top; and there he and Walsh spent several weeks together, discussing the Latin poets – Walsh had been correcting Pope's translation of Statius – pastoral verse, ancient and modern, and the finer points of English prosody. By the middle of September he was safely back in London; and Bridges hastened to inform Sir William that, one day strolling near the Temple, he had encountered 'little Pope'. They had conversed; and 'he would walk with me ... to the farther end of St James's Park, and all that way he plied me with criticisms and scraps of poetry'.

Both correspondents, the reader will notice, make free use of the word 'little'. It was a word that Pope became accustomed to hearing, employed

* Mary was also called Mercy.

1 Martha and Teresa Blount; 'two of the finest faces in the universe'. Artist unknown.

2 Arabella Fermor; 'Though gay yet modest, though sublime yet sweet'. She wears the jewelled cross that Pope describes. Portrait by Sykes.

by friends and foes alike – Wycherley had spoken, half tenderly, half condescendingly, of his 'little crazy carcase'; and, as his poetic development progressed, it acquired a peculiar hold on his imagination. In May 1707, he had celebrated his nineteenth birthday; but he still presented a strangely juvenile appearance; his large and noble head surmounted a diminutive body; his limbs were pathetically meagre, and his shoulders bowed. Four feet six inches was the adult poet's full height – a span that every student of his character should mark off on some convenient wall or door, and keep before him as he reads. True, the average Englishman in the eighteenth century was probably somewhat shorter than he is today. But there were many exceptions: Henry Fielding, for instance, was unusually tall and solid; Hogarth, the aggressive 'five foot painter', is depicted by contemporary caricaturists as an almost dwarfish personage; and Pope at four-and-a-half feet, would have appeared an *homunculus* in any gathering. Nor did his littleness, unlike Hogarth's, go with a muscular and well-proportioned body. His back was crooked – though just how crooked it is difficult to determine. Hogarth, in an early satirical engraving, which portrays Pope, William Kent, Lord Burlington and their fellow-leaders of Palladian taste, gives him a pronounced hump, whereas a pen-and-ink sketch by Hoare of Bath, showing the poet in his fifty-third year, drawn 'without his knowledge while conversing with Mr Allen at Prior Park', suggests that, despite the curvature of his spine, he retained a tolerably upright carriage. His head is neatly balanced on his shoulders; and, as he extends his right arm to emphasize a point he is making, he has an authoritative, energetic air.

Pope's was a resolute, passionately spirited nature; and an expressive face revealed his temperament. In youth, at least, it was a distinctly handsome face, with a long, high-bridged, finely shaped nose, a thoughtful, stubborn, yet sensuous mouth, and big melancholy blue-grey eyes. But his physical infirmities were beginning to leave their mark; and, as time went on, they were to scar him deeply. During no period of his adult existence can he have been altogether free of pain. Insomnia vexed him; neuralgia tortured him; and the great sculptor Louis François Roubiliac, who modelled his features about 1738, observed that 'his countenance was that of a person who had been much afflicted with headache; and that he should have known the fact from the contracted appearance of the skin above the eyebrows. . . .' Worse still, perhaps, was a galling sense of weakness, accompanied and accentuated by a sense of inward strength. How could he reconcile his weakness and his strength, keep the peace between turbulent emotional appetites and a sickly, undeveloped body?

For such a problem there could be no complete solution; and the story of Pope's attempts to solve it, and to achieve through art a harmony that life denied, is also the story of his poetic progress. Meanwhile, he was acquiring a defensive *persona*, the mask, more or less elaborate, behind which we hide our secret doubts and fears. The *persona* Pope adopted was that of an accomplished worldling. 'The little *Aesopic* sort of animal' patronized by Wycherley, and dressed 'à la mode' by Charles Wogan, was fast becoming a literary man of fashion, who could hold his own in the most rakish society and chose his acquaintances among London wits and beaus.

In a century that made a cult of friendship, Pope's friends were uncommonly numerous and varied. During the year 1707, for example, they included a famous English tragic actor. On Thomas Betterton had fallen the mantle of Burbage; and he had established his fame in such exacting rôles as Hamlet, Mercutio, Macbeth, Lear and Troilus. Pope had been 'acquainted with Betterton from a boy', he subsequently informed Spence. The actor, then aged about seventy, died in the year 1710; and their friendship must clearly have begun before the publication of Pope's earliest poems. Like Wycherley, this one-time hero of the Restoration stage provided a valuable link with the historic past. He had inherited many of the legends of the Jacobean green-room; and he often assured Pope that, although 'it was a general opinion that Ben Jonson and Shakespeare had lived in enmity ... there was nothing in it'. Betterton also talked of Sir William Davenant, who had sometimes claimed to be Shakespeare's natural son; of how he had criticized Dryden's poetic diction, and even persuaded him to omit from *The Spanish Friar* an image that Davenant considered 'mean'. His anecdotes may well have influenced Pope; for, when Betterton suggested that he, too, should become a dramatic poet, and 'would have had me turn my early epic poem into a tragedy', Pope prudently declined, 'seeing how much everybody that did write for the stage was obliged to subject themselves to the players and the town'. Betterton, moreover, seems to have been a daring irreligious wit; and Pope remembered and treasured his reply to Archbishop Tillotson,★ author of the celebrated *Sermons* and *Rules of Faith*. The prelate had asked him if he could explain why it was that, having composed 'the most moving discourse' and delivered it 'as feelingly as he was able', he still failed to move his assembled congregation nearly as much as Betterton stirred his audience. ' "That," says Betterton, "I think, is easy to be accounted for: 'tis because you are only *telling* them a story, and I am *showing* them facts." '

★ John Tillotson (1630–94).

Either through Betterton or through Wycherley, Pope became the friend of Henry Cromwell; and a correspondence began in the summer of 1707 that continued until the end of 1711, providing a regular interchange of scandal, views and literary discussion. Cromwell, a prosperous country gentleman who chose to bustle about the world of literature, had published a comic poem entitled 'Venus at Bath', and was now translating Ovid. Otherwise he remains a slightly mysterious personage; Johnson, at least, wrote that he could glean 'nothing particular' about him except 'that he used to ride a-hunting in a tye-wig',* and that he was 'fond, and perhaps vain, of amusing himself with poetry and criticism'. Gay, however, styles him 'honest Cromwell', and refers to his decorative red breeches and to his habit of frequently removing his hat. In 1707, he was some fifty-five years old, a tough, good-humoured literary roué. Though he had an estate at Beesly in Lincolnshire, he preferred to spend his time in London, where he kept his lodgings and occupied a 'speculative angle' – probably a convenient window-seat – at the Widow Hambleton's coffee-house in Prince's Street, near Drury Lane. From Pope's letters we learn that he loved nosegays, which he bought in Covent Garden, drank strong coffee and titillated his nose with 'Brasil', a particularly expensive brand of snuff. But, despite his fashionable whims and his assiduous pursuit of 'the Fair', he was not always very well-dressed. 'What an ascendancy,' exclaims his young correspondent, 'have you over all the Sex, who could gain the fair one's heart by appearing before her in a long, black, unpowdered periwig; nay, without so much as the very extremities of clean linen in neckcloth and cuffs!' For women were Cromwell's ruling passion; he liked to visit the theatres and hold gallant conversations behind the stage with actresses and figurantes; and he had a mistress, whom he had dubbed 'Sappho' – a minor poetess named Mrs Thomas – whom, on warm evenings, he would escort across the Thames to explore the leafy avenues of some suburban pleasure-ground. Pope, he assumed, must have the same interests; and the poet's literary neighbour Mrs Nelson – 'a very orthodox lady', Pope protested – Cromwell also nicknamed 'Sappho'. Similar jokes were exchanged by the correspondents on the subject of their amatory trials and triumphs, 'unmerciful, virtuous dames', 'Drury Lane damsels', and the ever-present risk of contracting a clap, and being disastrously 'burned' or 'fired'.

As in his correspondence with Wycherley, Pope proved an aptly imitative pupil. Again he made a courageous attempt to advertise his

* The curls of the tye-wig were tied back with a ribbon at the nape of the neck. Presumably most hunting men wore the more compact bob-wig.

masculinity, describing, for example, an encounter he had had amid the shadows of an 'uneasy stage-coach' that was carrying him home to Binfield. When the vehicle halted, he had heard the 'dreadful news' that he was to be joined in the carriage by a sick woman:

... I stood resigned with a stoical constancy to endure the worst of evils ... ! I was indeed a little comforted to find by her voice and dress, that she was young and a gentlewoman; but no sooner was her hood removed, but I saw one of the finest faces I ever beheld, and to increase my surprise, heard her salute me by my name. I had never more reason to accuse Nature for making me short-sighted than now ... and was utterly at a loss how to address myself, till with a great deal of simplicity and innocence she let me know ... that she was the daughter of one in our neighbourhood, lately married, who having been consulting her physicians in town, was returning into the country, to try what good air and a new husband could do to recover her. My father, you must know, has some-times recommended the study of physic to me, but *the Devil take me* if I ever had any ambition to be a doctor till this instant. I ventured to prescribe her some fruit (which I happened to have in the coach) which being forbidden her by her damned doctors she had the more inclination to. In short, I tempted and she eat; nor was I more like the Devil, than she like Eve.... I put on the gallantry of the old Serpent, and in spite of my evil form, accosted her with all the gaiety I was master of; which had so good effect, that in less than an hour.... her colour returned.... In a word, I had the pleasantest journey imaginable, so that now, as once of yore, by means of the *forbidden fruit*, the *Devil* got into *Paradise* – I should not have used this last phrase but that I know your civil apprehension will not put any ill construction upon it, and you will firmly believe that we were as modest – even as Sappho and Mr Cromwell.

The letter, from which this passage has been taken, is dated 11 July 1709; but, in its tone of determined flippancy, sharpened by an occasional hint of lubricity, it is characteristic of the whole exchange. Pope's first letter to Henry Cromwell was written on 12 or 13 July 1707, while he was preparing to set out for Abberley, a long rhyming epistle, full of learned allusions, scandalous references and entertaining private jokes. Apparently they did not write again until the beginning of the next year; and the most typical part of the correspondence was exchanged between May 1709 and December 1711, when Pope and Cromwell had a minor dis-agreement that brought it to a gradual close. Some biographers have solemnly deplored the friendship. Cromwell, they imply, was a wicked old trifler, whose mannerisms his young correspondent adopted with extremely bad results. Pope himself, seeing his letters printed – Cromwell gave them to Mrs Thomas, who sold them to the publisher Edmund Curll★

★ Curll published them in 1726, in the first volume of a Miscellany.

26

– must have felt that they called for some apology. 'My letters to Cromwell,' he assured Spence, 'were written with a design that does not generally appear; they were not written in sober sadness.' What his design was, it is no longer easy to decide; but Pope was never completely unaware of the literary effect he was creating, and believed that in his correspondence, as in everything else, a writer's style should be carefully suited to his subject. Letter-writing was a form of self-portraiture; and his letters to Cromwell produce a vivid composite impression of the young man's personality – at least, of the aspect of his personality that, for the moment, he felt most inclined to show. Simultaneously, they chronicle his daily life. Although he loved his parents, he was often bored and restive. 'Every day,' he wrote on 18 March 1708, 'is literally another tomorrow; for it is exactly the same with yesterday. It has the same business, which is poetry; and the same pleasure which is idleness.' Sometimes he pretended to regret that he was not a more productive scribbler. But 'why should a fellow like me, who all his life does nothing, be ashamed to write nothing? . . .' On occasions, he was tempted to sink back into the lulling atmosphere of Binfield House: 'Well, Sir, for the future I'll drown all high thoughts in the Lethe of cowslip-wine; as for fame, renown, reputation, take 'em Critics! . . . If ever I seek for immortality here, may I be damned! . . .'

That winter, he was still at Binfield – 'so well satisfied with the country ever since I saw you, that I have not so much as thought of the Town', and unperturbed by Tonson's delays over the publication of the *Pastorals*: 'I have been most mercifully reprieved by the sovereign power of Jacob Tonson from being brought forth to public punishment. . . .' Next year, his rustication continued; but he thought nostalgically of London pleasures: 'the time now drawing nigh, when you use, with Sappho, to cross the water in an evening to Spring Garden, I hope you will have an opportunity of ravishing her'; and he wished his friend, not only amorous diversions, but 'the best company, and the best coffee'. Meanwhile Cromwell, too, had been revising his Statius; and, on 10 June 1709, Pope acknowledged the receipt of a part of his translation and the critical 'remarks' that had accompanied it. In July he managed to visit the metropolis, and on his way home had his agreeable adventure in the uneasy stage-coach. Later that summer, Cromwell retired to Beesly, and Pope reported that he had 'caused an acquaintance of mine to enquire twice of your welfare, by whom I have been informed that you have left your Speculative Angle in the Widow's coffee-house, and bidding adieu . . . to all the rehearsals, reviews, gazettes . . . have heroically marched off into Lincolnshire. Thus I find you vary your life in the scene . . . though not in the action; for though life for the most part, like an old play, be still the same, yet now and then a new scene may make it more entertaining. As for myself, I would not have my life a very regular play; let it be a good merry farce* . . . and a fig for the Critical Unities!'

Binfield, of course, did not want its attractions; and, when he walked on the verges of the Forest, Pope enjoyed the companionship of a devoted dog. It resembled its master, being 'a little one, a lean one, and none of the finest shaped. He is not much a spaniel in his fawning; but has . . . a dumb surly sort of kindness, that rather shows itself when he thinks me ill-used by others, than when we walk quietly and peaceably by ourselves.' But Whitehill House was always apt to be dull; and, during a festival of the Catholic Church, family-life became extremely tedious. While his parents were celebrating Easter, they were scandalized if they saw their son writing; they 'take it for granted I write nothing but ungodly verses; and they say here so many prayers, that I can make but few poems. For in this point of praying I am an occasional conformist. So just as I am drunk or scandalous in town, according to my company, I am for the same reason grave and godly here.' Equally tiresome were bouts of sociability, marked by convivial gatherings of rustic neighbours. True, they had agreed to tolerate him: 'I am looked upon in the neighbourhood for a very sober and well-disposed person, no great hunter indeed, but a great esteemer of the noble sport. . . . They all say 'tis pity I am so sickly, and I think 'tis pity they are so healthy. But I say nothing that may destroy their good opinion of me. I have not quoted one Latin author since I came down. . . .' These cheerful people's knowledge of literature was confined to the drinking-songs of Tom Durfey:† 'he makes all the merriment in our entertainments. . . . Dares any man despise him who has made so many men drink? Alas, Sir! this is a glory which neither you nor I must ever pretend to. Neither you, with your Ovid, nor I with my Statius, can amuse a whole board of justices and extraordinary esquires, or gain one hum of approbation, or laugh of admiration! . . . 'Tis mortifying enough, it must be confessed; but however let us proceed in the way that Nature has directed us. . . .'

* Let the strict Life of graver Mortals be
A long, exact, and serious Comedy . . .
Let mine, an innocent gay Farce appear,
And more Diverting still than Regular . . .

Epistle to Miss Blount, with the Works of Voiture, 1712.

† Tom Durfey, 1653–1723.

So life went on, at a regular jog-trot pace, amid friends who loved and admired him, but with anguish or discomfort seldom far away. In the spring of 1710, during a visit to London, Pope once again fell dangerously ill. He recovered his strength; but 'almost continual illnesses' plagued him for the next few months; and he wrote philosophically that there was 'one good thing' that might be said about the state of sickness: 'it is the best cure in the world for ambition . . . it makes a man pretty indifferent for the future, provided he can but be easy, by intervals, for the present'. He had other troubles: Wycherley was growing sadly tired of Pope's interminable alterations. The sight of his manuscripts cruelly blotted and disfigured had begun to infuriate the disappointed author; and on 2 May, Pope had written, promising henceforward 'not to cross over, or deface the copy of your papers . . . and only to mark in the margin the repetitions, and not rectify the *method*, nor *connect* the *matter*. . . . So it really is my opinion, and desire, that you should take your papers out of my hands into your own'; and that no further changes should be made unless author and editor could make them jointly, 'when you may be satisfied with every blot. . . .' A diplomatic and well-intentioned proposal; but Wycherley's pride had been irremediably wounded; and Pope, with his deep regard for the affections, was distressed to see that he had lost a friend. 'I thank God,' he told Cromwell on 12 October, 'there is nothing out of myself which I would be at the trouble of seeking, except a friend; a happiness I once hoped to have possessed in Mr Wc. . . . I have for some years been employed much like children that build houses with cards, endeavouring very busily and eagerly to raise a friendship, which the first breath of any ill-natured bystander could puff away.' The association was never completely resumed; and Wycherley died in 1716 – but not before he had married a very young girl,* to deprive a nephew he disliked of the family inheritance. Pope, who remembered him with rueful tenderness, 'went to see him on his death-bed'.

'It is vanity,' Pope would afterwards observe, 'which makes the rake at twenty, the worldly man at forty. . . .' During the period that followed the writing of the *Pastorals*, Pope certainly adopted a rakish character – not perhaps, however, because he was uncommonly vain, but as a deliberate means of self-protection. A well-known frequenter of Will's

---

* She 'proved a cheat', Pope related to Spence, and 'was a cast mistress of the person who recommended her to him'. The evening before Wycherley's death, he 'earnestly entreated her not to deny him one request. . . . "My dear, it is only that you will never marry an old man again"'. He could not help remarking, Pope wrote to Edward Blount on 21 January 1716, that sickness, 'which often destroys both wit and wisdom, yet seldom has power to remove that talent which we call *humour*'. To Edward Blount, 21 January 1716.

was a notorious libertine named General Tidcombe, whose conversation eventually became so shocking that he was banished from the coffee-house. Pope, none the less, seems to have sought his company and to have appreciated his rough salacious wit. The General's 'beastly laughable life', he remarked to Cromwell, was both 'nasty and diverting'; and Tidcombe valued him, Pope was to inform a confidante, for his 'pretty atheistical jests'. Clearly when he wished to do so, he could beat such dissolute middle-aged gentlemen at their own preferred game; and in his letters to Cromwell he continues to play the game with increasing ease and self-assurance. But the assurance, of course, was superficial: even at this period, Pope the amorist and libertine humourist sometimes cuts a slightly dolorous figure. There is frequently a close connection between ideas of weakness and sickness and his defiant references to the pleasures of the flesh.

Thus, on 24 June 1710, when he had just shaken off a wretched ailment – the letter from Cromwell he now acknowledged had arrived while he was still in pain – he wrote a letter full of 'buffoonery', yet overcast by doubt and suffering. Death had again come very close; and, although he had escaped, 'I would not have you entirely lay aside the thoughts of my epitaph, any more than I do those of the probability of my becoming (e'er long) the subject of one. For Death has of late been very familiar with some of my size; I am told my Lord Lumley and Mr Lytton are gone before me; and . . . I may now . . . esteem myself the least thing like a man in England. . . .' He could not but be sorry, he added, that his two aristocratic counterparts had died 'inglorious in their beds . . . it had been a fate more worthy of our size, had they met with theirs from an irruption of Cranes or other warlike animals, that of old were enemies to our Pygmaean ancestors! You of a superior species little regard what befalls us, Homunciolos Sesquipedales. . . .'

That his fellow-men formed a superior species was an idea he could support with resolution; the sense of his insignificance became far less bearable if he saw himself reflected in a woman's eyes. Women, he knew, were inclined to laugh at him. The social standards of the age were lax; and it may be that they laughed aloud. Evidently they did not always spare his feelings; and 'the other day', continues his letter to Cromwell, after he had written of his Pygmy forebears, he had met 'a lady, who rallied my person so much, as to cause a total subversion of my countenance'. By way of revenge, he had composed a rondeau, which he had handed to her in quite a different gathering, and which he now transcribed for Cromwell's benefit, to be shown to Mrs Thomas. With its tone of rather forced indecorum and obsessive repetition of the damning epithet 'little', it is an unedifying, but highly curious effort:

> You know where you did despise
> (T'other day) my little eyes,
> Little legs, and little thighs,
> And some things of little size,
> You know where. . . .

Many famous poets, Tennyson included, have left behind them strange erotica; but Pope's verses have the unusual merit of embodying a deep-rooted conflict.

No doubt the rondeau amused Cromwell; but he did not hesitate to point out that Pope had been cleverly plagiarizing Voiture.* Pope accepted this mild rebuke; he had a regard for Cromwell's literary judgement; and he often consulted him, as he had consulted Trumbull and Walsh, both about the problems he encountered in his own writing and about more general questions of poetic style and finish. Their correspondence had an extremely serious side. Among subjects discussed were the merits of Ovid, 'who has an agreeableness that charms us without correctness, like a mistress whose faults we see, but love her with them all'; Priam's recovery of the corpse of his son, as treated respectively in the *Iliad* and the *Aeneid*; some lines from Persius; the rules of pastoral poetry; Rowe's translation of Lucan; and the use of the hiatus in modern English verse – 'every nice ear', Pope thought, must 'have observed, that in any smooth English verse of ten syllables, there is naturally a pause either at the fourth, fifth, or sixth syllable', as, for instance, in the poems of Edmund Waller. Both correspondents were also gravely concerned about the application of regular critical standards to contemporary English literature. Dryden himself had admitted that, in his youth, he was 'drawing the outlines of an art without any living master to instruct' him. The great English poets of the earlier seventeenth century had been brilliant and audacious spirits; but it was clear that they had lacked method; and since the Restoration there was a general feeling abroad that our literary criteria now demanded reappraisal. A host of critics had latterly invaded the scene; but their efforts served to irritate the poet rather than show him rules he cared to follow; and Pope, while he corresponded with Cromwell, was meditating how he could provide a remedy – a didactic poem that would scourge impertinent critics and, at the same time, set the art of criticism upon a right and proper footing.

* Vincent Voiture (1598–1648), a member of the literary circle that gathered at the Hôtel de Rambouillet.

So far the critics had handled him gently enough. When his *Pastorals* at length emerged, in May 1709, they had received a sympathetic welcome and, according to Wycherley on 17 May, had 'safely run the gauntlet through all the coffee-houses'. Thus Pope had no deep personal animus against contemporary critics and their works; it was merely a question of determining the rules under which modern criticism ought to operate. *An Essay on Criticism* was published anonymously in mid-April 1711; and the poet marked the title-page of his manuscript* 'written in the year 1709'. Pope was always inclined to antedate the composition of his works; and both Jonathan Richardson, who said that he had had it from the writer himself that the poem was written in 1707, and Warburton, who, perhaps with Pope's authority, announced that, at the time, he had 'not attained the twentieth year of his age', assigned the *Essay* to an even earlier period. There is a striking resemblance, however, between certain passages of the poem and some of the ideas he had recently expressed to Cromwell; and it seems likely that the project had not been completed much before the close of 1710. Meanwhile he kept his plan a secret; he refrained from mentioning the *Essay* to Cromwell until the volume was in circulation. Maybe he was deterred by a sense of his own temerity; a twenty-two-year-old poet, with a single sheaf of published works behind him, he was now proposing to lay down critical rules for the benefit of his literary elders and betters. *An Essay on Criticism* is, above all else, a young man's book – confident, assertive, dogmatic, as ambitious in its critical generalizations as it is uninhibited in tone and sharp in utterance.

Not that the theories propounded were strictly original; Pope's view of Nature, and of Man's relationship with Nature, can be traced back to the Middle Ages. Shakespeare had already absorbed it. Throughout the universe, medieval philosophers had taught, there extended a mysterious 'Chain of Being', from the heights of the fiery Empyrean, abode of the Creator himself and the immense celestial hierarchy, to the sublunary region inhabited by Man and the lowly plane occupied by animals and plants.† God was the ultimate source of order; and every detail of this complex edifice illustrated the workings of divine sagacity. Pope's was not a deeply religious mind; but he, too, at least in his *Essay on Criticism*, accepted the medieval view of Nature, and proceeded to exalt it as the

* Now in the Bodleian Library; the title page is drawn up in Pope's customary typographical style.

† 'As Nature has framed the several species of beings as it were in a chain . . .' 'On Reason and Passion', *The Spectator*, 18 June 1712.

fount and origin of all moral and aesthetic virtues. Let the creative artist look to Nature; for Nature alone provides an unerring standard:

> First follow NATURE, and your Judgement frame
> By her just Standard, which is still the same:
> *Unerring Nature*, still divinely bright,
> One *clear*, *unchang'd*, and *Universal* Light,
> Life, Force, and Beauty, must to all impart,
> At once the *Source*, and *End*, and *Test of Art*.
> *Art* from that Fund each *just Supply* provides,
> Works *without Show*, and *without Pomp* presides:
> In some fair Body thus th' informing Soul
> With Spirits feeds, with Vigour fills the whole,
> Each Motion guides, and ev'ry Nerve sustains;
> *It self unseen*, but in th' *Effects*, remains.

Even literary rules, Pope continues, were once derived from natural laws:

> Those RULES of old *discover'd*, not *devis'd*,
> Are *Nature* still, but *Nature Methodiz'd*. . . .

And he goes on to the yet more curious statement that the ancient poets, who discovered those rules, flourished in a Golden Age of poetry, far closer than our own to Nature, just as the shepherds of the Golden Age had partaken of its prevailing truth and innocence. Thus the young Virgil had looked up to Homer with regretful admiration:

> . . . When t'examine ev'ry Part he came,
> *Nature* and *Homer* were, he found, the *same*. . . .

Since that period, we had witnessed a steady decline of personal and poetic values; and, to check the decline, poets and critics should first learn to make a nice distinction between the complementary qualities that Pope distinguishes as 'wit' and 'judgement'. One is of little help without the other; for wit is the quality we nowadays call imagination; judgement, the critical sense that we acquire through studying the greatest masters:

> Be *Homer's* Works your *Study* and *Delight*,
> Read them by Day, and meditate by Night,
> Thence form your Judgement, thence your Maxims bring,
> And trace the Muses *upward* to their Spring. . . .

Not that he is inclined to denigrate wit –

> Great Wits sometimes may *gloriously offend*,
> And *rise* to *Faults* true Criticks *dare not mend*. . . .

33

– or would praise a work of literature merely because it is correct and smooth:

> A perfect Judge will *read* each Work of Wit
> With the same Spirit that its Author *writ,*
> Survey the *Whole*, nor seek slight Faults to find,
> Where *Nature moves*, and *Rapture warms* the Mind;
> Nor lose, for that malignant dull Delight,
> The *gen'rous Pleasure* to be charmed with Wit.
> But in such Lays as neither *ebb*, nor *flow*,
> *Correctly cold*, and *regularly low*,
> That shunning Faults, one quiet *Tenour* keep;
> We cannot *blame* indeed – but we may *sleep*.

No, true poetic excellence is always a reflex of Nature, tempered by the power of art:

> *True Wit* is *Nature* to Advantage drest,
> What oft was *thought*, but ne'er so well *Exprest*,
> *Something*, whose Truth convinc'd at Sight we find,
> That gives us back the Image of our Mind. . . .

Since every truth is already implicit in Nature, the poet should be content with an endless task of rediscovery and, as Walsh had advised, with giving established truths a more harmonious, more 'correct' form.

One of Pope's masters was evidently Boileau. The great French critic's treatise, *L'Art Poétique*, had appeared in 1674; and not only does Boileau expatiate on the poet's duties as a craftsman –

> *N'offrez rien au lecteur que ce qui peut lui plaire.*
> *Ayez pour la cadence une oreille sévère. . . .**

and on his obligations as a man of reason –

> *Quelque sujet qu'on traite, ou plaisant, ou sublime,*
> *Que toujours le bons sens s'accorde avec la rime. . . .*†

–but he insists that a successful writer must also be an *honnête homme*, civilized, generous, dignified, upright, innocent of petty deeds and vulgar thoughts:

> *Aimez donc la vertu, nourissez-en votre âme:*
> *En vain l'esprit est plein d'une noble vigueur;*
> *Le vers se sent toujours des bassesses du coeur.*‡

* Offer the reader only what may please.
  To every cadence lend a careful ear. . . .
† Whate'er your subject, frolic or sublime,
  Let sound good sense be married to the verse. . . .
‡ Love virtue then, and make your soul its home:
  In vain your wit may show a noble strength;
  Each baseness of the heart infects the line.

Pope, who acknowledges his debt to Boileau, draws an exemplary picture of the virtuous critic:

> But where's the Man, who Counsel *can* bestow,
> Still *pleas'd* to *teach*, and yet not *proud* to *know* . . .
> Tho' Learn'd, well-bred; and tho' well-bred, sincere;
> Modestly bold, and Humanly severe? . . . .
> Blest with a *Taste* exact, yet unconfin'd;
> A *Knowledge* both of *Books* and *Humankind*? . . . .
>   Such once were *Criticks*, such the Happy *Few*,
> *Athens* and *Rome* in better Ages knew.

Such, Pope might have added, was the writer that he meant to be. No account of the poet's development could pretend to do him justice if it omitted the moral side of his character, and the part that his moral impulses played in his long pursuit of poetic truth and beauty. Pope had always a deep regard for goodness; and he believed, with Boileau, that both a writer's intelligence and the qualities of his heart had an important influence upon his style. Writing, inevitably, was a method of teaching; the artist was a natural moralist; and *An Essay on Criticism* was planned by its author as, first and foremost, a didactic poem. It was also designed as an exercise in reasoning. 'They cannot be good poets,' Dryden had declared, 'who are not accustomed to argue well.' Pope's conduct of his argument, however, now strikes us as the poem's weakest point. He throws out a series of lively assertions, but fails to build up a system of original ideas; and his *Essay* is dazzling in flashes rather than impressive as a reasoned whole. Yet Addison, in a review published in that clever new journal *The Spectator* on 20 December, praised the poem very warmly; while Johnson was one day to observe that it exhibited 'every mode of excellence that can embellish or dignify didactic composition. . . .' Not until the early nineteenth century did the *Essay*'s stock begin to fall; Hazlitt considered it a wonderful achievement, a 'double-refined essence' of wit and sense; but De Quincey was inclined to regard it as the 'least interesting of Pope's writings . . . a mere versification, like a metrical multiplication-table, of commonplaces the most mouldy with which criticism has baited its rat-traps. . . .' Too many couplets, moreover, thanks to their gnomic appeal, soon became detached from their poetic context and, worn down by frequent quotation – 'a little knowledge' was clearly 'a dangerous thing' – were preserved and exhibited as literary fossils.

The true value of the *Essay* is to be found, not in Pope's handling of ideas, but in his exquisitely accomplished use of words. Here judgement is condensed into wit; and the resulting phrase, with its crystalline hardness and sharpness, arouses a sense of keen aesthetic pleasure. Pope's wit is frequently directed at writers who lack wit themselves. In principle he seems to approve caution; but cautious, correct, slow-paced versifiers are among his chief targets. They lack warmth; they are the slaves of correctitude:

> These *Equal Syllables* alone require,
> Tho' oft the Ear the *open Vowels* tire,
> While *Expletives*★ their feeble Aid *do* join,
> And ten low Words oft creep in one dull Line. . . .

Satirizing poets who round off a triplet by suddenly dropping into the Alexandrine measure, he produces a brilliant and harmonious parody:

> . . . *A needless Alexandrine* ends the Song,
> That like a wounded Snake, drags its slow length along.

Pope is at his best, not when he is instructing us how to write verse, but is writing poetry about poetry. To Cromwell, on 25 November 1710, he had already expressed the unoriginal opinion that 'a good poet will adapt the very sounds, as well as words, to the things he treats of. So that there is . . . a style of sound: as in describing a gliding stream the numbers should run easy and flowing, in describing a rough torrent or deluge, sonorous and swelling. . . .' That opinion he now enlarged and transfigured:

> *Soft* is the Strain when *Zephyr* gently blows,
> And the *smooth* Stream in *smoother Numbers* flows;
> But when loud Surges lash the sounding Shore,
> The *hoarse, rough Verse* should like the *Torrent* roar.
> When *Ajax* strives, some Rock's vast Weight to throw,
> The Line too *labours*, and the Words move *slow*;
> Not so, when swift *Camilla* scours the Plain,
> Flies o'er the unbending Corn, and skims along the Main.

In *An Essay*, Pope first emerges as a master of syllabic harmonies; and on this occasion his use of the Alexandrine – judged so contemptible in the work of others – brings the passage to a triumphant climax. Pentameters enclose his vision of the surging river and the labouring hero. Then the line expands and relaxes to produce a beautifully contrasted image – Camilla's weightless feet shining across the cornfield and down the path-

★ In the original sense, 'a word or syllable inserted for ornament or to fill up a vacancy'.

ways of the open sea – which he had derived from Virgil's portrait of the Volscian warrior-nymph in Book Seven of the *Aeneid*.*

The poem concludes with a heart-felt tribute to Walsh; for that knowing gentleman had died in 1708, the year after he had welcomed Pope at Abberley. Walsh, he declares, had provided a splendid exception to the general run of modern critics:

> Yet *some* there were, among the *sounder Few*
> Of those who *less presum'd*, and *better knew*,
> Who durst assert the *juster Ancient Cause*,
> And here *restored* Wit's *Fundamental Laws*. . . .
> Such late was *Walsh* – the Muse's Judge and Friend,
> Who justly knew to blame or to commend;
> To Failings *mild*, but *zealous* for Desert;
> The *clearest Head*, and the *sincerest Heart*.
> This humble praise, lamented *Shade*! receive,
> This Praise at least a grateful Muse may give!
> The Muse, whose early Voice you taught to Sing,
> Prescrib'd her Heights, and prun'd her tender Wing,
> (Her Guide now lost) no more attempts to *rise*,
> But in low Numbers short Excursions tries. . . .

Elsewhere the poet was a good deal more presumptuous. The *Essay* includes some bold reflections on the cultural influence of his own Church. Pope's Catholicism was always a little suspect; his faith was based upon domestic *pietas* rather than upon private piety; and, although he believed himself to be a good Christian in the most liberal meaning of the phrase, he once told Atterbury that, during his boyhood, he had been 'a Papist and a Protestant by turns', according to the latest book he read. Certainly he had adopted a Protestant view of monkish superstition and its attendant evils. The fall of Rome had involved the fall of learning:

> With *Tyranny*, then *Superstition* join'd,
> As that the *Body*, this enslav'd the *Mind*;
> Much was *Believ'd*, but little *understood*,
> And to be *dull* was constru'd to be *good*;
> A *second* Deluge Learning thus o'er-run,

* Lines 808–11.

> *Illa vel intactae segetis per summa volaret*
> *Gramina, nec teneras cursu laesisset aristas;*
> *Vel mare per medium, fluctu suspensa tumenti,*
> *Ferret iter, celeres nec tingueret aequore plantas.*

'She might have flown o'er the topmost blades of unmown corn, nor in her course bruised the tender ears; or sped her way o'er mid sea, poised above the swelling waves, nor dipped her swift feet in the flood.' (translated by H. Rushton Fairclough, 1954).

> And the *Monks* finish'd what the *Goths* begun.
> At length, *Erasmus*, that *great*, *injur'd* name,
> (The *Glory* of the Priesthood, and the *Shame*!)
> *Stemm'd* the *wild Torrent* of a *barb'rous Age*,
> And drove those *Holy Vandals* off the Stage.

Equally disturbing to his orthodox admirers was a hint that no single Christian communion held an exclusive monopoly of truth:

> Thus *Wit*, like *Faith*, by each man is apply'd
> To *one small Sect*, and All are *damn'd beside*. . . .

His Catholic friends – particularly the Abbé Southcote and a new friend, John Caryll, a member of the group of Catholic families who inhabited the Binfield neighbourhood – raised their voices in aggrieved protest; and it needed all Pope's considerable powers of diplomacy to convince his well-wishers that they had done him wrong.

Worse was his satirical description of a famous modern critic. John Dennis was a man of talent who believed himself to be a man of genius. Such writers often become reviewers; and Dennis is credited with having written one of the first genuine book-reviews ever published in the English language. When *An Essay on Criticism* appeared, he was fifty-four years old. Son of a London tradesman, a prosperous saddler, he had received a gentlemanly education at Harrow and Caius College, Cambridge; had been sent down from the university for stabbing a fellow undergraduate; had travelled abroad; obtained a minor post in the Customs (which he afterwards sold) through the good offices of the Duke of Marlborough; and had launched out, at the end of the century, as poet, dramatist and professional critic. Since 1697 he had written a series of poetic plays, of which the latest, *Appius and Virginia*, had been produced at Drury Lane only three years before the publication of the *Essay*. There is no doubt that his gifts were many and diverse; and, during the interregnum that followed Dryden's death, he is said to have ranked as 'incontestably the best judge of literature living in England'. Alas, he had a violent temper and a sullen, cross-grained disposition; Dennis was the type of cantankerous literary conservative, who feels that every new young writer has been specially sent to try his patience. He had lost his private fortune; he lived on a small annuity; none of the rewards that came his way were proportionate to his sense of his own value. His portrait, engraved by Van der Gucht, reveals an angry, disappointed visage – bulging cheeks divided by a formidable nose, lofty, contracted brow and pursed ungenerous mouth. He had already met Pope, perhaps

3 Robert, Lord Petre; Pope had heard that the young man was 'one of those lords that have wit in our days'. Artist unknown.

4 Alexander Pope by Charles Jervas, about 1714; the portrait engraved by Vertue in 1717 as frontispiece to Pope's *Works*.

at Will's; and their encounter seems to have been brief and hostile. Evidently the diminutive, ill-shaped youth, confronted with Dennis in full flow, had ventured to speak his mind instead of listening. In that musical, self-assured voice, of which the effect was accentuated both by his odd appearance and by the fashionable clothes he wore, it may be that he had even dared to argue. Dennis for the moment was dumbfounded; he had started back, and furiously scowled and reddened.

Pope had not forgotten the occasion; he possessed a keen pictorial memory. He was also a student of Dennis's plays; and he remembered how often, and how inappropriately, the dramatist employed the word 'tremendous'. A poet's head is always full of fragments for which he hopes one day to find the right place; and in the *Essay*, having written of critics who were at the same time civilized and honest men, Pope suddenly dredged up Dennis's picture:

> Fear not the Anger of the Wise to raise;
> Those best can *bear Reproof*, who *merit Praise*.
> 'Twere well, might Criticks still this Freedom take;
> But *Appius* reddens at each Word you speak,
> And *stares*, Tremendous! with a *threatning Eye*,
> Like some *fierce Tyrant* in *Old Tapestry*!

Nothing could have been more happily turned; every detail had a separate barb – Dennis's dramatic performances, which had received less applause than their quality deserved; his absurd affection for his favourite adjective; and, when Pope had caught him off his guard, the angry confusion that had overspread his face. Few middle-aged persons like to be told they have blushed; they are yet more disconcerted and annoyed if their informant is a very young man. And then, there was the charm of the poet's image. What could be more delightful than the comparison of Dennis, with his fierce eyes and his truculent attitude, to some figure of Herod or Xerxes in an old, moth-eaten tapestry, arms akimbo, buskined legs astraddle, blank orbs glaring down on the room from under a ridiculous dragon-crested helmet? Dennis was a poet himself; he could appreciate the simile and feel its sting.

His response was a passionate burst of invective. He, too, remembered his meeting with Pope; and he knew that this presumptuous dwarfish upstart had neither attended a university nor had had the classics beaten into his system at an English public school. He need not be reminded that the poet was both short and ill-shaped. Dennis hitherto had been a solemn academic writer, whose prose works had included treatises entitled *The Advancement and Reformation of Modern Poetry*, *The Grounds of Criticism in Poetry* and *The Genius and Writings of Shakespeare*. He was fond of applying the rules of Aristotle, which he described as 'nothing but Nature and Good Sense reduc'd to a Method', to the products of the modern stage. His critical approach was ponderous but dignified. Stung by Pope's slighting reference, however, he abandoned all decorum. Pope was to be destroyed – and, before he was destroyed, publicly humiliated. Thus, towards the end of June 1711, under the imprint of Lintot, who thoughtfully sent Pope a copy, he issued a pamphlet of thirty-two pages, with another five of introduction, styled *Reflections, Critical and Satyrical, upon a Rhapsody called an Essay upon Criticism*. Room was found for a number of critical points: though Dennis was a staunch supporter of the classics, he asserted that the essayist had been guilty of 'servile deference' to the Ancients and, ranging further afield, suggested that Pope was 'by politics a Jacobite'. But personalities were Dennis's strongest suit. He heaped ridicule on Pope's defective organism – 'As there is no creature in Nature so venomous, there is nothing so stupid and so impotent as a hunch-backed toad' – and remarked that the poet should be the last man to disparage another man's appearance. Let the reader hunt him down in his lair:

... If you have a mind to enquire between Sunning-Hill and Ockingham, for a young, squab, short gentleman ... an eternal writer of amorous pastoral madrigals, and the very bow of the God of Love, you will soon be directed to him. And pray as soon as you have taken a survey of him, tell me whether he is a proper author to make personal reflections on others; and tell him if he does not like my person, 'tis because he is an ungrateful creature, since ... I have always been infinitely delighted with his: so delighted, that I have lately drawn a very graphical picture of it. ... This little author may extol the Ancients as much and as long as he pleases, but he has reason to thank the good Gods that he was born a Modern. For had he been born of Grecian parents, and his father by consequence had by law the absolute disposal of him, his life had been no longer than that of one of his poems, the life of half a day.

It was cunning to include a mention of his father – 'a certain old gentleman in Windsor-Forest' – and to announce that, if Pope had been born in Greece, that devoted parent would probably have exposed his offspring, and thus insult, not only the poet himself, but a close relationship around which his life revolved. Pope loved his father; perhaps he was sometimes conscious of having disappointed him. Dennis had done his work thoroughly; and it is fortunate that Pope's character should have been both courageous and resilient. On 25 June, he wrote to John Caryll, enclosing 'Mr Dennis's Remarks ... which equally abound in just criticisms and fine railleries: the few observations in my hand in the margin are what only a morning's leisure permitted me to make purely for your perusal, for I am of opinion that such a critic ... is no way to be properly answered but by a wooden weapon. ... I can't conceive what ground he has for [so] excessive a resentment, nor imagine how those three lines can be called a reflection on his person, which only describe him subject a little to colour and stare on some occasions. ... If Mr Dennis's rage proceeds only from a zeal to discourage young and inexperienced writers from scribbling, he should frighten us with verse, not prose; for I've often known that, when all the precepts in the world would not reclaim a sinner, some very sad example has done the business. Yet to give this man his due, he has objected to one or two lines with reason, and I will alter them in case of another edition: I will make my enemy do me a kindness where he meant an injury. ... '

Cromwell, too, though he seems afterwards to have taken offence at Pope's treatment of his old friend Dennis, again proved a sympathetic ally. About this time, he suggested that he should visit Whitehill House, offering to bring as many pint bottles as he intended to remain days; and, when he arrived, he delighted the Pope family and dazzled the various neighbours whom they asked to meet him, with his sweeping old-fashioned civilities and rich fund of London gallantry and gossip. Pope's letter describing the effect he had produced, written on 15 July, contains his first mention of the name of John Gay. Evidently Cromwell had introduced the poets. 'Pray give my service,' Pope concludes, 'to all my few friends, and to Mr Gay in particular.' Gay repaid him with a fine poetic compliment; and, early next year – which was no less agreeable – in his dedication of the *Mohocks* he himself derided Dennis. Several reasons, he declared, had induced him 'to lay this work at your feet: the subject of it is *Horrid* and *Tremendous*, and the whole piece written according to the exactest rules of dramatic poetry, as I have with great care collected them from ... your elaborate dissertations. ... As we look upon you to have the monopoly of English criticism ... we hope you will very shortly chastise the insolence of *The Spectator*, who has lately had the audaciousness to show that there are more beauties than faults in a modern writer.' Meanwhile, a counter-attack on Dennis, of which Pope himself may or may not have been the author, and which pretended to announce an imaginary volume, entitled *The Mirror of Criticisme: or, The History of the Renown'd Rinaldo Furioso, Critick of the Woful Countenance*, had appeared in urban bookshops. It repaid insolence with insolence, jibed at the critic's 'tremendous' mannerisms, and noted how often he had failed to make his mark upon the stage.

Dennis's plan had clearly miscarried; as a serious man of letters, he had done himself more harm than good. Yet the poet did not escape un-injured; and in his existence, too, the hurt was lasting. Men and women who have had a happy childhood are sometimes particularly unprepared to meet the blows of later life. Pope's early childhood had been especially fortunate; no doubt he was a spoiled child; and the spoiled child had grown up into a clever, promising, much-flattered youth. Never had he lacked the affection he needed, or wanted encouragement and admiration. The world he inhabited as a young man was equally secure and dignified; at home, his parents continued to cherish him; and the intellectual stimulus they could not provide he enjoyed abroad among his friends. Only his body had persisted in playing him false; but, although sickness tormented him and the idea of his weakness haunted him, he had already learned to bear his burden. So long as he himself made light of his short-comings, and boldly adopted the rôle of 'little Pope', they could be supported with equanimity, even with a certain gaiety. It was much more difficult to stand up to public ridicule; Dennis had translated his darkest imaginings into ugly and opprobrious language – 'hunch-backed toad'; a 'squab, short gentleman', bent almost double like the bow of Love; an abortion whom any sensible father would have snatched from the cradle and cast forth to die. During his later life, Pope was inclined to dismiss the episode. When he first heard that Dennis had attacked him, the news, he said, had caused him 'some pain; but it was quite over as soon as I came to look into his book and found he was in such a passion'. Here perhaps he was not completely candid. The after-effects of this brutal attack were to remain with him throughout his whole existence. In his adversary's blustering abuse he had felt the fiery breath of real hatred.

3

Meanwhile Pope's friends far outnumbered his enemies, and the pleasures of society and successful authorship still outweighed the pains of living. That same year he had begun to fall in love, or had drifted into a pleasantly bemused state half-way between passion and affection. The latter months of 1711 seem to have been largely spent at home; and, towards the end of the year, he wrote an affectionate letter to Thomas Cromwell, apologizing for not having written earlier, but hoping that his correspondent would excuse the delay 'when you know what a sacrifice I make you . . . and that every moment my eyes are employed upon this paper, they are taken off from two of the finest faces in the universe'. Those faces almost certainly belonged to Teresa and Martha Blount, grand-daughters of Anthony Englefield, the Catholic owner of White-nights, who, with their widowed mother and unmarried brother, themselves lived at Mapledurham. Teresa was twenty-three in 1711, and her sister twenty-one. During her later life, Spence questioned Martha Blount as to exactly when she had first met the poet, suggesting that it must have been 'after his Essay on Criticism was published'; and Martha, whose memory was growing vague, supplied an unsatisfactory answer: 'O yes, Sir,' she replied, 'I was then a very little girl; my [grandfather] used to say much of him, but I did not much mind it then.' In fact, of course, she was two years younger than Pope. Her recollections of the poet, however, clearly went back to the days of childhood. The Catholic families established in that part of Berkshire formed a very close community; and old Mr Englefield of Whitenights – which stood some nine miles from Whitehill House – being, his grand-daughter asserted, 'a great lover of poetry and poets', must have been glad to welcome the prodigious stripling. Thus Pope had become a friend of the household; and soon he became a devoted attendant of the two attractive girls. Teresa apparently was his original favourite, a dark young woman with quick, uncertain moods. But his affection gradually shifted to Martha, nicknamed by her friends 'Patty', who was not only fresh and appealing, but particularly good-humoured.

Martha Blount had been 'blest with Temper'; nothing, Pope was to claim in later years – spleen, envy, sickness, even the destruction of a precious porcelain vase – could eclipse her radiant amiability. Her hair was blonde; her eyes were a luminous blue. At the outset, wherever his secret preference lay, Pope would appear to have courted both the Blounts. But we cannot tell what encouragement he received, or whether, apart from occasional literary tributes, he yet presumed to court them openly. As a lover, he could never forget his own defective size and shape; and on 25 January 1711, in the opening letter he addressed to John Caryll, he had remarked that, despite numerous compliments by which he had been duly gratified, he continued to regard himself as 'not the great Alexander Mr Caryll is so civil to, but that little Alexander the women laugh at'. Perhaps it was Martha's kindliness – her reluctance to laugh – that first established her in Pope's affections. Moreover, though she was pious and virtuous, Martha Blount was not at all a prude; and she did not shrink from the mildly improper raillery that he liked to slip into the pages of his letters. But in 1711 his approaches were tentative; she and her sister were merely the embodiment of a need that engrossed his heart and senses. Pope's nature was keenly sensuous; few English poets have written so feelingly of women and 'the woman's world'. He appreciated women, enjoyed their conversation, acquired an intimate knowledge of their thoughts and habits; and no doubt women, because they discounted him physically, were inclined to welcome him emotionally. He was neither a possible husband nor a prospective lover. They could entrust 'little Pope' with freedoms and confidences that they would not have granted to an ordinary man.

John Caryll may have encouraged the relationship; he was the friend of the whole Catholic circle that revolved around the Englefields and Blounts. In 1710 Pope had taken an immediate fancy to his shrewd and gifted co-religionist; and gradually his soberer, steadier influence over-shadowed that of Cromwell. Like Cromwell, he was already middle-aged, having been born in 1666. His uncle, who bore the same name, had received an earldom from the Old Pretender, and now lived abroad at the court of Saint-Germain, where he served the exiled King as Secretary of State.* But Pope's friend was a Sussex country gentleman, established at

* Lord Caryll died in France on 4 September 1711, and Pope composed a laudatory epitaph.

Ladyholt and West Grinstead, cultivated, active, gregarious, with a strong interest in modern Catholic affairs. The lengthy correspondence between Caryll and Pope began on 31 July 1710; and Pope's early letters are almost as studied and elaborate as those with which he had once favoured Wycherley. It is plain that he was determined to improve the acquaintance; and in January 1711 he sent Mrs Caryll his own picture of the Blessed Virgin. It was greatly admired: 'St Luke himself,' the recipient was said to have exclaimed, 'never drew such a Madonna'; and Caryll may therefore have been especially surprised when he looked into the pages of the *Essay* and noted that some of the lines he found there might be construed as offensive to the Catholic religion. Pope replied patiently and carefully, discussing every point raised. He asserted that his views had been misunderstood, suggested cunningly that he and his friend could afford to disregard his ill-informed opponents – who, he feared, 'understand grammar as little as they do criticism' – implied that 'our Church' would always command his allegiance, and promised that, 'if the alteration of a word or two will gratify any man of sound faith tho' of weak understanding, I will . . . comply with it: and if you please but to particularize the spot where their objection lies . . . that stumbling block, though it be but a little pebble, shall be removed out of their way'. His correspondent, none the less, continued laboriously picking over pebbles; and, a month later, on 19 July, having acknowledged the solicitude Caryll had shown 'for my reputation by the several accounts you have so obligingly given me of what reports and censures the holy Vandals have thought fit to make me the unworthy subject of', he added a bold profession of his personal beliefs:

I've ever thought the best piece of service one could do to our religion was openly to expose our detestation and scorn of all those artifices and *piae fraudes* which it stands so little in need of, and which have laid it under so great a scandal among the enemies. Nothing has been so much a scarecrow to them as the too peremptory and seemingly uncharitable assertion of an utter impossibility of salvation to all but ourselves, invincible ignorance excepted. . . . Besides the small number of the truly faithful in our Church, we must again subdivide, and the Jansenist is damned by the Jesuit, the Jesuit by the Jansenist, the strict Scotist by the Thomist, &c. There may be errors, I grant, but I can't think 'em of such consequence as to destroy utterly the charity of mankind, the very greatest bond in which we are engaged by God to one another. . . .

No declaration could have been better phrased, more firmly yet more reasonably argued; and the independence of Pope's line exemplifies his native courage. Caryll was the older man, and a friend he wished to keep;

he was also a member of the recusant aristocracy, whereas Pope was the son of a middle-class convert. But the same letter winds up with a copy of the improper *Rondeau to Phillis* that he had already copied out for Cromwell. It was sent, he writes, at Caryll's request. The fox-hunting Catholic squire must have been a tolerably broad-minded person; and Pope's tone in many subsequent letters is equally frivolous and uninhibited. Caryll, however, unlike Cromwell, was much concerned with good works; and during 1711 he and Pope became jointly involved in the affairs of two 'unfortunate ladies', both of whom were unhappily married and exposed to public spite and ridicule. One was Caryll's first cousin; and, on 19 July, Pope wrote that he was 'infinitely obliged for your bringing me acquainted with Mrs Cope, from whom I heard more wit and sense in two hours, than almost all the sex ever spoke in their whole lives'. Mrs Cope's husband had deserted her, and was afterwards to contract a bigamous marriage abroad. Meanwhile she was poor and lonely, leading a cheerless, hand-to-mouth existence. Similarly hard, though she had money and social standing, was the lot of Mrs Weston, sister to Sir Thomas Gage of Firle* and the ill-treated wife of John Weston, a Catholic gentleman, of Sutton Place, near Guildford. Perhaps she had inherited a somewhat eccentric strain; her younger brother, a noted adventurer and speculator, was destined to acquire such enormous wealth through his dealing in Mississippi shares that he once offered to purchase the Polish crown, together with the entire island of Sardinia, which he intended to use, he said, merely as a plot for growing vegetables. At all events, Mrs Weston had left her husband, had quarrelled with an unkind guardian, and was on difficult terms with a number of fellow Catholics, among whom were the Englefields of Whitenights and Pope's sister and brother-in-law, the Racketts. Pope warmly supported her cause; and Caryll promised he would approach her guardian and let his friend know the results of the conference for transmission to the injured lady. Evidently his attempts at peace-making failed; and, towards the close of June, Pope admitted that there seemed little hope of reconciling Mr and Mrs Weston, 'tho' they may be brought together: 'tis an easy thing (we daily find) to join two bodies, but in matching minds there lies some difficulty'. Mrs Weston had a 'lofty' character; and it is clear that she was sufficiently attractive to touch her younger champion's heart. 'I cannot but join with you,' he told Caryll on 2 August, 'in a high concern for a person of so much merit, as I'm daily more and more convinced by her conversation that she is; whose ill fate it has been to be cast as a pearl before swine. And

* Created 1st Viscount Gage in 1717.

he who put so valuable a present into so ill hands shall (I own to you) never have my good opinion. . . . God grant he may never be my friend! and guard all my friends from such a guardian!'

Both episodes reveal not only Pope's generosity but his imaginative grasp of human suffering. He understood what it was to be solitary and unfriended. Mrs Weston, he would write next year, had gone to visit her aunt Lady Aston, 'with that mixture of expectation and anxiety with which people usually go into unknown or half discovered countries, utterly ignorant of the dispositions of the inhabitants'. He trusted she would have the welcome she deserved; 'the unfortunate of all people are the most unfit to be left alone; yet we see the world generally takes care they should be so, by abandoning 'em: whereas if we took a right prospect of human nature, the business and study of the happy and easy should be to divert and humour, as well as pity and comfort, the distressed. I cannot therefore excuse some near allies of mine for their conduct of late towards this lady, which has given me a good deal of anger as well as sorrow. All I can say to you of them at present is, that they have not been my relations these two months.' The relations he complained of were his sister and brother-in-law, who had sided with the Englefields and with Mrs Nelson, whom Cromwell had once dubbed his 'Sappho', against the ill-used Mrs Weston. By December 1712, Pope's championship of the runaway wife had exposed him to 'the misconstruction of some of my neighbours', who were 'whispering away' his reputation. Local gossips impugned his secret motives; they allowed themselves 'little lecheries of the tongue' that were soon reported for the poet's benefit. ' 'Tis a common practice now,' he reminded Caryll on 8 January 1713, 'for ladies to contract friendships as the great folks in ancient times entered into leagues. They sacrificed a poor animal betwixt 'em. . . . So now they pull some harmless little creature into pieces, and worry his character together very comfortably; Mrs Nelson and Mrs Englefield have served me just thus. . . .' The scandal his officious neighbours had aroused was extremely difficult to live down; but Pope concluded, on 12 June, that 'the best way of overcoming calumny and misconstruction is by a vigorous perseverance in every thing we know to be right, and a total neglect of all that ensue from it'. He refused to abandon his unfortunate protégée, who eventually rejoined her husband – on what terms history does not say; she died at Sutton Place in October 1724. But the episode had important literary consequences; Mrs Weston and Mrs Cope, with some help no doubt from other hapless females, provided a type of romantic misfortune that he would afterwards crystallize in a moving and melodious poem.

47

Here we must return to the story's starting point. For Pope the summer of 1711 was a particularly active period, when his interests were divided between many different projects and commissions. Richard Steele, who may have been introduced by Caryll, and was presently to introduce him to his powerful collaborator Joseph Addison, wrote soliciting the young man's help. Would not Pope produce some verses to go with the musical score of Thomas Clayton, for a series of concerts that author and composer were promoting at a London music-room? 'The desire I have to gratify Mr Steele,' he informed Caryll, 'has made me consent to this request; tho' 'tis a task that otherwise I'm not very fond of.' Whether he completed the verses we do not know; they have not been preserved among his published works.* Meanwhile he was both busy and solitary. Around the walls of his chamber he had hung portraits of Shakespeare, Milton and Dryden, 'that the constant remembrance of 'em may keep me always humble'; and under their protection he waged an unending struggle, which, in the stately Augustan fashion, he personified as his diligent courtship of the Muses. Often the goddesses eluded him: 'Those Aerial Ladies just discover to me enough of their beauties to urge my pursuit, and draw me on in a wandering maze of thought. . . . We grasp some more beautiful idea in our brain, than our endeavours to express it can set to the view of others. . . . The gay colouring which Fancy gave to our design at the first transient glance we had of it, goes off in the execution; like those various figures in the gilded clouds, which while we gaze long upon, to separate the parts of each imaginary image, the whole faints before the eye, and decays into confusion.'

Now and then, his courtship was interrupted. Christmas, 1711, was spent away from home, 'with some honest country gentlemen', he explained to Steele, 'who have wit enough to be good-natured, but no manner of relish for criticism or polite writing, as you may easily conclude when I tell you they never read the Spectator'. Back at Binfield, he quickly returned to his pursuit of the elusive goddesses. 1712, which was even more fully occupied than the previous year, saw the publication of two major poems and the elaborate revision of a third; but, as usual when we are dealing with Pope, their chronological sequence is somewhat difficult to follow; for the third, entitled *Windsor-Forest*, though rounded off and finally given to the public in March 1713, incorporates a large quantity of much earlier material; and one version of the poem seems to have been completed by the previous May. Certainly, it recalls an early

* The *Ode for Musick*, however, published by Lintot as a separate pamphlet in July 1713, may have been written for Thomas Clayton.

work; Pope has not yet broken through the poetic spell of his seventeenth-century predecessors; he adopts, as he had done in his juvenile verses, a conventional approach to a time-honoured theme. 'This poem,' noted Pope on a manuscript copy, 'was writ mostly after the Pastorals . . . but the last hundred lines . . . were added . . . soon after the ratification of the Treaty at Utrecht.'

The original poem was to have been dedicated to Sir William Trumbull; and the elder statesman, during their rides through the Forest, may have suggested that Pope should produce a description of the landscape that they both loved. Pope was further enlarging and revising his text towards the end of 1712, when he wrote to Caryll that 'the poem of *Windsor-Forest* has undergone many alterations and received many additions since you saw it. . . .' That winter was especially severe; all his senses were congealed in ice. He suffered acutely; 'I feel no thing alive but my heart and head; and my spirits, like those in a thermometer, mount and fall thro' my thin delicate contexture just as the temper of the air is more benign or inclement. In this sad condition I'm forced to take volatile drops every day: a custom I have so long continued, that my doctor tells me I must not long expect support from them, and adds that unless I use some certain prescriptions my tenement will not last long above ground.' While the snow-drifts banked up outside his windows, he had 'turned his studies to those books, which treat of the descriptions of the Arctic regions'; and he remembered two lines, by his rival pastoralist Ambrose Philips, that 'seem to me what the French call very *picturesque*'* –

> All hid in snow, in bright confusion lie,
> And with one dazzling waste fatigue the eye.

Amid this radiant ice-bound prospect, 'that sets my very imagination a shivering', he endeavoured 'to raise up round about me a painted scene of woods and forests in verdure and beauty . . . I am wandering thro' bowers and grottos . . . and while my trembling body is cowering o'er a fire, my mind is expatiating in an open sunshine'.

Thus his old work received its final revision. Lively contrasts would always appeal to Pope; the use he made of elaborate antitheses became an important feature of his poetic style; and some of the poem's warmer and more luxurious passages may have been added in December 1712, when only his imagination appeared to move and breathe, and Nature itself to

---

* Pope to Caryll, 21 December 1712. Pope's use of this important word is only the second recorded in the *Oxford English Dictionary*. The first occurs nine years earlier in Steele's *Tender Husband*: 'That circumstance may be very picturesque'.

be asleep or dead. True, considered as a whole, *Windsor-Forest* lacks vitality. Again Pope was following an established pattern; and here the pattern had been laid down by the courtly versifier Sir John Denham* – better known to readers of Gramont for his matrimonial mishaps – whose long moralistic poem, *Cooper's Hill*, had first appeared in 1642. Oddly enough, it owed much of its fame to a supremely happy after-thought. Into the edition of 1655 Denham had written the mellifluous quatrain that enchanted all Augustan readers, his memorable tribute to the genius of the River Thames –

> Oh could I flow like thee, and make thy stream
> My great example as it is my theme!
> Though deep, yet clear; though gentle yet not dull;
> Strong without rage; without o'erflowing, full.

– lines that innumerable critics have praised and many eighteenth-century poets, among them Pope, took the opportunity of parodying. Denhams' poem, however, in its entirety, is somewhat ponderous and sententious stuff. Though it is classed by literary historians as a topographical poem, *Cooper's Hill* bears little direct relation to the landscapes it sets out to cover. All the scenes that the poet introduces – Ludgate Hill and the noble bulk of St Paul's, with the city rising around them 'like a mist': Windsor and its antique fortress: Cooper's Hill and a meadow beneath its slopes where Denham, in happier days, had admired a Stuart King among his huntmten and his courtiers – are presented for their symbolic significance rsaher than for their living beauty. The text is full of political and historical allusions; Denham was an impassioned Royalist, and wrote in the opening year of the English Civil Wars; his descriptive passages serve merely as the framework of his topical and controversial message. Yet his 'majesty' delighted the Augustans; and Pope, too, when he revised his early poem, gave the work a strong didactic colouring. The last hundred lines that he added were concerned with war and peace – the peace that a Tory cabnet had determined to force through against the opposition of their belliciose Whig opponents.† Pope's dedicatee was not Sir William Trumbull, who may possibly have inspired, and been promised the dedication of the earliest drafts, but George Granville, now the first Lord Lansdowne – the same Granville who had offered to introduce his friend Harry to an extraordinary young modern poet – today an important member of the

* Poet, dramatist, diplomatist and architect, 1615–69.

† The War of the Spanish Succession, in which England, Holland and the Emperor were ranged against France and Bourbon Spain, had broken out in 1701.

Tory administration that had planned and negotiated the Peace of Utrecht.

Granville is said to have 'commanded' the poem; and Pope's dedication is appropriately effusive:

> Thy Forests, *Windsor*! and thy green Retreats,
> At once the Monarch's and the Muse's Seats,
> Invite my Lays. Be present, Sylvan Maids!
> Unlock your Springs, and open all your Shades.
> *Granville* commands: your Aid O Muses bring!
> What Muse for *Granville* can refuse to sing?

Here, as elsewhere, the tone is firmly conventional. But then, the employment of poetic conventions was in no way displeasing to a perceptive eighteenth-century reader. The quality he looked for was a poem's *organization* – the skill with which traditional themes were combined to produce a new effect of grace, the ingenious interplay of allusion and description, of literary learning and creative fancy. Pope's object was not to depict his individual response to Nature or, as the Romantic poets would do, record his own perplexed emotions, but to portray a universe that enclosed and completed both the aspiring thoughts and the triumphant works of Man. Yet Pope's poem is much less stylized than its cumbrous seventeenth-century model; despite his reverence for 'majestic Denham', he had an infinitely freer, more widely ranging spirit; and between the classic urns and stately colonnades, the artificial ruins and picturesque grottos, that he plants up and down the Berkshire meadows, we catch sudden glimpses of a very different landscape, large, windy, irregular, unconfined, where he had ridden as a boy beside Sir William Trumbull. Part of the charm of the Forest he knew lay in its mazy walks and unexpected prospects, its stag-antlered oaks and secret grassy glades, its patches of wild heath and stretches of placid farmland, with cloud-shadows sweeping across the hills and the darkened battlements of Windsor Castle far ahead above the trees:

> There, interspers'd in Lawns and opening Glades,
> Thin Trees arise that shun each other's Shades.
> Here in full Light the russet Plains extend;
> There wrapt in Clouds the blueish Hills ascend:
> Ev'n the wild Heath displays her Purple Dies,
> And midst the Desart fruitful Fields arise,
> That crown'd with tufted Trees and springing Corn,
> Like verdant Isles the sable Waste adorn.

The setting of *Windsor-Forest* is half baroque and half romantic. Nature herself is beautiful and admirable; but, when Man pays his court to Nature, he does so with superb assurance, and with none of the doubt and trepidation that characterized a nineteenth-century poet.

Its author's statement that *Windsor-Forest* was written 'mostly after the Pastorals', and that the political ending was attached 'soon after the ratification of the Treaty of Utrecht', need not perhaps be taken very literally. The treaty was ratified on 11 April 1713, and the poem – for which Bernard Lintot paid him the sum of £32 5s. 0d. – was published on 7 March of the same year. The text, we know, had undergone 'many alterations' during the course of the previous twelve months; and, from start to finish, it is an ingenious piece of carpentry, in which the new is cleverly married to the old. But all Pope's technical cleverness could not quite disguise the lack of any real imaginative design; it consists of a series of poetic episodes, summarily linked together. The result, however, with its historical and topical references, its descriptive passages and scraps of mythology, was well-calculated to delight the age. Queen Anne receives some fitting compliments; a picture of Norman barbarism, when William the Conqueror had enlarged his hunting forests by levelling towns and emptying villages, emphasizes the blessedness of the present period, when

> Rich Industry sits smiling on the Plains,
> And Peace and Plenty tell, a STUART reigns.

This cheerful view of the present suggests an enthusiastic vision of the future. Now that peace has been established, predicts the deified Thames, British commerce will embrace the globe, and outlandish vessels drop their anchors beneath the warehouses of London merchants:

> The Time shall come, when free as Seas or Wind
> Unbounded *Thames* shall flow for all Mankind. . . .
> Then Ships of uncouth Form shall stem the Tyde,
> And Feather'd People crowd my wealthy Side,
> And naked Youths and painted Chiefs admire
> Our Speech, our Colour and our strange Attire!
> Oh stretch thy Reign, fair *Peace*! from Shore to Shore,
> Till Conquest cease, and Slav'ry be no more:
> Till the freed *Indians* in their native Groves
> Reap their own Fruits, and woo their Sable Loves,
> *Peru* once more a Race of Kings behold,
> And other *Mexico's* be roof'd with Gold.

Such visions have today an ironic appeal, rather than a prophetic interest; we are more attracted by the lyrical-descriptive asides, and by the parade of mythological beings with whom the author populates his woods and fields. Thus the River Lodon, which flows into the Thames near Binfield, becomes the Ovidian nymph Lodona; and elsewhere a whole catalogue of local streams, including the Lodon itself, is recited in the style of Ausonius's poem on the River Moselle:

> The *Kennet* swift, for silver Eels renown'd;
> The *Loddon* slow, with verdant Alders crown'd:
> *Cole*, whose dark Streams his flow'ry Islands lave;
> And chalky *Wey*, that rolls a milky Wave:
> The blue, transparent *Vandalis*★ appears;
> The gulfy *Lee* his sedgy Tresses rears:
> And sullen *Mole*, that hides his diving flood;
> And sullen *Darent*, stain'd with *Danish* Blood.†

Pope was also imitating Ausonius in his impressive catalogue of fishes:

> Our plenteous Streams a various Race supply;
> The bright-ey'd Perch with Fins of *Tyrian* dye,
> The silver Eel, in shining Volumes roll'd,
> The Yellow Carp, in Scales bedrop'd with Gold,
> Swift Trouts, diversify'd with Crimson Stains,
> And Pykes, the Tyrants of the watery Plains.

Another passage – the description of the 'impatient courser' pawing the ground: 'And ere he starts, a thousand Steps are lost' – had been adapted from the *Thebaid*. Pope's recollections of the books he had read, however, are here constantly interwoven with vivid memories of things seen; the acute visual sense that would encourage him to become a painter was now pressed into the writer's service; and in *Windsor-Forest* he is looking back, not, as in *Pastorals*, to an imaginary Golden Age, but to the romantic background of his own boyhood. Thus he remembers the vocal hunt, riders bent on their horses' necks, as it streams across the Forest; spaniels quartering the stubble-fields and crouching obediently when they scent a partridge; the painted pheasant that whirrs through the boughs and drops in broken splendour to the earth:

> See! from the Brake the whirring Pheasant springs,
> And mounts exulting on triumphant Wings:
> Short is his Joy! he feels the fieryWound,
> Flutters in Blood, and panting beats the Ground.

★ The Wandle.
† Nearby the Danes had been bloodily defeated in the year 1016.

Ah! what avail his glossie, varying Dyes,
His Purple Crest, and Scarlet-circled Eyes,
The vivid Green his shining Plumes unfold;
His painted Wings, and Breast that flames with Gold?

Later, he recalls the sportsman out in the frost-bound woods, or ranging the water-meadows and the heathy commons –

Where Doves in Flocks the leafless Trees o'ershade,
And lonely Woodcocks haunt the wat'ry Glade.
He lifts the Tube, and levels with his Eye;
Straight a short Thunder breaks the frozen Sky.
Oft, as in Airy Rings they skim the Heath,
The clam'rous Lapwings feel the Leaden Death:
Oft as the mounting Larks their Notes prepare,
They fall, and leave their little Lives in Air.*

Among those who enjoyed and admired the poem was a new admirer, Jonathan Swift, who, on 9 March 1713, when Lintot's book was only two days old, informed Esther Johnson that 'Mr Pope has published a fine poem called Windsor Forest', adding the command 'read it', in his usual gruff, peremptory fashion. Though it proved somewhat less popular than a poem by Thomas Tickell, also concerned with *The Prospect of Peace*, which had appeared a few months earlier, during the course of the next two years *Windsor-Forest* ran through three editions.† Another product of this auspicious period was the work, entitled *Messiah: A Sacred Eclogue*, that had appeared in *The Spectator* on 14 May 1712. From the twentieth-century point of view, it is one of its author's least successful efforts; but Pope was always glad to demonstrate his versatility; and, at the time, he may have been anxious to write a poem that would please his good friend John Caryll, and satisfy the doubts that had been raised in Caryll's mind by the publication of the suspect *Essay*. Certainly Caryll was delighted and relieved; he found Pope's choice of subject very proper; church-music, he wrote on 23 May, was for him 'the most ravishing of all harmonious compositions', and 'sacred subjects, well-handled, the most inspiring of all poetry'. Pope, however, seems to have handled his subject in the spirit of a conscientious craftsman. The early eighteenth century was not an age of faith; since the death of Henry Vaughan in 1695, something had gone out of English devotional verse. Gone were John Donne's

* For this last image, Pope had a model in the *Georgics* – a line translated by Dryden as: 'From clouds they fall, and leave their souls above'.

† During the same period, Tickell's poem ran through six editions. Pope paid it a generous tribute. See Pope to Caryll, 29 November 1712.

troubled fervour, Herbert's exquisite delicacy and gentleness, Crashaw's incandescent passion, the haunting lyricism of Vaughan and Traherne, two poets who had translated their intense religious emotions into a pantheistic sense of natural beauty. Addison's well-known hymn, which appeared in *The Spectator* during the same year as Pope's sacred eclogue –

> The Spacious firmament on high,
> With all the blue ethereal sky,
> And spangled heavens, a shining frame
> Their great Original proclaim.

– illustrates the Augustan conception of religious poetry: a form of Loyal Address presented to the Divine Sovereign, rather than the record of a private spiritual adventure.

Pope's *Messiah* has a similarly official tone. The editor – Steele in this issue of *The Spectator* – published it without the author's name, but added that it had been composed 'by a great genius, a friend of mine, in the country; who is not ashamed to employ his wit in the praise of his Maker'. Based on Virgil's fourth *Eclogue*, inscribed to Pollio, through which, according to his Christian admirers, he had prophesied the birth of Jesus, it was also coloured by the poet's study of Isaiah. In some passages he follows the prophet closely. Thus Isaiah's dream of a peaceful future world – 'That which was dry land, shall be as a pool, and the thirsty ground as fountains of waters. In the dens, wherein dragons dwelt before, shall spring up the greenness of reed and bulrush' – is expanded in three splendid couplets:

> The Swain in barren Desarts with surprize
> See Lillies spring, and sudden Verdure rise;
> And Starts, amidst the thirsty Wilds, to hear
> New Falls of Water murm'ring in his Ear:
> On rifted Rocks, the Dragon's late Abodes,
> The green Reed trembles, and the Bulrush nods.

Elsewhere Jewish and classical, secular and devotional imagery form a not altogether harmonious pattern. Even in the eighteenth century Pope's 'florid epithets' and 'useless circumlocutions' sometimes aroused unfavourable comment; while, during the nineteenth, his use of a stylized 'poetic diction' – which led, for example, to the production of the weakly tautologous line:

> As the good Shepherd tends his fleecy Care

would be denounced by Wordsworth as 'extravagant and absurd'.

Yet, for all these shortcomings and obvious inequalities, both *Windsor-*

Forest and *Messiah* mark an important stage in Pope's development; and, when he wrote them, he had already begun a poem that would at length reveal the adult writer. In the years 1712 and 1713 his imagination was extraordinarily alert; though, during the same period, he was often seriously ill or slowly recovering from a breakdown. He had been ill in the spring of 1712, and remained 'excessively weak' throughout the summer. A long holiday in Sussex, presumably among the Carylls, was followed by another bout of illness as soon as he returned to Binfield. The savage winter season of 1712, with its icy blasts and heavy snowfalls, evidently left him tired and languid; and, on 8 January 1713, he reported to Caryll that he had been 'indeed much indisposed of late, rather weak and faint than sick'. He added, however, that he would willingly come to London, if there were any hope that they could arrange a meeting; and, before February was over, he felt sufficiently strong to take the road. His London holiday lasted for several months, until the latter part of July; and, having arrived there, he immediately renewed his association with the metropolitan literary world. 'I have just now stolen myself,' he told Caryll in February, 'from a tumult of acquaintance at Will's, into my chamber, to enjoy the pleasing melancholy of an hour's reflection alone. There is an agreeable gloominess which instead of troubling, does but refresh and ease the mind. . . .' *Windsor-Forest* had recently been sent to the press; and, at the same time, he had had 'the entertainment of reading Mr Addison's tragedy of *Cato*'. Addison, he later informed Spence, had brought him the play once it was finished, 'and desired to have my sincere opinion of it, and left it with me for three or four days. I gave him my opinion sincerely, which was "that I thought he had better not act it, and that he would get reputation enough, only by printing it". . . . Some time after Mr Addison said that "his own opinion was the same with mine: but that some particular friends of his, whom he could not disoblige, insisted on its being acted".'

Despite his doubts about its theatrical qualities, Pope thereupon agreed to write a prologue; and, at the end of April, he attended the first night, when *Cato* was enacted 'with the greatest applause'.* As Addison was a determined Whig, and partisan feelings were now running high, his somewhat pedestrian drama, which showed a great patriot sacrificing his life to freedom's sacred cause, became the focus of intense political excitement. 'The numerous and violent claps of the Whig party on the one side of the theatre,' reported Pope, 'were echoed back by the Tories

---

* *Cato* had an almost unexampled run of thirty-five performances; the text was translated into French, Italian and Latin.

on the other, while the author sweated behind the scenes with concern to find their applause proceeded more [from] the hand than the head. This was the case too of the prologue-writer, who was clapped into a staunch Whig sore against his will, at almost every two lines.' Then, between the acts, the Tory leader, Lord Bolingbroke, called Booth, the actor who played Cato, into his box and handed him a purse of fifty guineas, 'in acknowledgment . . . for his defending the cause of liberty so well against a *perpetual dictator*'; whereat the Whigs, reluctant to be outdone, arranged to furnish Booth with a similar gratuity; 'so betwixt them, 'tis probable that Cato (as Dr Garth expressed it) may have something to live upon, after he dies'. Cato, indeed, was 'not so much the wonder of Rome itself, in his days, as he is of Britain in ours'; and conspicuous among the audiences it attracted was a certain 'young gentleman of Oxford', who made it 'the sole guide of all his actions, and subject of all his discourse', and who had fallen in love with Mrs Oldfield 'for no other reason than because she acted Cato's daughter!' The text of the play had already been published; 'the town is so fond of it, that the orange wenches and fruit women in the Park offer the books at the side of the coaches, and the Prologue and Epilogue are cried about the streets by the common hawkers'.

Voltaire was afterwards to praise Addison as 'the first English writer who composed a regular tragedy and infused a spirit of elegance through every part of it', though he admitted that the heroines were feebly drawn;* but Dennis complained that the dramatist had clung with ridiculous perseverance to the classic doctrine of 'unity of place', so that the entire action, political or emotional, is staged in a single 'large hall in the governor's palace of Utica'; while Johnson was to remark that the public – which, whenever it thinks long on a subject, 'commonly attains to think right' – had 'not unjustly determined' that the play was 'rather a succession of just sentiments in elegant language than a representation of natural affections, or of any state probable or possible in human life'. Very wisely, the writer of the Prologue had decided to concentrate on the justice of Addison's sentiments:

> Our Author shuns by vulgar springs to move,
> The hero's glory, or the virgin's love. . . .
> Here tears shall flow from a more gen'rous cause,
> Such tears as Patriots shed for dying Laws. . . .

* 'La partie carrée des deux filles de Caton dans Adisson [sic] fait voir que les anglais ont souvent pris nos ridicules.' Voltaire to Panckoucke, 8 January 1768. Elsewhere Voltaire describes Addison's heroines, in verse, as 'insipides personages'.

and to advocate the emancipation of our national drama:

> Our scene precariously subsists too long
> On *French* translation, and *Italian* song.
> Dare to have sense your selves; assert the stage,
> Be justly warm'd with your own native rage.

But good Dr Garth, who contributed the Epilogue, preferred to strike a comic note; and, Cato having bade his solemn farewell, attended by Portius, Marcus and Juba, all in flowing modern periwigs, Mrs Porter, who played the part of Lucia, delivered a lengthy tirade against the folly of man and the frailty of 'fantastick' woman:

> Our hearts are form'd as you yourselves would chuse,
> Too proud to ask, too humble to refuse:
> We give to Merit, and to Wealth we sell;
> He sighs with most Success that settles well.
> The Woes of Wedlock with the Joys we mix;
> 'Tis best repenting in a Coach-and-Six.

– verses that must have sent the audience home duly relieved of the sense of terror and pity.

Pope's contribution to the success of *Cato*, however, was only one of many current interests. Five or six writers, far less celebrated than Addison, had recently seized upon him, begging him to criticize their works; the proofs of *Windsor-Forest* had to be corrected; he had 'an affair with Mr Steele' – no doubt the production of Steele's new paper, *The Guardian* – 'that takes up much consultation daily, and to add to all this a law business, which my father uses me in. Guess if I have time upon my hands. . . .' Early in April, he meant to retire to Binfield; but either the visit was postponed or he soon returned to London; and there, in June, he somehow found time to embark on a fresh course of studies. The visual arts had always attracted him – even as a boy he was devoted to painting and drawing; and, earlier that year, Caryll, whose wife had so much admired Pope's picture of the Virgin Mary, had suggested that it was time to cultivate his gifts. Pope therefore entered the studio of Charles Jervas, Kneller's industrious but untalented pupil, now a fashionable portrait-painter, whose women (observes a twentieth-century art historian) 'all look astonishingly alike and resemble a robin or one of the birds of the finch tribe'. Nearly every morning he repaired to the studio; his evenings, he said, were usually passed 'in the conversation of such as I think can most improve my mind, of whatever party or denomination they are'; and Jervas obligingly gave him the freedom of his private lodgings at Bridgewater House, Cleveland Court, next to St James's Palace, which for some while remained his address as often as he visited London. Pope, according to Spence, 'learned to draw of Jervas for a year and a half'. It proved a remarkably fruitful experience; there was a moment when he is said to have hesitated whether he should become a painter or a poet; and, Spence having demanded whether poetry or painting gave him more delight, he replied that each was 'extremely pleasing', and that the question was almost impossible to answer. Certainly he acquired some skill; and we know that he specialized in drawing heads. Besides a portrait of Betterton, copied from a canvas by Kneller, he afterwards informed Caryll, he had produced and thrown away no less than 'three Dean Swifts, two Duchesses of Montagu, one Virgin Mary, the Queen of England ... half a score Earls and a Knight of the Garter'. In painting as in poetry, he was a diligent reviser of other men's work; and once, when he visited Lord Radnor and saw a landscape by Peter Tillemans* standing unfinished on an easel, it was with great satisfaction that he appropriated the artist's brushes and 'stole some strokes' that he felt the picture needed.

Simultaneously, he was learning to write prose. Between the beginning of February 1712 and the end of September 1713, Pope published a dozen articles in *The Spectator*, followed by fourteen in *The Guardian*.† All are occasional essays, neatly and pleasantly turned, fair imitations of the style of Montaigne, though they lack both the French essayist's penetrating originality and his incomparable gift of self-analysis. But, here and there, Pope describes his own surroundings or includes a reflection of his deepest feelings. Thus, in 'A Dream of the Seasons', he depicts a garden that may very well have been his father's – entered from the house by a flight of stone steps that descend 'into a large square divided into four grass plots, in each of which is a statue of white marble', and bordered by a low wall, whence 'thro' a pair of iron gates, you are led into a long broad walk of the finest turf, set on each side with tall yews. ...' Pope's last contribution to *The Spectator* appeared in November 1712. That winter, we know, he was ill and weak; but, as soon as he returned to London, he again became a journalist and gave Steele such characteristic productions as 'Against Barbarity to Animals', 'The Club of Little Men', 'On a Dream of a Window in his Mistress's Breast', and an essay on the art of gardening.

* Died 1734; renowned as a 'master of panoramic landscape', author of many views of Newmarket Heath.

† All these articles are either unsigned or signed with a pseudonym. Sometimes their attribution to Pope is based on stylistic grounds alone. See Norman Ault, *The Prose Works of Alexander Pope*, 1936.

Pope's tenderness for the brute creation was unusual in Augustan England. Cruelty, he wrote, was nowadays 'almost a distinguishing character' of the jovial, unthinking British race: 'we should find it hard to vindicate the destroying of anything that has life, merely out of wantonness; yet in this principle our children are bred up, and one of the first pleasures we allow them, is the license of inflicting pain upon poor animals. . . .' Just as bulls are baited and cocks set fighting, so 'there are other animals that have the misfortune . . . to be treated as common enemies wherever found. The conceit that a cat has nine lives has cost at least nine lives in ten of the whole race of 'em. . . . Whether the unaccountable animosity against this useful domestic may be any cause of the general persecution of owls, (who are a sort of feathered cats) or whether it be only an unreasonable pique the moderns have taken to a serious countenance, I shall not determine.'

Still more evocative of the author's own emotions is a two-fold essay entitled 'The Club of Little Men'. A small man, Pope observes, is inevitably self-conscious; and to self-consciousness he often adds a certain tincture of aggressiveness: 'I remember a saying . . . concerning persons in low circumstances of stature, that their littleness would hardly be taken notice of, if they did not manifest a consciousness of it themselves in all their behaviour . . . I question not but that it will be pleasing to you to hear, that a set of us have formed a society, who are sworn to *Dare to be Short*, and boldly bear out the dignity of littleness under the noses of those enormous engrossers of manhood, those hyperbolical monsters of the species, the tall fellows that overlook us.' The idea is then developed in comic and pathetic detail, with special reference to the President of the Club, a diminutive poet named Dick Distick, 'a lively little creature with long arms and legs', who 'stoops as he walks' and, to make himself appear even more inconspicuous, generally wears a black suit; 'a spider is no ill emblem of him. He has been taken at a distance for a small windmill.' If Dick climbs into an elbow chair and 'his arms are spread over it', he resembles 'a child in a go-cart'. When the club is gathered around a table, their chins scarcely clear the pewter dishes; and the President was once almost eclipsed by a large flask of Italian wine. Since that day their meeting-place has been appropriately refurnished and the entrance made a good deal lower, 'so as to admit no man of above five foot high, without brushing his foretop, which whoever does is utterly unqualified to sit among us'. Also disqualified for membership is any man that 'strives to get above his size, by stretching, cocking or the like; or . . . hath stood on tiptoe in a crowd. . . . If any member shall take advantage from the fulness or length of his wig . . . or the immoderate extent of his hat . . . to seem larger and higher than he is, it is ordered, he shall wear red heels to his shoes and a red feather in his hat, which may apparently mark and set bounds to the extremities of his small dimensions. . . .'

Elsewhere Pope discourses on the evils of newspaper-reading, a passion particularly widespread in the London coffee-houses, whose frequenters 'read the advertisements with the same curiosity as the articles of public news; and are as pleased to hear of a piebald horse that is strayed out of a field near Islington, as of a whole troop that has been engaged in any foreign adventure. In short, they have a relish for everything that is news . . . or to speak more properly, they are men of voracious appetite, but no taste.' Pope's most important essay, however, was his mock-review of Ambrose Philips. When his pastoral verses first appeared, Pope had paid his fellow-pastoralist a handsome tribute; but he had since been hurt by invidious comparisons between his own and Philips's lines. In April, 1713, he therefore composed an ironic appreciation of his rival's gifts, emphasizing all the errors he detected by pretending to regard them as conspicuous virtues. 'Mr Pope's' merits were elaborately played down. Whereas 'Philips hath given us manifest proofs of his knowledge of books', his competitor, though it must be admitted that he had 'imitated some single thoughts of the Ancients well enough, if we consider that he had not the happiness of a university education', had 'dispersed them, here and there, without that order and method which Mr Philips observes. . . .' Mr Pope, moreover, 'hath fallen into the same error with Virgil. His clowns do not converse in all the simplicity proper to the country: his names are borrowed from Theocritus and Virgil'; while 'Philips, who hath the strictest regard to propriety, makes choice of names . . . more agreeable to a reader of delicacy; such as *Hobbinol, Lobbin, Cuddy* and *Colin Clout*'. Philips's 'beautiful rusticity' is applauded, his 'simplicity of diction, the melancholy flowing of the numbers', and his ingenious employment of antique English proverbs. True, Philips sometimes confuses the seasons and introduces wolves into a modern English landscape; but he would not, writes the essayist, 'have a poet slavishly confine himself (as Mr Pope hath done) to one particular season . . . one certain time of the day, and one unbroken scene in each eclogue . . . Mr Philips, by a poetical creation, hath raised up finer beds of flowers than the most industrious gardener; his roses, lilies and daffadils blow in the same season.'

Such minutiae were often debated by orthodox Augustan critics; and Pope had so cleverly adopted their tone that his first biographer, William Ayre,* having noted that, when his *Pastorals* appeared, some cri-

* *Memoirs of the Life and Writings of Alexander Pope, Esqr., 1745.*

their vote to Philips, published extracts from the parody as a perfectly genuine piece of criticism. More surprising, the essay deceived Steele. According to Warburton, Pope had caused his manuscript to be delivered 'by an unknown hand'; and, gravely perturbed, the editor had consulted Pope, explaining that he would never publish an article in which one of his associates 'was complimented at the expense of another'; whereupon Pope 'told him he was too delicate, and insisted that the paper should be published in the *Guardian*'. Only Addison is said to have recognized the fraud and, taking Pope aside, remarked, 'in his agreeable manner', that he had put his friends 'in a very ridiculous light. . . .' But Spence had it from the poet that Addison was himself deceived. As for Philips, he soon detected the fraud, and registered extreme annoyance.

Pope, no doubt, was delighted with the success of his parody. The whole episode, nevertheless, throws a disconcerting light upon his adult character. During his youth, it had seemed singularly straightforward; he was generous, warmly attached to his friends, and showed a sensitive appreciation of their individual moods and feelings. Now, for the first time, we meet him in a very different guise – as the literary strategist, a master of subterfuge, prepared to sacrifice a friend if, by doing so, he could score an easy triumph. Steele was an ingenuous, good-humoured man; and it was neither kind nor, indeed, was it wise to exploit his simple nature. The stratagems employed – the use of an unknown emissary and an assumed handwriting – had done their author small credit; and, although the parody was a highly successful joke, it must have wounded Steele and exasperated Addison – both fellow-writers whom he had every reason to regard – at least as much as it offended Philips. Perhaps an explanation is to be found in his essay on 'The Club of Little Men'. Dick Distick could not forget his size. 'Those enormous engrossers of manhood', 'the tall fellows that overlook us', were bound to rank among his hereditary enemies. He might admire, but he could not entirely trust them; and the sense of solitude that sometimes enveloped Pope was now beginning to breed the habit of suspicion, which, as the years went by, would gradually prevail against his kindlier and gentler instincts. John Dennis had taught him the meaning of hatred; henceforward he was to envisage the artist's life as a state of martial preparation, in which nothing must be left to chance, and each move carefully planned and mounted.

It is significant that, towards the end of 1712, he had already decided to collect his letters. According to English law, a personal letter ranks as 'an original literary work'. That, unquestionably, was Pope's view; and, on 19 November, he had written to Caryll admitting his interest in their correspondence. His letters, he protested, were 'scribbled with all the carelessness and inattention imaginable: my style, like my soul, appears in its natural undress before my friend. . . . There's no dragging your dignity about with you everywhere, as if an alderman should constantly wear his chain in his shop.' But his postscript includes what he himself admits to be 'an odd request' – that, if Caryll had 'ever thought any of my epistles worth preserving, you will favour me with the whole cargo, which shall be faithfully returned to you'. His excuse was that they might be of some assistance in an undertaking – presumably his essays for *The Guardian* – on which he happened to be currently at work: 'I never kept any copies of such stuff as I write; but there are several thoughts which I throw out that way in the freedom of my soul that may be of use to me in a design I am lately engaged in, which will require so constant a flux of thought and invention, that I can never supply it without some assistance, and 'tis not impossible but so many notions . . . may save me a good deal of trouble.' Clearly, his real reasons were somewhat more complex. His letters were to form part of the elaborate defensive system that he was gradually building up around his own genius.

As a controversialist, Pope had tasted blood; and, just three months after his brush with Philips, he launched a full-scale attack on Dennis, his alleged provocation being the veteran critic's *Remarks upon the Tragedy of Cato*, recently issued under Lintot's imprint. Dennis had known that his remarks would be taken ill: 'I pass for a man,' he grumbled, 'who is conceitedly resolved to like nothing which others like.' But he could not have expected, nor did he quite deserve, the scurrilous assault that followed. He had published his criticism on 11 July; on 28 July Pope issued a threepenny pamphlet entitled *The Narrative of Dr Robert Norris, concerning the strange and deplorable Frenzy of Mr John Denn—s An Officer of the Custom-house*. Dr Norris was a well-known mental specialist, whose advertisements, declaring that he had been 'many years experienced in the care of lunatics' and offering 'suitable attendance' at his private house, frequently appeared in London newspapers. Having borrowed the physician's name and functions, Pope gave the public a so-called 'exact account' of how he had done his best to treat the frenzied critic. It is a wild story, told with ferocious gusto. Summoned to Dennis's lodgings by an agitated charwoman, the narrator had found both the patient and his room in a condition of extreme disorder: 'His eyebrows were grey, long, and grown together, which he knit with indignation when anything was spoken, insomuch that he seemed not to have smoothed his forehead for many years. His flannel nightcap, which was exceedingly begrimed with sweat and dirt, hung upon his left ear; the flap of his breeches dangled between his legs, and the rolls of his stockings fell down to his ankles.'

Next Pope makes somewhat self-complacent fun of the squalor in which needy critics live, and adds a wounding reference to his previous portrait: 'I observed his room was hung with old tapestry, which had several holes in it, caused, as the old woman informed me, by his having cut out the heads of divers tyrants, the fierceness of whose visages had much provoked him. . . . By the fireside lay three-farthings-worth of smallcoal in a *Spectator* . . . . There was nothing neat in the whole room, except some books on his shelves very well bound and gilded, whose names I had never before heard of. . . .* The whole floor was covered with manuscripts, as thick as a pastry-cook's shop on a Christmas Eve.† On his table were some ends of verse and of candles; a gallipot of ink with a yellow pen in it, and a pot of half-dead ale covered with a Longinus.'

Attending the lunatic are his publisher, Bernard Lintot, and 'a grave elderly gentleman . . . the latitude of whose countenance was not a little eclipsed by the fulness of his peruke', thought to stand for Henry Cromwell. It is the success of *Cato* that has driven Dennis mad; and his ravings concern his injured professional dignity: 'Is the man who settles poetry on the basis of antiquity mad? Dares any one assert that there is a *peripaetia* in that vile piece that's foisted upon the Town for a dramatic poem? That man is mad, the Town is mad, the world is mad. See Longinus in my right hand, and Aristotle in my left. I am the only man among the moderns that supports them.' The encounter concludes in a scene of knockabout farce, when Cromwell, who has also begun to show signs of derangement, breaks down the door of the closet into which he has been locked for safety, and, brandishing 'a vast folio', attacks the doctor and the publisher, while Dennis, wielding a peruke-block, helps to drive them from the room. As a means of resolving a serious literary argument, Pope's *Narrative* is an inexcusable production; and Dennis, not altogether unjustly, was to denounce the pamphlet as 'a Billingsgate libel'. It is redeemed by the writer's comic verve, and by his Hogarthian mixture of imaginative and realistic details. Dennis's squalid study seems to have been drawn from life – the papers on the floor, the scattered candle-stumps, the pot of flat beer and the yellow quill. No less vivid is the picture of Dennis himself with his thick ragged grey eyebrows and perpetually aggrieved expression.

The pamphlet, of course, was issued anonymously; and Addison, on

* These volumes were Dennis's own work.

† Wastepaper was used to line pie-dishes. See Dryden's *MacFlecknoe*, where Shadwell's poems are said to have been employed for these, and even humbler purposes.

first reading it, felt that, much as he had resented Dennis's *Remarks*, it was a joke in very poor taste. He therefore instructed Steele to write a disclaimer, which was sent to Bernard Lintot, informing him that 'Mr Addison . . . wholly disapproves the manner of treating Mr Dennis in a little pamphlet by way of Dr Norris's account. When he thinks fit to take notice of Mr Dennis's objections to his writings, he will do it in a way Mr Dennis shall have no just reason to complain of.' If Pope knew that Addison disapproved, he remained entirely unrepentant. His social life was as busy and 'rambling' as ever; and in August he informed Caryll that he divided his time between conversations with the Arian astronomer William Whiston, who lectured him on the plurality of worlds, and ribald coffee-house talk with the outrageous General Tidcombe: 'You can't wonder my thoughts are scarce consistent, when I tell you how they are distracted! . . . This minute, perhaps, I am above the stars . . . looking forward into the vast abyss of eternity. . . . The next moment I am below all trifles, even grovelling with Tidecombe in the very centre of nonsense: now I am recreating my mind with the brisk sallies and quick turns of wit, which Mr Steele . . . darts about him . . . Good God! what an incongruous animal is Man? how unsettled in his best part, his soul; and how changing and variable in his frame of a body? . . . What is Man altogether, but one mighty inconsistency?'

At the end of August he was still in London, and still diligently working in Jervas's studio, where every day he discovered 'beauties that were till now imperceptible to me', and, as he drew or painted, the 'corner of an eye, or turn of a nose or ear, the smallest degree of light or shade on a cheek', had power to warm his heart and stir his fancy. In September he left London for a week at Whitehill House, accompanied by the dramatist and editor Nicholas Rowe,* whose natural 'vivacity and gaiety' made him a peculiarly delightful companion. But on the 20th he was back at Cleveland Court, 'taking a solitary walk by moonshine in St James's Park', for the moment quietly meditative, 'full of the reflections of the transitory nature of all human delights', and once more haunted by the idea of the starry worlds above his head. In October, he received the agreeable news that Count Anthony Hamilton, author of the *Memoirs of the Comte de Gramont*, now nearly seventy years old, had translated his *Essay on Criticism* into French, and wrote to thank him for his good offices, adding a characteristic reference to his own defective shape: 'if I am now a good figure, I must consider you have naturalized me into a country which is

* Pope wrote an epilogue for Rowe's tragedy, *Jane Shore*, which was performed in February 1714.

famous for making every man a fine gentleman'. Meanwhile Cromwell seemed to have taken offence at his recent caricature of Dennis, though Pope had cautiously denied the authorship. The quarrel, however, had been patched up; and he hoped they were 'very far from being enemies. We visit, criticize, and drink coffee as before.' Such a multitude of varying occupation evidently over-taxed his strength; and, during the latter part of October, he was 'troubled with sickness' and a prey to philosophic melancholy. But he did not leave London. He intended, Caryll was informed, to 'go into the country about a month hence. . . . I am deeply engaged in poetry, the particulars whereof shall be deferred till we meet.'

His poetic projects at the time were twofold. In October, he had entrusted Addison with an important literary secret – always anxious to extend his poetic scope, he had decided to produce a versified rendering of the *Iliad*; and Addison had courteously approved, offering to promote subscriptions. The second project was of even greater importance. Pope was now refashioning and enlarging a poem that Lintot had already published, an elegant *jeu d'esprit* entitled *The Rape of the Lock*, on a topical subject that he owed to Caryll. The completion of the poem in its enlarged form marked the end of his apprenticeship. Hitherto he had been slowly learning his trade, progressing from the facile lyricism of the *Pastorals* to the critical and didactic *Essay*, thence to the elaborately organized landscape of *Windsor-Forest* and the solemn measures of his 'Sacred Eclogue'. In each he had displayed his mastery, his extraordinary sensitiveness to the value of words and his almost unfailing command of verbal music; in each he had carefully selected a theme, then developed its possibilities with conscientious literary artifice. Each perhaps might be described as a trial-run, that carried him a little further towards the conquest of his medium; but he had still to achieve a perfectly harmonious alliance between his imaginative gifts and his intellectual powers. His new poem had been embarked on carelessly; its real significance only emerged when he set about his task, developing even brilliantly once he had begun to enlarge his original design. His other early works attest his ambition and skill, his devoted absorption in the art of letters. Here his mood was happy, carefree and bold. He was writing a poem primarily to please himself.

4

'Most little poems,' Pope instructed Spence, 'should be written by a plan', adding, in the course of a different colloquy, that 'a poem on a slight subject requires the greater care to make it considerable enough to be read'. During the latter part of 1711 he had drawn up a plan for one of his slightest and lightest, but solidest and richest works, had completed it 'in less than a fortnight's time' and, early next year, had sold it to Lintot, who published it among *Miscellaneous Poems and Translations*, where it appeared with Pope's versions of the opening book of Statius's *Thebaid* and Ovid's *Vertumnus and Pomona*, his delightful address *To a Young Lady* and some relatively unimportant pieces. The occasion was curious. Pope had always taken a keen interest in England's ancient Catholic families; and Caryll, who had many links with their world, told him of a ridiculous domestic feud that had recently broken out between the Fermors and the Petres, because the seventh Lord Petre, Caryll's ward and protégé, had stolen a cherished lock from the head of his kinswoman, Arabella Fermor. The details of his theft remain uncertain: whether it was committed, as Pope declares, at Hampton Court, or in a London drawing-room. But there seems no doubt that the harum-scarum young man did indeed snip off the treasured curl – the kind of serpentine side-curl that Hogarth would afterwards describe as 'too alluring to be strictly decent'; that Arabella was enraged by her loss; that the elder Fermors were astonished and offended; and that various subsidiary members of the clan, including Sir George Browne and a Mrs Morley, who may or may not have been Sir George's sister, took up arms in the ensuing squabble.

All the protagonists were closely connected: the Petres referred to Caryll as their cousin; and Lord Petre was particularly fond of him and regarded his '*cher Tuteur*' as a second sire. Caryll had been much concerned about the young man's foolish 'frolick'; for Petre had a winning disposition, and Pope had heard that he was 'one of those lords that have wit in our days'.* But it was evident that his frolic had gone too far; and Caryll, having discussed the problem with Pope, now suggested that he should act as peace-maker and proceed to furnish a poetic remedy. 'The stealing of Miss Belle Fermor's hair', Pope recorded, had caused an estrangement between the families, 'though they had lived so long in great friendship before'; and 'a common acquaintance and well-wisher to both desired me to write a poem, and laugh them together again'. Thus he sat down to produce *The Rape of the Lock*, which, as literary masterpieces are often apt to do, soon transcended its immediate object.

At the time he had not met Lord Petre; and it is doubtful if he was acquainted with his heroine, except presumably by reputation. Miss Fermor, then aged about twenty-two, eldest daughter of a Catholic squire, Henry Fermor, of Tusmore and Somerton in Oxfordshire, was already celebrated as a fashionable beauty; and, two years earlier, London's rhyming journalists had paid tribute to her charms and virtues – to the 'modest lustre' she dispensed on her walks across St James's Park; to her 'snowy breasts', the 'easy motion' of her neck, and the elegant propriety of her moral conduct:

> F—rm—r's a pattern for the beauteous kind,
> Compos'd to please, and ev'ry way refin'd;
> Obliging with reserve, and humbly great,
> Though gay yet modest, though sublime yet sweet.

– the last an encomium that Pope must certainly have read, since it had appeared in the same issue of Tonson's *Miscellanies* that had printed his own pastoral verses.

Three portraits of Miss Fermor still exist; and one shows her wearing the small jewelled cross – 'which Jews might kiss and infidels adore' – hung by the poet on Belinda's bosom. The artist was Sykes, a well-known portrait-painter of the day; but, like other successful portraitists, he was interested not so much in studying and commemorating a personality as in manufacturing a pleasant picture; and the young woman who looks out from his oval canvas merely reflects the Augustan conception of elegance – an egg-shaped face with a long and pointed nose, which runs down smoothly from the rounded forehead; big dark eyes beneath neatly-drawn eyebrows; a faintly simpering mouth, the lower lip somewhat

* Robert, Lord Petre, of Ingatestone, Essex, had been born in 1690, succeeded as seventh baron in 1706, married 'a great heiress' in 1712 and died of smallpox at his Arlington Street house in March 1713. He is said to have been a man of small stature, a detail that may have interested Pope.

protuberant; and a diminutive, slightly dimpled chin. Arabella's hair, we learn, was of a 'warm golden shade' or a 'fair auburn', whereas Belinda's fated lock was sable-black; and in Sykes's portrait she is wearing a lustrous blue-silk dress, which reveals a linen undergarment around the breast and sleeves. The picture was painted before 1714 or 1715, when she married a Catholic gentleman named Francis Perkins, of Ufton Court, Berkshire. It represents her at the zenith of her youthful attractions, as the proud, yet decorous and modest girl, whom her kinsman's misbehaviour had so gravely ruffled.

Pope, says his editor Warburton, made a diplomatic approach both to his hero and to his heroine before his poem reached the public; and Belinda had graciously approved the work and had given him her *imprimatur*. There is no doubt that, once it had been printed, he wrote, in May 1712, to a relation of Caryll, a Mr Edward Bedingfield, enclosing two advance copies, which he requested him to pass on; and Bedingfield replied that Miss Fermor was for the moment 'out of town and therefore all I can do is to leave her packet at her lodging. . . .' But, later that year, Arabella and some of the minor characters to whom it seemed to refer took a rather more unfriendly line. Sir George Browne was especially annoyed. 'Sir Plume blusters, I hear,' reported Pope to Caryll on 8 November 1712; 'nay, the celebrated Lady herself is offended, and, which is stranger, not at herself but me. . . .' Some audacious *double entendres* had hurt her modesty, and she was also exasperated by the poet's hint that Belinda had had a secret weakness for the Baron; while Sir George, who was her second cousin and a notably pompous and consequential personage, suspected with reason that the thumb-nail sketch of Sir Plume bore a distinct resemblance to his own traits. Other Catholic gentlemen were almost equally aggrieved; and 'upon the day that this poem was published', Pope noted in his subsequent *Key to the Lock*, 'it was my fortune to step in the Cocoa Tree, where a certain gentleman was railing very liberally at the author, with a passion extremely well counterfeited, for having (as he said) reflected upon him in the character of Sir Plume. Upon his going out, I enquired who he was, and they told me, a *Roman Catholic Knight*. I was the same evening at Will's, and saw a circle round another gentleman, who was railing in like manner, and showing his snuff-box and cane to prove he was satirized in the same character. I asked this gentleman's name, and was told he was a *Roman Catholic Lord*.'

Sir George's blusterings continued loud and violent; and, still flourishing his celebrated cane, he assured his coffee-house cronies that he meant to lay it across the wretched author's back. Pope accepted the news with cynicism. On 5 December 1712, he wrote to Caryll's son from Binfield; and, having admitted that he himself has been leading a dull and stupid life – 'confined to a narrow closet, lolling on an armchair, nodding away my days over a fire', at a time when Caryll was pursuing 'the sprightly delights of the field . . . rousing a whole country with shouts and horns' – he remarks that 'possibly some of my good friends . . . may give me a more lively sense of things. . . . Dull fellows that want wit, (like those very dull fellows that want lechery) may, by well-applied strokes and scourges, be fetched up into a little of either. I therefore have some reason to hope no man that calls himself my friend . . . will do me the injury to hinder these well-meaning gentlemen from beating up my understanding. Whipt wits, like whipt-creams, afford a most sweet and delectable syllabub to the taste of the town, and often please them better with the dessert, than all the meal they had before. So, if Sir Plume should take the pains to dress me, I might possibly make the last course better than the first.'

Sir George, whom Pope dismisses as a 'stale, cold fool' – not even a frothy syllabub – never carried out his threat. As for Arabella, she soon grew less indignant, and learned to accept her vicarious immortality with becoming *savoir-faire*. In 1775, Hesther Thrale, then touring France accompanied by her husband and Samuel Johnson, encountered a Mrs Fermor, the abbess of a Parisian convent, who 'remembered that Mr Pope's praise made her aunt very troublesome and conceited', and that the Fermors had quickly forgiven Pope and entertained him at their country house, where he proved a difficult and capricious inmate. Arabella was fully reconciled to her position before the end of 1713. That December, despite the protests of Addison – a warm admirer of the original poem, which he styled a 'delicious little thing' – Pope returned to *The Rape of the Lock* and produced a considerably enlarged version. In January 1714 it was announced for publication; and the new addition appeared, on 2 March, accompanied by a complimentary address 'To Mrs Arabella Fermor'. The first version had consisted of two cantos; another three were now added. In his address, Pope asserts that the original poem had 'found its way into the world' without his leave, and that, when he heard that an 'imperfect copy' had been offered to a bookseller, Arabella had had the good nature to authorize 'the publication of one more correct'; and that he had been obliged to publish it 'before I had executed half my design, for the machinery was entirely wanting to complete it'. This machinery he had since been able to provide. . . . But then, in questions of his own literary chronology, Pope was seldom altogether truthful; and there is no evidence to support his assertion that he had merely completed

5 Lady Mary Pierrepont by Charles Jervas, about 1714; 'I have made a perfect passion wrote her admirer) of preferring your present face to your past'.

6 Henry St. John, 1st Viscount Bolingbroke. Artist unknown.

a preconceived design. More probably, he had enjoyed re-reading his poem; and it gained a fresh hold on his imagination as he looked back through the printed pages.

The machinery he had chosen to supply was based, he told his dedicatee, on 'the Rosicrucian Doctrine of Spirits', as set forth 'in a French book called *Le Comte de Gabalis*, which both in its title and size is so like a novel, that many of the Fair Sex have read it for one by mistake'. The Sylphs, Gnomes, Nymphs and Salamanders of Rosicrucian lore, he goes on to explain, 'are the best-conditioned creatures imaginable. For they say, any mortal may enjoy the most intimate familiarities with these gentle spirits, upon a condition very easy to all true Adepts, an inviolate preservation of chastity.' Perhaps he felt fairly confident that Arabella would not pursue her own researches. Philip Ayres's translation of *Le Comte de Gabalis, ou Entretiens sur les Sciences Secrètes* had been published thirty-four years earlier; and the first French edition had appeared in 1670. Its author was as odd as the book itself. Born near Toulouse in 1636, the scion of an ancient Gascon family, l'abbé de Montfaucon de Villars had at an early age abandoned the Church to become a Parisian man of letters and, besides a philosophical-historical romance, had produced some bold attacks on the poetic style of Racine and Corneille – which amused Madame de Sévigné; though, judging by certain of the expressions he used, she suspected that the writer did not really 'know the world' – together with a series of controversial pamphlets aimed at Pascal and the Jansenists. In character, he seems to have been a true Gascon, impetuous, hot-headed, often blood-thirsty. Twice the local Parlement had convicted him of murder and sentenced him to the most dreadful of all deaths – to be broken on the wheel; in 1662, when he was accused of assassinating a neighbour, Paul de Ferrovil, sieur de Montgaillard; again in 1668, when he and his confederates had attacked and burned down a château that bore the name of the Montgaillard family, mortally wounding a maid-servant whom they happened to discover there.

Luckily, the jurisdiction of the Parlement de Toulouse did not extend as far as Paris. Villars escaped the torments of the wheel and, not long after he had committed his second crime, wrote that delightful book, *Le Comte de Gabalis*. It achieved an immediate and scandalous renown, thanks not only to the erudition it displayed, but to the fluent charm of the author's narrative and his touches of poetic and erotic fancy. The hero of the *Entretiens* is a learned German nobleman, absorbed in Rosicrucian studies; and Villars informs us that he has recently died, carried off by an apoplectic seizure. Some of his readers, he adds, will no doubt remark that such an end customarily overtakes those who have divulged the secrets of the Sages, and that, since the days of '*le Bien-heureux Raymond Lulle*',* an avenging angel has seldom failed to wring their necks. Strangely enough, a similar retribution would appear to have overtaken Villars; for he, too, died in highly mysterious circumstances, on the road from Paris to Lyon, towards the close of 1673, either slain by outraged Rosicrucians – France, during the closing decades of the seventeenth century, harboured a large number of occultists and practitioners of the secret arts – or struck down by friends of his old adversary, the ill-fated sieur de Montgaillard.

The book he left behind him certainly deserved its renown. In a period that saw the production of some of the greatest masterpieces of French prose, he was a lively, easy, energetic writer, who possessed an invaluable knack of springing headlong into the middle of his subject. He unfolds the story of how he had received an unexpected visit from the illustrious German in a few succinct paragraphs, quickly and neatly preparing the scene, then allowing the Count to tell his own tale. The universe, Gabalis assures him, is populated by an innumerable company of spirits. Nature abhors a vacuum; and the 'immense space, which is between the Earth and the Heavens, has more noble inhabitants than birds and flies; this vast ocean has also other troops besides dolphins and whales; the profundity of the earth is not only for moles; and the element of fire (more noble than the other three) was not made to be unprofitable and void.'

Overhead arches the romantic realm of the Sylphs, a countless multitude 'having human shape, somewhat fierce in appearance, but tractable upon experience. . . . Their wives and daughters have a kind of masculine beauty, such as we describe the Amazons to have.' During the Dark Ages, in the reign of King Pepin, a famous Cabalist had recommended the Sylphs to show themselves to mankind; and they had done so 'with great magnificence: these creatures appearing in the air, in human shape; sometimes ranged in battle, marching in good order, or standing to their arms, or encamped under most majestic pavilions; at other times, on airy ships of an admirable structure, whose flying navy was tossed about at the will of the zephyrs'. While the Sylphs haunt the regions of the sky, alert, intellectual, amorous, yet delicate and subtly diffuse as the element in which they move, the waters teem with a people whom ancient Sages called the 'Undians or Nymphs. They have but a few males amongst

* Ramon Lull (*c.* 1236–1315), Catalan poet and philosopher, translated by Caxton. Many works on magic and alchemy were attributed to his authorship.

them; but the women are there in great numbers. Their beauty is marvellous; and the daughters of men have nothing in them comparable to these.' The element of fire is the home of the Salamanders, who partake of its consuming purity. As for the dark and massy earth, it is 'filled almost to the centre with Gnomes', a race 'of small stature, the guardians of treasures, of mines, and of precious stones ... ingenious, friends of men, and easy to be commanded'. The females of the species, the Gnomids, are diminutive but prepossessing, and wear an extremely curious garb.

Some of these details – and Villars's conception of a universe alive with supernatural beings – were freely adopted by the English poet. In one important respect, however, he differs considerably from *Le Comte de Gabalis*. Whereas Pope had assured Miss Fermor that friendship 'with these gentle spirits' demanded 'an inviolate preservation of chastity', Gabalis announces that, although the Sylphs and allied spirits had an extraordinarily long life, after some centuries had passed they were bound to fade away and vanish, unless they could enlist the support of a human bedfellow, whose hopes of salvation and a blessed futurity they might then expect to share. Thus they are perpetually pursuing and seducing mankind; and many of the Sages had proved complaisant victims. To enjoy the embraces of an aetherial mistress, they gladly renounced more trivial human joys;* for the lovliest woman seemed coarse and earthy beside the meanest of the Sylphs, and no sense of disgust or satiety followed such sublime encounters. Gabalis thereupon proceeds to develop his theme with the assistance of three additional dialogues, in which the adept's burning enthusiasm is matched against his interlocutor's ironic wit, until we reach the conclusion of the fifth *Entretien*, and, just when we expect that Villars will describe an actual meeting between a Sage and a Sylphid, he prudently breaks off his tale.

In these learned fantasies and their erotic undertones Pope clearly took a keen delight; but, to frame his poem as a whole, he needed source-books of a different order. The mock-heroic poem was a well-established literary mode, derived from the *Margites*, or War of the Frogs and the Mice, that Greek critics, before the days of Aristotle, customarily attributed to the author of the *Iliad*. Among more recent specimens were Tassoni's *Secchia Rapita*, published in 1622, the description of a fierce struggle

* By way of contrast, Gabalis repeats an anecdote, gathered from the works of Paracelsus, about a German philosopher who had attempted to make the best of both worlds, and had kept an earthly, as well as a spiritual, mistress. '*Comme il dinait avec sa nouvelle maîtresse et quelques-uns de ses amis, on vit en l'air la plus belle cuisse du monde; l'amante invisible voulut bien la faire voir aux amis de son infidèle, afin qu'ils jugeassent du tort qu'il avait de lui préferer une femme. Après quoi la Nymphe indignée le fit mourir sur l'heure.*'

between the citizens of Modena and Bologna about a missing household bucket, and Boileau's famous poem, *Le Lutrin*, which he began half a century later and rounded off in 1683. Here the protagonists are a gaggle of angry clerics, who wage savage war over the appropriate position of an ancient reading desk. Boileau had first fixed the scene of his drama in a modest country church, but afterwards shifted it to Paris, and chose for his new setting the venerable Sainte-Chapelle. His disputants are the Chapelle's epicurean Treasurer and its vain, contentious Choir-master. Each is portrayed with true heroic gusto; as the drama gradually unfolds, their quarrel assumes Olympian proportions. The purpose of mock-heroic verse is to describe littleness in terms of greatness, and to make absurdity doubly absurd by placing it against a splendid legendary background; but, if the poet has a genuine imaginative gift, however ironically he may affect to treat his characters, a certain air of greatness clings. Thus Boileau's Treasurer – '*ce prélat terrible*' – becomes a figure of voluptuous dignity, a sensual demi-god, enshrined among swan-stuffed pillows, dozing through the day from meal to meal:

> *Dans le réduit obscur d'une alcôve enfoncée,*
> *S'élève un lit de plume à grands frais amassée . . .*
>
> *C'est là que le prélat, muni d'un déjeuner,*
> *Dormant d'un léger somme, attendait le dîner.*
> *La jeunesse en sa fleur brille sur son visage;*
> *Son menton sur son sein descend à double étage,*
> *Et son corps, ramassé dans sa courte grosseur,*
> *Fait gémir les coussins sous sa molle épaisseur.**

Samuel Garth, from whom Pope was not ashamed to borrow, undoubtedly admired *Le Lutrin*; he introduces the same stately personifications; and Boileau's picture of *la Mollesse* –

> *La Volupté la sert avec les yeux dévots,*
> *Et toujours le Sommeil lui verse des pavots.†*

* In the dark shelter of a deep-set alcove
  Rises a bed thick-stuffed with costly swansdown . . .

  'Twas there the Prelate, fortified by luncheon,
  Enjoyed a sleepy pause, awaiting dinner.
  The glow of youth shone brightly from his visage;
  His chin, two-tiered, descended to his bosom;
  His body, short and stout, lay gently drawn up,
  And his soft bulk weighed heavy on the pillows.

† Pleasure with reverent eyes obeys her bidding,
  And always Slumber pours his draught of poppies.

– must have inspired the portrait of Sloth that embellishes *The Dispensary*.★
Pope appears to have made good use both of the English copy and of the
French original; but it was Boileau, being the more serious artist, who
exercised the greater influence. Garth provided Pope with a decorative
detail here and there; what he took from Boileau was the whole conception of a modern mock-heroic poem, frivolous in subject, flippant in
approach, yet deeply imaginative in its range of thought and feeling.
Again and again, Boileau seems to have anticipated Pope, though his
ideas were worked out on a less imposing scale. He displays a similar
energy, gaiety, variety, and makes a similarly effective use of contrast;
as, for example, when he compares the noisy, triumphant reign of Louis
xiv with the delightful lassitude of the Merovingian court –

> *Hélas! qu'est devenu ce temps, cet heureux temps,*
> *Où les rois s'honoraient du nom de fainéants . . .*
> *Aucun soin n'approchaient de leur paisible cour:*
> *On reposait la nuit, on dormait tout le jour.*
> *Seulement, au printemps, quand Flore dans les plaines*
> *Faisait taire des vents les bruyantes haleines,*
> *Quatre boeufs attelés, d'un pas tranquille et lent,*
> *Promenaient dans Paris le monarque indolent.*†

– or describes the carillon of clamorous bells –

> *Les cloches dans les airs, de leur voix argentines,*
> *Appelaient à grand bruit les chantres à matines. . . .*‡

– that, while his clerics are still sluggishly abed, rolls out across the morning
sky.

Pope would have been the last to ignore his debt. As he once remarked,

★ Upon a Couch of Down in these Abodes,
   Supine with folded Arms he thoughtless nods;
   Indulging Dreams his Godhead lull to Ease,
   With Murmurs of soft Rills, and whisp'ring Trees.
   The *Poppy* and each numbing Plant dispense
   Their drowsy Virtue and dull Indolence.

† Alas! where is that time, that happy time,
   When monarchs bore the style of 'royal drones' . . .
   No carking care approached their quiet court:
   All day they slumbered, and all night reposed.
   Only, in spring-days, once across the country
   Flora had laid to rest the blustering breezes,
   Two yoke of oxen, slow and steady-footed,
   Would draw his lazy Majesty through Paris.

‡ Across the morning air, with silvery voices,
   The loud-toned bells called choristers to matins . . .

poets who borrowed were 'like trees which of themselves would produce only one sort of fruit, but by being grafted upon others may yield variety. A mutual commerce makes poetry flourish. . . .' Originality, in the later sense of the word, was not the Augustan poet's chief aim; his ambition was to adapt an old form and, by combining novel and traditional elements, invest it with a new attraction. Throughout *The Rape of the Lock* familiar themes abound; it is not only a wonderfully light-hearted, but an extremely learned poem. Besides its borrowings from contemporary verse and its erudite parodies of Homer and Virgil, it concludes with a reference to *The Lock of Berenice*, in which the Alexandrian court poet Callimachus had told how a tress of Queen Berenice's hair was once translated to the heavens.* This solemn framework of myth and history gives Pope's ephemeral heroine an added lustre. A creature of the fashionable present day, she has had her prototypes in the historic past; and her beauty, though doomed to fade and decay, will be recalled by future ages.

Discussing *The Rape of the Lock*, Johnson characterizes it as 'the most airy, the most ingenious, and the most delightful' of all its author's compositions. True to his precept that, the slighter a poem was, the more care it needed in the framing, Pope set himself a clear-cut plan, on which he built an exquisitely harmonious edifice. As we have seen, it was constructed in two efforts, the first occupying him for 'less than a fortnight', the second, during the course of December 1713, probably a good deal longer. Here we shall consider the second version of the poem; even if Pope was not entirely accurate when he said that he had always meant to add the Rosicrucian passages, they blend so easily into the accompanying episodes that they seem to have been implicit in his original design; and the structural unity of the completed narrative must rank among its greatest virtues. A mixture of airiness and solidity, of grace and strength, of light-hearted lyricism and scathing social wit, *The Rape of the Lock* is at once a hymn of praise addressed to Beauty and a lament for the transience of youth and the vanity of human wishes. Pope's handling of his subject reflects his private attitude towards the world of women. Though he had always observed the opposite sex with passion, and was fascinated by the smallest details of a woman's daily life, he remained perforce an imaginative outsider, too frail and insignificant himself ever fully to possess the beings he desired. Thus there is a touch of cruelty about his feminine portraits; women aroused in him a kind of loving hatred. That

* Except for a single fragment of the Greek text, this poem has survived only in a translation by Catullus.

every beauty must at length grow old and grey was evidently a poignant and saddening, yet not altogether an unwelcome thought.

The Rape of the Lock, wrote William Hazlitt, was a masterpiece over which the reader scarcely knew whether he should laugh or weep. As a Romantic critic, Hazlitt felt obliged to deplore its fashionable mannerisms and its undisguised frivolity: 'it is made of gauze and silver spangles. The most glittering appearance is given to everything. . . . Airs, languid airs, breathe around; – the atmosphere is perfumed with affectation. . . . No pains are spared, no profusion of ornament, no splendour of poetic diction, to set off the meanest things.' But then, Pope does not merely set off and embellish: he also enlarges and transfigures. To look through his eyes, Hazlitt had already remarked, 'is like looking at the world through a microscope, where everything assumes a new character and a new consequence, where things are seen in their minutest circumstances and slightest shades of difference; where the little becomes gigantic, the deformed beautiful, and the beautiful deformed'. Although Pope always remembers that he is parodying an epic poem, travestying an antique convention, and reducing the sublime to the ridiculous, he operates throughout upon a grandiose scale. His satirical adaptation of the epic mode itself possesses epic qualities; and 'the balance between the assumed gravity and the concealed irony is as nicely trimmed as the balance of power in Europe'.

Every epic must open with an invocation; and Pope invokes the Muse, but dedicates the poem to his friend Caryll. Then he moves straight into his heroine's innermost sanctuary. Behind white curtains, drawn to exclude the Sun God, who glimmers through them with a wavering and timorous ray, Belinda is discovered still safely asleep; while her guardian Sylph, present in a morning dream, breathes out his supernatural message. The poem is built up of five main dramatic episodes – Belinda's vision and her abrupt awakening, which takes place near the stroke of noon; the afternoon water-party, followed by the card-party at Hampton Court; Belinda's despair and recovery; the Homeric conflict, which becomes a Battle of the Sexes; and the last scene when the stars have assembled to witness the apotheosis of the Lock. But Pope attaches three subsidiary scenes – the Baron's sacrifice, celebrated before the sun has quite risen, Umbriel's descent into the underworld, and Sir Plume's confrontation of the outrageous ravisher. All are connected by the comings and goings of the Sylphs, who have their own distinctive melody: 'Pope,' it has been pointed out, 'associates the sylphs and sylphids with their short vowel *i*', and gives them such names as Brillante, Crispissa and Momentilla, which convey both their insubstantiality and their sparkling delicacy. Ariel's voice is pitched in a very different key from those of the men and women among whom he lives: Belinda's rises to a piercing scream: Sir Plume's is comically gruff and bluff: the Baron's, loud and manly and determined. It is not surprising that Pope should have felt that his introduction of Rosicrucian machinery had been a very happy after-thought, and that his success in making the two versions of the poem 'hit so well together' had been 'one of the greatest proofs of judgment of anything I ever did'.

Although Addison had feared that he might spoil the design, its harmony is maintained from start to finish; from the lyrical prologue, with its evocation of an idle sunny morning –

> *Sol* thro' white Curtains shot a tim'rous Ray,
> And op'd those Eyes that must eclipse the Day;
> Now Lapdogs give themselves the rowzing Shake,
> And sleepless Lovers, just at Twelve, awake:
> Thrice rung the Bell, the Slipper knock'd the Ground,
> And the press'd Watch return'd a silver Sound

– to the grand finale of the epilogue. At first the atmosphere is light and carefree; but Ariel's speech introduces a hint of tension. Pope had carefully studied *Gabalis*; Sylphs, Gnomes, Salamanders, Nymphs all reappear in Ariel's review of the celestial and infernal hierarchy; and the poet recollects Villars's account of how, during the reign of King Pepin, the Sylphs had shown themselves to men on earth:

> Know then, unnumber'd Spirits round thee fly,
> The light *Militia* of the lower Sky. . . .

Fierce, warlike spirits, however, did not entirely suit his purpose. He domesticates them, brings them down from the air, and assigns them various servile offices, even asserting – contrary to Rosicrucian belief – that some spiritual bodies may house the disembodied souls of women:

> Think not, when Woman's transient Breath is fled,
> That all her Vanities at once are dead:
> Succeeding Vanities she still regards,
> And tho' she plays no more, o'erlooks the Cards . . .
> For when the Fair in all their Pride expire,
> To their first Elements their Souls retire:
> The Sprights of fiery Termagants in Flame
> Mount up, and take a *Salamander*'s name.
> Soft yielding Minds to Water glide away,
> And sip with Nymphs their Elemental Tea.

By one of those swift transitions which give the poem its delightfully rapid movement, Ariel's discourse comes to an unexpected end, when Shock, Belinda's beloved lapdog – no doubt a shaggy Iceland terrier* – leaps up to rouse his dreaming mistress:

> This to disclose is all thy Guardian can.
> Beware of all, but most beware of Man!
> He said; when Shock, who thought she slept too long,
> Leapt up, and wak'd his mistress with his Tongue.

During the Second Canto, Ariel resumes his speech, this time apostrophizing not Belinda herself, by now immersed in worldly pleasures, but the 'lucid squadrons' of spirits who crowd around her gilded vessel:

> Some to the Sun their Insect-Wings unfold,
> Waft on the Breeze, or sink in Clouds of Gold.
> Transparent Forms, too fine for mortal Sight,
> Their fluid Bodies half dissolv'd in Light.
> Loose to the Wind their airy Garments flew,
> Thin glitt'ring Textures of the filmy Dew. . . .

He instructs them as to the duties they owe their charge, warns them of the unknown disaster that today hangs above her radiant head, but proceeds to threaten them, should they dare to neglect their office, with 'whole ages' of ignominious agony. Pope's imagination was as exquisitely attuned to pain as it was to sensuous pleasure. His 'most sensuous descriptive poetry', writes a modern critic, 'is seldom independent of physical irritation. It is the *suffering* eye† which stings Pope into his most elaborate luxuriance of vision'; and Ariel's inferno was clearly devised by a man who had himself acutely suffered:

> Whatever Spirit, careless of his Charge,
> His Post neglects, or leaves the Fair at large,
> Shall feel sharp Vengeance soon o'ertake his Sins,
> Be stopt in *Vials*, or transfixt with *Pins*;
> Or plung'd in Lakes of bitter *Washes* lie,
> Or wedg'd whole ages in a *Bodkin's* eye:

* The breed was popular in the eighteenth century; see the Countess's dog in Hogarth's *Marriage-à-la-Mode*. It was also called a 'shough', and was described by a seventeenth-century writer as 'curled and rough all over', so that it 'made show neither of face, nor of body . . .'

> † The suff'ring eye inverted Nature sees,
> Trees cut to statues, statues thick as trees . . .
> *Moral Essays: To Richard Boyle, Earl of Burlington*, 1731.

> *Gums* and *Pomatums* shall his Flight restrain,
> While clog'd he beats his silken Wings in vain;
> Or Alom-*Stypticks* with contracting Power
> Shrink his thin Essence like a rivell'd Flower.*

Pope's imagery always reflects his temperament – he is the least impersonal of eighteenth-century poets; and, when we are considering the symbolism of *The Rape of the Lock*, a further point deserves attention. Is there not a close affinity between the poet and the sylph? Pope's relationship with women was often that of a protective sprite, hovering around beauties whom he could not hope to capture, and advising and assisting 'unfortunate ladies', whose hearts had been given to other men, and who ultimately went their own way. As for Ariel, though he can read Belinda's mind, he is powerless to control her feelings; and, once he detects the emergence of an earthly lover, he sadly renounces his ungrateful mission:

> Just in that instant, anxious *Ariel* sought
> The close Recesses of the Virgin's Thought;
> As on the Nosegay in her breast reclin'd,
> He watch'd th'Ideas rising in her Mind,
> Sudden he view'd, in spite of all her Art,
> An Earthly Lover lurking at her Heart.
> Amaz'd, confus'd, he found his Pow'r expired,
> Resign'd to Fate, and with a Sigh retir'd.

Ariel's withdrawal from the scene prepares the way for an Homeric conflict, a prolongation of the warlike card-game already depicted in the Third Canto. One episode is designed to enhance the other; but the story of the card-party is particularly brilliant and effective. Under Pope's eyes the candle-lit card-table expands to the dimensions of a Trojan battle-field; the painted cards become heroic warriors; and a desperate life-and-death struggle rages back and forth across 'the velvet plain'. His account of the engagement shows a due regard for the existing rules of warfare. Ombre, the game he describes, had originated among the Spaniards and was said to have in it 'a good deal of the gravity peculiar to that nation'; but, towards the end of the seventeenth century, its vogue had been transferred to England; and, a few years after Pope had written his poem, it was recommended by the author of *The Court Gamester*, as 'the most delightful and entertaining of all games, to those who have anything in them of what we call the Spirit of Play'. At Ombre – *le Royal Jeu de l'Hombre* – the pack

* This passage, of course, embodies a recollection of *The Tempest* – Prospero's account of the torments from which he had saved an earlier Ariel.

consisted of forty cards; the Ace of Spades was known as *Spadille*, the Two of Spades as *Manille*, and the Ace of Clubs as *Basto*; and the black aces, together with an additional card, bore the style of *Matadors*. Pope had undoubtedly played it himself; the stratagems his contestants employ are worked out down to the very smallest details; and the reader, if he is also a card-lover, can follow the fortunes of the struggle hand by hand, as the heroine, through a series of epic vicissitudes, rushes ahead to final victory:

> The *Baron* now his *Diamonds* pours apace;
> Th'embroider'd *King* who shows but half his Face,
> And his refulgent *Queen*, with Pow'rs combin'd,
> Of broken Troops an easie Conquest find.
> *Clubs*, *Diamonds*, *Hearts*, in wild Disorder seen,
> With Throngs promiscuous strow the level Green.
> Thus when dispers'd a routed Army runs,
> Of *Asia's* troops, and *Africk's* Sable Sons,
> With like Confusion different Nations fly,
> Of various Habit, and of various Dye,
> The pierc'd Battalions dis-united fall,
> In Heaps on Heaps; one Fate o'erwhelms them all.
>   The *Knave* of *Diamonds* tries his wily Arts,
> And wins (oh shameful chance!) the *Queen* of *Hearts*.
> At this, the Blood the Virgin's Cheek forsook,
> A livid Paleness spreads o'er all her Look . . .
> And now, (as oft in some distemper'd State)
> On one nice *Trick* depends the gen'ral Fate.
> An *Ace* of Hearts steps forth: the *King* unseen
> Lurk'd in her Hand, and mourn'd his captive *Queen*.
> He springs to Vengeance with an eager pace,
> And falls like Thunder on the prostrate *Ace*.
> The Nymph exulting fills with Shouts the Sky,
> The Walls, the Woods, and long Canals reply.

The whole episode of the card-party had been inserted when Pope recast the poem; and this interpolation, like the others, was undoubtedly a decisive 'proof of judgement'. Not only were the thirty-eight new couplets in themselves a major *tour de force*; but they enlarged and enriched the structure of the work without impairing the original design. The earlier version had had human life as its subject. Pope added a new dimension when he opened up the aerial world of the Sylphs; and he further extended his range by describing the world of the Cards, which form

a miniature court inside a court, painted replicas of the courtly personages
who fill the room and press around the table:

> Behold, four *Kings* in Majesty rever'd,
> With hoary Whiskers and a forky Beard;
> And four fair *Queens* whose hands sustain a Flow'r,
> Th'expressive Emblem of their softer Pow'r;
> Four *Knaves* in Garbs succinct, a trusty Band,
> Caps on their heads, and Halberds in their hand . . .

If the human protagonists are epic heroes and heroines skilfully reduced to
comic size, the cards are reductions of reductions, the diminutive counterparts of already diminished figures.

The Rape of the Lock, we know, was intended primarily as a 'little poem'.
Yet, notwithstanding the slightness of its theme and the minute delicacy
of its execution – Hazlitt called it a marvellous piece of filigree – it is
indeed a work 'where the little becomes gigantic'. Both to its admirers
and to its detractors, the superficial lightness of the poem is usually more
apparent than its underlying weight and strength. Pope's lyricism has
a steel-hard edge of wit; and wit, we know, was regarded by Augustan
readers as an extremely serious literary virtue. Pope's wit is of several
different kinds. There is the verbal, zeugmatic wit that depends on
assembling discordant ideas within a single frame of words:

> Whether the Nymph shall break *Diana's* law,
> Or some frail *China* Jar receive a Flaw,
> Or stain her Honour, or her new Brocade,
> Forget her Pray'rs, or miss a Masquerade . . .

– the social wit, shared by modern novelists, that illuminates and trans-
forms an individual personality:

> She said; then raging to *Sir Plume* repairs,
> And bids her *Beau* demand the precious Hairs:
> (*Sir Plume*, of *Amber Snuff-box* justly vain,
> And the nice Conduct of a *clouded Cane*)
> With earnest Eyes, and round unthinking Face,
> He first the Snuff-box open'd, then the Case,
> And thus broke out – 'My Lord, why, what the Devil?
> Zounds? damn the Lock! 'fore Gad, you must be civil!
> Plague on't! 'tis past a Jest – nay, prithee, Pox!
> Give her the Hair' – he spoke and rapp'd his Box.
> 'It grieves me much (reply'd the Peer again)
> Who speaks so well shou'd ever speak in vain.'

– the erotic wit that offended his dedicatee, and makes an especially outrageous appearance in the last lines of the Fourth Canto; and the wit
grotesque and fantastic that inspires the story of Umbriel's descent into
the cavern of the Goddess Spleen:

> A constant *Vapour* o'er the Palace flies;
> Strange Phantoms rising as the Mists arise;
> Dreadful, as Hermit's Dreams in haunted Shades,
> Or bright as Visions of expiring Maids. . . .
>
> Unnumber'd Throngs on ev'ry side are seen
> Of Bodies chang'd to various Forms by *Spleen*.
> Here living *Teapots* stand, one Arm held out,
> One bent; the Handle this, and that the Spout:
> A Pipkin there like *Homer's Tripod* walks;
> Here sighs a Jar, and there a Goose-pye talks.★
> Men prove with Child, as pow'rful Fancy works,
> And Maids turned Bottels, call aloud for Corks.

Finally, there is his wit at its best, where observation is combined with
imagination, and gaiety, fantasy, irony with a poignant sense of human
drama:

> Mean while declining from the Noon of Day,
> The Sun obliquely shoots his burning Ray;
> The hungry Judges soon the Sentence sign,
> And Wretches hang that Jury-men may Dine;
> The Merchant from th'*Exchange* returns in Peace,
> And the long Labours of the *Toilette* cease. . . .

Than the last two couplets, it would be difficult to find a better example
of Pope's peculiar poetic method. In each, image is matched against image;
between the imagery of separate couplets there is an equally effective
contrast; and, after the preceding lines which are particularly light and
frivolous, the whole passage, with its references to the hungry justice on
the bench and the miserable prisoner at the bar, sounds a sudden note of
doom. Then, having achieved a dramatic crescendo, the impetus of the
verse falls away through a magnificent diminuendo. The hurriedly
sentenced wretch has been carted off to die; but the world he is leaving
behind him goes on about its daily business, the merchant deeply engaged
in the laborious task of self-enrichment, the fashionable woman just as
gravely absorbed in her unending schemes of self-adornment. But the

★ In a footnote, Pope explains that the second half of the line 'alludes to a real fact; a lady
of distinction imagined herself in this condition'.

placid harmony of the fifth line does nothing to prepare us for the protracted measure of the majestic line that follows it. The keynote is the adjective *long*; and these eight simple, ingeniously assorted words lend the trivial procedure of feminine rising and dressing an air of superhuman consequence. They remind us of the solemn 'rites of pride', a travestied version of ancient religious ceremonies, already depicted in the opening canto.

Pope points his effect with the help of alliteration – a device that he occasionally abused, but more often employed to splendid purpose. He uses it again in the apotheosis of the Lock, where sibilants are deliberately crowded together to evoke a picture of Belinda's ravished tress, coiling and uncoiling as it flies on its radiant serpentine course athwart the heavens. For their prize eventually eludes the contestants; after the hubbub of the battle has died down, it seems to have disappeared beyond recovery:

> The Lock, obtain'd with Guilt, and kept with Pain,
> In ev'ry place is sought, but sought in vain . . .
>   Some thought it mounted to the Lunar Sphere,
> Since all things lost on Earth, are treasur'd there.
> There Heroes' Wits are kept in pondrous Vases,
> And Beaus' in *Snuff-boxes* and *Tweezer-Cases*.
> There broken Vows, and Death-Bed Alms are found,
> And Lovers' Hearts with Ends of Riband bound;
> The Courtier's Promises, and Sick Man's Pray'rs,
> The Smiles of Harlots, and the Tears of Heirs,
> Cages for Gnats, and Chains to Yoak a Flea;
> Dry'd butterflies, and Tomes of Casuistry.

Pope, however, takes a much more sanguine view: the Lock has been translated to the firmament of the imagination, where it will be preserved for ever in immortal freshness:

> But trust the Muse – she saw it upward rise,
> Tho' mark'd by none but quick Poetic Eyes . . .
> A sudden Star, it shot thro' liquid Air,
> And drew behind a radiant *Trail of Hair*.
> Not *Berenice's* Locks first rose so bright,
> The Heav'ns bespangling with dishevel'd Light.
> The *Sylphs* behold it kindling as it flies,
> And pleas'd pursue its Progress thro' the Skies.

On Belinda herself, though condemned to physical extinction –

> When those fair Suns shall sett, as sett they must,
> And all those Tresses shall be laid in Dust. . . .

84

– the poet, as poets have always done, promises to confer undying youth. It was an engagement he faithfully carried out; and Arabella showed appropriate gratitude; so proud was she of the homage paid by a celebrated poet to her second self that she became, according to her niece the abbess, 'very troublesome and conceited'. Otherwise her life was unadventurous. When she married Francis Perkins, his country house, Ufton Court, is said to have been 'much-refashioned and enlarged' to provide her with a proper setting. Her marriage appears to have been happy; she bore her husband six children; and at Ufton, she is reputed to have played the part of literary hostess and 'received the wits of that Augustan Age', including Pope himself, Dr Arbuthnot and Lord Bolingbroke. When Mr Perkins died in 1736, he left his 'Loving Wife', beside more important bequests, 'all her wearing apparel, gold watch and jewels and her dressing plate, with the furniture of her closet and chamber'. Arabella's own interment was recorded, in the parish register of Ufton, on 9 March 1738.

5

Both *The Rape of the Lock* and *Windsor-Forest* make loyal reference to the reigning sovereign. Queen Anne had inherited the tastes of her great-grandfather, King James I; she was, noted Swift, 'a mighty hunter, like Nimrod', and, when she had become too infirm to ride, would follow the hunt 'in a chaise with one horse, which she drives herself, and drives furiously. . . .' Thus *Windsor-Forest* compares her to the goddess Diana, than whom she is no less pure and no less brilliant; while *The Rape of the Lock* presents us with a glimpse of the Queen during the summer months at Hampton Court, the huge rose-red Tudor palace that Sir Christopher Wren had recently restored and remodelled, where

> . . . Thou, Great *Anna*! whom three Realms obey,
> Dost sometimes Counsel take – and sometimes *Tea*.

The impression produced is festive and dignified. In fact, the middle-aged Queen was now an obese and sickly woman, swollen with dropsy, tortured by gout, and gradually sinking beneath a life-time's sorrows. Her children were all of them dead; her closest friend, the fascinating, intolerable Duchess of Marlborough, had been transformed into her bitterest enemy. Nor was she happy in her ministers. The General Election of August and September 1713 had returned another Tory government; and between the Tory leaders, Oxford and Bolingbroke, a savage private feud had developed, which was growing steadily more and more explosive. That Christmas the Queen fell ill; and, although she recovered, the problem of the succession – was it to be Catholic or Protestant, Stuart or Hanoverian? – immediately acquired a new importance. Those who favoured the chances of a Stuart sovereign admitted that they were unprepared to act; and James's announcement, early in 1714, that he would neither change nor dissimulate his faith – his advisers, he exclaimed, were asking him to play the villain – made their prospects

7 Lady Mary Wortley Montagu by Jonathan Richardson, senior.

8 Pope's Villa; from an engraving of 1749, which shows the riverside lawn and the entrance to his subterranean passage.

doubly doubtful. The Queen's own attitude was somewhat ambivalent. 'There is no indication,' writes a modern historian, 'that Anne ever wished to be succeeded by a Roman Catholic King'; but she had strong family feelings, a certain reluctant affection for her 'poor brother', and little regard for the Hanoverian claimants, who kept pressing her to help them establish their claims, and to allow the Electoral Prince, the future George II, already created Duke of Cambridge, to take his seat among his English peers. Not every Tory was a Jacobite – the party had its Hanoverian wing; but Oxford and Bolingbroke were in regular clandestine touch with James. Lacking themselves, however, a definite policy, they left their partisans hopelessly confused and divided.

Pope was by tradition a Tory, by personal preference, no doubt, a Jacobite. But since Dennis had accused him of Jacobitism, he was always careful to conceal his sympathies; and, whereas Steele boldly leapt into the arena and published a pamphlet entitled *The Crisis*, suggesting that the present government had designs against the Protestant Succession, which caused his fellow-members to expel him from the House of Commons, Pope very wisely stood aside and quietly pursued his own poetic business. The early part of the year 1714 was occupied with the 'grand undertaking' that he had launched the previous autumn. All his friends were enlisted as helpers; and Caryll and Swift gave particularly valuable support. The Dean had gone to work among his political connections; Caryll canvassed the social world at large, and, early in May 1714, was still 'soliciting with all his might'. For Pope hesitated to put pen to paper until his project had begun to bear fruit, and he knew that a sufficient number of sub-scribers had actually paid down their guineas. Should the project fail, he had told Caryll on 15 December 1713, his failure would not occasion him 'any great mortification, considering how much of life I am to sacrifice if it succeeds'. Now and then, the idea alarmed him; but, at all events, his labours would 'keep me a poet (in spite of something I lately thought a resolution to the contrary) for some years longer'. Still, it was 'no comfortable prospect to be reflecting' that he had to live through the whole story of the siege from Achilles' wrath and retirement to the recovery of Hector's body. Yet he must confess that 'the Greek forti-fication does not appear so formidable as it did upon a nearer approach; and I am almost apt to flatter myself, that Homer secretly seems inclined to correspond with me, in letting me into a good part of his designs. These are, indeed, a sort of underling auxiliars to the difficulty of the work, called commentators and critics. . . . These lie entrenched in the ditches, and are secure only in the dirt they have heaped about 'em with great pains. . . . But I think we have found a method of coming at the main works by a more speedy and gallant way than by mining under ground; that is, by using the poetical engines, wings, and flying thither over their heads.'

The real labour of translating the *Iliad* was not begun until the early summer; and, as he gathered in subscriptions and distributed receipts, Pope continued to make the most of his last few months of social freedom. Thus, in December 1713, he had dined at the house of the ageing poetess Lady Winchilsea,★ where after dinner a play was read aloud, but he had 'sat in great disorder with sickness at my head and stomach'. This disorder may perhaps have been caused by the quantity of claret he liked to consume and the fashionable hours he kept; for, although Caryll had recently given him a horse, no doubt to encourage a habit of taking healthful daily exercise, he was now so fond of frequenting London taverns that, on 6 March 1714, his oldest mentor, Sir George Trumbull, felt obliged to address the young poet in a very serious strain, earnestly imploring him 'to get out of all tavern-company. . . . What a misery it is for you to be destroyed by the foolish kindness . . . of those who are able to bear the poison of bad wine, and to engage you in so unequal a combat! As to *Homer*, by all I can learn your business is done; therefore come away and take a little time to breathe in the country.' Sir George also congratulated him on *The Rape of the Lock*, of which he had received a presentation copy. 'You have given me,' he wrote, 'the truest satisfaction imaginable, not only in making good the just opinion I have ever had of your reach of thought, and my idea of your comprehensive genius; but likewise in that pleasure I take as an Englishman to see the French, even Boileau himself in his *Lutrin*, outdone in your poem: for you descend, *leviore plectro*, to all the nicer touches, that your own observation and wit furnish, on such a subject as requires the finest strokes, and the liveliest imagination.'

Pope's new poem, indeed, had run into a second edition, having sold three thousand copies within four days. It was generally applauded; and still more flattering than Sir George's approval was a letter from the Reverend George Berkeley, author of the *Treatise concerning the Principles of Human Knowledge* and the celebrated *Dialogues*, written on 1 May from Leghorn. He had 'accidentally met with your *Rape of the Lock*', announced the philosopher, and it had surpassed his expectations: 'Style, Painting,

★ Anne Finch, Countess of Winchilsea (1660–1720); author of *The Spleen* and many other poems. She had shone at the court of James II as one of Mary of Modena's Maids of Honour. Her husband, who succeeded to the earldom late in life, was President of the Society of Antiquaries.

Judgment, Spirit, I had already admired in others of your writings; but in this I am charmed with the magic of your *Invention*, with all those images, allusions, and inexplicable beauties, which you raise so surprisingly, and at the same time so naturally, out of a trifle.' Berkeley added a recommendation that Pope himself should leave England; for, when they had met earlier, 'I remember to have heard you mention some half-formed design of coming to Italy.' And 'what might we not expect from a Muse that sings so well in the bleak climate of England, if she felt the same warm sun and breathed the same air with Virgil and Horace?'

Pope's half-formed design was never to be carried out; and in May 1714, while the siege of the *Iliad* still awaited his direction, the best he could do was to fall back on Berkshire. Early that month he retired to Whitehill House; and again he took with him a congenial literary guest. Thomas Parnell, the friend of Gay and Swift, was a sensitive, sympathetic Irish clergyman;* and, like Cromwell before him, he seems to have captivated the entire family, accomplishing 'several miracles', Pope informed him afterwards: he had made old people fond of a young and lively person, 'and inveterate Papists of a clergyman of the Church of England'. Even Pope's venerable nurse, Mary Beach, was 'in danger of being in love in her old age. . . .' As Parnell's scholarship was somewhat solider than his host's, he was able to advise Pope on Homeric problems; and in their leisure moments they composed facetious letters – a joint letter addressed to Gay, describing the enjoyments of a country life, and a similar letter to Charles Ford, another of Swift's private circle, headed 'From the Romantic World. . . . By Sunshine', in which they gave an account, parodying epic mannerisms, of the various beauties of a rural landscape.

In July, Parnell returned to Binfield; and he and his host set off on a visit to Swift, then staying at Letcombe, near Wantage, with his old friend the Reverend John Geree. Distracted by the quarrels of Bolingbroke and Oxford, the Dean had temporarily deserted London. But his mood was cheerful; he scolded the two friends in his usual loud, decisive way, treated them to a pint of Bolingbroke's 'Florence', followed by draughts of local cider, and roasted them coffee 'with his own hands in an engine for the purpose. . . . He talked of politics over coffee, with the air and style of an old statesman, who had known something formerly; but was shame-

---

* Thomas Parnell (1679–1718); despite Pope's account of his cheerful behaviour, he was suffering at the time from the loss of his wife, 'whom he tenderly loved'. Sorrow drove him to dram-drinking; and he expired, writes Pope's editor, 'in some measure a martyr to conjugal fidelity'. Ruffhead suggests, however, that his end was hastened by the death of Queen Anne, which destroyed all his hopes of ecclesiastical preferment.

fully ignorant of the three last weeks. When we mentioned the welfare of England he laughed at us, and said Muscovy would become a flourishing empire very shortly.' Between Swift and Pope there had by now developed a close and affectionate relationship. Each recognized not only the other's genius but the native singularity of his private character. In 1714 Jonathan Swift was forty-seven years old, a renowned satirist and political pamphleteer, who had risen to a position of high importance as the literary spearhead of the Tory party. By nature he was fiercely impatient and arrogant; 'all my endeavours from a boy', he was afterwards to tell Pope, 'were only for want of a great title and fortune, that I might be used like a Lord by those who have an opinion of my parts. . . .' In 1714, he had reached the zenith of his career. Used as a lord by lords, flattered and cherished by the greatest ladies, he surveyed the patrician world *de haut en bas*. Never a man to be trifled with, he assumed, as he grew older and angrier, an increasingly dictatorial expression. 'Dr Swift,' wrote his biographer Orrery, 'had a natural severity of face, which even his smiles could scarce soften, or his utmost gaiety render placid and serene: but when that sternness of visage was increased by rage, it is scarce possible to imagine looks, or features, that carried in them more terror and austerity.'

Yet the terrible black-browed Dean was also sensitive and warmly generous; and here again the 'mazy turnings' of his character often puzzled those who knew him well. 'Of all mankind,' decided Lord Orrery, 'Swift perhaps had the greatest contrasts in his temper.' He enjoyed aristocratic society, for example, but was devoted to 'scenes of low life'. Towards a few women his attitude was that of a tenderly protective tutor; yet he regarded most of their sex as unmistakably 'beasts in petticoats'. He would become a tireless champion of the Irish people's rights, without ceasing to despise the ordinary run of humanity as a race of pestilential Yahoos. Although he was a lonely man and yearned for affection, he usually mistrusted an unsolicited tribute; an acquaintance who had declared that he loved him was summarily dismissed as an arrant fool; and Pope recollected having spoken to him of a lady 'that longs to see you, and admires you above all things'; which provoked the immediate rejoinder: 'Then I despise her heartily!' But, during the first period of his friendship with Pope, his spirit had not yet been warped by exile, disappointment and disease. His physiognomy might be solemn and severe; yet it showed, now and then, an unexpected radiance. Under his heavy brows shone 'very particular eyes . . . quite azure as the heavens'. There was 'a very uncommon archness in them' that revealed his whimsical, fantastic bent and his sardonic sense of humour. When Pope and Parnell visited him at Letcombe, they found him engaged in an unexpected pastime. He kept a magnifying glass on a sunny window-ledge, which he employed to burn 'curious little holes' through a collection of important state papers.

No doubt the pastime had a symbolic significance: Swift, who foresaw the ruin of the Tories, which would mean the extinction of his own hopes, was preparing to abandon the splendid part he had played and withdraw into a life of exile. Soon he and Pope were to be separated, after a preliminary period of friendship that seems to have lasted less than eighteen months. Just how early they had met is difficult to determine from their published correspondence; but Pope's first letter to Swift, which shows that they were already on good terms, is dated 8 December 1713; and, that November, Bishop Kennett,* who did not like or admire Swift, wrote a vivid account of how he had watched him, 'the principal man of talk and business', in the sovereign's ante-chamber at Windsor Castle: 'He stopped F. Gwynn, Esq., going in with the red bag to the Queen, and told him aloud that he had something to say to him from my Lord Treasurer. He talked with the son of Dr Davenant to be sent abroad. . . . He turned to the fire, and took out his gold watch, and . . . complained that it was very late. A gentleman said he was too fast. "How can I help it," says the Doctor, "if the courtiers give me a watch that won't go right?" Then he instructed a young nobleman, that the best poet in England was Mr Pope (a Papist), who had begun a translation of Homer into English verse, for which he must have them all subscribe; "for," says he, "the author shall not begin to print till I have a thousand guineas for him." ' Swift may or may not have been personally acquainted with Pope when, in March 1713, he ordered Esther Johnson to read *Windsor-Forest*; but evidently it was his enthusiastic support of Pope's 'grand undertaking' that helped to make them close friends.

In the spring of 1714, both became members of a newly-founded literary club. The social history of Augustan England is closely bound up with the history of its clubs, of which the earliest was the famous Kit Cat, established about 1700, whose membership included Congreve, Addison, Steele, various politicians like Sir Robert Walpole, and the club-portraitist, Sit Godfrey Kneller. But the Kit Cat had a distinctively Whig colouring; and in 1711 The Brothers was organized as an opposition stronghold, where Tory partisans could sit over their wine composing topical ballads

---

* White Kennett (1660–1728); Bishop of Peterborough; voluminous writer and vehement Whig partisan. This description of Swift at Court was printed by Sir Walter Scott in his *Life of Swift*. Johnson also quotes from it.

and political pamphlets. Swift, however, though for a while he had been its Secretary, soon felt that it had outlived its purpose; and the Scriblerus Club was projected as a literary and critical, rather than a political, assembly, composed of poets and wits devoted to the sacred cause of modern literature. All were shocked – or professed to be shocked – by the current flow of bad writing, by the slipshod illiteracy of Grub Street and the ponderous lucubrations of so-called learned authors. They contemplated, therefore, launching a joint attack against Dullness under its many different guises, parodying a journal entitled the *History of the Works of the Learned* that had recently ceased publication, in an account of the *Works of the Unlearned*, in which (wrote Pope to Gay) every meritorious new book 'shall be depreciated ironically' and 'the high productions of Grub-Street' should be damned with extravagant applause. Pope also planned to write the memoirs of a grotesque pedant named Martinus Scriblerus, the representative of 'false tastes in learning', a dilettante 'that had dipped into every art and science . . .' Neither plan was completed at the time; but the idea aroused much lively discussion and helped to promote some pleasant meetings. Swift had greatly approved of the scheme; and, according to Pope, it was from a part of the unfinished memoirs that he 'took his first hints for Gulliver'.

Besides Swift and Pope, the founding fathers of the club were Arbuthnot, Gay and Parnell; and they usually met at Dr Arbuthnot's rooms, up a flight of dark stairs in St James's Palace. John Arbuthnot, a tall, slouching, energetic Scot, fond of literature and practical jokes, but so absent-minded that Swift once described him as 'the King of inattention', had been born in 1667. His *Essay on the Usefulness of Mathematical Learning* had appeared in 1700; and since then he had published many vigorously written Tory pamphlets, among them being the *Art of Political Lying* and his best-known work, the *History of John Bull*.* A Fellow of the Royal Society and of the Royal College of Physicians, in 1709 he had been appointed physician in ordinary to the Queen; and he had now risen to become her favourite medical attendant. Pope valued the Doctor's professional advice as much as he enjoyed his company. Between 20 March and 12 June 1714 Arbuthnot seems to have presided over at least five meetings of the Scriblerus Club; and on each occasion, the Club despatched an invitation to their distinguished patron the Lord Treasurer, begging in doggerel verse that he would join their party. Two of the Treasurer's replies have been preserved; and both contain a warm accep-

* Arbuthnot, if he did not invent, certainly popularized this famous folk-hero. *The Art of Political Lying*, though unsigned, is generally attributed to his authorship.

tance. Oxford's appetite for diversion seldom flagged, even in the present crisis of his political career, when his fellow-minister was exerting all his strength to hurl him out of public office. The Tory government, remarked Swift, were like a ship's company quarrelling in a storm. Yet, amid daily and hourly tribulations, Oxford maintained his epicurean composure; and, in the last note he addressed to the Scriblerus Club, he hinted broadly that he had lost the will to govern.*

It seems doubtful if Pope, at this time, had yet felt the magnetic charm of Bolingbroke; the Lord Treasurer's boon-companion would not have been numbered among the Secretary's closest friends. Bolingbroke was one day to fascinate him as a creature 'more than mortal'. Meanwhile, during the heyday of the Club, he acquired a genuine respect for Oxford – 'a steady man', who had 'a great firmness of soul', and who 'talked always very kindly to me, and used often to express his concern for my continuing incapable of a place';† though, at the same time, Oxford attempted to dissuade him from setting to work upon the *Iliad*, saying that 'so good a writer ought not to be a translator'. But Oxford's noble 'firmness of soul' was counterbalanced by his idleness of mind. He was naturally drawn towards literature and learning – he had already laid the foundations of the magnificent Harleian Library – and (according to Bolingbroke, a prejudiced observer) 'took great delight in repeating hard Greek verses'; yet he is said to have remained 'very ignorant of Greek', and was less a scholar than a dilettante. As a parliamentarian, he cut an awkward figure, mumbling and stammering 'with serpentine convolutions, numerous hypotheses, and long involved periods'. He was 'huddled in his thoughts', remembered Pope, 'and obscure in his manner of delivering them'. Among his literary friends, 'he talked of business in so confused a manner that you did not know what he was about. . . .'; and, now that his star was declining, he grew steadily lazier and less effective. Always fond of drinking, he was apt to enter the Queen's presence, if not downright fuddled, by no means altogether sober – a spectacle she much resented. 'He used to send trifling verses from Court to the Scriblerus Club' and, almost every night, would visit Arbuthnot's rooms, where he drank and 'talked idly'.

Two politicians more remarkable, and more curiously contrasted, than Robert Harley, first Earl of Oxford and Earl Mortimer, and Henry

* '. . . He that cares not to rule will not fail to obey – When summoned by Arbuthnot, Pope, Parnell and Gay.' 5 June 1714.

† As a Catholic, Pope was incapable of holding any of the sinecures that Oxford might otherwise have procured for him.

St. John, first Viscount Bolingbroke, have rarely occupied the same stage, Oxford's temperament was saturnine; Bolingbroke was 'the man of Mercury'. Both were dissipated, but, whereas Oxford's drunken habits produced a vague, lethargic indolence, Bolingbroke's excesses, amatory and alcoholic, seem to have heightened his natural energy and fire. As a minister, he was indefatigable; 'whenever he thought it necessary', recorded Swift, he would display 'prodigious application' and 'plod days and nights like the lowest clerk in an office'. At other moments, he affected to despise politics; 'his arrogance and excessive fiery temper', the Austrian envoy had written in 1711, 'are increasing . . . to such an extent that one cannot penetrate his real ideas. . . . He is given to the bottle and debauchery to the point of almost making a virtue out of his open affectation that public affairs are a bagatelle to him. . . .' During the last struggles of the Tory government, while Oxford's attitude, both towards the sovereign and towards his fellow-ministers, was rapidly becoming more and more sullen and neglectful, Bolingbroke overflowed with spirits and himself bragged that 'in one day he was the happiest man alive, got drunk, harangued the Queen, and at night was put to bed to a beautiful young lady, and was tucked up by two of the prettiest young peers in England. . . .'

Nature had bestowed on Bolingbroke not only an iron constitution – born in 1678, he was now approaching middle age – but an attractive and impressive body. All his life he was voted extraordinarily handsome; and to good looks he added peculiarly winning and distinguished manners. His mind was large; his interests were wide-spread. Yet the constitution of this patrician nonpareil was flawed through and through by some mysterious defect. He dazzled, but he failed to govern; he inspired devotion, but he could not inspire trust; and in his public career he encountered a long series of humiliating disappointments, as the power that he had laboured and intrigued to gain was snatched away before he could enjoy its fullness. Although he thought hard and boldly, Bolingbroke did not plan constructively; perhaps the encircling radiance of his talents disguised the lack of any real genius; and it may be that, despite his astonishingly varied gifts, he remained an incomplete and ill-adjusted character. In 1714 his gifts were uppermost; he used them, however, to the worst advantage. Besides pressing on with the notorious Schism Bill, designed to abolish Dissenting schools and academies,* he conducted a savage personal campaign against his abominated colleague the Lord Treasurer, who,

* This Bill itself formed part of Bolingbroke's campaign against Oxford, who had many connections with the Non-Conformists.

suddenly aroused from his lethargy, put up a no less fierce resistance. His friends had nicknamed Oxford 'the Dragon' – true, they sometimes murmured that he would have been better named 'Dagon' after the Canaanites' clay-footed idol; and now, confronting defeat and disgrace, he revealed himself in a lurid majesty. 'The Dragon dies hard,' noted Dr Arbuthnot on 26 June. 'He is . . . kicking and cuffing about him like the Devil'; and so strenuously did he defend his position that for another month, until 27 July, he could not be dislodged from office. Then the Queen, 'harangued' by Bolingbroke and 'teased' by her designing favourite, Oxford's former protegée Lady Masham, consented to dismiss her minister; and Oxford went out in a blaze of fury. At the last council both ministers attended, each loudly upbraided and denounced his rival; while their sovereign, sick and exhausted, sat powerless to control the hubbub, broke down, burst into tears and was carried fainting from the room.

Two days later, the Queen, 'complained of a pain in her head'; the seven royal doctors, including Arbuthnot, pronounced that the gout that had crippled her lower limbs had now 'translated itself upon the brain'; and by 20 July they admitted that her case was hopeless. Thus Bolingbroke's enjoyment of his new position had lasted only two whole days; and he was faced with a sudden dynastic change for which he and his partisans were completely unprepared. Jacobite hotheads urged decisive action; the Duke of Ormond promised the support of the army; the Bishop of Rochester was said to have undertaken to proclaim King James III at the Royal Exchange and Charing Cross. Then, while Bolingbroke hesitated and temporized, two important opposition noblemen, the Duke of Somerset, representing the English, and the Duke of Argyle the Scottish Whigs, entered the council chamber uninvited. They were exercising, they said, their privilege as Privy Councillors; and they were duly received and made welcome by their accomplice, the Hanoverian Duke of Shrewsbury. During the course of an unrecorded debate, it was agreed 'to move the Queen that she would constitute the Duke of Shrewsbury Lord Treasurer'. Having ascertained from the dying woman's attendants that she was still 'in a condition to be spoke to', her ministers now despatched a deputation which filed into the royal presence; and at one o'clock the Queen gave the Treasurer's staff to the Duke of Shrewsbury, Lord Harcourt, the Lord Treasurer, 'holding her hand to direct it to the Duke'. That done, the Privy Council, though half its members were 'in some sort or degree Jacobites', could set to work preparing the way for the peaceful accession of a Hanoverian monarch; and, at Kensington Palace, the last of the Stuart line was allowed to resume her interrupted journey. She died early on the morning of 1 August 1714. Soon afterwards the Elector of Hanover, Duke of Brunswick-Luneburg, was solemnly proclaimed King. There were rejoicings and festivities throughout the metropolis; and Lord Bolingbroke – it was thought that he feared the mob - provided a bonfire 'and the finest illuminations in town at his house in Golden Square'.

Pope was rusticating with his parents at Binfield when he received news of the Queen's death; and, 'moved by the common curiosity of mankind, who leave their business to be looking upon other men's', he felt that he 'could not but take a trip to London'. He quickly returned; the business that now engaged his attention allowed him very little respite; he was withdrawing his mind, so far as he could, 'from all the present world, its customs and its manners, to be fully possessed and absorbed in the past'. For days on end, he seldom spoke to his family. 'When people talk of going to Church,' he told Jervas on 28 July, 'I think of sacrifices and libations; when I see the parson, I address him as Chryses priest of Apollo . . . . While you in the world are concerned about the Protestant Succession, I consider only how Menelaus may recover Helen. . . .' At the moment, too, he was 'perpetually afflicted with headaches, that very much affect my sight'; and, now and then, he was deeply depressed both by the *taedium vitae* and by the *taedium scribendi* . . . 'Half the things that employ our heads deserve not the name of thoughts; they are only stronger dreams . . . our schemes of government, our systems of philosophy, our golden words of poetry are all but so many shadow images and airy prospects. . . .' Long habit and weariness might reconcile him to abandoning literature; 'I should be sorry and ashamed to go on jingling to the last step, like a waggoner's horse in the same road, to leave my bells to the next silly animal that will be proud of them'.

Often he envied his friends who remained behind in London, remembering the pleasures of Pall Mall and St James's, and of good French claret at 3s. 6d. a bottle. Although he had ceased temporarily to play a part in the world, he could not quite escape from its disturbing influence. He was a Catholic, a suspected Jacobite; and, whereas Protestant patriots impugned his loyalty, some of his more ardent co-religionists questioned the sincerity of his faith. 'I find by dear experience,' he wrote to Caryll, 'we live in an age, where it is criminal to be moderate; and where no man can be allowed to be just to all men. The notions of right and wrong are so far strained, that perhaps to be in the right so very violently, may be of worse consequence than to be easily and quietly in the wrong.' Pope was too discreet to make any direct comments either on the Queen's death or on the general prospects of the new reign; 'I thank God,' he remarked, 'that as for myself, I am below all the accidents of state-changes by my circumstances, and above them by my philosophy'; and the greatest fear he had as 'a poor Papist' was that, if the new government were again to put into force the anti-Catholic legislation introduced during the reign of William and Mary, the palfry that Caryll had given him – its value exceeded five pounds; and no Catholic subject could nominally acquire a more expensive beast – might at once be confiscated. But possibly the new turn in affairs, he hazarded, would have an excellent political result, by bringing to an end the strife between Whig and Tory, and might thus enable the warring parties 'to love each other as well as I love them both, or at least hurt each other as little as I would either. . . .' Now that the Catholics were powerless – his reflections were confided to John Caryll – 'our own people' would perhaps be left in peace.

Some of his associates thought very differently. Swift, who had never been a moderate, and had thrived on the excesses of party warfare, now gloomily prepared to leave England; Oxford retired into private life, where he awaited the enemy's next move with his customary *sang-froid*. The Whigs had returned in strength; they would continue to dominate the public scene for another forty-six years. As modern historians have repeatedly reminded us, political alignments during the eighteenth century were often determined not so much by issues of principle as by the activities of opposing personal factions. But, at the beginning of the age, the division between Tory and Whig was still comparatively clear-cut, the Whigs representing the 'moneyed interest', which had supported Britain's lengthy struggle against her chief commercial adversary France and had bitterly resisted the negotiation of the Peace of Utrecht; the Tories championing the interest of the lesser country gentry, whose revenues were derived from land, and on whom war-time taxation imposed a particularly heavy burden. Sir Roger de Coverley was, of course, a Tory; whereas Addison, who held him up to gently patronizing ridicule, expressed the point of view of the mercantile class, which, under the shrewd direction of Sir Robert Walpole, would soon establish the City of London as the greatest trading centre in the whole of Europe. Pope, the friend of Oxford, presently developed a keen dislike for Walpole; and henceforward he made no attempt to attach himself to Court or government.

The new government, however, if not the new sovereign, showed some interest in gaining the support of a distinguished modern man of letters; and Pope claimed that both Lord Halifax,* who then headed the Treasury Commission, and, later, that intrepid young politician James Craggs,

* Charles Montagu, Earl of Halifax (1661–1715), patron of Congreve, Addison and Prior.

who in 1717 became Secretary at War, made him flattering advances, which he felt obliged to turn down.* During the early days of the new reign, he declared, Halifax had sent for him 'of his own accord', said that he had 'often been concerned that I had never been rewarded as I deserved; that he was very glad it was now in his power to be of service to me; that a pension should be settled on me, if I cared to accept it; and that nothing should be demanded of me for it'. This overture, according to Johnson, Pope 'seems to have received with sullen coldness'; whereas he himself asserted that he had thanked his admirer, but asked for time to consider the suggestion, and after some three months had finally replied 'that all the difference I could find in having or not having a pension, was, that if I had one, I might move at large in town, and that if I had not, I might live happily enough in the country. . . .' Craggs's proposal, when it arrived, was even more accommodating; he offered both a pension of three hundred pounds and complete freedom from all official ties, since he was ready to pay the pension from secret-service funds at his disposal, 'without anyone's knowing that I had it'. This offer he repeated several times, 'and always used to insist on the convenience that a coach would be of to me. . . .' But Pope as often declined, reflecting that, once he had got into the way of keeping a coach, were his pension suddenly withdrawn, it would be disagreeable to have to break the habit.

Thus he preserved his liberty; independence was an essential condition of the task that he had set himself. During the last two hundred years, few middle-class English writers had escaped some form of servitude; poets had depended for their livelihood on minor bureaucratic posts, on the Church, on the capricious patronage of great men, or on their ill-paid work as hireling dramatists. Among his contemporaries, Pope alone was associated with no political party, benefited from no official or clerical appointment, and was indebted to no aristocratic patron. Here circumstances, of course, had favoured him. Although, between February 1712 and February 1714, the poems so far published by Lintot had earned him less than ninety pounds, he could always count on a good-natured father. But now his father's revenues appeared to be dwindling. Part of the elder Pope's capital was invested in French government securities;† and the rate of interest they yielded had recently been much reduced. Pope, therefore, had had a double motive when he decided to translate the *Iliad*. Not only was it a bold experiment that would strengthen and enlarge his

---

* James Craggs (1686–1721) was said to have owed his advancement to his relationship with Countess Platen, mistress of George I.

† As a Catholic, he would have found it difficult to invest in English stock.

reputation; but it would provide the solid financial backing that he needed as an upright freelance writer.

In both respects he was remarkably successful. Besides producing a book that gained immediate popularity, thanks to the businesslike contract he had signed with Lintot, on 23 March 1714, he laid the foundations of a modest personal fortune. But the effort required was tremendous. If *The Rape of the Lock* had been a poetic holiday, his translation of the *Iliad* was a long, exhausting battle. Headaches clouded his eyesight; nightmares haunted him. 'What terrible moments,' he reflected in later years, 'does one feel after one has engaged for a large work! In the beginning of my translating the *Iliad*, I wished anybody would hang me, a hundred times. It sat so heavily on my mind at first, that I often used to dream of it, and so do sometimes still.' He would dream, for example, that he had been condemned to prosecute an interminable journey, and 'was puzzled which way to take, and full of fears he should never get to the end of it'. The 'great pain and apprehension' he had suffered left a lasting scar upon his memory.

Homer's opening books, were, of course, the most formidable; and, once he had surmounted them, the long road that he was travelling began to grow a little smoother. He would start work before he had risen from his bed, translate thirty or forty verses and then 'piddle' with them throughout the morning hours. Having adopted this method, he found that the business 'went on easy enough'; and, as soon as he had thoroughly mastered the system, his fears subsided and he 'did the rest with pleasure', dashing off a preliminary draft, which he proceeded to correct by referring both to the original text and to other translations – Chapman, Ogilby, Dacier – last of all reading and revising it 'for the versification only'. In the process, he found, he was apt to sink into a deep abstraction; his work, he wrote to Jervas on 16 August, preoccupied him so entirely that it almost cut him off from the ordinary affairs of life; and 'I scarce see what passes under my nose, and hear nothing that is said about me. To follow Poetry as one ought, one must forget father and mother, and cleave to it alone.' But twice at least he abandoned his books and manuscripts – for a brief expedition to Oxford, where the dons, 'all very honest fellows', gave him hospitable entertainment; and late in September, on a visit to Bath, where the physicians, whom he had no doubt consulted about his headaches, had suggested he should take the waters. It was his first visit to the gay and decorative city; and he now 'stared at the Bath, and sneaked along the walks, with that astonished and diffident air which is natural to a modest and ignorant foreigner'. Parnell was his travelling companion; they took up residence at a crowded inn; and the noise of ten people gathered around a tavern table did not much improve his headaches. Still, he felt well enough to join the local amusements, attend plays and pump-room assemblies, make the prescribed round of the chocolate-houses and raffling shops, and cultivate the acquaintance of a one-time beauty, Lady Sandwich, 'who has all the spirit of the last age, and all the gay experience of a pleasurable life. . . . She is, in a word, the best thing this country has to boast of, and as she has been all a woman of spirit and delight could be, so she still continues that easy, lively, and independent creature that a sensible woman always will be.'

From Bath Pope moved on to Longleat, at the invitation of his friend Lord Lansdowne;* and thence, by way of London, after attending the Coronation of King George I, he travelled slowly home to Binfield. Late in October, however, he wrote to inform Caryll that he would shortly be returning to London 'to set Homer forwards in the press'. The original draft of the translation – Pope was a shrewd domestic economist – had been written on odd scraps of paper; but, once a fair copy had been made, he tactfully solicited the advice of various cultivated great men, including Halifax and the fallen leader Bolingbroke. Pope apparently was still undecided as to whether he should accept a pension; and about this time Halifax desired that he might have the pleasure of hearing the work read aloud. There followed a somewhat comic scene; Pope, at any rate, gave the incident a comic twist when he was telling Spence the story. Addison, Congreve and Garth attended the reading; and Lord Halifax, who was 'rather a pretender to taste than really possessed of it', felt obliged, in the presence of such distinguished literary personages, to assume a suitably judicious air and, on four or five occasions, interrupted the author to admit that he was not altogether satisfied: 'I beg your pardon, Mr Pope,' he would say, 'but there is something in that passage that does not quite please me. Be so good as to mark the place . . . I'm sure you can give it a better turn.' Pope was both puzzled and mortified; and, on the journey home in Dr Garth's chariot, he complained that, having thought over the passages criticized, he could not understand the Minister's objections. Garth, however, 'laughed heartily' and 'said I had not been long enough acquainted with Lord Halifax to know his way yet. . . . "All you need do," says he, "is to leave them just as they are; call on Lord Halifax two or three months hence, thank him for his kind observations on those passages, and then read them to him as altered." ' Pope obeyed the Doctor's instructions; and 'his lordship was extremely pleased' to observe that his

* Lansdowne had married the widow of Lord Weymouth.

criticisms had proved so effective, exclaiming that the passages he had singled out were now everything they should be.

More practical help came from William Broome, who had agreed to examine and annotate the learned commentaries of Eustathius,* which the translator needed for his Notes and found it difficult to plough through. But, while the translator's head buzzed with Homeric problems, his heart once again was in a state of pleasant unrest. No doubt his creative labours during the last few months had produced a mood of nervous excitement that demanded some emotional issue; and the letters he wrote to his beloved Blounts grew increasingly passionate and high-flown. From his opening message, addressed to both sisters, we learn that 'Mrs Patty' had a taste for theatrical performances and romantic novels; 'may she believe all the passion and tenderness expressed in them to be but a faint image of what I bear her, and may you (who read nothing) take the same truth.... You will both injure me very much, if you don't think me a truer friend than ever any Romantic Lover, or any imitator of their style, could be....' His next letter, which was written to Teresa while he was exploring Bath, contains an account of its aquatic fashions – the voluminous buckram overalls assumed by modest eighteenth-century bathers: 'Ladies, I have seen you often, I perfectly know how you look in black and white, I have experienced the utmost you can do in *any* colours; but all your movements, all your graceful steps, all your *attitudes* and postures, deserve not half the glory you might here attain, of a moving and easy behaviour in buckram: something betwixt swimming and walking, free enough, yet more modestly-half-naked than you appear anywhere else.' The letter concludes with a declaration of feeling, none the less serious because Pope gave it a facetious turn: 'You are to understand, Madam, that my *violent* passion for your fair self and your sister has been divided with the most wonderful regularity in the world. Even from my infancy I have been in love with one after the other of you, week by week; and my journey to Bath fell out in the three hundred and seventy-sixth week of the reign of my sovereign Lady Martha. At the present writing hereof, it is the three hundred and eighty-ninth week of the reign of your most serene majesty, in whose service I was listed some weeks before I beheld her. This information will account for my writing to either of you hereafter, as she shall happen to be Queen Regent at that time.'

* Byzantine scholar, Archbishop of Thessalonica during the second half of the twelfth century. His 'Commentary on the Iliad and Odyssey of Homer' includes valuable extracts from the lost works of earlier Homeric scholars. Johnson believed that his crabbed Byzantine Greek would certainly have defeated Pope.

Like Pope, the Blount family had been in London for the Coronation; while she was there, Martha contracted smallpox, the disease that every woman dreaded; and Pope, after his own return, wrote an anxious letter to her sister – 'a month ago I should have laughed at any one, who had told me, my heart would be perpetually beating for a lady that was thirty miles off' – in which he assured her that the poor invalid was seldom absent from his thoughts and prayers; and that, 'whatever ravages a merciless distemper may commit, I dare promise her boldly . . . she shall have one man as much her admirer as ever'. Teresa, he knew, had shown her a 'generous tenderness'; and Martha made a quick and happy recovery. But, as soon as she had begun her convalescence, her family decided she must leave London; and the two girls therefore missed the festivities that followed in the Coronation's wake. The new monarch, with his son the Electoral Prince, henceforward Prince of Wales, and his strange Hanoverian attendants, who included his *maîtresses en titre*, the cadaverous Countess Schulenburg and the elderly but voluptuous Countess Kielmansegge, having reached England on 18 September, the Coronation itself had been solemnized on 20 October. Teresa apparently attended the spectacle; but Martha, no doubt already ailing, seems to have been left behind in bed. While London was still full of excitement, both were hurried back to Mapledurham; and Pope did his best to console them for their loss by writing an occasional poem in his lightest and gayest vein, as elegant a production as his *Epistle to Miss Blount* which he had published three years earlier.*

Each has a comic-didactic turn, and reveals Pope's fascinated preoccupation with women, and with their ways and moods and sufferings. Again, as in some passages of *The Rape of the Lock*, we note an astringent touch of sexual jealousy – the jealousy inspired by the 'enormous engrossers of manhood' who play their brutal part as ordinary lovers and husbands. Thus, in the first *Epistle*, he warns Miss Blount – whether she was Martha or Teresa we do not know – against the wretchedness of modern marriage. Man-made restrictions vex a woman's youth; thence she escapes into a yet more dismal servitude:

> Marriage may all those petty Tyrants chace,
> But sets up One, a greater, in their Place;
> Well might you wish for Change, by those accurst,
> But the last Tyrant ever proves the worst.

* This was the poem, then entitled *To a Young Lady, with the Works of Voiture*, that had appeared in Lintot's miscellany on 20 May 1712, together with the first version of *The Rape of the Lock*.

9 Stanton Harcourt: the haunted Lady Pool. Beyond the Church rise Pope's Tower (flying a flag) and the ancient kitchen.

10 Richard Boyle, Earl of Burlington, collector, builder and general arbiter of taste; portrait by George Knapton.

> Still in Constraint your suff'ring Sex remains,
> Or bound in formal, or in real Chains. ...
> Ah quit not the free Innocence of Life!
> For the dull Glory of a virtuous Wife!

The same threatening shape appears in the second poem – this time the personification of gross, self-centred masculinity, the robust country gentleman who arrives with a present of game and administers loud smacking kisses –

> Or with his hound comes hollowing from the stable,
> Makes love with nods, and knees beneath a table;
> Whose laughs are hearty, tho' his jests are coarse,
> And loves you best of all things – but his horse.

It was an intolerable thought, that the poet might lose a creature he had once adored in the embrace of such an earth-bound tyrant. He preferred that a woman should be remote and pensive, and feed upon romantic day-dreams, even if her dreams happened to be chiefly concerned with the vanished amusements of a Coronation. The second *Epistle* seems to have been addressed to Teresa; but Martha, though she had not witnessed the Coronation herself, might have found it almost equally applicable. It concerns a young woman who has been snatched away from London, and relegated to a simple country round:

> She went, to plain-work, and to purling brooks,
> Old-fashion'd halls, dull aunts, and croaking rooks,
> She went from Op'ra, park, assembly, play,
> To morning walks, and pray'rs three hours a day;
> To pass her time 'twixt reading and Bohea,
> To muse and spill her solitary Tea,
> Or o'er cold coffee trifle with the spoon,
> Count the slow clock, and dine exact at noon. ...

Finally, Pope compares the beloved's solitude, haunted by transient visions of the pleasures she has forfeited, with his own isolation amid London crowds:

> So when your slave, at some dear, idle time
> (Not plagu'd with headache, or the want of rhime)
> Stands in the streets, abstracted from the crew,
> And while he seems to study, thinks of you:
> Just when his fancy points your sprightly eyes,
> Or sees the blush of soft *Parthenia* rise,

H

Gay pats my shoulder, and you vanish quite;
Streets, chairs, and coxcombs rush upon my sight;
Vext to be still in town, I knit my brow,
Look sow'r, and hum a tune – as you may now.

When, in 1769, Owen Ruffhead published his *Life of Alexander Pope, Esq*, he announced that he had under his hand 'the original copy of these verses', including 'sixteen additional lines, which immediately follow the last line of the printed copy', and which the poet, on reflection, had evidently thought it proper to suppress. That suppressed passage was communicated to the *St James's Chronicle* in August 1775 by a writer signing himself G.R., who claimed that they had been 'transcribed from the original, in the handwriting of Mr Pope', and remarked that he heartily wished he 'could apologise for their licentiousness as easily as I can prove their authenticity'. Pope, indeed, would appear to have been the author; but the additional lines accord so ill both with the mood and with the imagery of the previous twenty-five couplets that they may perhaps have once formed part of some completely different poem. There is at least a possibility, however, that they were addressed about this time either to Teresa or to Martha Blount. The occasion upon which they were written was clearly very much the same: a young woman's withdrawal to the country has left her poetic admirer lonely and disconsolate. In the published *Epistle* he describes himself dreaming and musing; but here he is also depicted running hot-foot after mercenary pleasures and finding such consolation as he can among the London bawdy-houses, which include the Park Place establishment of the notorious Mother Needham.*

'Thus, Madam, most Men talk, and some Men do.' Pope apparently was numbered with those who did; for the last line contains an unabashed reference to the horrid risks involved: 'And if poor *Pope* is cl—pt, the Fault is yours.' Seldom has a romantic admirer paid a more strangely indirect tribute! No doubt Pope never intended that it should reach the Blounts' eyes. It still provides a curious sidelight on his relationship with his beloved friends – and on his relationship not only with Martha and Teresa, but with the whole family at Mapledurham. The sisters were well-brought-up Catholic girls, living under the supervision of a widowed mother and an unmarried brother. Why, then, were they permitted to receive letters, always romantic and frequently libertine in style, from a

* Mother Needham was the long-lived meretrix represented by Hogarth in the first episode of *The Harlot's Progress*. In 1731 she was convicted of keeping a disorderly house and sentenced to stand in the pillory. There she was 'pelted in an unmerciful manner' and, having been committed to prison, died soon afterwards.

young poet who professed to be a rake, and whom even the estimable John Caryll considered somewhat irreligious? Can their correspondence have been clandestine? The Blounts were surrounded by their pious, inquisitive kinsmen; and the arrival of the post-bag was an important event in any eighteenth-century household.

The most probable explanation is that none of the Blounts, excepting Martha, who was sensitive and soft-hearted, took his protestations very seriously; and that Pope exploited the privileges accorded him as a hopeless invalid and as a man of genius. By the end of 1714, Teresa's image was being eclipsed by that of Martha. He had already fallen into the perilous habit of writing letters when he was a little tipsy – early in the year, he had written a letter to Miss Betty Marriot which seems afterwards to have caused him some embarrassment;* and during November he apostrophized Martha Blount in an equally euphoric style: 'Most Divine! 'Tis some proof of my sincerity towards you that I write when I am prepared by drinking to speak truth. . . . Wine awakens and refreshes the lurking passions of the mind, as varnish does the colours that are sunk in a picture, and brings them out in all their natural glowings.' He had also been inspired, he admits, by Martha's 'two obliging letters . . . That which begins with "Dear Creature," and "my charming Mr Pope", was a delight to me beyond all expression. You have at last entirely gained the conquest over your fair sister. . . .' Teresa had shocked him 'on several accounts', not least by her irritating displays of prudery; and he enlarges on the superior qualities of his correspondent's blithe, unruffled spirit: ''tis true you are not handsome, for you are a woman and think you are not; but this good humour and tenderness for me has a charm that cannot be resisted. That face must needs be irresistible which was adorned with smiles even when it could not see the Coronation.' Meanwhile Martha's kinsfolk at Whitenights had been harbouring a dramatic secret; it was only the other day that he had 'heard of Mrs Fermor's being actually, directly and consummatively, married'. Thus the ethereal Belinda herself had gone the ordinary way of womankind; but, if Pope was pained or aggrieved, he managed to conceal his feelings; and, as a poet who, after his death, would 'certainly be spoken of' because he had once admired her beauty, he wrote to congratulate young Mrs Perkins with peculiar charm and good grace.

* 'I hope I uttered no such absurdities in the letters to the ladies as were utterly unpardonable; for all I remember of them is, that I was not quite sober when I writ them.' Pope to William Broome, 30 May 1714. The Marriots lived at Sturston, where Broome was then the parish priest.

6

No writer likes correcting his proofs; it is often a moment of acute anxiety; and Pope, we learn from a letter to Trumbull, was still drudging with printer's sheets as late as mid-February, 1715. At the time, the translator's sensations may well have been particularly anxious. Of the formidable journey he had to make, only a sixth yet lay behind him; since he had promoted a lucrative subscription,* he could not hope to leave the road; and everything now depended on the success or failure of the first four books. But he remained uncommonly gay and social; and, that same February, having returned to London, he much enjoyed the visit he paid to a 'reigning curiosity' of the metropolis, a young hermaphrodite, 'the production of the joint endeavours of a Kentish parson and his spouse', then being exhibited as a public side-show. He had never, he said, 'tasted a monster to that degree I have done this creature'; and he sent allusive, and slightly salacious descriptions both to the tolerant Blounts and to the long-suffering Miss Betty Marriot, whom he had already entertained with an over-gallant epistle dashed off when he was 'not quite sober'. During the same month, he issued a new poem – or, rather, an old poem that, according to later editions, he had 'written in year 1711'. Now it was resurrected and, no doubt, revised; and Lintot, who had paid him a fee of £32 5s. od., announced *The Temple of Fame* on 1 February.

In newspaper announcements it was styled 'A Vision'; and Pope's 'Advertisement', attached to the text, explained that 'the hint of the following piece was taken from *Chaucer's House of Fame*', but that the design had been 'entirely altered', and that 'the descriptions and most of the particular thoughts' were the modern poet's own. Pope had a deep regard for Chaucer, and in the past had published modernized adaptations of 'The Merchant's Tale' and 'The Wife of Bath her Prologue'; but like

* See Appendix B.

other eighteenth-century critics, including Horace Walpole, who, despite his love of Gothic antiquity, preferred to enjoy the *Tales* in Dryden's version, he felt that the medieval poems were 'too much clogged with trivial circumstances' and old-fashioned crudities to be altogether palatable. Pope's poem is an extremely free improvisation on a theme supplied by Chaucer. For the Gothic mannerisms of *The House* he substitutes the architecture of the High Baroque; and to later editions Lintot added a headpiece, the work of the engraver Gribelin,* which shows Fame enshrined in a circular building that recalls the Roman Pantheon, beneath a canopy with serpentine columns, strongly suggestive of the columns that support Bernini's *baldachino*. No less Baroque are many of Pope's lines:

> The Temple shakes, the sounding Gates unfold,
> Wide Vaults appear, and Roofs of fretted Gold:
> Rais'd on a thousand Pillars, wreath'd around
> With Lawrel-Foliage, and with Eagles crown'd . . .
> As Heaven with Stars, the Roof with Jewels glows,
> And ever-living Lamps depend in Rows.

The poet's acute pictorial sense is constantly employed throughout the Vision; and some of its more elaborate passages seem to anticipate the architectural *capriccios* of Piranesi and Pannini, or suggest a dramatic landscape drawn from the imagination of Salvator Rosa:

> *Amphion* there the loud creating Lyre
> Strikes, and behold a sudden *Thebes* aspire!
> *Cythaeron's* Ecchoes answer to his Call,
> And half the Mountain rolls into a Wall:
> There might you see the length'ning Spires ascend,
> The Domes swell up, the widening Arches bend,
> The growing Tow'rs like Exhalations rise,
> And the huge Columns heave into the Skies.

The Temple is founded on a towering 'rock of ice'; and Pope, who, during the hard winter of 1712, had amused himself at snow-bound Whitehill House with books 'which treat of descriptions of the Arctic regions', clothes the prospect in tremendous majesty:

> So *Zembla's* rocks (the beauteous Work of Frost)
> Rise white in Air, and glitter o'er the Coast;
> Pale Suns, unfelt, at distance roll away,
> And on th' impassive Ice the Lightnings play;

* Simon Gribelin (1661–1733); a French artist who worked in England from about 1680 onwards.

Eternal Snows, the growing Mass supply,
Till the bright Mountains prop th' incumbent Sky:
As *Atlas* fix'd, each hoary Pile appears,
The gather'd Winter of a thousand Years.

But the poem's general construction is weak; when he wrote it, Pope had not yet learned the art of organizing a long poetic narrative; and, although his genius appears in single passages or in splendid isolated lines –

As to the Sea returning Rivers roll,
And the touch'd Needle trembles to the Pole . . .

– the allegory, or 'fable', is an awkward piece of contrivance, where Fame stands not only for Renown but for Rumour, Report and even Gossip, and a splendid procession of prophets, priests and heroes is succeeded, after nearly two hundred couplets, by a rabble-rout of modern votaries; at which the poet makes a sudden descent into brisk contemporary satire.*

Both Martha Blount and Sir William Trumbull received advance copies of their friend's Chaucerian poem. With John Caryll, then at home, suffering from an attack of gout, he was still in regular correspondence; and on 3 March he wrote to describe the gratifying success of Gay's new farce, a whimsical production entitled *The What d'ye Call It*. Other letters he despatched to Ladyholt – sometimes Pope and Gay collaborated – gave an account of London characters and doings. Cromwell was deaf, and had grown slightly absurd; the outrageous Tidcombe, once exiled from Will's because his 'beastly' conversation was fast becoming unbearable, had now been 'restored to the great joy of Cromwell, who was at a great loss for a person to converse with upon the Fathers and Church History'; Mr Jervas, at Cleveland Court, was busy painting Mr Addison's portrait; Mr Rowe's tragedy of *Jane Grey* would be performed in Easter Week, and Garth's new topographical poem, *Claremont*, would appear about the same time; the coffee-houses, where Pope and Gay often met, were full of noise and dense tobacco-smoke. Pope himself was agreeably dissipated, sat up every night until one or two o'clock over burgundy and champagne, and had become, he confessed, 'so much a modern rake that I shall be ashamed . . . to be thought to do any sort of business'. After such disorderly interludes he usually sought the calm of Binfield; and early that June he was back with his family, plunged once again in work and silence. 'My Muse,' he wrote to Caryll, 'is now an old stale wife, and I make bitter

* There is a close connection between later passages of *The Temple of Fame* and some portions of *The Rape of the Lock*, both in its first and in its second form. See, for example, line 393 of *The Temple* and line 16, Canto III, of *The Rape*.

dry drudgery of it. This jade of mine, that is so fruitful of abortions, will lie in her month, whatsoever she brings forth, tho' it were but a sooterkin:* for so the state and ceremony of the matter requires.' Meanwhile he was concerned with purchasing an annuity at the cost of about £500 – a project in which his 'unfortunate state of health might be', he supposed, 'of some advantage . . .'.

It was a rainy spring; and, although the first volume of the *Iliad* had been scheduled to come out in March, Lintot was obliged to hold up publication because the printed sheets could not be dried. The volume eventually appeared on 6 June 1716; but, two days earlier, Pope had received an infuriating piece of news – a version of Book I by Thomas Tickell, under Tonson's imprint, would be appearing almost simultaneously. Pope already knew that such a version existed; for Addison, who had done so much to encourage his own work, had given him a timely warning. After a dinner party at Button's, Pope explained to Spence,

Addison said that he had wanted for some time to talk with me, that his friend Tickell had formerly, whilst at Oxford, translated the first book of the *Iliad*, that he now designed to print it, and had desired him to look it over. He must therefore beg that I would not desire him to look over my first book, because if he did it would have the air of double dealing. I assured him that 'I did not at all take it ill of Mr Tickell . . . that he certainly had as much right to translate any author as myself, and that publishing both was entering on a fair stage'. I then added that 'I would not desire him to look over my first book . . . but could wish to have the benefit of his observations on my second, which I had then finished, and which Mr Tickell had not touched upon'. Accordingly, I sent him the second book the next morning, and Mr Addison returned it . . . with high commendations.

What Pope evidently did not expect was that Tickell's translation would appear so soon;† and Addison's subsequent behaviour was by no means reassuring. When the rival translations appeared, he affected an air of bland impartiality, announcing that each of them was good in its way, but that Tickell's was probably the more Homeric. Pope now began to grow suspicious. Had Tickell really composed his translation while he was still an undergraduate? Assuming that it was a much more recent work, might he not have received some help from Addison? A chance

* 'An imaginary kind of afterbirth formerly attributed to Dutch women': *Oxford English Dictionary*.

† Nor did Pope know that, on 31 May 1714, Tickell had signed with Tonson an agreement to translate the whole *Iliad*. Addison, however, must surely have been let into the secret.

conversation with Dr Young, he claimed, and 'what Steele has said against Tickell in relation to this affair', made it seem 'highly probable that there was some underhand dealing in that business. And indeed Tickell himself [he added], who is a very fair, worthy man has since in a manner as good as owned it to me.' Pope had known that he could not escape attacks; soon after he had signed an agreement with Lintot, the hackwriter Charles Gildon, in an anonymous dialogue entitled *A New Rehearsal*, or *Bays the Younger*, had heavily ridiculed the whole project; and a series of similar attacks had followed, one of the sharpest being by Thomas Burnet, son of the well-known anti-Catholic bishop. All impugned the translator's scholarship; some suggested that he was a money-grubbing scribbler. It now occurred to Pope that Addison and his 'little senate' at Button's – the group of admirers and sycophants that included Tickell, Eustace Budgell, Henry Carey and the conceited poetaster Ambrose Philips – might have been the secret agents of this venomous campaign. Philips, of course, was an old enemy; he had never forgiven the pretended review of his pastorals that Pope had managed to impose on Steele, had talked loud and long of 'the scurrilous treatment he had received', and was reported afterwards to have bought a rod, which he 'stuck up at the bar of Button's coffee-house', declaring that, if he encountered his rival, he intended to use it for the proper purpose. But Addison was a man he had esteemed and respected. At heart Pope may not have liked him; still, he had never failed to do him justice.

Now he rebelled; and naturally there were gossiping acquaintances who, once hostilities had broken out, did their best to keep the feud alive. Thus Lord Warwick, Addison's future son-in-law, a somewhat foolish young man, informed the poet, either then or later, 'that" it was in vain for me to endeavour to be well with Mr Addison; that his jealous temper would never admit of a settled friendship between us". To convince me of what he had said, he assured me that Addison had encouraged Gildon to publish those scandals, and had given him ten guineas after they were published.' On the appearance of Tickell's translation, Pope's friends immediately rallied to his side. 'Mr Tickle's book,' wrote his publisher, was 'already condemned here, and the malice and juggle of Button's is the conversation of those who have spare moments from politics'. Swift applauded his work; Garth bade Gay tell him 'everybody is pleased with your translation'; and Berkeley reported that 'some days ago, three or four gentlemen ... sate in judgement upon the two translations of the first *Iliad*', and had all given 'the preference where it was due; being unanimously of the opinion that yours was equally just to the sense ...

and without comparison more easy, more poetical, and more sublime'. Addison, however, according to Garth, who had his information straight from Steele, now proclaimed that Tickell's version 'was the best that ever was in any language'; and Garth added that he had heard that 'at Button's your character is made very free with as to morals, &c.' Pope thereupon sprang to his own defence and, assembling his previous impressions of the enemy's character, transfixed Addison in a memorably savage portrait.

The quarrel had had a long history. 'Of the gradual abatement of kindness between friends, the beginning,' observes Johnson, 'is often scarcely discernible by themselves, and the process is continued by petty provocations and incivilities. . . .' Despite the courteous gestures they were always careful to exchange, the young poet and the middle-aged essayist – Addison was Pope's senior by sixteen years – had slowly been drifting towards an open breach. Not only were their ambitions opposed, but they were men of contrasted character and outlook. Pope was decisive; Addison was magisterial. Pope spoke his mind boldly and freely; Addison uttered solemn pronouncements, then sat back with grave composure while they reverberated around his listening synod. The younger man possessed imaginative genius; the older, a high degree of talent. One was a Catholic and a Tory; the other, a Protestant, a Whiggish moralist and an arbiter of middle-class commercial taste.* Yet, although Addison could be awkward and pompous, he had, if he cared to employ it, a personal attraction that there was no gainsaying. Among his intimates, Pope remembered, he was 'perfect good company . . . and had something more charming in his conversation than I ever knew in any other man: but with any mixture of strangers . . . he seemed to preserve his dignity much, with a stiff sort of silence'.

Perhaps because he was secretly shy and reserved, he was apt to assume a prim, parsonic mien; he resembled 'a person in a tye-wig', wrote the satirist Bernard Mandeville; while Jacob Tonson, with whom he had quarrelled, 'used frequently to say of him: "One day or other, you'll see that man a bishop! I'm sure he looks that way; and, indeed, I ever thought him a priest in his heart." ' But, at the outset, Pope had enjoyed his society, and had been glad to join his daily round: 'Addision usually studied all the morning: then met his party at Button's, dined there, and stayed five or six hours – and sometimes far into the night. I was of the company for about a year, but found it too much for me. It hurt my health and so I

* 'During these years an Establishment was formed in London, and Addison and Steele . . . helped to clarify its responses to the world in which it found itself': J. H. Plumb, *The Spectator*, 21 January 1966.

quitted it.' Finally, Addison's nature, Pope felt, concealed a touch of latent malice; now and then, he would make a disparaging reference to Dryden, whose superior fame aroused his envy; and, notwithstanding his genuine affection for Steele, he was apt to tease his devoted colleague in a not altogether kindly fashion; at which the invariably good-humoured Steele never showed the least annoyance. As a public personage, Addison was bound to succeed. For many years a respected Member of Parliament, in 1706 he had become an Under Secretary of State to Lord Sunderland; in 1709, secretary to the Lord Lieutenant of Ireland; and in 1716 he was to crown his social career by marrying the dowager Countess of Warwick, a marriage that, like Wycherley's similar alliance with Lady Drogheda, is said to have caused him much disquietude.

From the relations of Pope and Addison emerged two very different works, both published after Addison's death.* Although the poem, addressed *To Mr Addison, occasioned by his Dialogues on Medals*, was not printed until 1720, the greater part of it must have been written before their breach in 1715. Two years earlier, the July issue of *The Guardian* had included an essay by Addison on medals; and the essayist was already planning a *Dialogue* – it was published posthumously in 1721 – of which Pope, no doubt, had seen the manuscript. These papers may have stirred his imagination; but Pope proceeded to develop the subject along particularly individual lines. He was fascinated, we know, by the idea of littleness, which he associated with ideas of delicacy, subtlety and spiritual or intellectual grace. A medal is small, yet extraordinarily lasting. Huge monuments, like huge men, for all their pride and overweening solidity must soon decline and disappear; while a gold or silver disc, lying in the hollow of the hand, is an imperishable record of human strength and beauty:

> Ambition sigh'd; She found it vain to trust
> The faithless Column and the crumbling Bust;
> Huge moles, whose shadow stretched from shore to shore,
> Their ruins ruin'd, and their place no more!
> Convinc'd, she now contracts her vast design,
> And all her Triumphs shrinks into a Coin:
> A narrow orb each crouded conquest keeps,
> Beneath her Palm here sad Judaea weeps . . .†
> A small Euphrates thro' the piece is rolled,
> And little Eagles wave their wings in gold.

* Addison died at Holland House on 17 June 1719.

† Here Pope refers to a coin commemorating Vespasian's conquest of Jerusalem, AD 70, with the inscription JUDAEA CAPTA.

Towards the end of the poem, Addison's name receives a flattering mention. In 1715, however, it had become synonymous for Pope with envy, malice and literary self-love. 'We have, it seems,' he wrote to James Craggs, 'a great Turk in poetry, who can never bear a brother on the throne; and has his mutes too, a set of nodders, winkers, and whisperers, whose business is to strangle all other offsprings of wit in their birth. The new translator of Homer is the humblest slave he has. . . .' Phrases that the letter-writer had first employed were often re-used by the poet; and, when Pope drew his portrait of Atticus, he remembered how he had already compared Addison to a jealous Turkish sultan. He had begun the portrait, he told Spence, after hearing from Lord Warwick that Addison had instigated Gildon's squib; 'the next day, while I was heated with what I had heard, I wrote a letter to Mr Addison to let him know that "I was not unacquainted with this behaviour of his; that, if I was to speak severely of him in return for it, it should be not in such a dirty way; that I should rather tell him himself fairly of his faults and allow his good qualities; and that it should be something in the following manner. . . ." ' He had then enclosed the preliminary draft of his verses, which so impressed the recipient that 'Mr Addison used me very civilly ever after'. The poet's account of the affair may not have been completely accurate; but there seems no doubt that the sketch of the portrait was drawn when Addison was still alive, and that, between 1715 and 1735, he gradually refined on and improved his work, until, in *An Epistle from Mr Pope to Dr Arbuthnot*, it emerged as a weighty and deadly, yet moving and beautifully balanced satire.

Atterbury, Johnson informs us, considered it Pope's masterpiece. Certainly it illustrates his unexampled gift of assembling a series of diverse images to form a single vivid pattern. Pope works like a mosaicist, building up his picture block by block. He does not minimize his victim; Addison, he admits, had been a great personage; perhaps his worst fault was that he did not sufficiently respect himself, and through lack of self-confidence had become a jealous sovereign ruling over a petty, sycophantic court. In the *Epistle* Pope precedes his attack on Addison with a sweeping review of pedants, plagiarists and Grub Street scribblers. They are soon dismissed as beneath the satirist's regard:

> Peace to all such! but were there One whose fires
> True Genius kindles, and fair Fame inspires;
> Blest with each Talent and each Art to please,
> And born to write, converse, and live with ease:
> Shou'd such a man, too fond to rule alone,

Bear, like the *Turk*, no brother near the throne,
View him with scornful, yet with jealous eyes,
And hate for Arts that caus'd himself to rise;
Damn with faint praise, assent with civil leer,
And without sneering, teach the rest to sneer;
Willing to wound, and yet afraid to strike,
Just hint a fault, and hesitate dislike . . .
Who but must laugh, if such a man there be?
Who would not weep, if *Atticus* were he!

Pope was always reluctant to lose a friend; the loss hurt his idealized
conception of how a virtuous man should live; but his friendship with
Addision had for several years been breaking up; and no doubt he
was somewhat relieved to abandon all his previous pretences. Tickell,
in the meantime, had proved a trifling adversary; his book, though it
had had its admirers, rapidly dropped out of public notice; while Pope's
Iliad was acclaimed, as in Johnson's words, 'the noblest version of poetry
which the world has ever seen'. That, at least, was the common reader's
opinion. Classical scholars, always a captious race, have often held a
slightly different view. According to an anecdote that may perhaps be
apocryphal, the celebrated Dr Bentley, on meeting the poet, once observed:
'It's a very pretty poem, Mr Pope, but you mustn't call it Homer'; and his
remark has set the tone of many later academic gibes. Pope's rendering
may be good verse; it is not a good translation, if in a translation we look
for a meticulous reproduction of a poem's style and spirit. But then, as
material for translation, the Homeric poems present peculiar difficulties.
The poets who produced the work were themselves describing a state
of society – the vanished Mycenaean Age – that they did not wholly
understand.* A gulf of several hundred years separated the poet from his
subject-matter; and, assuming that the *Iliad* and the *Odyssey* took their
definitive shape in the eighth century before Christ, at least a century
separates Homer's work from the earliest black-figure vase-paintings, on
which nowadays we are apt to base our mental picture of Homeric scenes
and backgrounds. Pope knew nothing of early Greek art, little or nothing
of the history of primitive literatures. He saw Homer's heroes in Graeco-
Roman guise; the austerity and dignity of his original was tempered by
Virgilian elegance; and, when he visualized Achilles, Hector or Priam,
he would probably have recollected some Roman copy of an indifferent

* It has been pointed out, for example, that, although the Homeric heroes own chariots,
Homer's generation did not remember their strategic purpose; and that warriors, having
driven to the front line, then dismount to fight on foot.

Hellenistic statue. But Pope was neither a classical scholar, nor was he an archaeologist. What stirred him was his instinctive appreciation of an even greater poet's genius, and the feeling, which had cheered him at the outset, that Homer, across the years, 'seems inclined to correspond with me', and would admit him to the secrets of his grand design. In the preface to his rendering of Ovid's *Epistles*, Dryden had suggested that a valid form of translation was a freely constructed imitation: 'I take imitation of an author ... to be an endeavour of a later poet to write like one who has written before him on the same subject; that is, not to translate his words, or to be confined to his sense, but only to set him as a pattern, and to write, as he supposes that author would have done, had he lived in our age, and in our country.' This was the principle that Pope had followed when he was adapting Chaucer's *Tales*; and, although, when he was dealing with the *Iliad*, he aimed at some degree of textual accuracy, he also sought to revive his author's genius – to produce a new epic based on the old – as he recast hexameters in heroic couplets.

Before we consider the result, we must begin by setting aside many of our twentieth-century beliefs and prejudices, and make our standard the conception of Homer's art that inspired his brilliant introductory essay. Homer, he declares, 'is universally allowed to have had the greatest Invention of any writer whatever'; and 'it is to the strength of this amazing Invention we are to attribute that unequalled Fire and Rapture, which is so forcible in Homer, that no man of a true poetical spirit is master of himself while he reads him. What he writes is of the most animated nature imaginable; every thing moves, every thing lives, and is put in action. . . . The course of his verses resembles that of the army he describes. . . . *They pour along like a fire that sweeps the whole earth before it.* . . . This Fire is discerned in Virgil, but discerned as through a glass, reflected, and more shining than warm, but everywhere equal and constant: in Lucan and Statius, it bursts out in sudden, short, and interrupted flashes: in Milton, it glows like a furnace kept up to an uncommon fierceness by the force of art: in Shakespeare, it strikes us before we are aware, like an accidental fire from heaven: but in Homer, and in him only, it burns every where clearly, and everywhere irresistibly.'

To demonstrate how 'this vast Invention' had been exerted, 'in a manner superior to that of any poet', was the critic's next aim. 'It seemed not enough to have taken in the whole circle of arts and the whole compass of Nature'; Homer had also 'opened a new and boundless walk for his imagination, and had created a world for himself in the invention of Fable. That which Aristotle calls the Soul of Poetry, was first breathed into it by

Homer.' Here Pope's view of the Homeric poems reflects inevitably the preconceptions of his age; he saw in Homer a mighty imaginative genius, a prodigious innovator; while today we are taught to regard the poet who gave the cycle its majestic final shape as the greatest of a lengthy line of bards, inheritors of a huge poetic corpus and all tellers of the same stories. Pope tends, therefore, to emphasize the poems' individual, rather than their traditional aspect, and to pay particular attention to the poet's heroes, each of whom 'has something so singularly his own, that no painter could have distinguished them more by their features, than the poet has by their manners'. Similarly, epithets and images we nowadays regard as traditional Pope applauded as brilliant poetic discoveries; Aristotle had had reason to say that Homer was the only poet who had 'found out *living words*. . . . An arrow is *impatient* to be on the wing, a weapon *thirsts* to drink the blood of an enemy. . . . Yet his expression is never too big for the sense, but justly great in proportion to it: 'tis the sentiment that swells and fills out the diction, which rises with it, and forms itself about it.' Homer, too, had revolutionized the Greek language, by combining different dialects – Ionic, Attic, Doric and Aeolic – 'to beautify and perfect his numbers . . .'.

Such was the word-master whom Pope revered – not a poet who had inherited a long tradition, but the first of modern poets, the discoverer who had opened up a world where none but he had yet trodden. He envisaged Homer, though at a respectful distance, as essentially a modern man. Hence the vigorous quality of his rendering and certain of its imperfections. There was little in the ancient poems that he could not hope to understand, little with which he did not sympathize. The breach between Achilles and Agamemnon resembled the quarrels that divide English governments; and sometimes he carried the resemblance so far that Thersites, the plague of the Grecian camp, is re-fashioned as the acrimonious wiseacre of a London coffee-house:

> Thersites only clamour'd in the throng,
> Loquacious, loud, and turbulent of tongue . . .
> Spleen to mankind his envious heart possest,
> And much he hated all, but most the best:
> *Ulysses* or *Achilles* still his theme;
> But Royal scandal his delight supreme . . .

Pope may occasionally nod; but, on the whole, throughout the entire twenty-four books, he maintains a regular and rapid pace; and just as the movement of Homer's verse 'grows in the progress . . . and becomes on fire like a chariot-wheel, by its own rapidity', his fast-flowing heroic couplets produce an effect of burning strength and speed. His use of the heroic couplet has often been criticized. How could a poet so sensitive to the sonorous dignity of Greek hexameters find the rhyming pentameter a worthy substitute? The measure that Pope adopted is sometimes dismissed as tamely uniform. But, in his hands, it develops an extraordinary range of verbal music; and, whatever virtues his rendering may lack, it cannot be said to lack variety. There are few more readable translations in modern European literature; and it long remained one of the most popular books on the shelves of any English library, enjoyed not only for its bursts of poetic splendour, but as a supremely moving and exciting narrative, which young and old devoured with equal passion.*

In every translation we know that we have lost something; in Pope's *Iliad* what we seem to miss is Homer's primitive dignity and his poignant sense of human tragedy. A tragic episode is apt to be merely grandiose; there is an Augustan stateliness about the diction that sometimes diminishes the story's impact. Pope is at best in the more richly decorative passages – in the great description of the Shield of Achilles, which concludes the eighteenth book; in the passage where the far-seen watch-fires are compared to stars in a moonlit summer sky:

> So many flames before proud *Ilion* blaze,
> And lighten glimm'ring *Xanthus* with their rays.
> The long reflections of the distant fires
> Gleam on the walls, and tremble on the spires.†

– in Homer's comparison of the advance of the Trojan host to the fabulous warfare of the Cranes and Pigmies:

> So when inclement winters vex the plain
> With piercing frosts, or thick-descending rain,
> To warmer seas the cranes embody'd fly,
> With noise, and order thro' the midway sky:
> To pigmy nations wounds and death they bring,
> And all the war descends upon the wing.

– in the romantic glimpse of the sanctuary of 'bleak Dodona'

* Pope's *Homer* was among the English classics on which Edward Gibbon and the young John Ruskin had been brought up.

† It is instructive, as an illustration of Pope's method, to compare these two couplets with a modern prose-translation: 'Such and so many were the Trojans' fires, twinkling in front of Ilium midway between the ships and the streams of Xanthus.' *The Iliad*, translated by E. V. Rieu, 1950.

Whose groves the *Selli*, race austere! surround,
Their feet unwash'd, their slumbers on the ground;
Who hear, from rustling oaks, thy dark decrees;
And catch the fates, low whisper'd in the breeze . . .

– or in the picture of the luxurious flowery nuptials of the Olympian ruler and his consort:

Gazing he spoke, and kindling at the view,
His eager arms around the Goddess threw.
Glad Earth perceives, and from her bosom pours
Unbidden herbs and voluntary flow'rs:
Thick new-born vi'lets a soft carpet spread,
And clustering *Lotos* swell'd the rising bed,
And sudden *Hyacinths* the turf bestrow,
And flamy *Crocus* made the mountain glow.
There golden clouds conceal the heav'nly pair,
Steep'd in soft joys and circumfused with air . . .

Yet Homer's tragic vision of existence is not entirely lost in Pope's rendering. He may somehow fail to convey the solemn pathos of the famous scene upon the Trojan wall, when the old men, at Helen's approach, praise the beauty of that 'fatal face' which spells their beloved city's ruin; but death is a subject that always quickens his imagination, whether it be the lonely end of the devoted mercenary soldier –

A faithful servant to a foreign Lord

– or the fall of Clytus, the gallant squire, picked off by Teucer's 'thrilling arrow' –

In youth's first bloom reluctantly he dies

– a line that, with its memorable adverb, we owe to the translator's unaided fancy: Homer's hero is described neither as reluctant to leave the world, nor, indeed, as very young. Pope often deliberately embroiders his theme. His translation is rooted in Homer; but, like an orchid rooted in the branch of a tree, it is also an independent organism, a poem arising from a poem, subject to its own poetic laws of growth. The 'bitter dry drudgery', about which he sometimes complained, had no effect upon his workmanship. 'Fire' and 'Invention' were the qualities he sought to emulate; in his verses, as in Homer's, 'everything moves, everything lives', though at a different pace, and with a different kind of vitality. We can well believe that, during his long struggle with the *Iliad*, he was often plunged into a waking dream, mistook the local clergyman for the

11 Mid-nineteenth-century engraving of Burlington House, Piccadilly, with its Palladian colonnade and famous gateway.

12 Allen Bathurst, 1st Earl Bathurst, by Sir Godfrey Kneller.

venerable priest of Apollo, and felt less concerned about the Protestant Succession than about the recovery of Menelaus's wife.

Now the problem of the Succession seemed to have been definitely solved; as he wrote, the world was changing. Jacobitism, however, still flourished in many parts of England, for example, in the University of Oxford; and the Stuart Pretender and his associates abroad were busily preparing to launch an armed descent. James's Scottish supporters did not rise until the early autumn; and meanwhile the Whig government had organized a vindictive campaign against the fallen Tory magnates. In January 1715, Pope mentions that he has 'passed . . . a few days with Lord Bolingbroke'. Then, on the night of 25 March, Bolingbroke, having made a public appearance in his box at Drury Lane, quickly slipped away across the Channel. But Oxford, more courageous or more lethargic, decided to await his punishment. On 8 July he spoke in the House of Lords; on the 16th he was committed to the Tower of London, where he was to live as a state-prisoner for two years.

Disaster became him. 'The Earl of Oxford,' wrote Pope to the Blounts, 'has behaved so bravely, that . . . he might seem above Man, if he had not just now voided a stone to prove him subject to human infirmities. The utmost weight of affliction from princely power and popular hatred, were almost worth bearing for the glory of such dauntless conduct. . . .' On 21 July the Duke of Ormond followed Bolingbroke's lead; and, on 27 July, all Catholics were enjoined to leave London and keep outside a ten-mile radius. Pope presumably obeyed this order; he remained in the country throughout the summer and the autumn, sometimes at Binfield, sometimes at Mapledurham amid the friendly Blounts. Before he left London, he had watched the martial preparations that now absorbed the whole metropolis. New regiments had been raised; tents sprang up in Hyde Park; and 'the sight of so many thousand gallant fellows', he told Teresa and Martha, 'with all the pomp and glare of war yet undeformed with battle, those scenes which England has for many years only beheld on stages, may possibly invite your curiosity. . . .'

Pope's letter, describing the encampment, which was written on 23 July, includes two casual mentions of a new acquaintance. 'I must stop here,' he remarks, 'till further advices from the Lady Mary Wortley, this afternoon.' At the bottom of the page, he adds that the promised advices have now arrived from Lady Mary's house in Duke Street, and that she relates the ridiculous story of Mr Thomas Gage, a persecuted Catholic, who had been deeply distressed by the official seizure of his Flemish coach-horses and, having watched a procession of splendid equipages rolling cheerfully beneath his windows, had felt that he could no longer bear his loss, and had rushed out, taken the Oath of Abjuration and, henceforward a loyal Protestant, had 'recovered his dear horses which carried him in triumph to the Ring';* while his more steadfast co-religionists, 'unhorsed and uncharioted', were still obliged to go on foot. The Blounts must already have heard of their dazzling rival Lady Mary, although, in the summer of 1715, Pope's friendship with her was not many months old. Possibly he had met her through Gay; but, as a youthful poet, he had known her father; for Lord Dorchester is listed among the grandees who had condescended to approve his early efforts. Lady Mary was one year younger than Pope; and, having lost her mother during early childhood, she had been brought up first by her grandmother in Wiltshire, then by Lord Dorchester himself, a careless, self-indulgent person, at Thoresby, his Nottinghamshire country house upon the verge of Sherwood Forest, and at his London residence near Piccadilly.

Of that upbringing she had vivid recollections – how, when she was a little girl, she had longed to catch the sun before it sank below the sky-line, which she could 'remember running very hard to do'; and how, at the age of six or seven, she had enjoyed the happiest moment of her whole existence. Her father, who was a Whig and a Kit-Cat, had commanded her nurse to dress the child in her most becoming clothes and bring her to a tavern-assembly of the Club, where she 'went from the lap of one poet, or patriot, or statesman, to the arms of another, was feasted with sweet-meats, overwhelmed with caresses, and, what perhaps already pleased her better than either, heard her wit and beauty loudly extolled on every side. Pleasure, she said, was too poor a word to express her sensations; they amounted to ecstasy. . . .' Such moments are never quite recaptured; and, even as a little girl, Lady Mary seems to have begun to learn the vanity of human wishes. The ecstatic moment passes beyond recall; it would have been 'a fine thing truly' to overtake and catch the setting sun. Experience, alas, 'soon shows it to be impossible'.

Not that at any period of her life she despaired; hers was a naturally ardent and demanding character; and nowadays we might well describe her as both a romantic idealist and an incorrigible exhibitionist. She yearned to succeed; she rejected the common round; and in her blue-curtained nursery with its three blue-covered beds, above her father's noble park and gardens, she had already begun to cultivate the art of literature, and was busily occupied reading, writing and copying out her

* The Ring in Hyde Park had the same degree of social importance as Victorian and Edwardian Rotten Row. The Gage family did, in fact, change their faith about this time.

own verses; of which the earliest collection – presently followed by her 'Entire Works' – had been produced by the year 1703, before she had achieved her fourteenth birthday. In other respects, too, she had had a privileged childhood. When she was seventeen, her father – plain Mr Evelyn Pierrepont at the time of her birth; Earl of Kingston since 1690 – was elevated to the rank of marquess; presently he would receive a dukedom. If Lady Mary had the tastes of a bluestocking, and had once aspired to found a private nunnery over which she could preside as lady abbess, she also enjoyed the benefits and absorbed the prejudices that went with her exalted station. Proud of her scholarship, she was no less proud of her lineage. But perhaps it was from her beauty and her gift of charming that she derived the keenest pleasure. She had, moreover, an unruly heart and a fund of strong emotions.

When she was about twenty, she decided that she had fallen in love, her choice being an attractive, solemn, self-centred personage, some eleven years her senior, Edward Wortley or Wortley Montagu, a close relation of the Earl of Sandwich, barrister, Member of Parliament, and the friend of Steele and Addison. Their courtship was carried on by stealth – Lord Dorchester, who was both obstinate and selfish, soon fell out with his future son-in-law concerning the question of the marriage settlement. If Lady Mary married against his wishes, she would forfeit a substantial dowry; and, although their correspondence has an agreeably romantic side, it also records the many 'useless disputes' that arose between these ill-assorted lovers – Edward Wortley, the cautious careerist, always mindful of his worldly chances, and Lady Mary, a modern Millamant, stubborn, high-spirited and mettlesome, perpetually balancing passion, to which it is clear that she was by no means insensitive, against the claims of sober reason. Neither of them could face a life of poverty; her reason, wrote Lady Mary, 'tells me that in any circumstances of life (wretched or happy) there is a certain proportion of Money necessary to the living in it'. Wortley agreed; and it was her irritated parent himself who eventually overcame their scruples – by attempting to force her into an odious marriage with the son and heir of a rich Irish viscount, as whose wife, she complained, she would 'enjoy every pleasure ... those of happiness excepted', and by ordering that, until she was wed, she should remain a prisoner in the country. Thereupon even her backward lover began to show a more heroic spirit; while Lady Mary declared that her resolution was taken, and merely begged that he would 'love me and use me well'. They eloped and were secretly married during the summer of the year 1712.

There seems no doubt that, in the early days of their marriage, the rash young woman loved her husband deeply. 'Pray, my dear,' she implored him, when they were first separated, 'write to me, or I shall be very mad.' She remained his, she wrote, *de tout mon coeur*. Soon she was pregnant; and their eldest child, who received his father's Christian name, was born on 16 May 1713. But gradually, once they were established in London, the young wife had grown a little less passionate, and the husband, who had never matched her ardour, more and more solemn and preoccupied. He was ambitious – in later years he earned the reputation of being coldly avaricious; while Lady Mary, so long as she lived, was a 'mighty gay and airy' personage, quick-thinking and quick-talking, with a sharp wit and an extremely savage tongue. Despite the cares of marriage and mother-hood, she was still an enthusiastic scribbler; and, since Addison was not only her husband's associate but her father's old acquaintance, it was seldom very difficult to get her literary productions published. Once the Hanoverian family had reached England, she developed a yet more profit-able diversion; she began to exercise her fascinating talents at Court; and, although her keen eye informed her that the new monarch was 'an honest blockhead', and his son, the Prince of Wales, an irascible martinet, who 'looked on all the men and women he saw as creatures he might kiss or kick for his diversion', she played her part among their outlandish courtiers with the utmost grace and self-assurance. Is it possible that she had some thoughts of founding her fortune – and her husband's fortune – as an accredited royal favourite? If that was her plan, she was unlikely to succeed, suggested a contemporary gossip. Lady Mary had a small and slender frame; and the King 'can't like anybody so little, let their mind be as large as it will'. The largeness of her mind and the restlessness of her wit was more valued in a different sort of company; she enjoyed collecting poets, artists and scholars; and a particularly agreeable acquisition was the celebrated Mr Pope.

Both Pope and Lady Mary had been painted by their friend Jervas – Lady Mary during her twenty-second year, when she was still Lady Mary Pierrepont. The arrangement of the picture is no less stiff and mannered than most of Jervas's compositions. He has portrayed his subject as what, in a letter to Pope, he would afterwards call 'one of my shepherdesses', holding a rustic staff, attended by a favourite lambkin, the elbow of an ill-painted arm vaguely at rest against a tree-trunk. But the face is charming and, besides the charm and the subtlety of youth, reveals a strongly indi-vidual character, with its smooth, lofty forehead, its delicate nose and chin, and long, dark, rather narrow eyes, set far apart above the cheek-bones. As an older woman, Lady Mary was often criticized for her Bohemian mode of dressing; and here the thick dark locks hang down to her shoulders, unornamented and unconfined, and a short, untidy wisp, which has surely defied the comb, strays across the left temple. It is not surprising that she should at once have captivated Pope; but we cannot tell how Pope's aspect and character struck the highly fashionable Lady Mary, an accomplished member of the London great world, who was just then much preoccupied with her own attractions and her own successes. About his appearance, despite his diminutive stature and his crooked back, certainly there was nothing that she need have found repellent. Jervas had painted his head and shoulders towards the end of 1714 – the portrait that, in 1717, was to be engraved as the frontispiece of his collected *Works*. Again the sitter's pose is conventional; but the effect that the face produces is extraordinarily alert and keen.

Pope, at the time, was twenty-six years old; and he has still the features of an energetic young man, though the shadows left by fatigue and ill-health have already begun to appear below the eye-lids. But his eyes themselves – bright and blue-grey – shine with a compelling lustre; they are as clear and cool as the sharp-cut mouth is sensitive and fine-drawn. It is a self-assured, almost an arrogant face, which suggests that the owner maintained his position in life by a deliberate exercise of will. Jervas has given the poet a suitably imperious attitude. Half turned to confront an unseen audience, his fragile shoulders boldly squared so as to correct their stooping outline, he lays the fingers of one elegant spidery hand across the breast of his dark-blue velvet coat; his fine linen shirt is open at the neck; and he wears a greyish-yellow wig, which heightens the darkness of the eyes and eyebrows. For all its dignity and distinction, it is not a reassuring face – though Jervas may perhaps have softened its contours, there are too many hints of inward strain; the lips have an acutely sensuous curve; and beneath the air of ascetic refinement we detect an angry gleam of pride and passion.

This was the young man who, during the spring or summer of 1715, had been drawn into Lady Mary's circle. When a writer courts a literary *femme du monde*, he usually begins by advising and flattering her about her own imaginative efforts. Clearly, it was the method Pope adopted; for, that autumn, he and Gay collaborated with Lady Mary in a series of three satirical 'town eclogues', which depicted courtiers and court-ladies as Virgilian nymphs and shepherds. 'The Basset Table', containing sketches of Cardelia, said to represent Lady Bristol, and Smilinda, the victim of an unfortunate passion, in whom it is thought she may have sketched herself, and 'The Drawing Room', a squib directed at the frivolous entourage of the new Princess of Wales, we owe to Lady Mary's talent; but her professional friends, no doubt, corrected her verses and added an image or an epithet here and there. If Smilinda's experiences were those of Lady Mary –

> With eager beats his Mechlin cravat moves:
> He loves, I whisper to myself, He loves! . . .
> My panting heart confesses all his charms;
> I yield at once, and sink into his arms

– her account of her fall, as Pope considered and revised it, may have had a disturbing effect on his imagination. Sharper, Smilinda's masterly lover, is believed to have stood for Lord Stair; and with Lord Stair, according to Horace Walpole, Lady Mary had just committed, or would soon commit, her first fashionable infidelity.

Pope, however, was seldom in London during the latter part of 1715. In August, he, Jervas, Dr Arbuthnot and 'Duke' Disney, one of Swift's Irish associates, planned an expedition to the West of England; but the scheme miscarried; and, towards the end of the month, Pope and Arbuthnot travelled to Oxford unaccompanied, the poet going on to Bath – a 'ramble' from which he returned to Binfield about the beginning of October. Meanwhile he had not lost touch with the girls at Mapledurham, whose future now caused him some concern, since their brother Michael had become engaged to the eldest daughter of Sir Henry Tichborne and, when he married, they might be obliged to leave his house. In August their admirer sent them a pair of fans, which had been chosen at his request by Jervas, thanked them for two bottles of elderberry wine, and protested that 'I am in love with you both as I am with myseif, and find myself most so with all three when I least suspect it'. But his letters contain very few references – and none direct – to the tragic episode of the Jacobite Rebellion. On 6 September the Scottish Jacobites had at length raised the standard of King James III. They were ill-prepared and notably ill-led, as were the Catholic gentlemen of northern England, who, following a new Pilgrimage of Grace, marched with their tenants into Lancashire. The English rising was quickly crushed at Preston; and on the same November day, at the battle of Sheriffmuir, the Earl of Mar's troops, though they greatly outnumbered the government forces led by the Duke of Argyle, encountered a decisive check, after which the Jacobite army gradually lost heart and scattered. The Pretender's appearance did little to encourage his champions. He arrived belatedly and departed abruptly, a lonely, lugubrious, ineffective figure.

By the close of October, Pope, who had been hard at work correcting his next volume, evidently felt that it would now be safe for him to return to Cleveland Court. His spirits were low; he was 'weary of translating', he told Caryll, weary of poetry, weary of prose, and had begun 'to hate to write at all, even letters . . .' And, once he had returned, he found London 'in so prodigious a ferment of politics that I, who never meddled with any, am utterly incapable of all conversation in it'. The metropolis was full of horrid sights and sounds; and on 9 December a procession of rebellious Catholic gentlemen, captured in Lancashire, their arms roped, their horses led by soldiers, filed through the London streets amid the cat-calls of an angry mob. But Pope's mood of gloom and perplexity had some deeper, more mysterious origin. Caryll, he hoped, would forgive his recent neglect; 'I should make you a very . . . extraordinary apology . . . if I were to tell you in what a wild, distracted, amused, buried state, both my mind and body have been ever since my coming to this town. A great deal of it is so odd, that it would hardly find credit. . . . It would move pity in you when you reflect how naturally people of my turn love quiet, and how much my present studies require ease. In a word, the world and I agree as ill, as my soul and body, my appetites and constitution, my books and business. So that I am more splenetic than ever you knew me, concerned for others, out of humour with myself, fearful of some things, wearied with all.' For an explanation we must look to a private sorrow; in mid-December he learned that the incomparable Lady Mary had been stricken down by an attack of smallpox. Although her friends surrounded her and the most celebrated London physicians, among them Garth and Sir Hans Sloane, immediately hastened to her bedside – Sloane offering her cordial draughts, Garth vowing he would restore her health and beauty – none of these well-wishers could bring a single gleam of comfort. Heavily masked against the injurious daylight, she lay abed and wept and trembled. In time she recovered and rose to face the world; but her morbid fears had not been unfounded. Jervas's maiden shepherdess had vanished beyond recall; her smooth skin was irremediably scarred; and she had for ever lost her long dark lashes.

The year 1712 had ended with a savage winter. Late in 1715, the surface of the Thames froze, and remained a rugged mass of ice from the beginning of December until the third week of January. For the first time since 1688, Londoners could enjoy the diversions of a Frost Fair; a whole village of canvas booths was built along this arctic causeway, where oxen were roasted over enormous bonfires, and the citizens met to drink and gamble. Even carriages ventured to cross the ice; while the watermen, who had lost their livelihood, 'pensive reclined' beside their useless oars. Gay depicted the scene in *Trivia*, his mock-heroic poem, published towards the end of January, on 'The Art of Walking the Streets of London'; and he also described – it was among his finest efforts – the tragedy of Doll, an unfortunate apple-seller who, once a dangerous thaw had begun to set in, had had her head chopped from her shoulders by a sheet of 'cracking crystal'.* Pope was obliged to postpone a visit to the Caryll family at Ladyholt; and meanwhile he felt greatly disturbed about the prospects of 'the Mapledurham ladies', now that it seemed likely that they might be forced to leave their old home. During the same month, he learned of the death of 'that eminent Comic Poet ... Wycherley', hard on the heels of his preposterous marriage. 'I saw our friend twice ...' reported Pope, and found him 'less peevish in his sickness than he used to be in his health; neither much afraid of dying, nor (which in him had been more likely) much ashamed of marrying'. Poor Wycherley had been, if not an entirely estimable, at least an admirably consistent character.

During February Pope was established in London; and he, Gay, Jervas and Arbuthnot, having assembled for a convivial evening at 'the chop

* 'The cracking crystal yields, she sinks, she dies,
　Her head, chopt off, from her lost shoulders flies:
　Pippins she cried, but Death her voice confounds,
　And Pip-Pip-Pip along the ice resounds.'
　　　　　　　　　　　　　　　　Trivia, Book II

13 Pope's Seat at Cirencester Park, one of Bathurst's architectural 'baubles'.

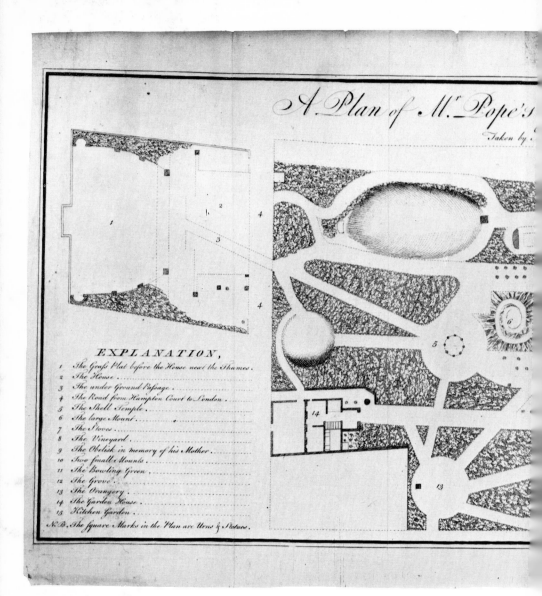

A Plan of Mr. Pope's

Taken by

EXPLANATION,

1 The Grass Plat before the House next the Thames.
2 The House.
3 The under Ground Passage.
4 The Road from Hampton Court to London.
5 The Shell Temple.
6 The large Mount.
7 The Stoves.
8 The Vineyard.
9 The Obelisk in memory of his Mother.
10 Two small Mounts.
11 The Bowling Green.
12 The Grove.
13 The Orangery.
14 The Garden House.
15 Kitchen Garden.
N.B. The Square Marks in the Plan are Urns & Statues.

14 A plan of Pope's gardens at Twickenham, 'taken by Mr. Serle his Gardener', 1745.

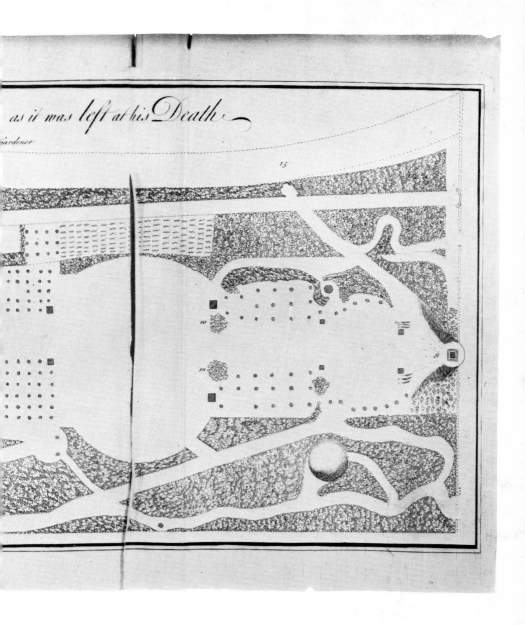

as it was *left* at his *Death*

Gardener

15

10

10

15 Pope at work in his Grotto; a drawing by Lady Burlington. Behind the poet shines his alabaster lamp.

house in Exchange Alley', wrote a joint letter* to Thomas Parnell, then languishing beyond the Irish Sea. Gay admits to having been 'sick with wine'; Jervas reports that he has engaged to paint a two-fold portrait of 'Pope's favourites', Martha and Teresa; Arbuthnot announces that 'Gay has got so much money by his art of walking the streets, that he is ready to set up his equipage', and that 'Mr Pope delays his second volume of his Homer till the martial spirit of the rebels is quite quelled, it being judged that his first part did some harm that way'; while Pope, in his share of the letter, reverts to his immediate Homeric problems, and to the learned treatise on Zoilus† that the good-natured Parnell was preparing for his benefit. All send their love to the 'dear Dean' who, they were told, was finding Dublin an extremely gloomy place of residence. Swift continued to lament the fall of the Tory leaders. 'You know how well I loved both Lord Oxford and Bolingbroke, and how dear the Duke of Ormond is to me,' he had already written during the previous summer: 'Do you imagine I can be easy? . . .' And, since he left England, he had been obliged to exist 'in the corner of a vast unfurnished house', his household consisting of 'a steward, a groom, a helper in the stable, a footman and an old maid . . . and when I do not dine abroad, or make an entertainment (which last is very rare) I eat a mutton-pie, and drink half a pint of wine. My amusements are defending my small dominions against the Archbishop, and endeavouring to reduce my rebellious Choir.' It was little enough for an intensely active spirit, who had once shone as 'the principal man of talk and business' in the royal ante-room at Windsor.

Pope had his own troubles, apart from the difficult business of translating Homer, his romantic preoccupation with Lady Mary and his anxious interest in the future of the Blounts. His family had decided that they would leave Binfield; and during March he revisited the Forest, to take his 'last look' at the place he had loved, and bid farewell to friendly neighbours. Perhaps the old Popes felt that the time had come when they must seek smaller, more convenient lodgings; and as Catholics, obliged to register their estates, they may have feared that, if they kept their land, they might soon be ruined by increasingly oppressive taxes. At all events, Whitehill House had been sold; and, some weeks later, they removed their goods to Mawsons' New Buildings in Chiswick, close to Chiswick House, the Jacobean residence of young Lord Burlington, which he was afterwards to demolish when he conceived the plan of raising his splendid

* According to George Sherburn, the writing of this letter is 'strongly redolent of wine'.
† Zoilus, a Macedonian professor of rhetoric (*c.* 400–*c.* 320 B C) called Homeromastix, or the Scourge of Homer.

Palladian villa. Before the house in New Buildings had been furnished and occupied, Pope passed two or three days of 'high luxury' as the great man's guest; 'we are to walk,' he told Martha Blount, 'ride, ramble, dine, drink, and lie together. His gardens are delightful, his music ravishing. . . .' In any period, Richard Boyle, third Earl of Burlington, fourth Earl of Cork, would have seemed a gifted and impressive figure: in the Augustan Age, thanks to his talents, his learning, his wealth and the brilliant society he gathered round him he became an exemplar of modern taste at its most advanced and most eclectic.

Pope already knew him well; when Burlington returned from the Grand Tour during the spring of 1715, he is reported to have had trouble with the Customs over the gifts he had purchased for 'Senr. Pope', which, as the officers wished to confiscate them, must have been bibelots of some value. Burlington's other luggage included porphyry vases, canvases by Maratta and Domenichino, and a dozen miniatures by Rosalba Carriera that had cost him 288 crowns; and he also brought back three Italians – presumably artists or musicians – a bass-viol, a pair of harpsichords and over eight hundred assorted trunks and boxes. In 1716 he was only twenty-two, and still more attracted by music and painting than by classical and Renaissance architecture; but, on his return home, he acquired a pair of folios that were to revolutionize his whole development – Colen Campbell's opening volume of *Vitruvius Brittanicus*, a pictorial survey of the work of modern architects, and Nicolas Dubois' translation of Giacomo Leoni's four-volume treatise, *The Architecture of A. Palladio*.

Such a neighbour Pope was bound to appreciate; and he may have considered that, once established at Chiswick 'under the wing of my Lord Burlington', a strong government-supporter and recently appointed Privy Councillor, he and his family would avoid some of the trials that now threatened other English Papists. Besides, he liked the Thames and its verdant background; and Chiswick was agreeably near St James's and the Wortley's house in Westminster. As soon as she could leave her bed, Lady Mary had returned to Court, where, despite the bad effect produced by 'The Drawing Room', that shrewd and tolerant woman the Princess of Wales gave not the smallest hint that she had taken umbrage. Lady Mary seemed as gay and talkative as ever; but her loss of beauty there was no disguising. When she first fell ill, said an amused acquaintance,* Edward Wortley had been especially alarmed; for that winter she stood high in favour with the King; and her disfigurement

* James Brydges, afterwards Duke of Chandos, to Colonel Bladen, 28 December 1715; quoted by George Sherburn, *The Early Career of Alexander Pope*.

would probably put an end to certain ambitious private schemes that he had already 'chalked out'. Yet he persevered; if Lady Mary must abandon every hope of becoming a royal favourite, her husband might still obtain an embassy. Early in April his efforts were rewarded, and he secured the interesting position of Ambassador Extraordinary to the Sublime Porte.* The post, it was true, had disadvantages; five years was usually the shortest period that a British Ambassador remained in Turkey; but Lady Mary, as she afterwards told Spence, was entirely undismayed by the idea of leaving England. Bred on travel-books and romantic stories, she was 'charmed with the thoughts of going into the East, though . . . 'twas a sort of dying to her friends and country. But 'twas travelling . . . 'twas wandering; 'twas all whimsical, and charming.' And she prepared to set forth 'with all the pleasure imaginable'.

Before she left, she was often in Pope's company; and, so far as prudence and decorum allowed, he made his admiration plain. Thus, in March, when Richard Graham published an edition of Dryden's translation of Dufresnoy's *Art of Painting*,† it included Pope's *Epistle to Mr Jervas*, in which he applauded his friend's delightful gifts and enumerated some of the beauties on whom the painter had conferred undying radiance:

> Beauty, frail flow'r that ev'ry season fears,
> Blooms in thy colours for a thousand years.
> Thus *Churchill's* race shall other hearts surprize,
> And other Beauties envy *Wortley's* eyes,
> Each pleasing *Blount* shall endless smiles bestow,
> And soft *Belinda's* blush for ever glow.‡

At the same time, Pope adopted the rôle of Lady Mary's literary champion. The 'Town Eclogues', after passing from hand to hand, had been somehow snapped up by a Fleet Street bird of prey, one of those booksellers who united the functions of bookseller, publisher and stationer, and often conducted a lucrative sideline in the sale of patent medicines.

Few English bookmen or journalists have been more abused than

* It was not, however, his first official appointment. Soon after the Hanoverian accession, Wortley, somewhat against his will, had accepted the post of Junior Commissioner, offered him by his relation Lord Halifax.

† Charles Alphonse Dufresnoy (1611–65), a friend of Mignard and himself both a painter and a poet.

‡ The 1st Duke of Marlborough had four beautiful daughters, 'Churchill's race', including the short-lived Countess of Bridgewater, mentioned elsewhere in the poem. For 'Wortley' Pope was later to substitute 'Worsley', Lady Worsley being the wife of Swift's friend, Sir Robert Worsley.

Edmund Curll, and have met general abuse and contempt with greater cynicism and equanimity. During the four decades that he spent in business, he experienced a long series of ignominious misadventures – pilloried, imprisoned, reprimanded on his knees at the bar of the House of Lords, even set upon and tossed in a blanket by the indignant pupils of Westminster School. Nothing deterred him; he continued to scavenge and publish. But, if he had little regard for the decencies of literature Curll would seem to have had a genuine love of books. He had also, we are told, a 'good natural understanding' and 'talked well on some subjects', especially on the English stage. His appearance was as bizarre as his character; and a contemporary journalist, probably Daniel Defoe, declared that, besides being 'scandalous in his fame', he was no less 'odious in his person'. Curll is said to have been 'very tall and thin, an ungainly, awkward, white-faced man. His eyes were a light grey, large, projecting, goggle and purblind.' Nor were his personal habits attractive; he was both debauched and avaricious; and, like other London booksellers, he kept a stable of impoverished hacks, including his needy translators who 'lay three in a bed at the Pewter Platter Inn in Holborn'. Though he produced some editions of respectable authors, many of the publications that issued from his Fleet Street shop, opposite St Dunstan's Church, had nothing to recommend them but their pornographic value; and, when pornography failed, he resorted to books and pamphlets that possessed a topical or controversial charm, announcing them in cunningly worded advertisements, designed to interest the news-hungry reader.

Thus, having secured the 'Town Eclogues' and, as a collection of *Court Poems*, had them quickly set up, he proceeded to surround their origin with a beguiling air of mystery. These verses, he asserted on the title-pages, had been discovered in a pocket-book left in Westminster Hall during the trial of the Jacobite Lord Winton; while, in an ingenious advertisement which occupied the first three pages, he threw off hints about their authorship. At the St. James's Coffee House, he wrote, they had been generally attributed to 'a Lady of Quality'; at Button's, to Mr Gay; whereas 'a Gentleman of distinguished Merit, who lives not far from Chelsea' – by which he evidently meant Addison – had pronounced that they could only have been written by 'the Judicious Translator of Homer'. It seems unlikely that Curll had consulted Addison; he was merely determined to bring into the affair as many well-known names as possible. But Pope was enraged; the publication of the poems might do Lady Mary harm at Court; the mention of Addison's name was a further irritant; and he may have disliked being credited with such frivolous and flimsy pieces. Possibly he would have preferred to thrash Curll; but then, the bookseller was a very tall man. He therefore devised, perhaps with Arbuthnot's help, a more elaborate means of punishment.

Court Poems made their appearance on Monday, 26 March; 'on the Wednesday ensuing, between the hours of ten and eleven', Lintot, who was evidently Pope's accomplice, solicited an interview with his fellow-bookseller to discuss a title-page, suggesting that they should meet at the Swan Tavern, and there take a friendly 'whet' together. The unsuspecting Curll duly arrived, myopic, gaunt and splay-footed; and, while they were still discussing their business, they were joined in the tavern-room by Pope. No doubt he expressed surprise; but, having met Curll, he reprimanded him 'with a seeming coolness . . . for wrongfully ascribing to him the aforesaid poems'. Curll, however, 'excused himself, by declaring that one of his authors (Mr Oldmixon by name) gave the copies to the press, and wrote the Preface'. Pope then affected to be satisfied, and each of the disputants toasted the other in a glass of sack. So far as colour and taste were concerned, the liquor 'differed not from common sack'; but into Curll's glass Pope had dropped a strong emetic. Dr Arbuthnot is thought to have mixed the draught; its effect on Curll's stomach and intestines showed how well he had studied the pharmacopoeia.

Once Pope had returned home, he hastened to commit the story to writing; and a threepenny pamphlet was almost immediately issued, under the title *A Full and True Account of a Horrid and Barbarous Revenge by Poison on the Body of Mr Edmund Curll, Bookseller*. As described by Pope, John Dennis's madness had been a trivial episode compared with the pangs that the unhappy Curll suffered; and his poisoner noted down every detail in his most wildly Rabelaisian style. No sooner had the bookseller regained his shop than his wife, 'observing his colour changed, said, "Are you not sick, my dear?" He replied, "Bloody sick"; and incontinently fell a vomiting and straining . . . the contents of his vomiting being as green as grass . . . Mr Lintot in the meantime coming in, was extremely affrighted at the sudden alteration he observed in him. "Brother Curll," says he, "I fear you have got the vomiting distemper, which (I have heard) kills in half an hour." ' But there is worse to come, when the bookseller's symptoms begin to include 'acute pains in the lower belly'; and Curll, having summoned his partner and dictated his last will and testament – a long list of books he had pirated and modern authors whom he had defrauded – retires to a near-by close-stool where the sad tale of his retchings and gripings is for the moment cut short.

Pope, however, was sufficiently pleased with his pamphlet to concoct a second essay, *A Further Account of the most Deplorable Condition of Mr Edmund Curll, Bookseller, since his being Poisoned on the 28th of March*, incorporating 'A True Copy of Mrs Curll's Letter to Mr Lintot':

You, and all the neighbours know too well, the frenzy with which my poor man is visited. I never perceived he was out of himself, till that melancholy day that he thought he was poisoned in a glass of sack; upon this, he took a strange fancy to run a vomiting all over the house, and in the new-washed dining-room. Alas! this is the greatest adversity that ever befell my poor man since he lost one testicle at school by the bite of a black boar.

Like his original attack on John Dennis, Pope's description of Edmund Curll's misfortunes does not lack a saving humour. Thus, in the second, Curll commands the presence of the troop of needy writers he employed, and explains where they may be run to ground – 'at a tallow-chandler's in Petty France, half way under the blind arch': 'at a blacksmith's shop in the Friars', a Pindaric writer in red stockings': 'at the Three Tobacco Pipes in Dog and Bitch Yard, one that has been a parson; he wears a blue camblet coat trimmed with black': 'the cook's wife in Buckingham Court: bid her bring along the similes that were lent her for her next play': 'call at Budge Row for the gentleman you used to go to in the cock-loft; I have taken away the ladder, but his landlady has it in keeping'. Once the hacks arrive, they present a recognizable picture of a crowded literary gathering:

They no sooner entered the room, but all of them showed in their behaviour some suspicion of each other; some turning away their heads with an air of contempt; others squinting with a leer that showed at once fear and indignation, each with a haggard abstracted mien, the lively picture of scorn, solitude, and short commons. So when a keeper feeds his hungry charge, of vultures, panthers, and of Lybian leopards, each eyes his fellow with a fiery glare. . . . Or as a housewife stands before her pales, surrounded by her geese; they fight, they hiss, they gaggle, beat their wings. . . . Such looks shot through the room transverse, oblique, direct; such was the stir and din, till Curll . . . spoke, (but without rising from his close-stool).

Pope was in no way ashamed of his stratagem, though inclined to gloss over the fact that he had written the ensuing pamphlets; and when next he addressed his friend at Ladyholt, he mentioned, among other items of news, 'a most ridiculous quarrel with a bookseller, occasioned by his having printed some satirical poems on the Court under my name. I contrived to save the fellow a beating by giving him a vomit, the history whereof has been transmitted to posterity by a late Grub-street author' whose narrative had 'much entertained the town'. So far as we can tell, none of Pope's contemporaries found his behaviour odd or unbecoming; the Augustan Age was accustomed to practical jokes of a somewhat coarse and heavy-handed kind; and this squalid tradesman neither deserved nor demanded the protection of polite society. The modern world may at heart be equally savage; it is unquestionably far more squeamish. However little we may sympathize with Curll, Pope's satirical pamphlets – in time they were followed by a third, the grotesque story of the bookseller's alleged conversion to the Jewish faith – set his admirers some disturbing problems.

The poet had always been jealous of his personal and poetic dignity; and now that he was about to issue the second volume of his *Iliad* – it made its appearance early in April – the place he occupied was particularly secure. Why, then, stoop to engage so vulgar an adversary upon his own unpleasant level? And, once Pope had decided to launch his attack, what was the state of mind that lent such a peculiar relish to his strange cloacal fooling? In his collected prose-works, the *Full and True Account* of his absurd revenge is immediately preceded by his splendid *Preface to the Iliad*; and we pass straight from an essay that shows the writer's intelligence at its noblest and most judicious to the least attractive, and, indeed, the least effective of his casually thrown-off controversial squibs. But their juxtaposition is not without significance. Pope, like many great artists, had a radically divided nature, composed of Pope as he meant and longed to be and of another self, crafty, suspicious, malevolent, that sometimes emerged if his passions were unduly excited or his physical organism was overstrained. These two selves had never been easy to reconcile; during the course of his lengthy Homeric labours, the breach grew more and more alarming. Henceforward that dark and devious self was very often to direct his conduct.

Certainly it had dictated his attacks on Curll; and, in the spring of 1716, the same unruly spirit encouraged him to write and hand around an improper parody of the First Psalm.* For a Catholic and suspected Jacobite, it was a remarkably imprudent move; but, just as, under the influence of wine, he was apt to compose unseemly letters, in some moods, when he was relaxed and unbuttoned, he was fond of scribbling ribald verses. Often the effect was gay and pointed. Thus, in 1715, he had written a facetious *Farewell to London*, complimenting or gently ridiculing his friends, and enlarging on the worldly delights that he was now resolved to forego:

* It was based on a metrical version of the Psalms, published in the same year.

Dear, damn'd, distracting Town, farewell!
Thy fools no more I'll teize:
This Year in Peace, ye Critics, dwell,
Ye Harlots, sleep at Ease! . . .

To drink and droll be *Rowe* allowed
Till the third watchman toll;
Let *Jervase* gratis paint, and *Frowd*★
Save Three-pence, and his Soul. . . .

Why should I stay? Both Parties rage;
My vixen Mistress squalls;
The Wits in envious Feuds engage;
And *Homer* (damn him!) calls. . . .

Why make I Friendship with the Great,
When I no Favours seek?
Or follow Girls Seven Hours in Eight? –
I need but once a Week.

Still idle, with a busy Air,
Deep Whimsies to contrive;
The gayest Valetudinaire,
Most thinking Rake alive. . . .

Laborious Lobster-nights, farewell!
For sober, studious Days;
And *Burlington's* delicious Meal,
For Sallads, Tarts and Pease! . . .

Pope's erotic revision of the First Psalm, adapted for the benefit of 'a young lady', is a far less entertaining trifle; the joke is rather forced and heavy. It provided, however, just the ammunition that his critics needed. Pope, at the time, was being incessantly harried by the journalists and pamphleteers; for both Curll and his associate Oldmixon, who contributed regularly to the *Flying Post*, were active and important figures in the literary underworld; and not only did the *Flying Post* print spiteful references to 'Mr Pope's *Popish* Translation of Homer', asserting that 'he neither understands the original, nor the author's meaning', which 'in several places he has falsified . . . on purpose'; but two ferocious lampoons, the *Catholick Poet* and *A True Character of Mr Pope and his Writings* – the

★ Philip Frowde, minor poet and member of Swift's circle.

latter probably the work of Dennis – came out towards the end of May. Simultaneously, the bookseller was doing his best to confound the poet through his own verses. He had procured copies of Pope's parody of the First Psalm and of some stanzas addressed *To Mr John Moore, Author of the Celebrated Worm-Powder*, another piece that had been privately circulating, in which Pope developed the unpleasant conceit that 'all human kind are worms', like the worms that Moore eradicated, and concluded with a savage jibe at the human maggots who bred and crawled in Button's. The address to Moore was printed during May; the *Roman Catholick Version of the First Psalm* – Curll, naturally, had added the offensive title – was announced by the *Flying Post* on 30 June. Their combined effect was decidedly damaging; and even Pope's admirers were embarrassed or annoyed. Until Curll and his allies had met the fate they deserved, the 'frolics of merry hours', wrote Swift from Ireland 'should not be left to the mercy of our best friends. . . .'

Pope may have been slightly abashed; and, on 31 July, he printed a disclaimer in the columns of *The Postman*, repeated on 2 August in *The Evening Post*. Certain scandalous libels having been published in his name, 'which I hope no person of candour would have thought me capable of', he was 'obliged to declare, that no genuine pieces of mine have been printed by any but Mr Tonson and Mr Lintot', and offered 'a reward of three guineas to anyone who shall discover the person or persons concerned in the publication of the said libel, of which I am wholly ignorant'. Whereupon he felt tolerably satisfied. 'If you have seen a late advertisement,' he wrote soon afterwards to Teresa Blount, 'you will know that I have not told a lie (which we both abominate) but equivocated pretty genteelly. You may be confident 'twas not done without leave from my spiritual director.' Teresa, no doubt, was expected to smile; it is improbable that any ghostly adviser had approved of Pope's lie; and by now she must have begun to understand his taste for genteel equivocation. That taste, which has often perplexed his admirers, sprang in part from a natural love of mystery. He enjoyed weaving ingenious webs, spinning plots to ensnare the foolish critic; and the success of his pretended tribute to Philips had already caused him keen amusement. Just as successful was the *Key to the Lock* that he had produced anonymously in 1715 – a solemn warning against 'the late poem, entitled the *Rape of the Lock*', which he proceeded to expose as a concealed attack, by an author 'professedly a Papist', on the Protestant administration, where Belinda represents Great Britain; the Baron, Lord Oxford; Thalestris, the Duchess of Marlborough; and Sir Plume, Prince Eugene of Savoy. Pope unfolds this fictitious symbolism with the greatest dexterity and good humour; but, as time went by, his taste for mysterious stratagems, and for the elaborate subterfuges they involved, was destined to become a ruling appetite. In the process of deceiving the gullible public, he would appear, now and then, to have deceived himself.

Yet he respected truth, valued his personal probity and, at least in his own estimation, remained a steadfast man of honour. If he equivocated, it must be the fault of his circumstances; he lived, surrounded by foes, in a difficult and dangerous period, when 'I suffer for my religion', he told Swift, 'in almost every weekly paper', and 'Truth is a kind of contraband commodity which I would not venture to export', even to a devoted friend across the Irish Channel. But there were other factors that made him oblique and evasive; his heart was over-clouded, and his nerves were troubled; he was suffering from the mood of inward frustration that had often visited him since his boyhood. Edward Wortley having received his credentials at the beginning of July, Lady Mary was due to leave England. Meanwhile she gave a farewell party. She had ordered him, wrote Jervas to Pope, 'by an express this Wednesday morning, sedente Gayo, et ridente Fortescuvio, to send you a letter or some other proper notice to come to her on Thursday about 5 a clock which I suppose she meant in the evening'. It was perhaps on this occasion that Lady Mary proposed they should write one of those joint letters their circle affected for the benefit of Lady Rich. Pope did as he was asked and, on returning the finished epistle, he dared at length to speak a lover's language:

Whether or no you will order me, in recompence, to see you again, I leave to you; for indeed I find I begin to behave myself worse to you than to any other woman, as I value you more. And yet if I thought I should not see you again, I would say some things here, which I could not to your person. For I would not have you die deceived in me, that is, go to Constantinople without knowing, that I am to some degree of extravagance, as well as with the utmost reason, Madam, your most faithful and most obedient humble servant, A. Pope.

Clearly, her presence had held him back; and, however desolating her departure, it may at the moment have seemed almost welcome. Accompanied by her husband and a score of liveried servants, Lady Mary set sail on 1 August, and boarded the yacht that was to carry her to Holland wearing a black full-bottomed wig. Not long afterwards the vessel ran into a storm; but, she assured the poet, she had been neither terrified nor sea-sick. Pope's opening letter, the prologue to a lengthy series, was written on the 18th. It has been suggested that the poet's 'epistolary homage', with which he followed her across Europe, had a conventional as well as a personal aspect, and that her admirer probably 'owed much to his reading of the French masters of the art'. The eighteenth-century letter-writer, we know, was expected to display both his learning and his social graces; and Pope obeyed the current mode. Yet, despite his attempts to remain a man of taste, he thought and felt like an unhappy lover.

Maybe he hoped that, as the miles between them lengthened, he could establish the sense of emotional proximity, arising from a real relationship between a man and a woman, that he had never achieved in her immediate presence. His letters, he said, were to be 'the most impartial representations of a free heart ... tho' of a very mean original. Not a feature will be softened, or any advantageous light employed to make the ugly thing a little less hideous. . . .' He proposed to 'think aloud' on paper; to open a casement in his breast through which she could observe his naked soul. 'You may easily imagine how desirous I must be of a correspondence with a person, who had taught me long ago that it was as possible to esteem at first sight as to love: and who has since ruined me for all the conversation of one sex, and almost all the friendship of the other. . . . Books have lost their effect on me.' Nowadays he could not pass her house 'but with the same sort of melancholy that we feel upon seeing the tomb of a friend. . . . I reflect upon the circumstances of your departure, your behaviour in what I may call your last moments, and I indulge a gloomy kind of satisfaction in thinking you gave some of those last moments to me.' Her generosity, he liked to assume, was not altogether accidental, 'but proceeded from a penetration which I know you have in finding out the truth of people's sentiments, and that you were not unwilling, the last man that would have parted with you, should be the last that did'.

If Pope hitherto had loved the idea of Love, and in his juvenile court-ship of the Blounts had pursued a visionary idea of Woman, his new passion was firmly fastened upon an individual human being, whom he not only desired and adored but had convinced himself he under-stood. No one, he told her, 'knows you better'. Reviewing their sub-sequent lives, we cannot resist the conclusion that, in fact, he knew her very slightly; for Virtue and Reason, he declared, were among her many dazzling attributes; and, although as a young woman she may have been moderately virtuous, at no period of her existence was Lady Mary strictly reasonable. What had attracted Pope, and fired his heart and mind, were, one suspects, some very different qualities – her brio, gaiety, enthusiasm and courage, all heightened by the underlying influence of a strongly sensual nature. But then, love thrives upon misunderstanding;

and Pope's delusive portrait of his beloved, as she receded over the wastes of Central Europe, grew every day more fresh and vivid. Two days after the despatch of his first letter, he decided that he must write again. In imagination he continued to keep her company; in spirit he was her perpetual guardian. He followed her through the pages of travel-books and investigated the smallest details of the journey 'with as much diligence as if I were to set out next week to overtake you'.

Yet he was not entirely wretched; he may, indeed, have been a great deal less unhappy than at a time when, radiant and unattainable, she was inhabiting a near-by street. Accustomed to solitude amid crowds, he soon took refuge in his ordinary social amusements. To Teresa Blount he explained that he was 'upon the whole . . . melancholy'; but that for the last ten days he had repeatedly dined out at one or other of the 'pleasant villas' whose gardens ran down to the Thames, and had played his part in the 'great entertainments' and the 'elegant company' they afforded. Lord Burlington, still the best of neighbours, was now hard at work re-modelling his domain. 'His gardens flourish, his structures rise, his pictures arrive,' wrote Pope to Charles Jervas in Ireland; and the young grandee's patronage of the arts was becoming daily more intelligent and generous. At the same time, Pope's health had improved; and the arrival of letters from Lady Mary – one written as soon as she landed in Holland, the second on 14 September, after she had reached Vienna – must certainly have cheered his heart. They were delightful letters, friendly, poetic, easy, and packed with diverting information. Viennese music was splendid, though such comedies as she had seen – a piece, for example, based on the legend of Amphitrion, where two of the performers 'very fairly let down their breeches in the direct view of the boxes' – proved eminently ridiculous. Pope meanwhile had been alarmed by a report that 'Mr Wortley thinks of passing thro' Hungary notwithstanding the war there', and begged that she would stay behind. As it happened, before he could cross into Hungary, the Ambassador was called away to Hanover; and there, at the end of a difficult journey, driving day and night along dangerous roads and through romantic snow-bound passes, the Ambassadress occasioned 'a great deal of discourse' among the jealous Hanoverian ladies, who noted that the old king, then enjoying a much-needed holiday from his irksome English kingdom, 'took but little notice of any other lady, not even of Madame Kielmansegge. . . .'

Pope's own adventures had been comparatively humdrum. During September and October, he visited York, in company with Lord Burlington, and Bath and the University of Oxford, whither he was accompanied by Lintot, whose rambling professional discourse – about printers and black-faced printer's devils, sheets, miscellanies and translators paid by the line – he reported for the great man's benefit. Much of the winter was spent at Bridgewater House. Jervas himself was still away in Ireland, busy turning out his stylish portraits; but Pope had the assistance of his faithful servants, Frank and Betty, his only companions in the cavernous old house, where, every time Frank unchained the door, the links rattled, the rusty hinges groaned; and the whole building, he told Jervas, seemed 'so sensible you are its support, that it is ready to drop in your absence. . . .' Among his other interests was his concern with the Blounts' affairs; and, on Teresa's behalf, he arranged to purchase stock in Lord Oxford's famous South Sea Company.* Its value was expected to fall; and Pope himself – which suggests that he had wisely put aside most of the profits of the *Iliad* – had 'kept a thousand five hundred pounds lying by me, to buy at such a juncture'. He had long been famous; now he was growing prosperous. Yet, beneath the surface of his successful public life, his heart and senses were in constant turmoil. His letters to Lady Mary became increasingly wild and rhapsodic; nor did he receive brief and chilly answers. 'I never . . .' she wrote from the Viennese court, 'was half so well disposed to take you in earnest, as I am at present, and that distance which makes the continuation of your friendship improabble, has very much increased my faith in it.'

Distance had a similar effect on Pope. His feelings, he admitted in October, were 'indeed so warm, that I fear they can proceed from nothing but what I can't very decently own to you, much less to any other. . . .' When he imagined that she was approaching the Mahomedan pleasures of Constantinople – he had not yet heard that she was still in wintry Hanover – he allowed his emotions even greater licence. Fascinating to picture his remote beloved in a strange, luxurious Eastern world! The Viennese court had been pagan enough – 'you have already (without passing the bounds of Christendom) out-travelled the sin of Fornication'; but she must by now be 'happily arrived at the free Region of Adultery'. One day he hoped to re-trace her footsteps. Here, he would be told, 'she practised to sit on the sofa'; there she learned to fold a turban. Here she was bathed and anointed; there she discarded her black full-bottomed wig. Lastly, he would be informed 'how the very first night you lay at Pera,

* In 1713 Oxford had proposed to pay off nine millions of the public debt by the ingenious expedient of allocating to the government's creditors stock of a newly founded company that was to have a monopoly of South American trade. The King himself became Governor of the Company; but the value of the shares it issued had at first declined.

you had a vision of Mahomet's Paradise, and happily awaked without a Soul. From which blessed instant the beautiful body was left at full liberty to perform all the agreeable functions it was made for.'

This was sufficiently bold – 'the mere pleasure of addressing to you makes me run on'; but he included some outrageous jokes about Middle Eastern tastes and habits. Not until the end of the year did Pope discover that his itinerant fancy had been travelling in the wrong direction; and then, that while he supposed she was 'going to Hanover', she was once again hurrying towards the Austrian capital, which she reached soon after Christmas. That same January 1717, the Wortleys left Vienna, bound for Belgrade. Although Lady Mary had been threatened, she wrote, 'with being frozen to death, buried in the snow, and taken by the Tartars, who ravage that part of Hungary I am to pass', they had a swift, and unadventurous journey, as the sleighs, that had replaced the wheels of the carriages, glided across a silent, snowbound landscape. On 16 February they ran into Belgrade, a strongly fortified Turkish city, where they were civilly received by the cultured Effendi Achmet Bey, and 'a whole chamber of Janizaries' mounted guard around their lodgings.

Three weeks later, they set out for Adrianople, the favourite residence of the Grand Turk. 'I am now got into a new world,' Lady Mary remarked at the beginning of April. Between Phillipopolis and their destination, 'vines grow wild on all the hills', and the country was extraordinarily fresh and spring-like. Sophia, 'situated in a large and beautiful plain on the river Isca, and surrounded with distant mountains', proved to be a populous city, well-known for its hot baths; and she immediately hired a Turkish coach – 'made a good deal in the manner of the Dutch coaches, having wooden lattices painted and gilded the inside . . . painted with baskets and nosegays of flowers, intermixed commonly with little poetical mottos' – and drove off to the local bath-house. What a pity that her old friend Mr Jervas had not been there to record the feminine paradise she found! She was in her travelling habit, 'a riding dress'; yet, not one of the women she saw 'showed the least surprise or impertinent curiosity' – although, as she afterwards told Spence, they were frightened by her whale-bone corsets – and behaved themselves far better, she thought, than most European court-ladies:

The first sofas were covered with cushions and rich carpets, on which sat the ladies; and on the second their slaves behind 'em, but without any distinction of rank by their dress, all being in the state of nature. . . . Yet there was not the least wanton smile or immodest gesture amongst 'em. They walked and moved with the same majestic grace, which Milton describes our General Mother.

There were many amongst them, as exactly proportioned as ever any goddess was drawn by the pencil of a Guido or Titian, and most of their skins shiningly white, only adorned by their beautiful hair, divided into many tresses ... braided either with pearl or riband. ... I was here convinced of the truth of a reflection I had often made, that if 'twas the fashion to go naked, the face would be hardly observed.

It was at Adrianople that she caught sight of the Grand Turk. Accompanied by the youthful French ambassadress, she looked down on the Sultan and his attendants moving solemnly towards the mosque – the janissary guard crowned with 'vast white feathers'; the multi-coloured Royal Gardeners, who 'appeared like a parterre of tulips'; the purple-robed Aga of the Janissaries; the guardian of the seraglio, the negro Kizlar Aga, or Aga of the House of Felicity, 'in a deep yellow cloth (which suited very well to his black face) lined with sables'; last of all, 'his Sublimity himself, arrayed in green, lined with the fur of a black Muscovite fox ... mounted on a fine horse....' The Sultan, she noted, was 'a handsome man about forty', somewhat 'severe in his countenance, and his eyes very full and black'. The cavalcade halted beneath the ambassadresses' window; and from those large dark eyes he glanced up 'very attentively' at the two unveiled young foreign women, so that they themselves had 'full leisure to consider him'. Pope at home – and perhaps it was as well – had received no account of the Turkish bath-house; but, on 1 April, she wrote him a charming description of the place in which she now lived. The River Hebrus ran beneath her casement:

My garden is full of tall cypress trees, upon the branches of which several couples of true turtles are saying soft things to one another from morning till night.... The summer is already far advanced in this part of the world; and for some miles round Adrianople the whole ground is laid out in gardens, and the banks of the rivers set with fruit trees, under which all the most considerable Turks divert themselves every evening.... A set party of 'em choose out a green spot, where the shade is very thick, and there they spread a carpet on which they sit drinking their coffee and generally attended by some slave with a fine voice, or that plays on some instrument. Every twenty paces you may see one of these little companies listening to the dashing of the river....

Better still, her quick imaginative insight noted all kinds of amusing comparisons between Turkish and Homeric modes. 'I have read over your Homer here,' she told him, 'with infinite pleasure, and find several little passages explained, that I did not before entirely comprehend the beauty of. . . .' Here, too, 'the Princesses and great ladies pass their time at their looms, embroidering veils and robes'; while 'the description of the belt of Menelaus exactly resembles those that are now worn by the great men, fastened before with broad golden clasps, and embroidered round with rich work. The snowy veil, that Helen throws over her face, is still fashionable; and I never see half a dozen of old Bashaws . . . with their reverend beards, sitting basking in the sun, but I recollect good King Priam and his counsellors.' Even the Turkish manner of dancing recalled Diana's dance beside Eurotas. Now and then she joined the measure; and we know that she sometimes adopted Turkish costume – a pair of drawers, which reached to her embroidered kid-skin shoes, 'of a thin rose-coloured damask, brocaded with silver flowers', beneath a wide-sleeved smock 'of a fine white silk gauze', through which 'the shape and colour of the bosom is very well to be distinguished', a damask waistcoat and a caftan, 'of the same stuff with my drawers' and 'exactly fitted to my shape'. For Pope she added some specimens of Turkish verse, remarking she found 'a good deal of beauty in them', and drawing his attention to some particularly vivid epithets; 'you see I am pretty far gone in Oriental learning, and to say truth, I study very hard'.

Before he had received her letter from Adrianople, it had already occurred to Pope that, since she had now 'been enlightened by the same sun that enlightened the Father of Poetry', she could give him 'great eclaircissements' upon Homeric scenes and images. Perhaps she would visit the windy plains of Troy, 'lay the immortal work on some broken column of a hero's sepulchre, and read the Fall of Troy in the shade of a Trojan ruin', or, at least, across the straits of the Hellespont, 'contemplate the fields of Asia, in such dim and remote prospect, as you have in my translation'. The third volume of the *Iliad* was published during early June, and despatched, with 'as many other things as fill a wooden box', to the British Embassy at Constantinople. Simultaneously, he was preparing an edition of his own collected *Works*, which, though advertised by Lintot in March, did not appear until the beginning of June; while, in July, he produced a miscellany for Lintot, entitled *Poems on Several Occasions*, which included some elegant 'trifles' by the literary Duke of Buckingham. He had also, earlier that year, tried his luck as a modern comic dramatist, and had assisted Gay and Arbuthnot to compose a somewhat feeble and improper farce entitled *Three Hours After Marriage*.

First staged on 16 January, it had a successful run, but, at the outset, was extremely ill-received; and many of its opponents pretended to detect Pope's hand in the more scandalous and malicious details. The story of how Fossile, a foolish old pedant, marries a young and attractive courtesan, and how a pair of her lovers, disguised as a crocodile and an Egyptian mummy, attempt to gain an entrance to the old man's rooms, aroused the indignation of the pit.* Fossile was assumed to be a caricature of Arbuthnot's rival, Dr Woodward; and Tremendous, the redoubtable critic, seemed evidently intended for John Dennis. Pope was taken aback by the public's cat-calls; and when, at the same London playhouse, he heard Colley Cibber, the well-known actor-manager and popular dramatist, make an impromptu reference to the crocodile, he felt that he had been personally insulted and, as Cibber afterwards informed the world, 'came behind the scenes, with his lips pale and his voice trembling, to call me to account for the insult, and fell upon me with all the foul language, that a wit out of his senses could be capable of. . . .' The comedian, however, a solid, self-confident personage, refused either to give him an apology, or promise in future to be less offensive; indeed, he declared that he would repeat his joke 'over and over again'.† Pope then retired; but he did not forget the episode; and henceforward Colley Cibber was to rank among his favourite enemies.

Otherwise, the opening months of the year 1717 were free from any serious vexation. He might be melancholy, if he allowed his thoughts to stray towards Constantinople; but he was always fully occupied – purchasing stock and advising his father about his mother's fragile health: 'to cure the bitterness she complains of', instead of taking a vomit, she would do well to chew rhubarb; corresponding with Parnell in Ireland and his former neighbour John Dancastle; drinking 'a dish of coffee' with Dancastle's domestic chaplain, the epicurean Father Philips; and attending 'ten or twenty parties' given by 'my Lord Burlington, Duchess Hamilton'‡ and Lord Jersey, which involved much gaiety and rustic 'rambling'. June and July were an especially crowded time; for, besides the appearance of his third *Iliad*, they saw the production of the volume that he regarded, he told Parnell, as his last will and testament, 'an entire collection of my own madrigals', in which he had given to the world 'all I ever intended to give. . . .'

During May, 1717, Pope had reached his twenty-ninth birthday; and

* Gay seems to have been responsible for both the mummy and the crocodile, and in a letter to Pope, written some time in January, suggests that, if he had omitted the crocodile, their comedy might have had a more friendly reception.

† The occasion was a revival of *The Rehearsal*. See Cibber's *Letter . . . to Mr Pope*, 1742.

‡ 'My Lady Duchess being drunk at this present . . . has commanded me to acquaint you that there is to be music on the water on Thursday next. . . .' G. Maddison to Pope, June, 1717.

his *Works*, a beautifully printed and spaciously proportioned book,* which included two prose essays, a long *Preface* and the early *Discourse on Pastoral Poetry*, is among the noblest and most dignified landmarks ever raised by a comparatively young writer. The *Preface*, which Joseph Warton described as a masterpiece of modern English prose, adopts a dignified, if somewhat disingenuous, tone: 'The Life of a wit is a warfare upon earth; and the present spirit of the world is such, that to attempt to serve it (any way) one must have the constancy of a martyr, and a resolution to suffer for its sake. I confess it was want of consideration that made me an author; I writ because it amused me; I corrected because it was as pleasant to me to correct as to write; and I published because I was told I might please such as it was a credit to please.' Very few items, he declared – a slightly misleading statement – 'were not written under the age of five and twenty'; and it was possible that he would not write again: 'If this publication be only a more solemn funeral of my remains, I desire it may be known that I die in charity, and in my senses; without any murmurs against the justice of this age, or any mad appeals to posterity. I declare I shall think the world in the right, and quietly submit to every truth which time shall discover to the prejudice of these writings. . . .' Pope, however, was confident of their worth, and at heart dreaded posterity's verdict almost as little as he feared contemporary critics.

At twenty-nine, he had taken his own measure, and felt his genius steadily rising and expanding. The *Works* included two new poems, both written during the previous twelve months, and both composed in what, for the author of *An Essay on Criticism* and *The Rape of the Lock*, was an entirely fresh and unexpected style. Pope remained a devoted pupil of the Ancients – 'It will be found,' he had announced in his *Preface*, 'that in every age, the highest character . . . has been obtained by those who have been most indebted to them'; but his taste was growing more and more eclectic; and Lady Mary's vivid account of her travels left a lasting impression on his mind. He had once, he admitted to Spence, 'had some thought of writing a Persian fable; in which I should have given a full loose to description and imagination', and which, if he had executed it, 'would have been a very wild thing. . . .' Eastern and Gothic scenes were equally

* The *Works* were advertised by Lintot on 3 June, as 'The whole Works of Mr Pope, containing all his genuine Pieces . . . in one volume . . . with several Ornaments in Copper, engrav'd by Mr Gribelin'. It appeared both in folio and quarto, the quartos themselves being unusually large. Among the lesser poems Pope decided to reprint were 'To a Young Lady. On her leaving Town after the Coronation', 'Epilogue to Jane Shore', 'On a Fan of the Author's Design', 'The Fable of Dryope from Ovid' and his epitaph on Sir William Trumbull, who had died in 1716.

'romantic' from an eighteenth-century point of view; and *Eloisa to Abelard* and the *Elegy to the Memory of an Unfortunate Lady* are both of them framed in the romantic mode. With romantic fantasy, as it was now beginning to emerge, goes a passion for the 'picturesque'; and of all picturesque subjects none was more attractive than a crumbling Gothic ruin. In previous centuries, few writers had been particularly drawn towards the architectural debris of the past, though Donne had written of the ruined English abbeys not without appreciation; while John Webster's *Duchess of Malfi*, first printed in 1623, had contained a splendid Gothic episode, which presents the widowed Antonio visiting a ruined sanctuary and, as he paces beneath its broken arches, listening to the echo of his voice:

> Now the echo hath caught you. . . .
> I told you 'twas a pretty one: you may make it
> A huntsman, or a falconer, a musician, or a thing of sorrow.

The heroine of the *Unfortunate Lady* is, indeed, 'a thing of sorrow', surrounded by all the imaginative apparatus – a darkling background, an air of suspense and mystery – that we find in later Gothic novels. A disconsolate phantom wanders through the dusk:

> What beck'ning ghost, along the moonlight shade
> Invites my step, and points to yonder glade?
> 'Tis she! – but why that bleeding bosom gor'd,
> Why dimly gleams the visionary sword?

At the time, the origins of this unhappy *revenant* provoked the keenest speculation; and Caryll, writing to Pope on 16 July 1717, did his best to draw the poet out, remarking that 'I think you once gave me her history', which, in the interval, he had, alas, forgotten. Subsequently, various tales were told – that her name was Wainsbury; that she was 'ill-shaped and deformed'; and, according to Ruffhead, whose story Johnson adopted that 'she was a woman of eminent rank and large fortune', separated from the suitor she loved and victimized by her unfeeling kin. In fact, so far as she had an original, the portrait of the Unfortunate Lady seems to have been based on the combined images of Mrs Cope and Mrs Weston, the two ladies Pope and Caryll had befriended six years earlier,* and one of whom, the cultured Mrs Cope, they continued to support with advice and charity until she died of a breast-cancer in 1728. Each had been miserable; each had been hardly used; Mrs Weston, like the Unfortunate Lady, had had a cruelly unsympathetic guardian. But Pope's heroine has

* See p. 46.

also some relationship with his idea of Lady Mary – not yet unfortunate, but exposed to constant dangers, driven by ambition, 'the glorious fault, of angels and of gods', and possessed by a bold unruly spirit that lifted her high above the common ranks of mankind:

> Most souls, 'tis true, but peep out once an age,
> Dull sullen pris'ners of the body's cage:
> Dim lights of life that burn a length of years,
> Useless, unseen, as lamps in sepulchres;
> Like Eastern Kings a lazy state they keep,
> And close confin'd to their own palace sleep.

Lady Mary's light had never been dim; she, too, was a woman made for some uncommon destiny.

In *Eloisa to Abelard* the relationship is even more apparent. The twelfth-century letters of Abelard and Eloise* supplied the basic hint he needed, with their story of star-crossed love, cruelty, separation and heart-broken exile. More than a year earlier, Pope had written to Martha Blount that 'the Epistle of Eloise grows warm, and begins to have breathings of the heart in it, which may make posterity think I was in love'. This conclusion is certainly inescapable; the poem is a hymn addressed to love – not to Christian love, idealized passion, but to love that is the child of 'rebel nature'. Eloisa, the passionate pupil, describes how her revered master had at length become her bedfellow:

> Guiltless I gaz'd; heav'n listen'd while you sung;
> And truths divine came mended from that tongue.
> From lips like those what precept fail'd to move?
> Too soon they taught me 'twas no sin to love.
> Back thro' the paths of pleasing sense I ran,
> Nor wish'd an Angel whom I lov'd a Man.

The memory of those pleasing paths returns to torment the cloistered abbess:

> Of all affliction taught a lover yet,
> 'Tis sure the hardest science to forget! . . .
> Unequal task! a passion to resign,
> For hearts so touch'd, so pierc'd, so lost as mine.
> Ere such a soul regains its peaceful state,
> How often must it love, how often hate! . . .
> Oh come! oh teach me nature to subdue,
> Renounce my love, my life, my self – and you.

* John Hughes's English translation had appeared in 1713.

Sometimes she envies her castrated lover:

> For thee the fates, severely kind, ordain
> A cool suspense from pleasure and from pain;
> Thy life a long, dead calm of fix'd repose;
> No pulse that riots, and no blood that glows.
> Still as the sea, ere winds were taught to blow,
> Or moving spirit bade the waters flow ...

The Paraclete, in which Eloise was imprisoned, had been built by Abelard himself. Pope invests it, nevertheless, with an atmosphere of grim antiquity, equips it with 'moss-grown domes', 'awful arches' and a rugged mountain background. The setting is Gothic and profoundly melancholic:

> The wandring streams that shine between the hills,
> The grots that eccho to the tinkling rills ...
> No more these scenes my meditation aid,
> Or lull to rest the visionary maid:
> But o'er the twilight groves, and dusky caves,
> Long-sounding isles, and intermingled graves,
> Black Melancholy sits, and round her throws
> A death-like silence, and a dread repose:
> Her gloomy presence saddens all the scene,
> Shades ev'ry flow'r and darkens ev'ry green,
> Deepens the murmur of the falling floods,
> And breathes a browner horror on the woods.

Pope's Gothicism may nowadays seem to have a somewhat artificial colouring. Yet *Eloisa to Abelard* is the most poignantly personal poem that he had yet composed and published. In April he had already known that Lady Mary would soon be leaving England; its theme is a guilty love – 'how glowing guilt exalts the keen delight!' – and the pangs that accompany an inevitable separation. The closing lines bring us suddenly back to the poet's own experience:

> And sure if fate some future Bard shall join
> In sad similitude of griefs to mine,
> Condemn'd whole years in absence to deplore,
> And image charms he must behold no more,
> Such if there be, who loves so long, so well;
> Let him our sad, our tender story tell;
> The well-sung woes will soothe my pensive ghost;
> He best shall paint'em, who shall feel'em most.

It is not surprising that the poem should have been warmly praised by

Byron, who had described poetry as 'the lava of the imagination', the product of passionate personal experience, which erupted to prevent an earthquake. Where, he demanded, was passion 'to be found stronger?' Pope had seized on the Ovidian Epistle – a particularly popular form since Dryden had translated the *Heroides* – and, without changing its accepted shape, had infused his medium with a new vitality. Despite their Gothic details and stately Augustan framework, his verses reflect the agonized confusion of an individual human heart; and, commending the poem to Lady Mary's notice, he remarked that it included 'one passage' that he could not decide whether he wished that she might fully understand.

8

By the end of May 1717, Lady Mary, her husband and their child were established in Constantinople. Before they left Adrianople, she had watched the departure of the Grand Turk, then setting out to join his armies, a long multi-coloured parade that lasted nearly eight hours, with an Effendi at the head, 'mounted on a camel, richly furnished, reading aloud the Alcoran', and around him 'a parcel of boys, in white', chanting verses from the holy book and throwing little cakes among the crowd. Again she had an extremely pleasant journey. Thirty baggage-waggons and five coaches, which contained her women servants, followed the ambassadorial carriage; and, the meadows that bordered the highway 'being full of all sorts of garden flowers, and sweet herbs, my berlin perfumed the air as it pressed them'. The Wortleys' new home was a palace at Pera, looking forth over 'the Port, the City, and the Seraglio, and the distant hills of Asia; perhaps . . . the most beautiful prospect in the world'. Edward Wortley had already proved himself a somewhat inexpert diplomatist – his attempts to reach an accommodation between the Sultan and the Emperor were agreeable to neither government; and the Austrians treated him with cold disdain. But Lady Mary continued to lead an unusually instructive and rewarding life. She visited antiquaries, collected Greek medals and fragments of classical art – 'I have a porphyry head (she reported) finely cut, of the true Greek sculpture' – and had bespoken an Egyptian mummy; 'which, I hope, will come safe into my hands, notwithstanding the misfortune that befell a very fine one, designed for the King of Sweden. . . .'*

Soon afterwards the heat of the early summer obliged the Wortleys to take refuge 'at a country house about ten miles from Constantinople',

* The superstitious Turks had suddenly refused to release it, fancying it 'to be the body of God knows who, and that the state of their empire mystically depended on the conservation of it'.

within easy distance of the Black Sea; and on 17 June she wrote to Pope, describing its Elysian situation, 'in the middle of a wood, consisting chiefly of fruit trees, watered by a vast number of fountains, and divided into many shady walks. . . .' Belgrade Village was 'only inhabited by the richest amongst the Christians, who meet every night at a fountain, forty paces from my house, to sing and dance. The beauty and dress of the women exactly resemble the ideas of the ancient nymphs. . . .' For herself she felt remote but happy; 'to say truth, I look upon my present circumstances to be exactly the same as the departed spirits. . . .' Although he did not receive her letter until the autumn, Pope responded in his most impassioned strain. He had found her description deeply moving and inspiring:

The poetical manner in which you paint some of the scenes about you, makes me despise my native country and sets me on fire to fall into the dance about your fountain in Belgrade-village. I fancy myself, in my romantic thoughts and distant admiration of you, not unlike the man in the Alchymist that had a passion for the Queen of the Faeries. I lie dreaming of you in moonshiny nights exactly in the posture of Endymion gaping for Cynthia in a picture. And with just such a surprise and rapture should I awake, if after your long revolutions were accomplished, you should at last come rolling back again, smiling with all that gentleness and serenity (peculiar to the Moon and you) and gilding the same mountains from which you first set out on your solemn, melancholy journey.

He wrote, he added, 'as I were drunk'; and the stimulant that Lady Mary provided was, indeed, of a very special kind. Considering that Pope had never been, and was never likely to become her lover, nothing is more remarkable in the letters they exchanged than the vein of strong imaginative sympathy that enabled her to catch his mood, and to supply the poetic hint he could develop into an elaborate literary pattern. But, whereas Pope's feelings were fixed on Lady Mary, the keenest emotions she experienced were focused on her own pleasures, which Pope's imagination merely reflected and returned, giving them a new effulgence. Meanwhile everything amused and delighted her. Even a ridiculous misadventure did not disturb the tranquillity of Belgrade Village. Perhaps because her complexion was pitted and scarred, she had tried a Turkish cosmetic known as 'balm of Mecca'; and 'my face was swelled to a very extraordinary size', she told a female correspondent, acquired an unbecoming flush and 'remained in this lamentable state for three days'; during which time Mr Wortley, always humourless and inclined to be pompous, 'reproached my indiscretion without ceasing'. Her foolish experiment, however, produced no lasting ill-effects; and, once the

16 Pope's Shell Temple at Twickenham; 'a kind of open temple . . . in the rustic manner'.
Drawing by William Kent.

17 Mrs. Howard, afterwards Countess of Suffolk. 'Civil to everybody, friendly to many . . .'. Portrait by Charles Jervas.

summer had passed, the embassy returned to Constantinople, whence, from a kiosk in her garden, she gazed down across the Golden Horn and 'an agreeable mixture of gardens, pine and cypress trees, palaces, mosques, and public buildings', arrayed in ascending tiers, 'with as much beauty and appearance of symmetry' as the bright objects clustered together in an English china-cabinet. Her little boy was now a charming companion; and early next year, she presently discovered, she could expect to bear a second child.

Why regret the 'smoke and impertinences' of London, though Pope assured her that she was much regretted by her friends? 'Mr Congreve,' he wrote, 'in fits of the gout, remembers you. Dr Garth makes epigrams in prose when he speaks of you. . . . Mr Craggs commemorates you with honour; the Duke of Buckingham with praise: I myself with something more. . . .' In 1717 Pope was suffering, as always, his full share of critical impertinences. John Dennis, for example, who had never relaxed his hold, had published in February a series of venomous *Remarks* on his translation of the *Iliad*; which, the critic asserted had 'neither the justness of the original . . . nor any beauty of language, nor any variety of numbers'; and in May Pope retaliated by helping Parnell to bring out his *Life of Zoilus*, accompanied by his rendering of the pseudo-Homeric *Battle of the Frogs and Mice*, and by a preface that enabled the translator to defend his use of rhyme: 'Let the French, whose language is not copious, translate in prose; but ours, which exceeds it in copiousness of words, may have a more frequent likeness of sounds, to make the unison of rhyme easier; a grace of music, that atones for the harshness our consonants and mono-syllables occasion.' Later in the year, on a somewhat different level, Pope himself set out to provoke an enemy, and published a pamphlet of the kind he particularly enjoyed producing, entitled *A Clue to the Comedy of the Non-Juror*. An attack on Colley Cibber's highly successful play, this 'odd piece of wit', Cibber afterwards wrote, set out to prove that the dramatist's Whiggish comedy was, in fact, 'a closely couched Jacobite libel against the government'. The pamphlet bore no signature; but it was 'so much above the spirit, and invention of the daily paper satirists that all the sensible readers' its victim met attributed it to Pope's authorship.

Pope, at the moment, could afford to tease his enemies: his friends were becoming more and more distinguished. Though Homer still lay heavy on his hands, he continued to enlarge his acquaintance with the fashionable world and pursue his usual round of visits. He had been 'indispensably obliged', he told Caryll in August, 'to pass some days at almost every house along the Thames. . . . After some attendance on my Lord Burlington, I have been at the Duke of Shrewsbury's, Duke of Argyle's, Lady Rochester's, Lord Percival's, Mr Stonor's, Lord Winchilsea's, Sir Godfrey Kneller's . . . and Duchess Hamilton's. . . . Then I am obliged to pass some days between my Lord Bathurst's, and three or four more on Windsor side. . . . I am also promised three months ago to the Bishop of Rochester . . . . I had forgot to tell you in my list of rambles . . . that I must necessarily go some time this season to my Lord Harcourt's in Oxfordshire. . . .' As an avowed Papist and a suspected Jacobite, Pope was excluded from the royal presence; but it was not a loss he much regretted. The sovereign was elderly and dull and firmly settled in his Hanoverian ways; his female favourites were old and hideous. The Prince and Princess of Wales maintained a far less unattractive household; some of the Princess's youthful Maids of Honour were particularly gay and elegant; and that September Pope described for the Blounts how he had gone to Hampton Court by water and had 'met the Prince and all his ladies (though few or none of his lords) on horseback coming from hunting'. Two of the prettiest Maids, Bellenden and Lepell, 'took me into protection (contrary to the laws against harbouring Papists) and gave me a dinner, with something I liked better, an opportunity of conversation with Mrs Howard' – the quiet, intelligent woman who was now the Prince's mistress:

We all agreed that the life of a Maid of Honour was of all things the most miserable . . . To eat Westphalia ham in a morning, ride over hedges and ditches on borrowed hacks, come home in the heat of the day with a fever, and what is worse a hundred times, a red mark in the forehead with a beaver hat; all this may qualify them to make excellent wives for fox-hunters, and bear abundance of ruddy-complexioned children. As soon as they can wipe off the sweat of the day, they must simper an hour, and catch cold in the Princess's apartment; from thence *to dinner, with what appetite they may* . . .

Despite the Maids' gaiety and beauty, Hampton Court was a solemn, oppressive place; 'no lone house in Wales, with a mountain and a rookery, is more contemplative than this Court. . . .' And he and Lepell, as they walked through the moonlit gardens, had met only the solitary King, who, under the shadow of a wall, was giving an audience to the Vice-Chamberlain. The last passage deserves especial note; for it evidently pleased its author; and next year, writing to Lady Mary, he decided to use it again, and added new romantic details: 'No lone house in Wales with a rookery is more contemplative than Hampton Court; I walked there the other day by the moon, and met no creature of any quality but the King, who was giving audience, all alone, to the birds under the garden-wall.' Like other famous letter-writers, Pope often reproduced the same images;

and, when his correspondents were Lady Mary and Martha Blount, he was especially inclined to share his wit between them. But it was for Teresa and Martha Blount that he drew a moving picture also a poetic night-piece, of how he had ridden across the hills to Oxford:

... After having passed thro' my favourite woods in the forest, with a thousand reveries of past pleasures, I rid over hanging hills, whose tops were edged with groves, and whose feet watered with winding rivers, listening to the falls of cataracts below, and the murmuring of winds above. The gloomy verdure of Stonor succeeded to these, and then the shades of the evening over-took me; the moon rose in the clearest sky I ever saw, by whose solemn light I paced on slowly, without company, or any interruption to the range of my thoughts. About a mile before I reached Oxford, all the bells tolled, in different tones; the clocks of every college answered one another; and told me, some in a deeper, some in a softer voice, that it was eleven a clock.

At Oxford, he was 'received with a sort of respect, which this idle part of mankind, the Learned, pay to their own species'; and, on his way home, he spent a night at Blenheim. As a friend of Burlington, the prophet of a new taste, Pope found nothing to admire in Vanbrugh's hugely grandiose conception. 'I never saw so great a thing with so much littleness in it. . . .' It is a house of entries and passages; among which there are three vistas through the whole, very uselessly handsome.' A series of cupolas and turrets 'make the building look at once finical and heavy. . . . In a word, the whole is a most expensive absurdity; and the Duke of Shrewsbury gave a true character of it, when he said, it was a great *Quarry of Stones above ground*.' Nor did he find much to say for its occupants, the mighty first Duke and his notorious consort Sarah. So he pressed on and, before the end of September, was safely back again at Chiswick. There old Mr Pope was laying out a new garden; their Binfield neighbour Mr Dancastle had promised him 'some white strawberry plants'; and, during the latter half of the month, the autumn days were mild and warm. Pope's father was now seventy-one, and apparently still in good health. Then, on the night of 23 October, he was struck down by a sudden seizure. Soon afterwards Martha and Teresa Blount received a brief and hurried message: 'My poor Father died last night. Believe me, since I don't forget you this moment, I never shall.' To Gay, Pope wrote at greater length; his father, he said, had 'died easily, without a groan, or the sickness of two minutes . . . as silently and peacefully as he lived'. The nineteenth century would be an age of filial revolt; the eighteenth was a period of sympathetic parents and devoted sons; and there is no doubt that, besides respecting and obeying, Pope had genuinely loved his father, the quiet, modest, pious old man, who had illustrated so many of his favourite virtues. For his idea of how an *honnête homme* should live – dignified, independent, reserved, remote from mundane cares and ambitions – he was deeply indebted to the older Pope's example.

His first thoughts concerned his mother's welfare; and he had decided, he told Caryll, that throughout the winter months it would be 'barbarity' not to remain at Chiswick. But Mrs Pope was neither a weak-spirited nor an unreasonably possessive mother; and, once she showed signs of recovery and had begun to sink into a 'dispirited state of resignation', he felt that he could again leave home. Meanwhile the newspapers had brought him exciting news. Mr Wortley's efforts to mediate between Austrian and Turk had still accomplished very little; and in September Addison, now Secretary of State, had announced that the British Government proposed to recall their ambassador. Early in November, his recall reached Constantinople; but the Wortleys did not embark on their homeward journey until 5 July 1718. During the interval, in February, Lady Mary bore a daughter; and, soon after she had risen from her bed, she took the brave step of having her son, though not her infant daughter, inoculated against smallpox. The theory of inoculation had already been discussed in London by members of the Royal Society; but Lady Mary had seen its results at first hand, and on 19 March she summoned an old Greek woman, who brought her needle and a supply of infected matter. The old woman's fingers were tremulous, and the needle she used was blunt and rusty. The child, then 'a very hopeful boy of about six years of age', reported the Embassy surgeon, cried a good deal; but within a day or two, Lady Mary wrote, he was singing and playing again, and 'very impatient for his supper'. Her bold decision had a far-reaching effect; at the beginning of the next decade it was imitated by the Princess of Wales herself; and, if Lady Mary had no other claim to celebrity she would occupy a minor niche in the history of English medical practice.*

Altogether, the opening months of the year 1718 were a particularly gay and successful period. Lady Mary continued to pursue what she called her 'rambling destiny'. Even in January, the weather was mild and warm; and, while her English friends, she supposed, were 'freezing over a sad sea-coal fire', she could throw her windows back to enjoy the sunshine; and 'my chamber is set out with carnations, roses, and jonquils, fresh from

---

* Inoculation, at the time, was extremely unpopular, particularly among physicians; and Lady Mary, wrote her grand-daughter, 'protested that in the four or five years immediately succeeding her arrival at home, she seldom passed a day without repenting of her patriotic undertaking', such was the persecution it brought upon her.

my garden'. Often she rambled abroad on visits to Turkish ladies of the Court, whose 'surprisingly rich' attire and pearl and emerald chains – 'the Sultana Hafiten, favourite of the late Emperor Mustapha', displayed a finely coloured emerald, no smaller than a turkey's egg – aroused her admiration and, no doubt, her envy. At the same time, she formed an intrepid project of examining the Byzantine splendours of St Sophia, 'which 'tis very difficult to see', and, accompanied by the Christian Princess of Transylvania, managed to slip across its threshold.* They were obliged, of course, to leave their shoes at the door; and going bare-footed, she afterwards told Spence, 'embarrassed Lady Mary extremely'; for, as she had been 'used to walk with high heels she tottered, and was ready to tumble down every moment'; so that she was obliged 'to return to the corner where she had left her slippers, and to steal 'em on again'. There was another awkward moment when the Princess, thinking of the Greek emperors who had reigned in Constantinople, and from one of whom she traced her own descent, burst into a flood of tears. Her companion scolded her in an urgent, passionate aside, and begged that she would 'leave off blubbering'; until the Princess 'wiped her eyes in private, and went on as well as she could' through the crowd of Muslim worshippers. Lady Mary was naturally amazed and dazzled. St Sophia exceeded her most romantic hopes; but the mosaic-work that lined the dome, she noted, was crumbling and fast falling. 'They presented me a handful of it; its composition seems to be a sort of glass. . . .'

About Turkish manners and morals she was equally inquisitive. The Sultan, of course, was an absolute monarch; but at any moment his ferocious janissaries might depose and strangle him. Turkish women of the upper classes lived an extraordinarily free and pleasant life, having 'at least as much wit and civility, nay, liberty, as among us'; but the 'customs that give them so many opportunities of gratifying their evil inclinations (if they have any) also put it very fully in the power of their husbands to revenge themselves, if they are discovered; and I do not doubt but they suffer sometimes for their indiscretions in a very severe manner'. Yet, as she informed an erudite correspondent, the Italian Abbé Conti, poet, philosopher and astronomer, whom she had met at the English Court in 1715, she was 'almost of opinion' that the Turks have 'a right notion of life. They consume it in music, gardens, and delicate eating, while we are tormenting our brains with some scheme of politics, or

* According to her letters, on the other hand, Lady Mary had duly obtained permission to visit the building, though not without some trouble; and the story she told Spence may have been a little over-coloured.

studying some science to which we can never attain. . . . We die or grow old before we can reap the fruit of our labours. Considering what short-lived weak animals men are, is there any study so beneficial as the study of present pleasure? I dare not pursue this theme; perhaps I have already said too much, but I depend upon the true knowledge you have of my heart.' Lady Mary's philosophic hedonism, strengthened by her glimpses of Turkish society, would have an important effect upon her later years; and no one was it better calculated to please than her epicurean friend at Chiswick, who, although his mind was far more subtle and penetrating, and his sense of virtue much more deeply rooted, had the same absorbing thirst for happiness.

At the moment, all his ideas of happiness were focused on Lady Mary's return to England. The pleasure he took in thinking of her return, he declared, 'transports me beyond the bounds of common sense and decency'. Between January and September, 1718, however, he seems to have written to her only twice – only two letters, at least, have been preserved; and in the first he explains that he had just suffered a severe illness, which had very nearly killed him, and that he was now writing against the advice of his doctor, who 'says, I must think but slightly of anything. Now I am practising if I can think so of You, which if I can, I shall be above regarding any thing in nature. . . . I may then look upon the sun as a spangle and the world as a hazel-nut.' His 'natural temper' was 'pretty much broke, and I live half a hermit within five miles of London. A letter from you soothes me in my reveries; 'tis like a conversation with some spirit of the other world. . . . The women here are – women. I can't express how I long to see you, face to face . . . Come for God's sake, come Lady Mary, come quickly!' As usual, he recovered and regained his zest for existence; but, during the course of the autumn, another serious illness laid him low. It is not surprising that 1718 should have been a comparatively unfruitful year, when his sole publication was the fourth volume of his *Iliad*, which he managed to see through the press by June. At the same time, old Mrs Pope had been 'in racking pains of the rheumatism'; and he was very often disturbed about their joint financial prospects. His father had not been a rich man; 'he has left me to the ticklish management of a narrow fortune, where every false step is dangerous'. Luckily, Pope was a good manager; and the funds he had earned from the *Iliad* were laid out with exemplary wisdom.

To these troubles was added the behaviour of the Blounts, who had now deserted Mapledurham, and were established at a London house; and, in a letter addressed to both girls, he complained that as often he called at

Bolton Street, one or other of them – probably it was Teresa he meant – contrived to puzzle him and wound his feelings; 'either I make her uneasy, or I see her unkind'. Towards the end of February 1718, there would appear to have been a fresh quarrel. Apparently, Pope entrusted to Teresa some important secret of his heart, which may perhaps have concerned his desire to marry Martha; 'you pretended so much generosity, as to offer your services in my behalf: the minute after, you did me as ill an office as you could, in telling the party concerned, it was all but an amusement occasioned by my loss of another lady'. Simultaneously Teresa had informed Pope that she was anxious to enlarge her income; and Pope thereupon arranged to pay her an annuity of forty pounds during the next seven years, provided that, during that time, she did not marry – a stipulation that she much disliked and received 'as if it were an affront'. The quarrel, however, did not permanently overcloud their friendship; and Pope continued to write to the Blounts as he moved around the country. In the spring he was often at home; but, once the summer had arrived, he visited Cirencester Park, where that genial dilettante Lord Bathurst needed advice about his new plantations; and, in late July or early August, now escorting his mother, he made his way to Stanton Harcourt, an ancient manor-house near Oxford, which Lord Harcourt had offered him as a place of literary and domestic refuge. There he could watch over old Mrs Pope and press forward with the unending siege of Troy. Simon first Viscount Harcourt – the same Harcourt who, in 1714, had 'directed' the dying Queen's hand when she passed the Treasurer's staff to Shrewsbury – was an adroit and successful politician. Swift called him 'trimming Harcourt'; he possessed, we are told, 'some forensic eloquence, more shrewd geniality' and a fund of 'most dexterous moderation'; but to Pope and Gay and other contemporary writers he proved a kind and sympathetic host.

What Pope needed was quiet, far from the social distractions that bedevilled Chiswick; and in the building today called 'Pope's Tower'* he could sit alone and write and read, as secure from disturbance as any monkish bookman. The fifteenth-century manor had long been neglected; and Harcourt had built himself a modern house at Cokethorpe; but, although the manor was decrepit and half-ruined, it provided a pleasant enough lodging for his Bohemian literary guests. Its air of antiquity delighted Pope; and he composed an elaborate literary description, which, varying his imagery here and there, he sent off both to the Duke of Buckingham and to Lady Mary. Stanton Harcourt, he wrote, afforded

* This tower had once formed part of the Harcourts' family chapel. For some years after the Reformation, they had remained loyal to the Catholic faith.

a 'true picture of an ancient country seat'. The plan of the house was strangely wild and irregular:

The whole is so disjointed, and the parts so detached from each other, and yet so joining again one can't tell how; that in a poetical fit you'd imagine it had been a village in Amphion's time, where twenty cottages had taken a dance together, were all out, and stood still in amazement ever since. A stranger would be grievously disappointed, who should ever think to get into this house the right way. One would expect, after entering through the porch, to be let into the hall. Alas nothing less – you find yourself in a brewhouse. From the parlour you think to step into the drawingroom, but opening the iron-nailed door, you are convinced by a flight of birds about your ears and a cloud of dust in your eyes, that 'tis the pigeon-house.*

As for the hall, when you finally gained admission, it was 'high and spacious, flanked with long tables' and 'ornamented with monstrous horns', broken pikes and other rusty weapons. 'Here is one vast arched window, beautifully darkened with divers scutcheons of painted glass . . . One shining pane bears date 1286.' Next the hall lay the tapestried parlour, containing 'a broken-bellied virginal, a couple of crippled velvet chairs, with two or three mildewed pictures of mouldy ancestors . . .' Such was the account he drew up for Lady Mary; for the Duke of Buckingham's benefit he added a sketch of the immense medieval kitchen, 'built in the form of a rotunda, being one vast vault to the top of the house; where one overture serves to let out the smoke and let in the light. By the blackness of the walls, the circular fires, vast cauldrons, yawning mouths of ovens and furnaces, you would think it either the forge of Vulcan, the cave of Polypheme, or the temple of Moloch.' The old hall, together with the 'shining pane' that interested Pope, was destroyed in 1750, when Lord Harcourt's successor removed the stone to build a more splendid seat at Nuneham; but the gatehouse remains, and so does the kitchen, a massive quadrangular pile – not a rotunda – with a lantern chimney and a vaulted octagonal roof, the vaults supported on fine sculptured bosses. A shaggy covering of thick-encrusted soot still clings to its medieval stonework; and the gardens and the haunted Lady Pool – a stew-pond during the Middle Ages – are still much as Pope and Harcourt knew them. Nor have the nearby parish church and Pope's Tower suffered any recent damage. Around the chancel of the church lie the alabaster effigies of early Harcourts – Sir Robert Harcourt, a victim of the Lancastrians, with long grey cloak and handsome clear-cut features, and his grandson, another Sir Robert, who

* Pope to Lady Mary Wortley Montagu; undated. The Walls of Thebes had arisen to the music of Amphion's lyre. See also *The Temple of Fame*.

had carried King Henry's standard on the field of Bosworth. Their tombs are surmounted by the Harcourt crest, a resplendent peacock in its pride.

Few places that the poet inhabited are more suggestive of his memory. We can follow him as he first ascended his tower, on the heels of a stiff old-fashioned steward, up 'dark winding stone-steps, which landed us into several little rooms one above another. One of these was nailed up, and our guide whispered to us as a secret the occasion of it. . . .' Here, 'about two centuries ago', a female Harcourt had been taken in adultery with a 'neighbouring prior, ever since which the room has been nailed up, and branded with the name of the Adultery-chamber. The ghost of Lady Frances is supposed to walk there,* and some prying maids . . . report that they have seen a lady in a fardingale through the key-hole. . . .' Pope's refuge, however, was on the fourth floor, immediately beneath the leads. Climbing the narrow, precipitous steps must have cost him an exhausting struggle; but, at their summit, he found a small, square, panelled room with five well-sized, diamond-paned windows, whence, if he chose to leave his desk, he could command a wide, delightful view – the grey stone-tiled roofs of the old manor, grouped around a grassy courtyard; the tower of the parish church, immediately opposite his own; the gardens, where Lord Harcourt had raised, or was soon to raise, some decorative urns and obelisks; the gleaming expanse of the Lady Pool; and, beyond them, a pattern of fields and hedges that stretched away towards distant Wytham Hill. While he worked, his calm, sensible old mother was making friends among their host's relations – 'a very good sort of woman', remarked one of them, 'who would make a very good neighbour . . .' Pope seems to have completed his task a little sooner than he had expected† – possibly it was the strain of overwork that brought on a second bout of illness; and by 1 September, when he wrote to Lady Mary, he and his mother had quitted Oxfordshire.

In another letter, dated 1 September, Pope describes a rustic tragedy that, while he was staying with Lord Harcourt, had occurred 'just under my eyes',‡ as he looked out from his tower casement. It was haymaking

---

* According to another version of the story, her name was Lady Alice; and she was murdered by her lover, the Harcourts' domestic chaplain. She is said to have haunted the Lady Pool (which was exorcised by the Bishop of Oxford in 1865) moaning pitiably if the level of the water fell and, if the Pool dried up altogether, wandering to and fro outside the chapel door.

† Preserved in the library at Stanton Harcourt is a fragment of glass, scratched with the words: 'In the year 1718 Alexander Pope here completed the fifth volume of Homer.'

‡ In letters of 6 and 9 August, addressed to Martha Blount and a 'Mr F—', Pope had already described the incident, in much the same phrases but with some further decorative touches.

time, and the villagers had gathered in a near-by common field. Suddenly the sky darkened, 'a terrible storm of thunder and lightning arose', and they were obliged to run for shelter. With them ran a certain John Hewet, a handsome young man about twenty-five years old, and Sarah Drew, 'a brown woman of about eighteen'. They were lovers; and 'their love was the talk, but not the scandal, of the whole neighbourhood. . . .' Sarah, 'frighted, and out of breath', had soon 'sunk down upon a haycock', and John, 'having raked two or three heaps together to secure her', had joined her in that sweet-smelling refuge, when a loud peal had reverberated through the heavens, and their friends, who had been calling to and fro, and got no answer from Sarah and John, hurried back across the meadow:

. . . They first saw a little smoke, and after, this faithful pair. John with one arm about his Sarah's neck, and the other held over her face as if to screen her from the lightning. They were struck dead. . . . There was no mark or discolouring on their bodies, only that Sarah's eyebrow was a little singed, and a small spot appeared between her breasts. They were buried the next day in one grave . . . where my Lord Harcourt, at my request, has erected a monument over them. Of the following epitaphs which I made, the critics have chosen the godly one. . . .

Pope's critics included the Bishop of Rochester, who complained that his reference to a fiery of Day of Judgement –

> Virtue unmov'd, can hear the call
> And face the Flash that melts the Ball –

was 'too apt to lead us into the image of a snowball'; and the version they chose was engraved on the tablet that Lord Harcourt caused to be let into the outer fabric of the church. Lady Mary alone, when she received Pope's letter, proved definitely unresponsive; this ridiculous incident in low life failed to touch her aristocratic heart. She saw no reason to imagine, she replied, 'that John Hughes [sic] and Sarah Drew were either wiser or more virtuous than their neighbours. . . . His endeavourings to shield her from a storm, was a natural action, and what he would certainly have done for his horse'; and she proceeded to compose some very different lines:

> Who knows if 'twas not kindly done?
> For had they seen the next year's sun,
> A beaten wife and cuckold swain
> Had jointly curs'd the marriage chain;
> Now they are happy in their doom,
> FOR POPE HAS WROTE UPON THEIR TOMB.

Pope himself, though he had been genuinely touched by the episode – the story was as romantic in the literary, as it was pathetic in the human sense – could not long resist the temptation of making it the subject of a ribald couplet:

> Here lye two poor Lovers, who had the mishap
> Tho very chaste people, to die of a Clap.

Stranger still, he sent his rhyme to the Blounts, who carefully preserved it among their private papers.

As Pope laboured at Stanton Harcourt, Lady Mary and her husband had been sailing home. Having dropped anchor between Sestos and Abydos, they disembarked to examine the site of Troy – the ruins shown to gullible travellers were probably, she decided, the remains of a city built by Constantine – ascended 'the famous promontory of Sigaeum . . . where Achilles was buried, and where Alexander ran naked round his tomb . . . which, no doubt, was a great comfort to his ghost', and viewed the course of the River Simois rolling down from Mount Ida, and the Scamander, an unimpressive stream, nowadays half choked with mud. Threading the Greek islands, they came to Tunis; and, towards the end of August, they left their ship at Genoa; whence, after a halt at Turin, they journeyed on towards 'those dreadful Alps'. They had a wearisome passage across the mountains; for, although Lady Mary enjoyed 'the prodigious prospect' as her party swung along in their light wicker chairs – the method of transport that Edward Gibbon was to find so amusing and exhilarating – 'the misty rains which fall perpetually' soon soaked through her heavy fur rugs, and, before they at last reached level ground, she complained that she was almost dead with cold. From Lyons they travelled direct to Paris; and of France she was extremely critical. The provinces seemed wretchedly impoverished; wherever they drew up to change horses, 'the whole town', she reported, 'comes out to beg. . . .' Nor, once they had gained the metropolis, did the odd fashions she observed in high society please her English sense of style: 'I have seen all the beauties,' she wrote, 'and such – (I can't help making use of the coarse word) nauseous creatures! so fantastically absurd in their dress, so monstrously unnatural in their paints! their hair cut short . . . and so loaded with powder, that it makes it look like white wool! and on their cheeks to their chins . . . a shining red japan. that glistens in a most flaming manner. . . . It is with pleasure I recollect my dear pretty countrywomen. . . .'

Yet the thought that she must presently rejoin her countrywomen often caused her some misgivings. True, she looked forward to the company of her friends; but, as she assured Pope in her letter of 28 September, she had grown impatient of the ordinary social round, 'when I consider that I must ... receive and pay visits, make curtesies, and assist at tea-tables. ...' There was no question, however, of turning back; and by 2 October she and Mr Wortley were once again in England. Pope had already sung his paean of welcome. He longed for her sonnets, he had written on 1 September, her observations and her Eastern learning; 'but I long for nothing so much as your Oriental Self. ... I expect to see your soul as much thinner dressed as your body; and that you have left off, as unwieldy and cumbersome, a great many damn'd European habits. Without offence to your modesty be it spoken, I have a burning desire to see your soul stark naked, for I am confident 'tis the prettiest kind of white soul in the universe.' His next message apparently reached her at Dover. It was impossible, he protested, 'to express the least part of the joy your return gives me'; and 'I excessively long to meet you'. Just now he was eighty miles from London; but 'I have given orders to be sent for the first minute of your arrival. ...' How and where they met we cannot tell. On 11 October, Pope was at Cirencester with Lord Bathurst, eating heartily, riding to hounds – a somewhat unexpected form of amusement – and helping him replan his park; and on the 18th, having left Cirencester, he wrote to Caryll that, since his return home, he had passed 'but one night in London, when I went to Mr Tempest's. ...' Inwardly, perhaps, he had begun to dread the meeting that, only a few weeks earlier, had been the subject of such exalted fancies.

For over two years his imagination had been busily occupied with Lady Mary's portrait, first endeavouring to fix its outlines, then, as she gradually receded, enlarging, ennobling and transfiguring. Now, at last, the moment had come when he must confront the portrait and the face. Were they reconcilable? He was surely far too sensitive a lover not to have felt some secret qualms. Evidently he hoped to find her unchanged; but he also hoped that, in her 'Oriental Self', he might meet a subtly different personage – even bolder, gayer and more magnetic, since her 'white soul' had broken free from its clumsy European trappings. Here he may well have been disappointed; Lady Mary's travels had enriched her mind; they had not altered or improved her character. She was still extravagant, capricious, volatile and, despite her professed contempt for London society, still very much a modern woman of the world. As a returned ambassadress, she was immediately summoned to Court, where once again she cut a brilliant figure; and at home she had a multitude of occupations to absorb her time and energy. It is a great deal harder pursuing a fashionable young woman, with two children, an ambitious middle-aged husband and a host of London friends, than paying distant, romantic homage to the ideal personification of Grace and Virtue. But, whatever obstacles may have arisen between them, before the year was out Pope and Lady Mary were back again upon the old terms; and, when the Wortleys, who had found temporary accommodation in Covent Garden, decided they would prefer a country residence, he promptly volunteered his aid. Sir Godfrey Kneller, the septuagenarian artist, had a villa, close to Twickenham village, that the poet recommended; and on their way to inspect the property, the Wortleys spent a night beneath his roof. After some argument, they agreed to lease the house, which Wortley bought in 1722.

At the time, Pope himself was moving. About March 1719, having decided to leave Mawson's New Buildings – no doubt the place was full of gloomy memories – he, too, settled near Twickenham,* in a house on the verge of the Thames that he would occupy for the remainder of his life. Pope the householder and landscape-designer is a subject that demands separate notice. The alterations and improvements he made were to become a source of endless pleasure; and by November 1719 he had already begun to take up gardening and had added a couple of acres to his original domain. The situation, he wrote, was airy yet warm; indeed, it was 'a sort of heaven'. He would have been happy if he were not so often ill – with a pain in his side, which obliged him to go to bed amid a heap of heated tiles and brickbats; while 'my mother too is fallen ill of her rheumatism. . . .' During the year 1719 he wrote comparatively few letters, and none that has been preserved to his neighbour Lady Mary. Early in 1720, however, he arranged to have the beloved's portrait painted. The artist he chose was old Sir Godfrey; and Kneller went out of his way to spare her all unnecessary trouble. He proposed, Pope told Lady Mary, 'to draw your face with crayons, and finish it up, at your own house in a morning; from whence he will transfer it to the canvas. . . . This, I must observe, is a manner in which they seldom draw any but crowned heads. . . .' Later, Sir Godfrey would attend 'to take a sketch of you in your dress'. The whole idea of commissioning her portrait excited him immeasurably; 'the picture dwells really at my heart, and I have made a perfect passion of preferring your present face to your past. I know, and thoroughly esteem, your self of this year. I know no more of Lady Mary Pierrepont, than to admire at what I have heard of her, or be pleased with

* Pope had, at one time, thought of building a small house in London on part of the Burlington estate, with James Gibbs as his architect; but Lord Burlington had dissuaded him.

some fragments of hers, as I am with Sappho's. But now – I can't say what I would say of you now – Only still give me cause to say you are good to me, and allow me as much of your person as Sir Godfrey can help me to.'

Between the young girl and the married woman there was, in fact, a sad difference. The portrait, when Sir Godfrey had supplied the last touches, showed very little of the charm and delicacy that had invested Jervas's pensive shepherdess. The face had grown coarser and fuller; Lady Mary was developing a double chin; only the big dark eyes, slanting at the corners, recalled her brilliant unspoiled beauty. But Pope was delighted with the portrait –

> The play full smiles around the dimpled mouth
> That happy air of Majesty and Youth. . . .*

– and immediately placed it on the wall of his 'Great Room', where it remained long after the former friends had ceased to meet or correspond. Under its benign influence, he at length completed the *Iliad*. In March he informed John Caryll that he had 'yet a fortnight's work with Homer'; and the two last volumes of this tremendous enterprise appeared during the second week of May. To celebrate the occasion Gay produced some particularly agreeable and light-hearted verses, *Mr Pope's Welcome from Greece*, which depicts the translator sailing home again after his 'six years' toil' beneath the ramparts of Troy and, as he enters the Thames, being greeted by gunfire and church-bells and the cheers of his friends who crowd the quayside. Gay enumerates over eighty persons, not including various absentees – Bolingbroke, 'sweet St John', nowadays perforce an exile; Oxford, who, although no longer imprisoned in the Tower, has been obliged to send excuses; and Swift who, much against his will, breathes the 'Boeotian air' of Ireland. The size and splendour of this extraordinary gathering bear witness both to the magnitude of Pope's fame and to the immense diversity of men and women – peers, politicians, ladies of the Court, country magnates, fashionable dilettantes, men of pleasure, writers, actors, painters, critics, clerics and miscellaneous coffee-house companions – who at that time formed his private circle. Even his corpulent crony Tidcombe waddles slowly into view; 'honest, hatless Cromwell' displays his red breeches; while John Dennis and Charles Gildon, hoping to turn a dishonest penny, hang uninvited upon the verges of the throng.

* *On Lady Mary Wortley Montagu's Portrait.* These verses, given in manuscript to Lady Mary, were not published during the poet's life.

It is the feminine part of the assemblage, however, that Gay describes in
the most elaborate detail; and to Lady Mary, of course, among those
'silken petticoats', the poet makes his first bow:

> What lady's that to whom he gently bends?
> Who knows not her? ah, those are Wortley's eyes.
> How art thou honoured, numbered with her friends;
> For she distinguishes the good and wise.
> The sweet-tongued Murray near her side attends:
> Now to my heart the glance of Howard flies;
> Now Hervey, fair of face, I mark full well
> With thee, youth's youngest daughter, sweet Lepell.
>
> I see two lovely sisters, hand in hand,
> The fair-haired Martha and Teresa brown;
> Madge Bellenden, the tallest of the land;
> And smiling Mary, soft and fair as down . . .
> See next the decent Scudamore advance
> With Winchilsea, still meditating song,
> With her perhaps Miss Howe came there by chance,
> Nor knows with whom, or why she comes along.

The lovely sisters Gay introduces were naturally the Misses Blount;
sweet-tongued Murray was Mrs Griselda Murray, renowned for her
mellifluous voice, who, a year later, would become involved in a particularly disturbing scandal;* decent Scudamore, the wife of Lord Scudamore
and a member of the Digby family; and Winchilsea, the veteran poetess.
But Henrietta Howard, Mary Lepell, Mary Bellenden and Sophia Howe
all belonged to the Prince of Wales's entourage, which, since the violent
domestic quarrel that had disrupted the royal family in 1717, was completely separate from the King's household. Sovereigns of the Hanoverian
line have seldom been on good terms with their eldest sons. George I
deeply resented his heir, and had an ever heartier detestation for his highly
accomplished daughter-in-law, 'cette diablesse madame la princesse'. Early
one morning, incensed by his son's behaviour, he had summarily ex-
pelled them from St James's Palace with their attendants and their
children; and they had been obliged to retire to Leicester House, a large
house off Leicester Fields, where they had established an opposition court.

* During the autumn of 1721, a young footman attempted to rape her in her father's
house; and the affair provoked some invidious journalistic comments. Lady Mary was said
to have contributed, though she hotly denied it, a ballad entitled *Virtue in Danger*, which
provoked a bitter quarrel between herself and Mrs Murray. She also produced an Ovidian
Epistle in a far more serious and romantic vein.

Since the days of Charles II, no English royal household had had such pretty Maids of Honour. The Prince's mistress, Mrs Howard, who was also his wife's Woman of the Bedchamber, might be less attractive than intelligent, discreet and charming; but the Princess Caroline's Maids were famous beauties – Mary Bellenden, smiling and delicate; Sophia Howe, with her pleasant vagueness and her wild inconsequential airs; Molly Lepell,* secretly married to one of the handsomest young men in London, John Hervey, a fascinating effeminate personage, who stands close beside her as she welcomes Pope. Howard, Bellenden and Lepell the poet had already met some three years earlier, when he had met the Prince's ladies as they jogged back from a day's hunting, and they had carried him off to dinner and complained of the hardships of a Maid of Honour's life. Subsequently, he seems to have improved the acquaintance; just before her marriage to 'Hervey, fair of face', we know that Molly Lepell was staying with the Popes at Twickenham.

Clearly, the new villa was soon in a condition to receive guests, though as late as September Pope would report that he was still surrounded by a horde of workmen. Improving the house and replanning the estate must have been a costly business; but, luckier or cleverer than many of his friends, he had escaped almost unscathed from the financial catastrophe of the South Sea Bubble. It was early in January 1720, that the Bubble had begun to mount, when the Directors of the South Sea Company announced their bold plan for assuming the entire burden of the national debt, provided that the government would grant them a monopoly of trade with the rich entrepôts of the Spanish colonial empire. A bill to that effect was hurried through Parliament, despite Walpole's energetic protests; and the value of South Sea stock, quoted at 128 in January, rose to 380 in March, and in April soared to 500. Meanwhile what Walpole had denounced as 'the pernicious practice of stock-jobbing' had become a universal craze; and a multitude of smaller projects, some of them strangely absurd,† were launched by the financiers of Change Alley. But, at this point, the government took alarm; legal measures were adopted to check the rapid growth of speculative companies; and, as those companies were suppressed or failed, investors who had borrowed on their holdings were obliged to sell out South Sea shares. Panic followed;

* Molly Lepell was married to the Hon. John Hervey, second son of the Earl of Bristol, who succeeded to his brother's courtesy title in 1723, on 21 April 1720.

† They included a scheme 'for effecting the transmutation of fluid mercury . . . into a solid and malleable body . . . of equal use, beauty and value with the purest standard silver'; and a device named 'Puckle's Machine Gun', designed to fire 'round and square cannon balls and bullets'.

18 Marble Hill, Twickenham; the north front. Designed for Mrs. Howard by her architectural friend, the future Earl of Pembroke.

19 Lady Bolingbroke, the statesman's second wife; medallion by Roubiliac at
Battersea Church.

South Sea stock declined; the glorious Bubble quivered and exploded. After the hysterical excitement of the last few months, Londoners sank into a mood of deep depression.

Pope could afford to be philosophic over the calamities of 'this miserable mercenary period'. While the Bubble ascended, he had indulged in the stock-jobbing mania, and had purchased South Sea shares both for himself and for Teresa Blount; but at a fairly early stage, he had decided to realize his holdings; and about May he was able to assure Caryll that personally he had 'very little in'. People told him, wrote Robert Digby on 9 July, that 'you was soon content; and that you cared not for such an increase as others wished you'. When the crash came '*like a thief in the night*', some of his paper profits disappeared; but he was among the few, he informed Atterbury, who had had 'the good fortune to remain with half of what they imagined they had. . . .' Thus he could continue to enjoy the pleasures of Twickenham, despite a cold and rainy summer, as he watched his 'Tuscan porticoes' arise and his stately colonnades expand their wings. Later that year, even the floods delighted him; the lawn that separated his house from the Thames had disappeared beneath the water, which now ran in to form 'an arm of the sea' between the two enclosing terraces; and river boats under full sail glided across the meadow opposite. The whole prospect was 'prodigiously fine'. He had found his house, he wrote to Teresa Blount, 'exactly like Noah's Ark in everything, except that there's no propagation of the species in it'. Whichever way the inhabitants looked out, they saw an unknown watery world; and, although the villa remained dry and comfortable, small fishes from the Thames were sometimes drawn in through the kitchen pipes.

9

Once he had returned from the siege of Troy, crowned with laurels and bearing golden spoils, Pope was free to take up life again as a great imaginative artist. But he decided otherwise; and for the next few years most of his time was spent on a variety of minor projects – a translation of the *Odyssey*, editions of the works of Parnell and the Duke of Buckingham, and a new edition of the works of Shakespeare. Perhaps his Homeric labours had temporarily worn him out. Perhaps he was experiencing one of those inward crises – sudden failures of courage and vital energy – which occur in every writer's life. Or he may have thought that by translating the *Odyssey* and publishing a new Shakespearian text, he could consolidate the small fortune he had already founded by his triumphant version of the *Iliad*. 1721 seems to have been largely passed at Twickenham, among the improvements he was still planning; and in December he published Parnell's *Poems on Several Occasions* – poor Parnell, a victim of intemperance, had died in 1718 – together with a stately *Epistle to Robert Earl of Oxford*. About the same period, he attacked the *Odyssey* and started work as a Shakespearian critic. Of learned editorship he had had no experience; but he knew the difficulty of translating Homer; and his first move was to recruit assistants. The henchmen he pressed into service were the Reverend William Broome, who had already helped him with the *Iliad*, and a worthy pedagogue, Elijah Fenton,★ both sound scholars and respectable versifiers, delighted to share the fame and (they hoped) the profits of a famous modern poet. Concerning the part they played, Pope was not averse from some polite deception; the *Iliad* he said that he had 'translated'; but, when he advertised his rendering of the *Odyssey*, he announced merely that he had 'undertaken' a translation, and referred

★ William Broome, 1689–1745: Elijah Fenton, 1683–1730. 'Fenton is a right honest man. He is fat and indolent, a very good scholar: sits within and does nothing but read and compose': Joseph Spence, *Observations, Anecdotes and Characters of Books and Men*.

lightly to 'two of his friends' who had been good enough to lend their help. In the upshot, neither felt that he had received his rightful share of cash or credit.

Meanwhile Pope was anxious that their collaboration should remain clandestine. In February 1722, a number of preliminary drafts arrived. Fenton's version of Book XII, he told Broome, undoubtedly required 'inspiriting'; but he added that there was nothing he would not do 'to make the whole as finished and spirited as I was able, by giving the last touches'. Next month, Fenton reported to Broome that 'Mr Pope is now in high spirits about Homer', and reminded him that the poet desired 'that the business . . . should be carried on with all the secrecy imaginable'. At the same time, Pope had not forgotten Shakespeare; and that May he published an advertisement in the columns of *The Evening Post*, requesting that 'if any person has any editions of *Tempest*, *Macbeth*, *Julius Caesar*, *Timon of Athens*, *King John*, and *Henry VIII*, printed before the year 1620', he would entrust them to the publisher, Jacob Tonson. These projects occupied his working hours; and evidently his friends complained. Caryll asked if he was no longer writing poems; and in October Pope replied that he had very different interests: 'I must again sincerely protest to you, that I have wholly given over scribbling . . . but am become, by due gradation of dullness, from a poet a translator, and from a translator, a mere editor.' Such was the poet's mood at the age of thirty-four. The ferment of youth had died down; he was content to pass the remainder of his life as a busy, distinguished man of letters; building and gardening, rather than poetry, gave him the creative outlet he had always needed. Every month Twickenham grew more beautiful; but one shadow barred that radiant prospect. His close neighbour and dearest associate appeared to be drifting off beyond recovery.

The process was gradual; and Lady Mary herself, much concerned at the moment with her private problems, may perhaps scarcely have noticed that their affection had begun to wane. In 1721 she had suffered serious annoyance from a disappointed French admirer; and the scandal that he threatened to provoke had caused her many weeks of misery. For once she had erred through good nature. Just as she was about to leave Constantinople in the early summer of 1718, she had received a letter signed by an unknown correspondent, a certain Nicolas-François Rémond de Saint-Mard. He was a friend, it appeared, of the Abbé Conti; and, having been allowed to read one of her letters to the Abbé on the subject of Turkish modes and morals, he felt obliged to express his warm regard both for the singularity of her character and for the 'infinite attractions' of her mind.

She replied; and he boldly declared his love; no other woman, he would have her believe, had been adored as he adored her. Lady Mary had never disliked flattery; on her way through Paris that year, she seems to have granted him an interview; and his amorous correspondence had continued after her return home. Then, during the heyday of the South Sea Bubble, Rémond had suddenly appeared in London. He was anxious to see her, but even more anxious that she should help him to increase his capital, '*ma petite fortune chancelante*'; and, although Lady Mary, now slightly annoyed, gave him at first a somewhat frigid welcome – Rémond, according to Saint-Simon, was a particularly gross and ugly man* – she thought that, since she had declined his advances, she could not decently refuse to act as his financial counsellor. Her advice succeeded; his purchase of South Sea Stock brought him in a satisfactory profit; and, when Lady Mary explained that 'his extravagancys made it utterly impossible for me to keep him company,' and hinted that he would do well to leave England, he begged that she would take charge of his winnings and re-employ them to the best advantage. She agreed; the Bubble collapsed; Rémond lost five hundred pounds. He had left her with 'tears and grimaces' and protestations of eternal passion; but presently furious letters began to arrive from Paris. Claiming that he was the victim of an impudent swindle, Rémond threatened that he would publish their correspondence and submit his case to Mr Wortley.

Lady Mary took immediate alarm. 'I am too acquainted with the world,' she wrote to her exiled sister Lady Mar, '. . . not to know that the most groundless accusation is always of ill consequence to a woman, besides the cruel misfortunes it may bring upon me in my own family.' Every post-day afforded her fresh anguish; but the letter that Rémond sent to her husband was held back by a good-natured emissary; and the aggrieved Frenchman at length gave up the struggle. As she had expected, however, her reputation suffered lasting damage. Lady Mary was one of those women who naturally attract gossip; scandal harried her throughout her long life; and, Rémond having told his story in Paris, it was rumoured that her unwary victim had been her lover before he became her dupe. Even Pope may have latterly grown suspicious. But during the summer and autumn of 1721 they were still upon familiar terms; and in a letter dated 21 September, written at Lord Bathurst's country house, he describes her

* '*C'était un petit homme fort du commun, et pis pour la figure, qui à force de grec et de latin, de belles lettres et de bel esprit, s'était fourré où il avait pu, puis, à force de débauche de toute espèce et de sentimens si malheureusement à la mode, était parvenu à voir des femmes, et quelque sorte de bonne compagnie.*' Elsewhere Saint-Simon describes him as resembling '*un biscuit manqué*' – an ill-cooked biscuit – with a big nose and large bulging eyes.

recent visit to his new garden. Amid the 'noble scenes, openings and avenues' of his host's immense domain, he had been proud to reflect 'what an honour it is to my Great Walk, that the finest woman in the world could not stir from it. That walk extremely well answered the intent of its contriver, when it detained her there.' During 1722, her visits were much less numerous; indeed, she rarely crossed his threshold; for, in April, she wrote to Lady Mar that nowadays she saw 'sometimes Mr Congreve, and very seldom Mr Pope', who, she understood, continued to embellish his house at Twickenham, and had built himself 'a subterranean grotto, which he has furnished with looking-glass, and they tell me it has a very good effect'. She also enclosed 'some verses addressed to Mr Gay, who writ him a congratulatory letter on the finishing his house' – verses that she had done her best to suppress in London and hoped that Lady Mar would not hand around in Paris:

> Ah friend, 'tis true – this truth you lovers know –
> In vain my structures rise, my gardens grow,
> In vain fair Thames reflects the double scenes
> Of hanging mountains, and of sloping greens:
> Joy lives not here; to happier seats it flies,
> And only dwells where WORTLEY casts her eyes.
>
> What are the gay parterre, the chequer'd shade,
> The morning bower, the ev'ning colonade,
> But soft recesses of uneasy minds,
> To sigh unheard in, to the passing winds?
> So the struck deer in some sequester'd part
> Lies down to die, the arrow at his heart;
> There, stretch'd unseen in coverts hid from day,
> Bleeds drop by drop, and pants his life away.

In its entirety, the poem was never published during Pope's life. At a less unhappy period he had made no secret of his passionate devotion to Lady Mary; but this poignant record of how his devotion had failed was intended only for a few good friends. Despite the elaborate artistry of the seventh and eighth lines – Pope was seldom to produce a more enchanting cadence – and the somewhat commonplace image with which the poem closes, its effect on the reader's mind is almost painfully direct and personal. He had planned his gardens as a kind of decorative trap, a labyrinth of alleys and avenues in which he had hoped that Lady Mary might consent to lose her way. Now she rarely visited his Great Walk; and the exquisite web that he had woven around her seemed a piece of empty artifice. Yet there were moments when she chose to reappear; and, that July, the mother of her one-time friend, Griselda Murray, reported, among other extremely spiteful references to Lady Mary's erratic mode of life, that 'she and Pope keeps so close . . . that they are a talk to the whole town'. Servants, carrying books and notes, still frequently passed to and fro. Lady Mary was an inveterate borrower; and in April 1723, she despatched a brief message, remarking that, as she had carefully sent back his copy of *Arcadia*, she hoped that he would trust her 'with a volume of Shakespeare's plays, which I shall take the same trouble to restore'. In December he received a second message, informing him that, if he were 'not well enough to come hither, I will be with you tomorrow morning, having something particular to say to you'.* Pope treated these notes a great deal less respectfully than he might have done in days past. Both of them were used as scrap paper; and on their blank spaces he jotted down rough drafts for his translation of the *Odyssey*.

Lady Mary never wrote again. Between them fell a deathly silence. During the last three or four years she had acquired a multitude of new friends, and now preferred to pass her days among 'a small snug set of dear intimates'. A frequent visitor was the handsome young Duke of Wharton, with whom she flirted, joked and squabbled; her female favourites included a 'little satin thread beauty' whom she referred to as her 'dear companion', and Sir Robert Walpole's mistress, the enchanting Molly Skerrett. It was an 'easy indolent life', which became even easier once she had managed to shake off the outrageous Rémond. Twickenham was the scene of unending concerts; in 1721 Lord Burlington's protégé, the composer Buononcini, the celebrated *prima donna*, Anastasia Robinson, and the famed *castrato*, Senesino, all took lodgings in the village and often supped at Lady Mary's table. Pope must sometimes have joined her parties; but her solemn, preoccupied husband usually remained aloof. 'They say a great many things,' Mrs Murray announced, 'of her using Mr Wortley like a dog'; since 1721, we know, she had begun to lose patience with what she today called 'the forlorn state of matrimony', and could only suppose, she sighed, that, however discordant earthly marriages might seem, they would eventually 'come right in Heaven'. Until then she was content to pursue her pleasures, while Mr Wortley cherished his political ambitions and prosecuted an absorbing round of business. Pope may perhaps have regretted him. To a lover, especially a platonic lover, a husband's presence is sometimes not un-

* Both notes are unsigned; but Lady Mary's handwriting has been identified by Dr Robert Halsband.

welcome; a useful Cerberus, who keeps other admirers at bay, he also provides a salutary check upon the beloved woman's vagrant fancies. Once Mr Wortley relaxed his guard, new friends were bound to bring new perils. No doubt Pope was both alarmed and excited; and in these unsettling circumstances he may have made a foolish gesture.

A variety of stories were afterwards told to explain why Pope and Lady Mary parted. One concerns an absurd domestic quarrel; she is said to have borrowed a pair of sheets from old Mrs Pope, that provident middle-class housekeeper, and then thoughtlessly sent them back unwashed. In another version, which Lady Mary preferred, the poet was himself responsible: 'at some ill-chosen time . . . he made such passionate love to her, as, in spite of her utmost endeavour to be angry and look grave, produced an immoderate fit of laughter; from which moment he became her implacable enemy'. Each story is slightly unconvincing; Pope must have been well aware of Lady Mary's vague and careless habits; and Lady Mary cannot have been surprised to learn that his feelings were not entirely innocent. She also told Lady Pomfret, who passed on the tale to Spence, that Pope had become unreasonably jealous of the attentions paid her by the Duke of Wharton. Their quarrel, if a definite quarrel took place, probably originated not in any single episode, but in the very nature, the secret stresses and strains, of their curiously unequal friendship. For Lady Mary, it had been an amusing literary diversion: for Pope, an all-absorbing passion. Pope had the pride that goes with genius; Lady Mary possessed a considerable share of talent, and, to the self-esteem that usually accompanies talent, she added the strain of levity and light-hearted cruelty that she derived from her education as a woman of the world. Most love affairs are based on a misunderstanding; but Pope, being a great imaginative artist, had raised his private delusions to a high poetic level. When they parted, Lady Mary lost a valued friend, a flattering and gifted courtier: Pope, a whole complex array of precious memories and associa-tions. We can only measure his pain by the extraordinary degree of violence with which, in later years, he was to attack her image.

For the moment, however, he held his hand. Lady Mary's portrait continued to embellish his drawing-room and radiate its 'happy air of majesty and youth'; but its subject, today a little coarsened and discredited – a one-time fashionable lady, at whom the London grand monde had begun to sneer – no longer figured in his correspondence. To the heart-stricken, work is a palliative, if not always an unfailing remedy; and Pope's relish of hard work was as deeply rooted as his social instincts. With his translation of the Odyssey and his edition of Shakespeare, he had enough to occupy him for many months to come; and in 1723 he ran into serious trouble over a comparatively unimportant undertaking. Two years earlier, John Sheffield, third Earl of Mulgrave, first Duke of Buckingham, literary patron, courtier and man of pleasure, had died at the age of seventy-three.* Once Dryden's friend and himself a prolific author, he had left behind him a large accumulation of miscellaneous verse and prose, including an *Essay on Satire*, an *Essay on Poetry*, a modernized version of *Julius Caesar*, to which he had thoughtfully added some affecting love-scenes, and a prose *Account of the Revolution*, written, his critics claimed, from a strongly Stuart point of view. Through his third wife, the illegitimate daughter of James II and Catherine Sedley, he had had a close connection with the Stuart line; and it was the Dowager Duchess, a proud and eccentric personage, who had requested Pope, as an old acquaintance, to produce a suitable edition of her husband's writings. He was glad to do so. 'That,' he had told Caryll in 1722, 'will be a very beautiful book, and has many things in it you will be particularly glad to see in relation to some former reigns.' Unluckily, these references to former reigns attracted the notice of the Whig government. The volumes were promptly impounded, and not released for publication until tendentious passages had been cut out; while Pope was obliged to equivocate in his customary genteel manner. Although he had hinted that his co-religionist Caryll was likely to be interested by the author's views, writing to Lord Carteret, a Principal Secretary of State, he protested that, at the time when the printer applied for a licence, he had 'never looked into those papers, or was privy to the contents of 'em'. Simultaneously, he sought the advice of Harcourt, who recommended that he should steer clear of politics and quietly pursue his work at home.

Buckingham's *Works* were suppressed by the government in January, 1723; and, at the beginning of May, he experienced a second crisis. During recent years, the Bishop of Rochester had become a fast friend. Now over seventy years old, Francis Atterbury was both a celebrated preacher and a formidable controversialist, whose eloquent defence of the Reformation had been warmly praised by Bishop Burnet. He was also much admired – despite an unfortunate clash with Dr Bentley over the spurious *Epistles of Phalaris†* – as a scholar and a modern critic; and Pope had often visited him at Bromley, to discuss poetic and religious questions. When the poet's

* To the Duke of Buckingham, and to six or seven others, Pope attributed 'the nobleman look' he had already admired in Wycherley. 'Mr Pope altered some verses in the Duke of Buckingham's *Essay on Poetry*, as he did many in Wycherley's poems.' Spence, op. cit.

† These letters threw a favourable light on the ferocious tyrant who had ruled over sixth-century Agrigentum. They were exposed as forgeries by Richard Bentley (1662–1742).

father died in 1717, Atterbury had even suggested that, since the main obstacle to his conversion had been removed, he might reasonably become a Protestant; to which Pope replied that, although one parent was dead, he must still respect the other's feelings; and that, for Mrs Pope, her son's apostasy would be the most grievous of all imaginable blows. So far as his own opinions were concerned, 'I am not a Papist, for I renounce the temporal invasions of the Papal power . . . I am a Catholic in the strictest sense of the word'; and meanwhile he was content to enjoy the benefits of the admirable British constitution, under a sovereign who was 'not a King of Whigs, or a King of Tories, but a King of England'; which, he added, 'God of his mercy grant his present Majesty may be. . . .' It is possible that, when he wrote, Pope knew that, in official quarters, his friend the Bishop was already suspect. As the leader of the High Church party, Atterbury was strongly opposed to the Hanoverian establishment; and in 1717 he had embarked on a secret correspondence with the exiled Stuart court. That correspondence was at length betrayed by the Regent duc d'Orléans; and in August, 1722, Atterbury was arrested and committed to the Tower of London, where he remained a close prisoner for the next eight months, until the spring of 1723.

Pope visited him in the Tower; and thence, on 10 April, the Bishop wrote to him, and managed to smuggle the letter out of prison. Besides thanking him for 'all the instance of your friendship, both before and since my misfortunes', he announced that he was considering whether, when his case was tried, he should call the poet as a witness, 'to say somewhat about my way of spending my time at the Deanery, which did not seem calculated towards managing plots and conspiracies'. Pope's reply was generous and heart-felt; he assured the Bishop of his complete devotion, and promised him that, 'even though it were death to correspond with you', he would still find an effective means of registering his love and gratitude. He was deeply perturbed, nevertheless, by the prospect of appearing in person before the House of Lords. A poor speaker, he dreaded public appearances. He was afraid, moreover, that the Lords might interrogate him about his own religious tenets. Again he consulted Lord Harcourt, and scribbled some notes – which he shortly afterwards lost – of Harcourt's advice as to how he should set about answering particularly inconvenient questions. Then, on 8 May, amid a solemn assemblage of lords temporal and lords spiritual, in ermine and scarlet and snowy lawn sleeves, the poet stood to give his testimony. Although the first row – 'which was all I could see' – were mostly, he remembered, 'all of my acquaintance', and he had 'but ten words to say . . . I made two or three blunders'. The House treated him indulgently and, 'between the speaking', he was allowed to sit down. Proceedings continued four days, from the 6th to the 11th and Atterbury delivered a lengthy and impressive speech. But, on the 16th, when a vote was taken, a Bill of Pains and Penalties was passed against him; and, having been condemned and stripped of his benefices, he retired into perpetual exile.

Pope believed that he himself might presently be obliged to leave England; for he assumed that the government would launch a further vindictive campaign against Catholics and suspected Jacobites; and early in 1723, he was also disturbed and saddened by the condition of his mother's health. That winter, she had fallen seriously ill; the 'melancholy office of attending her', he observed, was 'much like that of watching over a taper that is expiring; and even when it burns a little brighter . . . is but the nearer burning out'. Mrs Pope, however, was to cling to existence for another ten years; and her son, who had inherited her strength of spirit, soon recovered from his tribulations. Thus, in August, writing to Swift, he gave a singularly optimistic account of his current way of life, 'which has been infinitely more various and dissipated than when you knew me, among all sexes, parties and professions'. At the moment, he had had enough of society; and 'the merry vein you knew me in, is sunk into a turn of reflection, that has made the world pretty indifferent to me'. But his mood was neither violent nor sour; and 'I have acquired a quietness of mind which by fits improves into a certain degree of cheerfulness. . . .' Although he had always refused to flatter the Great, and, as a rule, 'carefully avoided all intercourse with poets and scribblers' – nowadays his only literary enemies were persons he had never seen – he was still continuing to enlarge the circle of his private friendships.

In 1723, the poet's new friends included an elderly retired general and an attractive young unmarried woman. Charles Mordaunt, third Earl of Peterborough – or Peterborow, as Pope spelled his title – had been born in 1658, and was one of those fascinating patrician amateurs who have left so bold a mark on English history. Whatever he did was done with elegant bravado. In 1705, for example, despite his complete lack of any proper military training, he had led the victorious expedition that attacked and captured Barcelona. He owed his appointment to the Duchess of Marlborough's support; but, during the siege, he had shown the courage and resolution of an experienced professional soldier. When panic swept through the Allied ranks, and his troops turned and fled beneath the citadel of Montejuich, Peterborough, we learn, 'fell into the horriblest passion that ever man was seen in', and, snatching Lord Charlemont's baton, himself stormed furiously up the hill, followed by his shame-faced infantry. No less characteristic, once he had taken Barcelona, was his chivalrous treatment of the Spanish garrison. As they left the city, having been granted the honours of war, they were surrounded, and might have been massacred, by indignant Catalan separatists, had not Peterborough immediately galloped to their aid and, under a hail of fire – a bullet pierced his periwig – managed to reach them and drive back the mob. In Peterborough's composition there was something of Don Quixote; something, too, of Don Juan. Before he was twenty-one, he claimed, he had committed three different crimes, all of which involved the death-penalty; and in his later years he became the type of aristocrat who can afford to laugh at social prejudices. On his visits to Bath, he preferred to do his own marketing, and would walk the streets, wearing his star and blue riband, but carrying a cabbage and a plucked fowl.

As a sexagenarian, he was still uncommonly handsome – spare, swarthy, of middle height, with thick black eyebrows above dark and penetrating eyes. He had recently wedded a beautiful singer, Lady Mary's acquaintance Anastasia Robinson; but he had not yet acknowledged the marriage – his wife maintained a separate household – and was laying romantic siege to Mrs Howard, the Prince of Wales's well-conducted mistress. It was Mrs Howard who inspired Lord Peterborough's only memorable poem;* and the verses he addressed to her were accompanied by a long series of strangely elaborate and effusive letters. Though he had voted for Atterbury's banishment, Pope regarded him with almost filial affection; and during the years 1722 and 1723 – apparently he had abandoned Cleveland Court – when the poet came to London he very often stayed at Peterborough's house in Bolton Street. His second new friend, Miss Judith Cowper, was a member of much the same circle; he had been introduced to her either by Mrs Howard or by the flighty Maid of Honour, Miss Sophia Howe. A niece of the Lord Chancellor, Earl Cowper, she suffered from literary pretensions and from some fashionable kind of nervous melancholy. But she was young and enthusiastic and sufficiently attractive to make a welcome correspondent; and Pope embarked on one of those

* 'I said to my heart between sleeping and waking,
  "Thou wild thing, that always art leaping or aching,
  What black, brown or fair, in what clime, in what nation,
  By turns has not taught thee a pit-a-patation? . . ."
  O wonderful creature! a woman of reason!
  Never grave out of pride, never gay out of season;
  When so easy to guess who this angel should be,
  Would one think Mrs Howard ne'er dreamt it was she?'

epistolary courtships for which he had a special aptitude, flattering, advising, teasing, with a hint, thrown in here and there, that she had seriously perturbed his heart. He may have hoped that, as the relationship developed, she would take the place of Lady Mary. Indeed, soon after the correspondence began, he drew a comparison between his new and his old love to Lady Mary's disadvantage. Both of his favourites possessed poetic gifts; himself he preferred the gentler spirit:

> Tho sprightly Sappho force our Love and Praise,
> A softer Wonder my pleasd soul surveys,
> The mild Erinna, blushing in her Bays.*

But it is clear that his private opinion of Miss Cowper's talents was a good deal less favourable, and that he was not at all anxious to be obliged to play the part of literary mentor. Should she beg for his views on her manuscripts, he turned the question aside with exemplary tact and kindness: '... Your writings,' he assured her, 'are very good, and very entertaining, but not so good, nor so entertaining as your life and conversation. One is but the effect and emanation of the other. It will always be a greater pleasure to me, to know that you are well, than that you write well. . . .' He pursued his courtship, with undiminished devotion, until November 1723. Then, in December, she finally severed the link by marrying a Captain Martin Madan.

Many of Pope's letters to Judith Cowper were written from his country house. He was often too busy to leave home; and, as time passed, his lawns and walks and groves, though Lady Mary no longer honoured them, were becoming a symbolic place of refuge. There, at least, he could realize his personal vision of a happy and harmonious world; and there, on a miniature scale, he emulated the triumphs of far more grandiose modern planners. But the theories he put into practice did not lack originality; both his own designs and the precepts he laid down were soon to secure him an important position in the history of English taste. That taste was rapidly changing; and among those who had done most to change it was his Chiswick neighbour Lord Burlington. In 1719 the great man had completed his second cultural tour of Italy, having spent some months at Venice and Vicenza, where he had studied and measured, and recruited local architects 'to draw all the fine buildings of Palladio'. With him he brought home not only the composer Buononcini – he was still

---

* This triplet Pope very rightly discarded; the following lines, which first appear in a letter to Judith Cowper dated 18 October 1722, were afterwards adapted to form part of his *Epistle to a Lady*. Erinna, authoress of the *Distaff*, flourished in the fourth century B C.

passionately devoted to music – but the versatile Yorkshireman William Kent, whom he immediately installed in Burlington House, where, surrounded by every comfort that his host could furnish, Kent would remain until he died. After a decade of Italian peregrinations, 'the Signior', as his acquaintances called him, had developed a highly critical attitude towards the aesthetic standards of his native country, denounced the lamentable achievements of the Age of Anne, and thundered against the 'damned gusto that has been with us for this sixty years past'. English art and architecture must be reformed, English parks and gardens re-designed. Sir Christopher Wren had been a false prophet; St Paul's Cathedral, finished in 1710, was an architectural abomination. The time had come to remember Inigo Jones and revert to a pure Palladian style, substituting Roman correctitude for the neo-Baroque extravagances that Wren, Vanbrugh and Nicholas Hawksmoor had favoured. The late Lord Shaftesbury had supplied the new movement with its philosophic text-book;* and it was now subsidized and directed by Burlington, who employed Kent as his chief lieutenant and Pope as his poetic aide. Together they founded the critical coterie that was presently to infuriate William Hogarth.

In 1716 Burlington House was already undergoing restoration. The old seventeenth-century house had been built for Burlington's grandfather by the poet-architect Sir John Denham. But it no longer satisfied its owner's taste; and James Gibbs was commissioned to produce a more harmonious structure. Next year, Gibbs, being an obstinate disciple of Wren, was abruptly replaced by Colen Campbell, who rebuilt the front of the house according to Palladian principles, raised the main gate which opened on Piccadilly, and threw out the magnificent curving colonnade that afterwards reminded Horace Walpole 'of one of those edifices in fairy-tales . . . raised by genii in a night's time'. Simultaneously, assisted first by Charles Bridgeman, then by Kent, Burlington was replanning the gardens around his villa at Chiswick. For the moment, he left the house unchanged; but its setting was 'taken in hand' as soon as he had returned home from his original visit to Italy. Together with unbounded enthu-siasm and energy, he possessed an enormous private fortune. Even Burlington's resources were sometimes strained – in a single year his outlay exceeded eighteen thousand pounds; and, during his later life, he fell into debt and was obliged to sacrifice his Irish properties; but the

* Anthony Ashley Cooper, third Earl of Shaftesbury (1671–1713); a pupil of Locke; author of a volume of essays, critical and philosophical, *Characteristics of Men, Manners, Opinions, Times*, published in 1711, which included some stern criticism of Wren's City churches.

lavish scale on which he built and gardened made him the paragon of contemporary connoisseurs. Despite his generosity, however, Burlington was a cool, impassive man – very unlike his perpetual guest, the free-spoken and uninhibited Kent, who 'often gave his orders when he was full of claret', and would frequently abandon his labours to enjoy a prolonged holiday at his patron's Chiswick house, where he lolled and drank beneath the trees, solacing himself with 'syllabubs, damsels and other benefits of nature'.

Burlington's portrait suggests a chilly temperament – hooded eyes, a thin unsmiling mouth, and an aquiline patrician nose. He can never have found it easy to unbend; but under the frigid mask he had a warm and kindly spirit. Undoubtedly, he loved the Signior – by the Burlington circle also called 'Kentino'; and, when in 1721, at the age of twenty-seven, he married Lady Dorothy Savile, daughter of the Earl of Halifax, she, too, became the Signior's ally. Burlington's domestic existence was not untroubled; though she had a deep affection for her husband, whom in her letters she usually styled 'my dear boy', 'my dear child' or 'my dearest life', Lady Burlington was a capricious, unbalanced woman, and is said to have shown a savage temper.* But nothing could ruffle Burlington's dignity or cloud his Olympian air of mild detachment. In art as in life, harmony, symmetry, classical elegance were the virtues that he most esteemed; and, as a gardener, the effect to which he aspired was based on a delicate equipoise between Man and the surrounding universe. Lord Shaftesbury had taught that taste and conduct formed part of the same moral pattern; the âme bien née was inevitably a man of taste, and the aesthete was perforce a moralist; finely proportioned buildings and beautifully laid-out gardens had a spiritual and philosophic, as well as an aesthetic value. In everything it was balance that counted; the demands of society must be balanced against the wishes of the individual; human altruism and human egoism, which, if reconciled, were productive of true morality, must learn to run in double harness. Thus Burlington envisaged a landscape where Man improved on the materials that had already been supplied by Nature; while Kent believed that his function in landscape-gardening was not to create new beauties, but merely to 'brush Nature's robe'. Hitherto, a garden – the French gardens imported by Le Nôtre, the Dutch gardens popularized by William III – had been carefully cut off from the neigh-

---

* See James Lees-Milne's admirable book, *Earls of Creation*. Lady Burlington, from her box at the opera, once engaged in an abusive dialogue with her musical antagonist Lady Pembroke, while two rival *prima donnas* were fighting on the stage. Lady Burlington's habit of cursing and blaspheming was recorded both by Horace Walpole and, earlier, by Lord Hervey:

'Let Dame Palladio, insolent and bold,
Like her own chairman, whistle, stamp and scold'.

bouring fields and woods, formal arrangements of box and yew and stone, spread out like exquisite floral chessboards with their intersecting paths and alleys. Kent, wrote Horace Walpole, 'saw that all nature was a garden', and boldly over-leapt the fence – that is to say, he abolished the boundary-line, pushed out his gardens towards the distant wooded horizon, and persuaded the natural sweep of the country to enfold the house itself.*

Yet, in the Augustan period, Art was never neglected; and it was Man who provided the final decisive touches, planting a term here, a sphinx or an obelisk there, or 'improving' a corner of the landscape to recall a picture by Lorrain or Poussin. This blend of the natural and the artificial was particularly characteristic of Lord Burlington's gardens at Chiswick, which included temples, statues, columns, tombs, as well as irregular spinneys and mossy serpentine walks, designed to produce the effect of 'agreeable disorder' that both the great man and his chosen artists loved. Pope had long been advocating this new technique; and in the year 1712, among his journalistic pieces, he had published an ambitious disquisition on the modern art of gardening, where he ridiculed the masterpieces of tailor-made topiary-work prized by the old-fashioned gardener, and re-commended a freer and more natural style. He was not alone; for, during the same year, Addison himself had produced an interesting horticultural essay: 'Writers,' he observed, 'who have given us an account of China, tell us the inhabitants of that country laugh at the plantations of Europeans, which are laid out by the rule of line', and had a word 'in their language by which they express the particular beauty of a plantation that strikes the imagination at first sight, without discovering what it is that makes so agreeable an effect'. His information Addison seems to have derived from Sir William Temple's essay *Upon the Gardens of Epicurus*, written as early as 1685. The Chinese, Temple had announced, scorn our European way of planting, in which our walks and trees are arranged 'so that they answer one another, and at exact distances . . . Their imagination is employed in contriving figures where the beauties shall be great, and strike the eye, without any order'; and '*Sharawadgi*', he added, was the word they used to designate the charms of elegant irregularity.†

* This practice had been anticipated by Burlington's original landscape-gardener, Charles Bridgeman, inventor of the ha-ha, or sunken fence.

† This word was once believed to have been Temple's own invention (see Hugh Honour, *A Vision of Cathay*, 1961). But, during his embassy at the Hague, he must have talked with Dutch merchants who had visited the Far East; and I am informed by my friend Professor Ivan Morris of Columbia University that, although there is no such word, or anything that resembles it, in Chinese, *Sharawadgi* may well be based on the Japanese *Sorowaji*, meaning 'does not match', 'is irregular'. He adds, however, that for a Japanese the word has no aesthetic connotation.

Pope would one day sum up his beliefs, and those of the whole Palladian coterie, in the majestic *Epistle* that he addressed to Burlington:

> Consult the Genius of the Place in all,
> That tells the Waters or to rise, or fall,
> Or helps th'ambitious Hill the heav'n to scale,
> Or scoops in circling theatres the Vale,
> Calls in the Country, catches op'ning glades,
> Joins willing woods, and varies shades from shades,
> Now breaks, or now directs, th'intending Lines,
> Paints as you plant, and, as you work, designs.
>   Still follow Sense, of ev'ry Art the Soul,
> Parts answ'ring parts shall slide into a whole,
> Spontaneous beauties all around advance,
> Start ev'n from difficulty, strike from chance. . . .

In conversation, he often discussed his theories; and to Spence he remarked how 'the lights and shades in gardening are managed by disposing the thick grove work . . . in a proper manner: of which the eye is generally the properest judge. Those clumps of trees are like the groups in pictures, (speaking of some things in his own garden). You may distance things by darkening them, and by narrowing the plantation more and more towards the end . . . as 'tis executed in the little cypress walk to that obelisk.' On another occasion, he described his project for remodelling an entire mountain, following the classic example of Dinocrates, who had proposed to remodel Mount Athos in the form of a gigantic effigy of Alexander; 'if anybody would make me a present of a Welsh mountain . . . I would undertake to see it executed. . . . The figure must be in a reclining posture, because of the hollowing that would otherwise be necessary. . . . It should be a rude unequal hill, and might be helped with groves of trees for the eyebrows, and wood for the hair. The natural green should be left whenever it would be necessary to represent the ground he reclines on.'

Thus Pope, no less than Burlington and Kent, could claim to have conceived and created the eighteenth-century *jardin anglais*. 'Our skill in gardening or rather laying out grounds,' wrote Thomas Gray in 1763, had become apparent less than forty years earlier; and Burlington by that time had largely reconstructed Chiswick, while Pope's Thames-side garden was already an accomplished work of art. A fellow enthusiast, of course, was Bathurst, whose operations at Cirencester Pope had first admired when he visited him in 1718. It was an 'immense design' that he had undertaken. Bathurst, indeed, had anticipated Pope's dream of remodelling an entire landscape, as he levelled slopes, scooped out amphitheatres, substituted plantations for meadows and corn-fields, and felled ancient groves and coverts to open up gigantic rides. While he improved the natural beauties of his park, he added interesting architectural 'baubles', among them the rusticated edifice today called 'Pope's Seat', a 'Silvan Bower' and a Gothic folly, named 'Alfred's Hall', in a glade where the Anglo-Saxon king, disguised as a musician, was said to have overheard the secrets of a Danish war-council. Bathurst's Broad Ride, which extends for six miles, is still the longest avenue in Great Britain. His achievement, however, was not merely large and grandiose; and something of the solemn splendour of the park, with its great grassy prospects cut through the thickness of the woods, and the artfully irregular alleyways that circulate between the main avenues, must have been due to Pope's directing influence.

As often as he visited Cirencester, he suggested numerous alterations, bidding his friend 'consult the genius of the place' and aim, whether he felled or planted, at a living arabesque of variegated light and shade. Bathurst took these criticisms good-humouredly; he was a particularly genial and good-natured man.* Whereas Burlington was cool, reserved and chaste – perhaps a trifle prim in aspect – Bathurst had the habits and temperament of a fashionable man of pleasure. In 1714 he had been one of the 'pretty young peers' who had helped to tuck up Bolingbroke with his latest young mistress; and, although since 1704 he had been happily married and had begun to found a large family, he remained, we are told, an adventurous lover and a prolific sire of natural children.† Unpunctuality and a strain of selfish inconstancy would appear to have been his worst faults; he was perpetually in search of new amusements, and soon grew tired of old diversions. But nothing could impair his extraordinary gift for friendship; and among the friends he cherished and assisted were some of the greatest writers of his age. Still robust, sanguine and pleasure-loving, he was to die at last in his ninety-second year, having accorded Laurence Sterne the same warm-hearted welcome that he had once bestowed on Swift and Pope and Gay.

His achievements at Cirencester dazzled and astonished Pope, but now and then left him slightly discontented with his 'own little *colifichies*', which, amid these huge prospects and 'noble scenes', he found that he 'despised, and totally forgot. . . .' By comparison, his property at Twickenham was indeed a small place – it covered only five acres; and its situation

* 'Bathurst was negative, a pleasing man', Johnson told Mrs Thrale in May, 1778. Boswell, *Life of Johnson*.

† In a letter to Lord Bathurst, tentatively dated 1725, Pope describes him as 'a patriarch of great eminence, for getting children, at home and abroad', and mentions his interest in 'strange women'. Bathurst had four legitimate sons and five daughters.

was somewhat unpromising; for the noisy and crowded London road ran immediately behind the house, and cut off the villa and its riverside lawn from the long and rather narrow garden. But beneath the road Pope decided to construct a romantic subterranean passage. The idea of this project annoyed Johnson; he considered it singularly 'frivolous and childish'. A grotto, he declared, was 'not often the wish or pleasure of an Englishman, who has more frequent need to solicit than exclude the sun; but Pope's excavation was requisite as an entrance to his garden, and, as some men try to be proud of their defects, he extracted an ornament from an inconvenience. . . .' An ornament it certainly became; of all the designs that he executed, none gave the poet so much pleasure; and on none did he spend so many months before it was built and decorated to his satisfaction. During the spring of 1722, Lady Mary reported that it already had 'a very good effect'; but Pope continued to enlarge and improve it until the summer of 1725, when he announced that he had 'put the last hand to my works of this kind, in happily finishing the subterraneous way and grotto', and described the beauties, both natural and artificial, of his impressive man-made cavern.

Exactly how it was constructed we cannot tell. But, a year after its builder's death, his gardener, John Serle, published a detailed plan of 'Mr Pope's Garden', which indicates that 'the under ground passage', besides cutting beneath 'the road from Hampton Court to London', slanted diagonally beneath the house. This is confirmed by the poet's own description; clearly, his chief object had been to unite the lawn before the house and the garden behind in a single comprehensive scheme. Pope employed a private waterman, the loquacious tosspot Bowry; and a new acquaintance, allowed to use his boat, would have seen the villa at its most imposing. It did not occupy a very secluded position; Lady Ferrers's domed summer-house stood up beyond the London road; and on either hand rose the gables and chimneys of a small, untidy village. Landing at the foot of a lawn flanked by terraces and hedges, the visitor would have approached a dignified but modest edifice, with a three-storeyed central block above a solid basement structure. In the basement, which gave the façade a curiously Venetian aspect, under the porticoed *piano nobile*, opened the jaws of a broad round-headed arch; and this, according to Serle's plan, was the riverside exit of the subterraneous passage, It provided a direct view, beneath the villa's foundations, to the Shell Temple in the distant garden – a view that especially delighted Pope, who was always fond of vivid, dramatic contrasts: 'From the river Thames,' he wrote, 'you see through my Arch up a walk of the wilderness to a kind of open temple, wholly composed of shells in the rustic manner'; while, from the Shell Temple, 'you look through a sloping arcade of trees, and see the sails on the river passing suddenly and vanishing, as through a perspective glass'. The effect was wonderfully strange and enlivening; and, in their own way, no less attractive and odd were the decorations of the famous grotto. Here Pope had constructed a private underworld, to set off the sunny prospect of lawns and sails and trees.

For its builder it had a two-fold charm; not only did it appeal to the more romantic and fantastic side of his literary imagination – whence had already sprung such poems as *Eloisa to Abelard* and the *Elegy to the Memory of an Unfortunate Lady*; but it satisfied the love of secrecy and mystery, of evasion, subterfuge and concealment, that was now deeply rooted in his private character. The grotto offered him a shadowy retreat from life; it was a place, observed Johnson, 'from which he endeavoured to persuade his friends and himself that cares and passions could be excluded'. At either end of the grotto, doors shut out the real world; but, since he did not wish to lose the vision entirely, he had found room for an ingenious optical device. Once the doors were closed, the gloomy cavern became 'on the instant . . . a *camera obscura*; on the walls of which all the objects of the river, hills, woods, and boats, are forming a moving picture in their visible radiations. . . .' When the doors were thrown open, however, 'it affords you a very different scene. . . .' A subterraneous way, tunnelled in damp soil, beneath a house and a road, might well have been somewhat cold and cheerless; and Pope had therefore encrusted the passage with a rough mosaic of luminous mineral bodies – Cornish diamonds, knobs of metallic ore, lumps of amethyst, spiky branches of coral, coloured Brazilian pebbles, crystals and quartzes, slabs of burnished flint, and rare and interesting 'fossile' specimens, amid a rich embroidery of rustic shell-work and scraps of looking-glass cut into angular designs.* On the roof shone a looking-glass star; and, dependent from the star, a single lamp – 'of an orbicular figure of thin alabaster' – cast around it 'a thousand pointed rays'. Every surface sparkled or shimmered or gleamed with a smooth sub-aqueous lustre; and, while these corruscating details enchanted the eye, a delicate water-music had been arranged to please the ear; the 'little

---

* See Pope's *Verses on a Grotto* . . . , 1740:
> Thou who shall stop, where *Thames'* translucent Wave
> Shines a broad Mirrour thro' the shadowy Cave;
> Where lingering Drops from Mineral Roofs distill,
> And pointed Crystals break the sparkling Rill,
> Unpolish'd Gemms no Ray on Pride bestow,
> And latent Metals innocently glow. . . .

dripping murmur' of an underground spring – discovered by the work-men during their excavations – echoed through the cavern day and night.*

Connected to the grotto, we learn, were 'two porches, with niches and seats; one toward the river, of smooth stones . . . the other towards the arch of trees, rough with shells, flints, and iron ore'; and no doubt it was behind the garden-porch that Pope had made his central sanctuary. Here he was visited by Lady Burlington. Among her other gifts, she was a clever draughtswoman, who often caricatured her husband's friends; and her sketch of Pope in his Grotto is a particularly bold and lively effort. With the help of dark washes and heavy pen-strokes, she gave the scene that she committed to her sketch-book a brooding, supernatural air. Framed by an arch of rugged masonry, the poet sits hunched over the antique tomb or altar that serves him as a writing-desk. From the groined roof hangs the 'orbicular' lamp, which sheds a dim, mysterious glow; and, behind his seat, daylight filters in along a narrow vaulted passage. As he crouches there, secluded and self-absorbed, Pope suggests a ghostly spider; while an owlet and a pair of strange insects flutter and beat their wings above his head. The effect is eminently 'Gothick' and romantic; Pope intended that his grotto should produce a sense of 'pleasing melancholy', and that the visitor, when at length he emerged, should feel that he had been re-born into a new existence. Horace Walpole, for one, thought that he had achieved his end, and much enjoyed the sudden contrast; 'the passing . . . from the grotto to the opening day', he declared, was 'managed with exquisite judgement', as was the layout of the garden beyond, with its 'retiring and again assembling shades', its dusky groves and its cypress-bordered walks.

True, the place, he thought, was almost absurdly small;† 'it was a little bit of ground of five acres', he told Sir Horace Mann, 'enclosed with three lanes and seeing nothing. Pope . . . twisted and twirled, and rhymed and harmonized this, till it appeared two or three sweet little lawns', one leading to another, 'and the whole surrounded with thick impenetrable

---

* See Garth's topographical poem *Claremont*, 1715:
      A Grott there was with hoary Moss o'ergrown,
      Rough with rude Shells, and arch'd with mouldring Stone.
      Sad silence reigns within the lonesomeWall;
      And weeping Rills but whisper as they fall.

† 'I am as busy in three inches of gardening, as any man can be in three-score acres. I fancy myself like the fellow that spent his life in cutting the twelve apostles in one cherry-stone. I have a theatre, an arcade, a bowling-green, a grove . . . in a bit of ground that would have been but a plate of sallet to Nebuchadnezzar, the first day he was turned out to graze. – Pope to Lord Strafford, 5 October 1725.

woods'.* In fact, the details of Pope's layout were considerably more ambitious. A straight walk ran through the Wilderness to the rustic Shell Temple; which was succeeded by a large mount and a symmetrical plantation named The Grove, followed by an extensive bowling green, two smaller mounts and an avenue of cypresses that stretched to the garden's shady end, where one day he would commemorate his mother by raising an impressive obelisk. The scheme also embraced a vineyard and an orangery, 'stoves' or hothouses, a kitchen-garden stocked with 'fenochio' and broccoli, and an adjoining Garden House. In the correct Burlingtonian style – Nature must be brushed and trimmed and embellished – Pope had added many urns and statues. The view of neighbouring cottages had, of course, been thickly planted out – hence Walpole's reference to 'impenetrable woods'; and the result was a contemporary *hortus conclusus*, all the more pleasing and reassuring because the scale was so diminutive. The Villa itself was by no means large – Walpole writes it off as 'small and bad'; but a 'Great Room', with parlours on either hand, extended across the main frontage; and its decorations, besides Lady Mary's portrait, included three huge pictures in *grisaille* of an Apollo, the Venus de Medici and the Farnese Hercules, a farewell gift from the artist, Sir Godfrey Kneller, which Pope eventually bequeathed to Lord Bathurst.†

Eighteenth-century men of taste showed a remarkably unselfish spirit. Between them there was a constant exchange of ideas – and not of ideas alone, but of more important and substantial offerings. Sometimes they would provide a friend with plans for a house; sometimes, with young trees to improve his prospect; sometimes they loaned him the services of a particularly skilful gardener. Pope was always generous with advice and help; and in 1724, now that his own projects were nearing completion, he became much concerned about the design of Mrs Howard's house at Marble Hill. Like Pope's villa, it was to be a place of refuge. Mrs Howard dreamed of retiring from the Prince of Wales's court, where her long servitude, as the Prince's mistress and his consort's Bedchamber Woman, had recently grown more and more oppressive. Neither of her employers had treated her well; she was a delicate, intelligent, thoughtful person, condemned to a life of sexual and social drudgery. The Prince did

---

* Horace Walpole to Mann, 20 June 1760. Walpole is writing of the disastrous changes effected by Sir William Stanhope, who had recently purchased the villa, and had 'hacked and hewed' Pope's sacred groves, and 'wriggled a winding gravel walk through them with an edging of shrubs, in what they call the modern taste. . . .'

† These pictures are still in the possession of the present Lord Bathurst, but now on loan to the Bristol Museum. See '*To Sir Godfrey Kneller, on his painting for me the statues of Apollo, Venus, and Hercules*', 1727.

not love her, though he regularly visited her – so regularly and punctually that he would walk up and down his chamber, watch in hand, until the hour had struck when he was accustomed to enjoy her embraces; but he cherished 'a silly idea', reports another courtier, that some display of domestic infidelity befitted a powerful royal personage, and that a prince without a *maîtresse en titre* had a very poor appearance; while his wife encouraged the relationship because she knew that she still retained his love, and that Mrs Howard – her 'good Howard', who handed her basins and combs, and accepted reproofs so quietly and patiently – had none of the qualifications of a genuine rival. Nor was the favourite dangerously young. Born in 1681, bereft at an early age of both her parents,* married in 1706 to Charles Howard, the spendthrift younger son of Lord Suffolk, in 1713, after bearing an only child, she had accompanied the drunken and quarrelsome Howard to the Hanoverian Court, at which they hoped they might ingratiate themselves with the future King of England. They had succeeded; Mrs Howard's qualities had made her 'extremely acceptable' to the aged Electress Sophia, mother of the prospective George I; and the Electress's grandson soon marked her out for conquest. On Queen Anne's death, the Howards returned home, closely following the new sovereign.

At first sight, it might have appeared a somewhat ignominious record; yet Mrs Howard, as all her contemporaries allow, was a woman of unusual dignity and charm. 'Good sense, good breeding and good nature,' admitted Lord Hervey, 'were qualities which even her enemies could not deny her. . . . She was civil to everybody, friendly to many, and unjust to none; in short, she had a good head and a good heart, but had to do with a man who was incapable of tasting the one or valuing the other. . . .' Among writers, she was devoted to Pope and Swift, and among connoisseurs to Lord Herbert,† the distinguished patrician architect whose achievement equalled that of Lord Burlington. Herbert was her adviser at Marble Hill, the small estate she had purchased near Richmond through another helpful friend, Lord Ilay. It had been bought with the profits of servitude, from a settlement of just over eleven thousand pounds, which the Prince, in some uncommonly generous mood, had bestowed on her a year earlier; and there she looked forward to establishing a private citadel of peace and harmony. Herbert was aided in his work by a professional architect, Roger Morris; but what Morris had been instructed to

* Her father, Sir Henry Hobart, of Blickling Hall, Norfolk, had been killed in a duel when his daughter was ten years old.

† In 1733 Lord Herbert was to become the ninth Earl of Pembroke. His masterpiece, of course, is the famous Palladian Bridge at Wilton.

supply was 'the naked carcass of a house'; and Herbert's function was to clothe its bare walls in the shining armour of Palladian grace. Pope, meanwhile, had promised to help with the gardens; 'my head,' he wrote in September, 1724, 'is still more upon Mrs Hd. and her works, than upon my own'. As for the house, Marble Hill, he reported during the course of the same letter, 'waits only for its roof – the rest is finished'. But a true Palladian enthusiast was hard to satisfy; and the structure had not been completed and approved until the summer months of 1729.*

Before it had reached this stage, Lord Bathurst had joined Mrs Howard's coterie of advisers, and had suggested how she should lay out her lawns. Marble Hill, like other Palladian houses, was planned, not so much as a separate, self-sufficient building with gardens draped around its feet, but as part of an aesthetic ensemble in which architect and gardener had collaborated to produce an all-embracing pattern. Grassy terraces sloped up from the banks of the Thames; and, since Nature invariably required embellishment, Bridgeman, whom Mrs Howard had also called in, had provided a decorative formal *parterre*.† Dark ilex trees, planted on either side, set off the clear-cut simplicity of Herbert's classic garden-front. The opposite frontage, which incorporated the main entry, though no less distinguished, was somewhat more elaborate, with Ionic pilasters supporting the pediment and a chastely rusticated central section. Its stuccoed walls had been painted a gleaming white;‡ and the roof, in the shape of a low pyramid, was surmounted by a golden globe. Seen from the river, the whole effect of the building is beautifully compact and trim; and, although Herbert had adapted a plan by Palladio, and intended to produce a miniature version of a sixteenth-century Italian villa, the design of Marble Hill is in perfect accord with its umbrageous English setting. Among Mrs Howard's greatest charms was her quiet, unassuming courtesy; and one of the most agreeable features of the house she built is its air of unobtrusive elegance.

She did not plan for elegance alone; the long years she had spent in draughty palaces had left her with a taste for comfort. Marble Hill must be sufficiently spacious to accommodate a few old friends, but so arranged

---

* Marble Hill, now under the care of the Greater London Council, was extensively restored in 1966. For a detailed description of the house, see James Lees-Milne, op. cit., and *Marble Hill House*, a booklet, abbreviated from a full-length monograph by Mrs Marie P. G. Draper, issued by the Greater London Council in 1966.

† In their final form, Mrs Draper has discovered, the gardens at Marble Hill included more than one grotto, presumably inspired by Pope's.

‡ The underlying structure was of brick; Morris had been a bricklayer before he became an architect.

that it was unlikely to attract a horde of careless, noisy visitors. A breakfast parlour, a dining parlour, a 'Paper Room' and a housekeeper's bed-chamber occupied the ground floor; and from the entrance hall ascended a fine staircase, built of the new-fangled wood mahogany.* On the first floor Mrs Howard had her Great Room, her bedroom and her dressing room, a Damask Room and a chamber afterwards reserved for her great-niece Miss Hotham. It was in the Great Room she would have received her guests – a splendid apartment that Herbert had created to recall Inigo Jones's famous Double and Single Cube Rooms at Wilton, all white-and-gold, with contemporary copies of Van Dyke portraits let into the moulded panelling, a sculptured chimneypiece and a lofty over-mantel, topped by a pair of golden cherubs. The furniture she had installed was particularly rich and various – marble tables, silver-gilt sconces, green and yellow damask chairs, India screens, Japan cabinets and fragile ivory pagodas. In the Great Room and in the adjacent bedroom, where Ionic columns guarded her bed, Mrs Howard had her private kingdom; a twisting iron stairway, behind a concealed door at the head of the main stairs, gave access to the rooms above. By comparison with her own apartments, they were by no means large; and it seems clear that Mrs Howard was not one of those insatiable hostesses who encourage lengthy visits.

Sometimes her enemies claimed that she had a cold, self-centred nature; and even Pope's attitude towards his valued friend was not entirely unprejudiced. In 1725 she was forty-four years old; and at no period of her existence had she ever been a beauty. But, if she failed to dazzle, she could always be sure of charming. Her body, we learn, was correctly propor-tioned; her expression, mild and pensive; and she had 'the finest light-brown hair'. Moreover, she was 'remarkably genteel', and dressed with the utmost 'taste and simplicity'. To these qualities did she add a heart? In Pope's verses Mrs Howard – Lady Suffolk, as she afterwards became – is portrayed under two different guises. His occasional poem *On a certain Lady at Court*, which concludes with a delicate allusion to the fact that she was now growing deaf, presents a serene, unshadowed picture:

> I know a thing that's most uncommon;
> (Envy be silent and attend!)
> I know a Reasonable Woman,
> Handsome and witty, yet a Friend.

* A supply of mahogany had been presented to Mrs Howard by the King, who had had it cut in the forests of Honduras and brought home on a naval vessel. At Marble Hill and Sir Robert Walpole's Houghton, it was used in England for the first time.

Not warp'd by Passion, aw'd by Rumour,
Not grave thro' Pride, or gay thro' Folly,
An equal Mixture of good Humour,
And sensible soft Melancholy.

'Has she no Faults then (Envy says) Sir?'
Yet she has one, I must aver:
When all the World conspires to praise her,
The Woman's deaf, and does not hear.

Among his *Epistles to Several Persons*, however, in the wonderful *Epistle to a Lady* which he addressed to Martha Blount, he throws a much more searching light on the problem of Mrs Howard's character. True, none of his savage vignettes seems to depict an individual woman – like a novelist, he built his portraits by taking a detail here and a detail there; but Mrs Howard undoubtedly contributed to his sketch of the impassive Cloe, decent, reasonable and well-conducted, yet frigid and innately selfish:

'With ev'ry pleasing, ev'ry prudent part,
'Say, what can Cloe want?' – she wants a Heart. . . .
Virtue she finds too painful an endeavour,
Content to dwell in Decencies for ever.
So very reasonable, so unmov'd,
As never yet to love, or to be lov'd.
She, while her Lover pants upon her breast,
Can mark the figures on an Indian chest;
And when she sees her Friend in deep despair,
Observes how much a chintz exceeds mohair. . . .
Would Cloe know if you're alive or dead?
She bids her Footman put it in her head.

The last couplet, Warton informs us, 'alludes to a particular circumstance'; at dinner with Mrs Howard, 'Pope heard her order her footman to put her in mind to send to know how Mrs Blount, who was ill, had passed the night'. This incident, though it no doubt suggests that she was often vague and self-absorbed, does not necessarily support the charge that she lacked all human feelings. Indeed, during her later life, she performed a singularly disinterested and generous action – by choosing as a second husband her decrepit old admirer, George Berkeley.

 **IO**

He must own, wrote Pope to Bolingbroke on 9 April 1724, that he had already arrived at 'an age which more awakens my diligence to live satisfactorily, than to write unsatisfactorily . . . more to consult my happiness than my fame; or (in defect of happiness) my quiet. . . . What you call a happy author is the unhappiest man. . . . To write well, lastingly well, immortally well, must not one leave Father and Mother and cleave unto the Muse? . . . 'Tis such a task as scarce leaves a man time to be a good neighbour, an useful friend, nay to plant a tree, much less to save his soul.' In Pope's mind there had always been this conflict between the rival demands of art and life; and, when he embarked on the *Odyssey* and Shakespeare, and told Caryll that he had 'given over scribbling', he may have thought that life had at last prevailed, and that he could now settle down, amid his duties and pleasures, to lead a calm and dignified existence. At the outset, his modest plan succeeded. Besides pushing forward with his work as a translator and a 'mere editor' – his *Odyssey* had begun to go to press by the end of February 1724; and, on 31 October, he could inform Broome that 'Shakespeare is finished', and that he had 'just written the preface' – he was able to plant and build, and advise his friends about their gardens, care for his mother, who again fell seriously ill, and undertake a romantic ramble, which extended far into the wilds of Dorset; where he visited Sherborne, the seat of the Digbys – a venerable Elizabethan house 'in a park, finely crowned with very high woods', full of prospects 'inexpressibly awful and solemn', surrounding the ivy-grown ramparts of a ruined keep.

Yet, only a few months later, all his hopeful schemes miscarried; just at the moment when, like Odysseus, he thought that he was reaching harbour, he found that he was obliged to set out upon another long and dangerous voyage. His edition of Shakespeare, published in March 1725, was followed in April by the first fourteen books of the *Odyssey*, the remaining books being held back until June 1726. But neither of these works received a particularly warm welcome; Pope's virtues by now were taken for granted; and critical journalists were delighted to observe that each had certain obvious defects. Thus, it was immediately clear that he should never have tried his hand at editing. Not that the hard-pressed poet had altogether shirked his task; he had advertised, we know, for early quartos, and had even considered holding a series of evening routs where his guests would be asked 'to collate the several editions of Shakespear's single plays . . .' But he was a poor scholar: 'to declare the truth', Johnson remarked, both Pope and his predecessor Nicholas Rowe were 'very ignorant of the ancient English literature. . . . The observation of faults and beauties is one of the duties of annotator'; and 'for this part of his task' – and for this alone – 'was Mr Pope eminently and indisputably qualified'. Much of the scholastic drudgery, indeed, he had been glad to leave to Elijah Fenton, who, having fallen behind with his Homeric assignment, seems to have been turned loose on Shakespeare.* Even Pope's preface, though an eloquent piece of writing, is much less graceful and impressive than his introduction to the *Iliad*.

As for the *Odyssey*, it was now well known that the translator had employed assistants; Broome, proud of his commission, had been talking far too freely; and, on 4 December 1724, Pope wrote him a reproachful letter, announcing that it was 'impossible I should do what you desire me, namely to proceed in the affair of Homer, as if there were no person concerned in it but myself'. Naturally, his critics took immediate advantage of this amusing piece of information. They alleged that he was both lazy and avaricious, and had employed 'hackney-hands' chiefly 'for the sake of idleness'. In fact, out of the twenty-four books of the *Odyssey*, Pope had himself translated twelve – the third, the fifth, the seventh, the ninth and tenth, the thirteenth to the fifteenth, the seventeenth, the twenty-first, the twenty-second, and the twenty-fourth; while Broome had handled the second, sixth, eighth, eleventh, twelfth, sixteenth, eighteenth and twenty-third; and Fenton had dealt with the remaining four. But Pope had corrected and 'inspirited' the whole, as the manuscripts were delivered to him; and he could justly claim that he had left his imprint on every detail of the whole production. It would be rewarding to know the method by which he had divided up the work – why Pope, for example, though he himself took Homer's descriptions of Ulysses at

---

* Another assistant was Gay, who received £35 17s. 6d. for his services; while the publishers, at Pope's request, paid out various sums to 'a man or two . . . at Oxford to ease me of part of the drudgery. . . .'

the court of Alcinoüs and of his adventures with the Lotos-Eaters and the Cyclops, allocated to Broome such highly poetic episodes as the hero's descent into the Underworld and his meeting with Nausicaa. Perhaps the sacrifice was reluctant, made because he wanted time; already, in September, 1724, he had told Broome that it was 'scarely credible how fast the press plies me'. More understandably, he was delighted that Broome should provide the annotations.

'The shares of the three colleagues,' wrote a Victorian biographer, are 'not to be easily distinguished by internal evidence.' Pope was a patient director; and both Broome and Fenton – particularly Broome – soon learned to turn out heroic couplets in the great man's mood and style. But the general effect of this collaboration was inevitably deleterious; Pope could not hope to raise his colleagues to his own exalted level; and their assistance had a slightly lowering effect on the standards that he himself adopted. Beside his *Iliad*, his translation of the *Odyssey* is a comparatively pedestrian work. The more various and lively of the two Greek poems, in Pope's version it re-appears as the less inspiring and the less dramatic. The postscript that he attached to his last volume suggests that he had always preferred the *Iliad*. 'The *Odyssey*,' he wrote, 'is a perpetual source of poetry'; but it resembled a broad, gentle stream that, after 'foaming and thundering . . . from rocks and precipices', flows 'through peaceful vales and agreeable scenes of pasturage'. Unlike the genius that Homer showed in the *Iliad*, it no longer 'strikes, amazes and fills the mind'. And then, in the *Odyssey*, 'Homer seems to have taken upon him the character of an historian, antiquary, divine, and professor of arts and sciences, as well as a poet. In one or other of these characters he descends into many particulars, which as a poet only perhaps he would have avoided. All those ought to be preserved by a faithful translator . . . and all that can be expected from him is to make them as poetical as the subject will bear.'

The more primitive aspects, the 'plainer parts', of the *Odyssey*, Pope evidently found embarrassing; and many of Homer's vivid rustic images – for example, the comparison, with which the last book opens, of the Suitors' ghosts to clustered bats that stir and squeak in the roof of a dusky cave – defeat all the translator's attempts to 'dignify and solemnize them'. Still, he tried his hardest; and 'some use', he explained, 'has been made to this end of the style of Milton. A just and moderate mixture of old words may have an effect like the working old abbey stones into a building, which I have sometimes seen to give a kind of venerable air, and yet not destroy the neatness, elegance, and equality requisite to a new work. . . .'

He had taken great pains to be 'easy and natural'. But Pope's ideas of ease and naturalness are not those of a modern reader; and often the effect he produces is almost as formal and static as one of John Flaxman's early-nineteenth-century illustrations. At this best, he had recreated the *Iliad*; he was content merely to reflect the *Odyssey*; there was no secret correspondence, we feel, between the translator and the ancient poet. Only now and then does he strike out a splendid line. Thus, in the fifth book, where Ulysses, we are told, has lost all his passion for Calypso and yearns to make his way home:

> Absent he lay in her desiring arms . . .

And where the demoralized chieftains are summoned to attend a council:

> Sour with debauch, a reeling tribe they came.

Or when the Suitors prepare to defend their lives;

> All arm, and sudden round the hall appears
> A blaze of bucklers, and a wood of spears.

Again Pope shows his gift of compressing emotion into a single noun or adjective.

Certain extended passages, too, were obviously composed with keen enjoyment. As a horticulturalist, Pope was at home in the legendary garden of Alcinoüs:

> Close to the gates a spacious Garden lies,
> From storms defended and inclement skies.
> Four acres was th'alloted space of ground,
> Fenc'd with a green enclosure all around,
> Tall thriving trees confess'd the fruitful mould;
> The red'ning apple ripens here to gold.
> Here the blue fig with luscious juice o'erflows,
> With deeper red the full pomegranate glows,
> The branch here bends beneath the weighty pear,
> And verdant olives flourish round the year.

He was also – himself a way-worn traveller – deeply moved by his contemplation of the hero's weariness and solitude; and Ulysses' return to his native island, which at first he does not recognize, provokes two carefully balanced and exquisitely melodious couplets:

> Now all the land another prospect bore,
> Another port appear'd, another shore.
> And long-continu'd ways, and winding floods,
> And unknown mountains, crown'd with unknown woods.

Here Pope, as he had sometimes done in the *Iliad*, applies to the original text a much more modern form of sensibility. Ulysses' disappointment, as Homer describes it, has been caused by the goddess Athena's clever stratagem* – the mist she has spread around the sleeping hero disguises the familiar Ithacan landscape; Pope's verses hint at the essential loneliness of life, and at the great gulf that separates Man from an unthinking and unfriendly universe.

When the first instalment of his work emerged in 1725, Pope may have felt more than ever inclined to sympathize with the misfortunes of Ulysses. Critics descended on him like a tribe of Laestrygonians; and during July *The London Journal* printed a letter signed 'Homerides', in which he and his publisher Lintot were accused of perpetrating a scandalous literary fraud. 'We have frequently heard,' wrote the contributor, 'of celebrated poets, who have published their light unfinished pieces under some subordinate name. . . . But I thought the natural pride of a good author would not suffer him, upon any account, to father the works of one less famous than himself; and for that reason I thought we were safe from any such imposition. But if once avarice gets the better of pride . . . we may live to see the most eminent writers keep half-a-dozen journeymen apiece. . . .' Other 'railing papers about the *Odyssey*' must at the time have been added to the large collection of abusive articles and pamphlets, all directed against his work or character, that he had put aside and presently had bound up, with the inscription, 'Behold my desire is that mine adversary had written a book', in a series of four impressive volumes. His collaborators, too, received some harsh treatment; and on 20 November 1725, Fenton wrote to Broome, lamenting that 'we have been but coarsely used this last summer, both in print and conversation'. Meanwhile Pope's dream of a tranquil well-ordered existence had dissolved and disappeared. The later books of the *Odyssey* had still to be got through. 'My cares are grown upon me,' he told Broome, 'and I want relaxation. But when shall I have it? Hurry, noise, and the observances of the world, take away the power of just thinking or natural acting.' Even his beloved house and garden had ceased to be a place of refuge; and, for the next few weeks, he considered retiring into Buckinghamshire – probably his goal was to be Lord Cobham's Stowe – in search of the peace and quiet that eluded him so long as he remained at Twickenham.

The year 1725, however, provided one invaluable consolation; that

* 'As a result everything in Ithaca, the long hill-paths, the quiet bays, the beetling rocks, and the green trees seemed unfamiliar to the King.' *The Odyssey*, translated by E. V. Rieu, 1946.

spring, after a decade of exile, Bolingbroke returned from France. For some time, through the agency of his second wife, a clever and attractive Frenchwoman, he had been remitting large bribes to the sovereign's mistress, the aged Duchess of Kendal, as Countess Schulenburg was now styled; and in 1723 he had felt sufficiently secure to pay his English friends a brief visit. In 1725, his position was guaranteed; thanks to the Duchess of Kendal's secret influence and Lady Bolingbroke's judicious lobbying, a Bill was passed that confirmed his pardon and restored his private property. But Sir Robert Walpole, who, much against his better judgement, had agreed to push the Bill through, insisted that, on no account, should Lord Bolingbroke be allowed to resume his place among his peers; and once more he found that he had achieved his aim, yet, as he did so, missed his real objective. 'Here I am', he told Swift, 'two thirds restored . . . but the attainder is kept carefully and prudently in force.' He was safe, but almost impotent; and power, to Bolingbroke's taste, was the keenest and noblest of human joys. Since he left England, he had struggled hard to regain it; and, although when he first arrived in Paris, he had endeavoured to play a double game – and had made simultaneous advances to the British Ambassador and the Jacobite leader, the Duke of Berwick – he had soon definitely transferred his allegiance to the Pretender's petty court at Saint-Germain, where James had accorded him a gracious welcome and appointed him his Secretary of State. In that rôle, Bolingbroke had helped to organize the Jacobite invasion, and displayed his usual skill and energy. But the failure of the assault on England was soon followed by his own downfall. James's Scottish courtiers detested him; it was alleged that, while he was in his cups, he had spoken disrespectfully about the exiled sovereign; and the death of Louis xiv – 'the best friend the Chevalier ever had' – helped to convince him that the Jacobite cause was hopeless. He had then retired into private life, and begun to amuse himself, at a secluded country house, with various gardening and building projects.

His companion there was a new mistress, Marie Clare Descamps de Marcilly, marquise de Villette, a seductive and experienced personage whom he had met in 1716. At the time, she was forty-one, three years older than Bolingbroke; but she possessed all the hard-wearing charm that often distinguishes the women of her race, together with a pretty neck, an elegantly decided nose and a beguiling air, which she retained to the end, of sensuous gaiety and good humour. As a school-girl actress performing in Racine's *Esther*, she had been applauded by the King himself; and at Saint-Cyr she had also attracted the attention of an elderly but engaging marquis, who had taken her from the convent to become his wife. Monsieur de Villette had died before she was thirty-three, leaving her a large fortune. When she met Bolingbroke, she occupied a pleasant little *hôtel* in the Faubourg Saint-Germain, where she held court, like other ladies of her kind, among attentive men of fashion and admiring men of letters.

Almost immediately Bolingbroke made her conquest; and they had set up house together at the Château de Marcilly, a dilapidated medieval fortress, but presently removed to the Château de la Source, a comparatively modern building, long and low and dignified, surrounded by a huge park, in the flat, sandy country just outside Orléans. Close to the château emerge the springs of the Loiret, a romantic offshoot of the Loire, which Bolingbroke described to Swift as 'the biggest and clearest stream perhaps in Europe'. Having leapt from the underworld to fill a deep basin, over twenty feet broad, and run, strong and smooth, beneath his windows, it formed, he wrote, 'a more beautiful river than any which flows in Greek or Latin verse'.* Above the fountain-head he hastened to build a temple and place the statue of a river god. But he added an elegant Latin inscription, chastely commemorating his own virtues, describing how he had been obliged to leave his country 'by the frenzies of an outrageous faction', recalling 'his unstained fidelity to his queen', and his strenuous efforts to establish peace in Europe. Before he deserted La Source, both the house and its gardens had been liberally strewn with such commemorative tablets.

Another distraction was receiving visitors; and among those who wished to pay him homage came, in 1721, the young poet, Arouet de Voltaire, author of the *Henriade*. Bolingbroke praised that somewhat indigestible epic; and Voltaire was surprised and delighted by Bolingbroke's mastery of the French language, which he spoke '*avec plus d'energie et de justice*' than any foreigner whom Voltaire had yet encountered. '*J'ai trouvé dans cet illustre anglais*,' he declared, '*toute l'erudition de son pays en toute la politesse du nôtre. Cet homme, qui a passé toute sa vie dans les plaisirs et dans les affaires, a trouvé pourtant le moyen de tout apprendre et de tout retenir.*' Not only did he know the history of the ancient Egyptians as well as he knew that of England; but he was equally conversant with Virgil and Milton, and appeared to love every form of poetic literature, English,

* After many years of neglect, the estate was recently purchased by the City of Orléans and has now been divided up between a new university (not yet completed), a new housing development and a particularly hideous 'Floral Park'. The source of the Loiret is today the starting-point of a noisy model railway; and all Bolingbroke's works have long since vanished. The Loiret is, in fact, not a tributary of the Loire, but an offshoot, which suddenly plunges underground and then rejoins its parent river.

20 Jonathan Swift; bust by Roubiliac in Trinity College, Dublin.

CARMINA, PICTURAS, ET DÆDALA SIGNA

JOSEPH SPENCE

21 Joseph Spence 'the sweetest tempered gentleman breathing'; an engraving by Vertue.

Italian or French. When Bolingbroke had set his mind on pleasing, none could do it more efficiently. He was now much concerned to present to the world an advantageous personal image; and, soon after Voltaire's visit, he further adorned his image by marrying his faithful mistress. His neglected and ill-used first wife, Frances, had died in October 1718; in May 1722, at a Protestant ceremony – Madame de Maintenon's old *pensionnaire* had renounced her former faith – the marquise de Villette was duly recognized as Lady Bolingbroke.

His new respectability caused him considerable pleasure. He was nowadays, he informed Swift in August 1723, far less irregular and dissipated 'than when you knew me and cared for me; that love which I used to scatter with some profusion, among the whole female kind, has been these many years devoted to one object'. He pretended, moreover, that since his retirement he had completely given up ambition; 'the hoarse voice of Party was never heard in this quiet place; gazettes and pamphlets are banished from it. . . .' Alas, in winter, the surroundings of La Source were apt to be somewhat damp and gloomy, drenched by heavy rain-falls and swept by icy north-east winds. Bouts of colic plagued Lady Bolingbroke; despite her natural gaiety, she suffered moments of acute depression. There were dull evenings, passed beside the fire, and dark mornings, as when the exile, whose temper had never been good, complained furiously of the detestable cook to whom some foolish neighbour had presumed to give a reference: 'his sauces are so black, so thick and so bitter' – while his soups and *entremêts* smelt of burnt grease – that 'my friend Devaux must have a very bad opinion of our style of living if he thinks this slovenly cook can satisfy me'. In short, Bolingbroke continued to long for England – for English dinner-parties and English intrigue and the endlessly fascinating world of high politics. Lady Bolingbroke, a true Frenchwoman, had made her husband's interests her own; and, having first established a link with the sovereign's favourite, she even dared a Channel crossing. Arrived in London, she canvassed ministers and courtiers and did her best to charm the King. George grumbled that the lady was far too talkative; but during the early months of 1725 Bolingbroke obtained his pardon.

That April the pair returned; and Bolingbroke's political hopes were disappointed. The King agreed to grant him an audience; and he seized the opportunity of launching a fierce attack against Sir Robert Walpole. But the King, who trusted Walpole, had been taught to regard Bolingbroke as an accomplished villain; and his attitude throughout the tirade was singularly unresponsive. Again Bolingbroke knew that he had failed; again he was obliged to retire to the country; and on this occasion he acquired an estate in Middlesex, not many miles from Pope's villa, near the little market-town of Uxbridge. Dawley was a large and noble house, a red-brick block encompassed by formal gardens, built some twenty or thirty years earlier. But Bolingbroke called it his 'Farm', and did everything he could to give it an appropriately rustic air; in 1728, for example, he would commission an artist to embellish his hall 'with trophies of rakes, spades, prongs', and other homely agricultural implements, and add the kind of inscription he favoured, extolling the beauties of a country life. Here he remained until 1734 – an English Coriolanus rather sketchily disguised as Cincinnatus; and from Dawley he poured out a flood of advice to his political and literary friends. Pope was an especially favoured friend; some time before Bolingbroke left France, he had become concerned about the poet's prospects; and the letter in which Pope declared that he felt nowadays more anxious 'to live satisfactorily, than to write unsatisfactorily', answered a letter from Bolingbroke, dated 18 February 1724, that had contained a particularly strenuous reproof.'. . . Sure I am,' he had declared, 'that you must not look on your translations of Homer as the great work of your life. You owe a great deal more to your self, to your country, to the present age, and to posterity. Prelude with translations if you please, but after translating what was writ three thousand years ago, it is incumbent upon you that you write, because you are able to write, what will deserve to be translated three thousand years hence into languages as yet perhaps unformed.'

This sound advice he immediately followed up by countering a possible objection. Why, the poet might ask, should he 'write for fame in a living language which changes every year, and which is hardly known beyond the bounds of our island?' . . . Certainly, the English language was still in a period of flux. But 'continue to write, and you'll contribute to fix it', just as Virgil had helped to fix Latin, and as Homer – writing 'for a parcel of little states who composed in his days a nation much inferior every way to what our nation is in yours' – established the groundwork of a great poetic style. Pope must agree that his own theatre was 'vastly more considerable than that of Hesiod and Homer', and that he could cherish 'much more reasonable hopes than they could entertain of immortality'. Bolingbroke's admonitions, conveyed in a message that runs to well over two thousand words, throw a vivid light upon his character; they illustrate his learning and wit and his extensive range of intellectual interests; but, at the same time, they reveal his long-windedness, his love of parading his accumulated erudition, his self-importance and his vanity. Every opinion Bolingbroke arrived at he felt obliged to proclaim with solemn eloquence.

Once an agnostic, he informed Pope, he had now accepted Deism. He professed no definite system of philosophy; for he knew of none that had not been pushed to unreasonable and unnatural lengths. Yet, 'far from despising the world, I admire the work, and I adore the Author. . . .' When Pope composed his *Essay on Man*, he was to dovetail into the structure of the poem many of his friend's theories.

There the magnetic influence that Bolingbroke exerted was not entirely beneficial. But it was his character, rather than his ideas, that really stimulated Pope's imagination; and his return to England in the spring of 1725 had been peculiarly well-timed. By the autumn of the year Bolingbroke's advice and encouragement had already begun to bear fruit. Pope was drawing up new poetic plans; and in September he wrote to Swift to congratulate him on his 'Travels' – the story of Gulliver's voyages, of which he had lately heard reports – adding: 'my own, I promise you, shall never more be in a strange land, but a diligent, I hope useful, investigation of my own territories. I mean, no more translations, but something domestic, fit for my own country, and for my own time.' These plans, however, he could not execute until he had finally written off the *Odyssey*. Meanwhile he had to contend against a series of irritating domestic problems.

One such problem involved a family shrine. His old acquaintance Sir Godfrey Kneller had died in 1723; and the widowed Lady Kneller, a large, masterful, aggressive woman, now proposed to embellish Twickenham Church with a suitably imposing monument. She herself, sculptured on a life-size scale, was to stand beside her husband; and she wished to make room for them by dislodging the elder Pope's monument, 'in which', he told Lord Harcourt, 'my mother also is to lie'. The poet, she alleged, during the course of his last visit to poor Sir Godfrey, had undertaken to resign the place – an allegation he firmly denied; 'the utmost I said . . . was merely not to disturb a dying man'. Lady Kneller then petitioned the Ecclesiastical Courts, where she eventually lost her suit. For Pope it had been a painful and troublesome business; and, apart from consulting Lord Harcourt, he was obliged to canvas Lord Strafford, whose wife and children occupied a pew just beneath the Pope memorial: 'If your Lordship,' he wrote, 'should really chance to take no great pleasure in beholding my name full before your eyes . . . yet at least (dangerous as that name is, and dreadful to all true Protestant ears) it cannot incommode you so much as a vast three-hundred-pound-pile, projecting out upon you, overshadowing my Lady Strafford with the immense draperies and stone petticoats of Lady Kneller, and perhaps crushing to pieces your Lordship's posterity!' He had been assured, he said, that the weight of the proposed monument was likely to bring the church-wall down in ruins.

Another imbroglio – no doubt, equally painful – affected his relationship with Martha Blount. She and her sister continued to live in London, at their mother's house in Bolton Street; for although their mode of existence was gay and gregarious, and they had always frequented the 'best company', neither of them had yet married. His beloved Patty was now thirty-five, by eighteenth-century standards a middle-aged woman. Teresa, of course, was two years older; and, whereas Patty remained good-natured and equable – the summery sweetness of her disposition still shone from radiant blue eyes – Teresa, always the more passionate, was becoming cross and violent; and it was said that, during domestic quarrels, she frequently ill-used their mother. Their friend the poet often visited them – but less often than in days gone by; perhaps his well-known attachment to Lady Mary had temporarily overcast the old affection. The exact nature of that affection – both before he encountered Lady Mary and after he had bidden her farewell – has never ceased to puzzle Pope's admirers. Many of his contemporaries believed that Patty Blount was either his mistress or his unacknowledged wife. She was charming and apparently disengaged; he was famous, reputed to be rich, and made up in gallant assiduity what he lacked in strength and size; he had written her a long series of letters and sent her amusingly improper verses.

To support this conclusion, however, we have very little solid evidence. Pope was strongly attracted towards women, liked sharing their interests and secrets, and enjoyed breathing the heady atmosphere of the self-centred world in which they lived. At one period of his existence, he had professed a romantic cult for both the Blounts; and it is possible that, as his devotion shifted, he had confided to Teresa (who selfishly betrayed his confidence) that he sometimes dreamed of marrying Patty. But he did not persist; the vision, if it took definite form, must have very soon evaporated; and not only for Patty's sake but for his own – so incongruous a match would have delighted his enemies; and, above all else, he dreaded ridicule – he may have considered that their relations had best remain on the safe and dignified footing of an *amitié amoureuse*. Nor, in the circumstances, does it seem probable that he could, at any stage, have been her lover. Her closest friends were also his friends; and those friends, as we shall see, were watchful moralists. Pope was no Lovelace; his libertinism was of the mind and heart. Finally, his affection for Martha had a domestic, as well as a passionate and romantic colouring. They had grown up together in the Forest; she belonged to the landscape of his happy childhood.

Thus he was deeply offended by the scandalous reports that reached him late in 1725. He had known, of course, that London gossips had, now and then, married him off to Martha Blount or had talked of their engagement; and he had done his best to scotch these ridiculous stories; while Martha herself had asserted, firmly enough, that 'no such thing could ever happen'. The present rumours were far more damaging; and, with a degree of indignation that suggests he was completely sincere, he wrote on 25 December to John Caryll. Having mentioned 'the railing papers about the *Odyssey*' that had not seriously disturbed his peace, he spoke of a worse attack – 'one that concerns my morals, and . . . the good character of another person', in whom both he and Caryll had a tender interest:

A very confident asseveration has been made, which has spread over the town, that your god-daughter Miss Patty and I lived 2 or 3 years since in a manner that was reported to you as giving scandal to many: that upon your writing to me . . . I consulted with her, and sent you an excusive alleviating answer; but did after that privately and of myself write to you a full confession; how much I myself disapproved the way of life, and owning the prejudice done her, charging it on herself, and declaring that I wished to break off what I acted against my conscience, &c; and that she, being at the same time spoken to by a lady of your acquaintance, at your instigation, did absolutely deny to alter any part of her conduct, were it ever so disreputable or exceptionable. Upon this villainous lying tale, it is farther added . . . that I brought her acquainted with a noble lord, and into an intimacy with some others, merely to get quit of her myself, being moved in consciousness by what you and I had conferred together, and playing this base part to get off.

From Pope's letter (of which a fragment is quoted above), it would appear that he had had some earlier correspondence with Caryll on the subject of the injured woman, and that his candid replies had completely satisfied his friend; while Mrs Caryll – the 'lady of your acquaintance' – had 'also expressed the same thing to her kinswoman'. Mrs Caryll had evidently approached Martha; and Martha's reponse had set her mind at rest; for a letter survives in which she warmly acknowledges her thankfulness. She had, she admits, heard 'a good deal of what the pratting part of the world had babbled out'; and she had 'never given any more ear to it than to the wind', until 'I found my own dear took something to heart, in good earnest, that related to the two . . . he heartily loves, and wishes so well to. . . .' The fact that, so far as the good-natured Carylls were concerned, the whole upsetting business had been satisfactorily cleared up made the revival of these malicious stories particularly hard to bear; and no less unpleasant tales had filtered down through the 'polite world' into the underworld of London journalism. There, in 1724, a notorious gossip-writer, Eliza Haywood, had published a catch-penny *roman-à-clef*, describing the adventures of a certain Marthalia (identified as 'Mrs Bl—t') and her paramour, the necromancer Lucitario, supposed to represent that rakish politician James Craggs.

We cannot tell whence these spiteful legends arose. Was James Craggs one of the deleterious acquaintances to whom the gossips alleged that she had been purposely introduced by Pope? But, as an unmarried woman, living among beaus and wits, Martha occupied an extremely vulnerable position; and Eliza Haywood's attack would seem to suggest that her behaviour had been at least imprudent. Some of the criticisms she incurred had came, we are told, from members of her own family. Her god-father, on the other hand, was convinced that she had been grossly wronged; she herself displayed exemplary courage – 'she keeps all in silence', wrote Pope to Caryll, 'and suffers, not opening her lips'; and after a time the scandal died down. Pope, however, had a very long memory; and Mrs Haywood and her kind would receive suitable punishment in the burning pages of *Dunciad*.

Pope's determination to launch a full-scale campaign against the monstrous confraternity of Dunces, though the original idea may have dated back as far as the early meetings of the Scriblerus Club, was certainly strengthened by his unhappy experiences during the years 1724 and 1725; and when Swift, his fellow Scriblerian, returned from Ireland, the project became more and more attractive. After his ten years of Boeotian exile, the Dean had shaken off his 'scurvy sleep'; and, even before he appeared, his letters to his English friends were beginning to rumble with impatient energy. Like Pope, he was now full of 'grand designs' – so full, he wrote in July 1725, that 'I believe I shall never bring them to pass. . . .' But these doubts were very soon overcome; and, at the close of September, he was able to report that he had just been engaged 'in finishing, correcting, amending and transcribing my Travels'; which were 'intended for the press when the world shall deserve them, or rather when a printer shall be found brave enough to venture his ears. . . .' He, too, had been exceedingly pleased to learn that Pope was now 'done with translations. Lord Treasurer Oxford* often lamented that a rascally world should lay you under a necessity of misemploying your genius for so long a time.' As to his private schemes, 'the chief end I propose to myself in all my labours is to vex the world rather than divert it. . . . I have ever hated all nations, professions

---

* The first Earl of Oxford, Bolingbroke's colleague and Queen Anne's Lord Treasurer, had died in 1724. His son, the second Earl (1689–1741), also became the poet's friend.

and communities; and all my love is towards individuals. . . . Principally I hate and detest that animal called Man, although I heartily love John, Peter, Thomas and so forth. . . . Upon this great foundation of misanthropy . . . the whole building of my Travels is erected.'

Swift had thrown out hints that he thought of revisiting England late in 1725; not until mid-March 1726 did he finally reach English shores. Having arrived, one of the first expeditions he undertook was to stay with Pope at Twickenham, where he remained for several weeks. But he found time to visit Bolingbroke at his 'Farm' and, accompanied by Pope, called on Oxford and Bathurst at their respective country houses; while, in London, Dr. Arbuthnot 'took him a course thro' the town' and he saw 'Lord Chesterfield, Mr Pulteney, &c', and Peterborough and Harcourt even proposed 'to carry him to Sir R. Walpole', the political epitome of all that he and Pope detested. Through Arbuthnot, he received overtures from that gifted woman the Princess of Wales, who, as Swift afterwards asserted, was so anxious to make his acquaintance that she had sent him ten or eleven invitations before he would agree to cross her threshold. In the Princess's rooms, he encountered the celebrated Wild Boy – the strange and pathetic being lately brought over from Germany, where he had been discovered in the depths of a forest near Hanover, running on all fours and eating grass and roots among the other sylvan creatures. Peter the Wild Boy was a scientific curiosity of the kind that eighteenth-century enquirers relished. His arrival, wrote Swift to Tickell on 16 April, 'hath been the subject of half our talk this fortnight. He is in the keeping of Dr Arbuthnot, but the King and Court were so entertained with him, that the Princess could not get him till now. I can hardly think him wild in the sense they report him.' Under Dr Arbuthnot's learned guidance, 'the ablest masters' were engaged to teach him how to speak and write; meanwhile, looking, we are told, 'extremely uneasy' in a new blue suit and smart red stockings, he ran the gauntlet of the Princess's friends. But, when all efforts to civilize him failed, his well-wishers lost hope and interest. A 'comfortable provision' was then made for him, and he was settled at a Hertfordshire farmhouse, 'where he continued to the end of his inoffensive life', dying a bearded patriarch in February, 1785.*

Now that she had seen a German wild boy, Swift had remarked on being presented to the Princess, he supposed that she was anxious to see

---

* Peter's tomb stands opposite the south door of St Mary's Church, Northchurch. Just inside the door is a brass tablet, with a small engraved portrait and an inscription, from which some extracts are printed above, recording his death on 22 February 1785, when he was 'supposed to be aged 72'.

a wild Irish dean; and Caroline, who did not dislike a joke, would appear to have received him in her easiest, most ingratiating manner. Perhaps he hoped she might become his ally – she was already well-known as the patroness of learned men; but no such hopes were ever realized. Similarly agreeable and equally disappointing was his reception by Sir Robert Walpole. Provided Walpole would change his views on Ireland, Swift was ready to forgive his past offences; and then, with the Minister behind him, he might be translated, if not to a noble bishopric, at least to a well-found English deanery, far from 'wretched Dublin, in miserable Ireland', where he had spent so many years of self-destructive solitude. But, although Walpole proved an amiable listener, on the subject of Irish government, and on the economic restrictions required to keep the Irish in their proper places, his keen opportunist mind had long ago been made up. Thus Swift's eagerly awaited visit brought him little real advantage; and he was to leave England, as he had arrived, a grimly disappointed man. Only his friends provided some measure of comfort – Pope, Bolingbroke, Arbuthnot, Gay and the always charming and beguiling Mrs Howard. Pope was an especially attentive friend. He had spent the last two months, Swift reported to Tickell on 7 July, 'for the most part in the country, either at Twitenham with Mr Pope, or rambling with him and Mr Gay for a fortnight together. Yesterday My Lord Bolingbroke and Mr Congreve made up five at dinner. . . .' Pope was careful to arrange amusements that, he felt, would suit the Dean's tastes; 'and Mr Gay and I', Swift told Lord Oxford, 'find ourselves often engaged for three or four days to come . . . Accordingly this morning we go to Lord Bathurst; on Tuesday company is to dine here. However, I will certainly attend your Lordship towards the end of the week.'

Swift's letter to Tickell concludes with a reference to his Irish background: 'I find the Ladies make the Deanery their Villa'; and he had learned, at the same time, 'that Mrs Johnson's health has given her friends bad apprehensions. . . .' The ladies, of course, were Esther Johnson and her companion, Rebecca Dingley, joint recipients of the extraordinary *Journal to Stella* that he had kept for their benefit between August 1710 and June 1713. Just as Pope's contemporaries sometimes assumed that he had secretly married Patty Blount, several of Swift's intimates believed that, in 1716, he had contracted a secret alliance with Esther Johnson, thereby breaking the heart of Hester Vanhomrigh, the gifted ill-fated 'Vanessa', who had played Héloise to Swift's reluctant Abelard since their meeting nine years earlier. Though the details of his friendship with Stella remain obscure, it certainly dominated Swift's existence; it was the fixed point round which his emotions revolved through endless vicissitudes of love and liking, while he teased her, bullied her, instructed her, seemed to draw her into a loverly or fatherly embrace and then summarily thrust her off, bidding her sharply 'Drink your coffee', or calling her 'slut', 'quean', 'huzzy' or 'agreeable bitch'. Vanessa had died in 1723; and, on the eve of Swift's departure for England, *Cadenus and Vanessa*, his poetic account of their frustrated passion, had been surreptitiously published and distributed by a Dublin bookseller.* To Stella's feminine pride it was a deeply wounding blow; the brilliant Vanessa had always aroused her jealousy; and the condition of her health now made her doubly sensitive. Swift believed that she must very soon die. Her lungs, he well knew, were riddled with tuberculosis.

Among the various reasons that had brought him over from Ireland was his fear of attending Stella's death-bed. He did not seek to excuse his own cowardice; but, his state of mind being what it was, he could not, would not watch her die. He had arranged, however, that their friends should keep him informed; and in July, while he was settling down as best he could among a round of English pleasures, he received reports from a pair of helpful clergymen, Thomas Sheridan and John Worrall. To Worrall, whose report was the more alarming, he replied, on the 15th, that 'what you tell me of Mrs Johnson I have long expected with great oppression and heaviness of heart. We have been perfect friends these 35 years. Upon my advice they both came to Ireland and have been ever since my constant companions. . . .' Stella he had 'esteemed upon the score of every good quality that can possibly recommend a human creature;' and her death would leave him desolate; but 'I would not for the universe be present at such a trial as seeing her depart. . . . Pray write to me every week, that I may know what steps to take, for I am determined not to go to Ireland to find her just dead or dying. . . . Let her know that I have bought her a good repeating watch for her ease in winter nights. I designed to have surprised her with it, but now I would have her know it, that she may see how my thoughts were always to keep her easy.'

Sometimes he revolted against his servitude to an attachment that could only end in sorrow. He believed, he said, 'that there is not a greater folly than to contract too great and intimate a friendship'; and, to another correspondent: 'I think that there is not a greater folly than that of entering into too strict and particular a friendship, with the loss of which a man

* 'The thing you mention which no friend would publish was written fourteen years ago at Windsor, and shows how indiscreet it is to leave anyone master of what cannot without the least consequence be shewn to the world.' Swift to Tickell, 7 July 1726.

must be absolutely miserable. . . . Besides, this was a person of my own rearing and instructing, from childhood, who excelled in every good quality. . . .' Swift had a naturally reticent spirit; and it seems doubtful whether, even to Pope, he had yet told the story of his fears and griefs. Yet, had he broken his silence, no one would have heard him out more readily or counselled him more sympathetically. As imaginative writers, Swift and Pope were men of very different genius – Swift, a nihilist, whose hatred of the human brute implied a complete rejection of the existing social system: Pope, a poetic moralist, who felt himself to be a necessary and important part of the civilization under which he lived. The mass of humanity, he agreed, was corrupt and debased; but the free poet, standing above the crowd, could still hope to perform an extremely useful social service; and 'useful' was the adjective he applied to the poems he was now planning.

Swift's disgust with the world, he suggested, was a little too extravagant; he would rather, he had already told the cynic, 'have those that out of such generous principles as you and I despise it, fly in its face, than retire from it'. Yet, temperamentally and emotionally, the two old friends had many of the same traits. Each required and demanded affection; each distrusted or despised the world at large, but was capable of developing a keen attachment for individual human beings. Swift had adored and cherished Stella; Pope's life was involved in a close web of obligations and domestic duties. Having once shouldered an obligation, he never willingly discarded it; and in 1725, for instance, he had again been consulting with Caryll about the unhappy affairs of Mrs Cope.★ Any member of his household had an established place in his heart; and when, during November 1725, Mary Beach, his 'poor old nurse, who had lived in constant attendance and care of me since I was an infant', succumbed to her infirmities at the age of seventy-seven, her disappearance caused him genuine sorrow. 'Surely,' he mused, 'this sort of friend is not the least, and this sort of relation . . . superior to most that we call so'; and he commemorated Mary in his Elzevir *Virgil*, where he recorded such personal losses, as *Nutrix mea fidelissima*.

Although Pope may not have understood the secret origin of Swift's distraction, he must, now and then, have observed its outward signs. The Dean was still capable of exhibiting tremendous energy and occasional flashes of his former gaiety; but it was evident that the burdens he carried had at last begun to break his spirit. He was troubled nowadays both by

★ Until her death, Mrs Cope seemed to have received financial assistance from both Pope and Caryll. See Pope to Caryll, 19 January 1726.

increasing deafness and by mysterious attacks of giddiness – symptoms of Ménière's Disease, the affection of the inner ear that, during the last few years of his existence, would gradually drive him mad. Pope, too, was in indifferent health and, while his guest rambled and dined out, often laid up by 'a very ill-timed misfortune, a lame thigh, which keeps me from these parties. . . .' Both writers had begun to feel their years; and Swift, at the age of fifty-nine, already thought himself an old man; yet, once they were alone together, they continued to lead a vigorous intellectual life. Not only did they plan a series of joint *Miscellanies*★ – collections of such occasional pieces as they enjoyed re-reading and considered worth publishing – but they discussed the great satire in which Pope intended to destroy the whole troop of mercenary modern scribblers. Swift would afterwards claim that the basic idea was his; that it was he who had 'put Mr Pope on writing the poem called the Dunciad'; and Pope agreed that 'Dr Swift . . . may be said in a sort to be the author of the poem'; for, while they were looking through their miscellaneous works, and discussing what they should eliminate, he had snatched the original draft from the fire, and had 'persuaded his friend to proceed in it' – a service that Pope had gratefully recognized when he came to write the dedication.

Strangely enough, although Swift had arrived with *Gulliver* 'in his pocket', he seems to have omitted to show his friend the manuscript. Pope, who had long ago heard of the 'Travels', must surely have expressed his interest; but the following December – Swift's masterpiece had been published at the end of October – he wrote to Caryll, whom no doubt it had shocked and offended, that 'you suspect me unjustly as to Gulliver's book. Upon my word I never saw it, till printed.' Perhaps Pope was deliberately deceiving that high-minded Catholic gentleman; but Swift's character had always included a suspicious and secretive strain; and he may have determined that, before his most critical English associates had begun to study *Gulliver* – a book that contained so much of his secret self – he would retire across the Irish Channel.† It was on 15 August that he finally set out from London; and, always anxious to avoid unnecessary suffering, he told Pope that, now they were parted, he meant to think of him as seldom as he could. Yet Pope, he implied, had a special hold on his affections; 'I love and esteem you for reasons that most others have little to do with, and would be the same although you had never touched a pen. . . .'

★ The first two volumes of the Pope–Swift *Miscellanies* appeared in June, 1727; the third, called 'the last', in March 1728.

† Swift may possibly have made an exception for Bolingbroke, who, on 23 July 1726, wrote a letter to Swift, Pope and Gay, addressing them as 'The Three Yahoos of Twickenham'.

A second letter was written soon after he arrived in Ireland. Pope, he declared, had taught him to dream, 'which I had not done in twelve years further than by inexpressible nonsense; but now I can every night distinctly see Twitenham, and the Grotto, and Dawley, and Mrs. B.,* and many other et cetera's. . . .' Three nights since he had dreamed of beating good Mrs Pope at the card-table or the backgammon-board.

Pope, we may assume, was now busily reconsidering the rough draft of his projected satire; but even with Swift's encouragement, he might have continued to postpone the scheme, had it not been for the outrageous intervention – outrageous, at least, in the poet's view – of yet another hostile critic. Pope was severely shaken. Hitherto the 'critical impertinences' from which he had suffered had come from unimportant journalists; Lewis Theobald was a serious scholar, qualified to speak with authority upon his proper subject. Nor could it be said that he was activated by malice alone; whatever his private prejudices, he had a genuine case to put forward. Born like Pope in 1688, the son of an attorney and himself a member of the same profession, Theobald was an exceedingly versatile bookman, whose works included English renderings of Homer, Plato and the Greek dramatists, poems, essays, biographies, a play entitled *The Perfidious Brother*, and a series of mythological pantomimes that had been put on to the stage by the celebrated impressario John Rich. But Shakespeare, for whom he proclaimed 'a veneration almost rising to idolatry', was the literary lawyer's chief interest. He had long considered producing his own edition of Shakespeare,† and for that reason had not replied to Pope's advertisement when he saw it in the public press. The edition that appeared under Tonson's imprint infuriated him beyond all measure – a slovenly piece of work, foisted off on the public beneath the protection of a well-known writer's name.

Yet his attack was cautious. He began by acclaiming Pope's genius, and mentioning the delight with which he had originally heard that the poet proposed to edit Shakespeare. Pope, however – possibly through 'a religious abhorrence of innovation' – had declined his most important office; he had done nothing to improve the text; and Theobald listed over a hundred passages in which the text of *Hamlet*, as Pope had allowed it to appear, might be emended and elucidated, adding an appendix where he applied the same method to certain of the other plays. *Shakespeare*

* Presumably Martha Blount.
† This edition eventually appeared in 1734. Theobald's reputation as a Shakespearian critic has declined in recent years; but there is no doubt that he was a far more competent editor than Pope, and had a deeper understanding of Shakespeare's literary background.

Restored: or, a Specimen of the Many Errors, as well committed, as unamended, by Mr Pope in his late edition . . . appeared in March 1726; and Pope's response, if highly irrational, was completely understandable. He knew that Theobald's criticisms were often sound; and his anger may have been complicated by a secret sense of guilt. In none of the letters he wrote at the time does Theobald's book elicit the slightest reference; and we cannot tell if Swift was shown a copy; but the offensive scholiast now took his place among the worst of modern Dunces, fit companion for Denni and Curll, even for the scandalous Mrs Haywood.

Such were the personal origins of *The Dunciad* – the poem that he probably launched during the early summer of 1726, and carried on with growing enthusiasm throughout the whole of 1727. Twenty-six months would elapse between the appearance of *Shakespeare Restored* and *The Dunciad's* publication; and while he slowly shaped and polished his thunderbolt, Pope, having at last completed his *Odyssey*, seemed to be preparing to enjoy a life of leisure. As usual, he travelled, dined out and entertained distinguished guests. It was in 1726, for example, that he first received a visit from Voltaire. After the series of hideous humiliations recently inflicted on him by his own countrymen, Voltaire had said good-bye to France and was nowadays a fervent anglophile, flitting like some bright-winged insect around the sunlit English scene, admiring the liberality of our statesmen and the glory of our institutions no less than the beauty of the graceful equestriennes whom he had watched exercising their horses beneath the trees of Greenwich Park. Everything he saw delighted him. Was not England a country where true genius received universal recognition; where writers and scientists lived on familiar terms with peers and bishops; and rich merchants, like his friend Falkener,* had almost the dignity of European princes? According to Condorcet, Voltaire's discovery of England was the starting-point of his career as an intellectual revolutionist: '*dès ce moment Voltaire se sentit appelé à détruire les préjugés de toute espèce, dont son pays était l'esclave*'.† Another impressive feature of the English world was the lavish hospitality of its great men. Bolingbroke welcomed him; so did the excellent Lord Peterborough and the millionaire politician Bubb Dodington. Bolingbroke presumably introduced him to Pope, whose exquisite mock-heroic poem, which he considered superior to *Le Lutrin*, he had already much appreciated; and,

* To Everard Falkener he dedicated *Zaïre*; and later, wishing to praise King Stanislaus of Poland, he described him as 'a kind of Falkener'.

† The attitude persisted. '*Ce qui aiguillonnait encore nôtra vive impatience*', wrote the comte de Ségur, describing the restlessness of the French aristocracy before the Revolution, '*c'était la comparaison de notre situation présente avec celle des Anglais.*'

during his visit, he may perhaps have been invited to explore the Grotto – a whimsy that the hard-headed Frenchman can scarcely have found either amusing or attractive.

Voltaire's story of his visit, reported by Goldsmith, describes the 'succession of opposite passions' with which he had first observed the poet, pitiably deformed, wasted by sickness and study, yet, once his interest was aroused, a ready and melodious talker. The guest had been prepared to pity his host; 'but when Pope began to speak and to reason upon moral obligations, and dress the most delicate sentiments in the most charming diction, Voltaire's pity began to be changed into admiration, and at last even into envy. It was not uncommon with him to assert that no man ever pleased him so much in serious conversation, nor any whose sentiments mended so much upon recollection.' But there exists a second version of the story, which seems also to have been derived from Voltaire. During their original interview, we learn, both host and guest were '*fort embarrassés*'; Voltaire complained that Pope spoke very bad French, and that he himself, '*n'étant point accoutumé aux sifflements de la langue anglaise*', often became entirely unintelligible. Nor was Voltaire's social small talk altogether to his host's liking. As the day drew on and the hour of farewells approached, Pope suggested that he should remain for dinner; and at the dinner-table he met Mrs Pope, a plain, modest, round-faced old lady, now over eighty-four years old, who, in her motherly way (writes Owen Ruffhead) noticing that their foreign guest 'appeared to be entirely emaciated' and seemed to have a weak stomach, 'expressed her concern for his want of appetite'; at which Voltaire gave her 'so indelicate and brutal an account of the occasion of his disorder contracted in Italy, that the poor lady was obliged immediately to rise from the table'.

Pope reported this occurrence to 'one of his most intimate friends'; and, when the friend enquired 'how he could forbear ordering his servant John to thrust Voltaire head and shoulders out of his house', he answered, mildly enough, 'that there was more of ignorance in this conduct than a purposed affront; that Voltaire came into England, as other foreigners do, on a prepossession that not only all religion, but all common decency of morals, was lost among us.' But Pope would not have forgotten the episode that had so affronted and disturbed his mother. Worse still, he presently learned that, despite his attachment to Bolingbroke, Voltaire was coquetting with the Court party and had solicited the favour of Sir Robert Walpole, to whom he carried any tales that he could pick up about the sayings and doings of his Tory hosts. Early next year, Pope became convinced – and Bolingbroke and Swift afterwards shared his belief – that

Voltaire had agreed to spy for the administration. But during the autumn of 1726 they were still on friendly terms; and in September, when Voltaire heard that Pope had narrowly escaped death, he hastened to compose a friendly message:

I hear this moment of your sad adventure. That water you fell in, was not Hippocrene's water; otherwise it would have respected you. ... Is it possible that those fingers which had written the Rape of the Lock, and the Criticism, which have dressed Homer so becomingly in an English coat, should have been so barbarously treated? Let the hand of Dennis, or of your poetasters be cut off. Yours is sacred. ...

The sad adventure that Voltaire mentions had occurred a few days earlier, probably about 8 or 9 September,* while Pope was travelling alone in Bolingbroke's coach from Dawley. At Whitton, where a bridge had collapsed, the six spirited horses had taken fright, the coach had overturned, and he had been 'thrown out into the river with the glasses of the coach up'. Water poured in, nearly drowning him – before he could be hoisted out, he was 'up to the knots of his periwig'; and he had already failed to break or lower the window, when the footman, who had himself been stuck in the mud, managed to struggle free, smash the glass and pull the desperate poet clear; 'by which', Gay informed Swift, 'he thinks he received a cut across his hand. He was afraid he should have lost the use of his little finger and the next to it; but the surgeon whom he sent for last Sunday from London ... told him that his fingers were safe, that there were two nerves cut, but no tendon.' In later life, Pope was often inconvenienced by his partly crippled right hand, and obliged to employ an amanuensis; but, like other chronic invalids, he possessed remarkable powers of recuperation; and Gay added that he was now 'in very good health, and very good spirits', and that his wound was 'in a fair way of being soon healed'. To Spence, Pope was to describe the adventure as his third escape from violent death. First, he had been saved from the horns of a maddened cow at Binfield; secondly, when he was a very young man, an imprudent coachman, negotiating a dangerous ford, had almost driven him and his party into a deep hole in the river-bed; last of all, he had nearly been plunged to destruction with Lord Bolingbroke's hurtling coach-and-six. Pope was no coward; and he took his mishap calmly. It was 'a fine paid for my life', he said, 'which may now continue me some years longer'.

* Gay, writing to Swift on 16 September 1726, says that it had happened 'about a week ago'.

II

During the summer or autumn of 1726, a new critic entered Pope's existence – on this occasion, however, a wonderfully well-disposed critic, civil, cultivated, of engaging manners, who soon became a firm friend. Early in June, Pope had written to William Broome, mentioning 'a book lately published at Oxford . . . which you will have reason to be pleased with'; and he was sufficiently pleased himself to enquire the anonymous author's name. Having learned it, he quickly suggested a meeting. The writer proved to be Joseph Spence, a twenty-seven-year-old Fellow of New College and recently ordained clergyman; and his *Essay on Pope's Odyssey: in which some particular Beauties and Blemishes of that work are considered* was, from the translator's point of view, a highly interesting and deserving effort. After the quiet acerbity of Theobald's strictures, the tone that Spence adopted could not fail to charm – appreciative and handsomely eulogistic, with a touch of sensible criticism here and there, that lent his praise an added value. Spence suspected, indeed, that his discussion of 'blemishes' might perhaps have been a little bold; his essay, he felt, though certainly not ill-natured, was 'blunt, and rough enough in places'; and he had therefore dreaded meeting Pope. But, once he had finally reached the villa, his courteous reception set his mind at rest. 'I'm in love with Mr Pope,' he told a school-fellow; 'he has the most generous spirit in the world. . . .' Was it not strange to be thanked for criticisms, and 'have 'em corrected in a friendly manner by the very person whose writing occasioned them? But Mr Pope has too great a soul to act upon a level with mankind.'

Of the *Essay*, which was cast in the form of dialogues, only the opening volume had yet appeared; and Spence submitted the second volume to Pope, who read the text and made various small improvements. The author's gratitude lasted as long as he lived; and his admiration never died down. Thenceforward he was a frequent guest at Twickenham; and to no one else did the poet speak more freely about his own experiences of

22 Old houses in a court off Grub Street; an engraving of the later eighteenth century.

23 Pope during the last decade of his life; pencil portrait by Jonathan Richardson, dated January, 1737.

life and literature. Thin, short, invalidish, bright-eyed, Spence was said by an Oxford contemporary to have been the 'sweetest tempered gentleman breathing'; and, although Johnson declared that his scholarship was 'not very great' and his mind 'not very powerful', he admitted that Spence's criticism was 'commonly just', and that 'what he thought, he thought rightly'. Johnson also credited him with 'coolness and candour' – both virtues that would have attracted Pope, who always appreciated the qualities that he himself did not possess. In 1728, thanks to Pope's support, Spence was appointed Professor of Poetry at Oxford; during the same year, his old college procured him a comfortable Essex living; and, later, he was to tour the Continent, where he met and conversed with Lady Mary Wortley, as tutor and companion to young Lord Middlesex and the future Duke of Newcastle. But Twickenham remained his spiritual home, and Mr Pope his chief hero. It was under Pope's influence that he discovered his real vocation. English literature has been extremely well-served by its memorialists and anecdotalists – Drummond of Hawthornden, John Aubrey, John Nichols, Henry Crabb Robinson and, towering above his fellows, James Boswell, who raised literary anecdotage to the height of imaginative art. Spence was no Boswell; he had neither Boswell's genius nor his vices. But he had a similar gift of listening and remembering, and of drawing out his hero's talents. His first notes on Pope's conversation were made in the autumn of 1728; and, year after year, he added to them, until he had amassed the solid sheaf of *Anecdotes, Observations, and Characters of Books and Men, collected from the conversation of Mr Pope, and other persons of his time*,* that now provides our most vivid record of Pope as artist, theorist, and private citizen.

Encouraged by Spence, he managed to cover an extraordinary range of topics. Naturally, their conversation very often turned on writing. Thus, the great exponent of the heroic couplet admitted that he had 'nothing to say for rhyme, but that I doubt whether a poem can support itself without it in our language. . . .' As a poet, he attached an especial value to the inward music of his lines; 'I have followed . . . the significance of the numbers, and the adapting them to the sense, much more even than Dryden, and much oftener than any one minds it. . . . The great rule of verse is to be musical.' Virgil, he believed, had produced 'the softest couplet that was ever written';† and, in English, 'Sir John Denham's celebrated couplet

* The title of the *Anecdotes*, as they originally appeared in 1820, under the editorship of Samuel Weller Singer.

† *Te, dulcis conjux, te solo in litore secum,*
Te veniente die, te decedente canebat.
        Georgics, Book IV.

on the Thames owes a great part of its fineness to the frequency and variety of the pauses'. To arrive at this state of perfection needed constant hard work; Pope would 'turn his lines over and over again' in his head until he was satisfied that they produced exactly the right effect. Above all else, he was a perfectionist; 'middling poets', he announced, 'are no poets at all'. Among the writers of the past whom he regarded as 'authorities for poetical language' were Spenser, Shakespeare, Fletcher, Waller, Butler, Milton, Dryden, and, among the moderns, Swift and Prior. He had read *The Faery Queen*, when he was about twelve, 'with a vast deal of delight; and I think it gave me as much, when I read it over about a year or two ago'. As for Chaucer, though he was by no means an authority, Pope read him 'still with as much pleasure as almost any of our poets. He is a master of manners and of description, and the first tale-teller in his true enlivened natural way.'

While talking of his own projects, Pope often mentioned an idea that he did not live to realize – such as an epic poem outlining his theories of civil and ecclesiastical government, which would describe how the hero, 'our Brutus from Troy', having investigated the religious mysteries of Egypt, and acquired ambitious notions of religion and statecraft, founds an enlightened empire upon English soil. He also referred to a 'Persian fable', that 'would have been a very wild thing, if I had executed it, but might not have been unentertaining', and to a scheme he had once discussed with Gay for a series of 'American pastorals', where the inhabitants of the New World would have taken the place of the customary Grecian nymphs and shepherds. Nearly all these unrealized works would have included some didactic element; for the self-portrait that Pope draws is that of a dedicated artist who, like French poets of the later nineteenth century, seeks to 'raise poetry to the condition of music', yet is firmly persuaded that every work of art must perform a moral function, and that 'no writing is good that does not tend to better mankind some way or other'. The story of Brutus would certainly have been didactic; perhaps even the Persian fable would have had its message for contemporary Europe.

Equally revealing are the sidelights that Spence throws upon the poet as a private personage. During his youth, the memorialist learned, he had been 'excessively gay and lively'; but, when Spence knew him, were he to tell a story, 'he was always the last to laugh at it, and seldom went beyond a particular, easy smile on any occasion that I remember.' Tears he sometimes shed when he listened to verses he loved; and he confessed that there was one passage in Homer – 'where he makes Priam's grief for the loss of Hector break out into anger against his attendants and sons' – that he could never read without weeping. Spence himself was a tender-hearted, deeply impressionable man, who wrote that 'the happiness of life is so nice a thing, that, like the sensitive plant, it shrinks away even upon thinking of it'; and he was often moved by the strain of generosity, delicacy and humanity that he noted in his friend's character. Pope's affection for the natural world – 'a tree,' he declared, 'is a nobler object than a prince in his coronation robes' – extended to all sentient creatures; and he distrusted the worthy Dr Hales because he had learned that Hales practised scientific vivisection, and 'has his hands imbrued with blood'. Did Hales, asked Spence, cut up rats? ' "Ay, and dogs too!" – (With what emphasis and concern he spoke it.) – "Indeed, he commits most of these barbarities with the thought of its being of use to man. But how do we know that we have a right to kill creatures that we are so little above as dogs. . . ." ' Nor would he agree that dogs lacked reason: 'Man has reason enough only to know what is necessary for him to know; and dogs have just that too. . . . They must have souls too, as inperishable in their nature as ours. . . . Where would be the harm to us in allowing them immortality? . . .'

Similarly humane were Pope's views on social life, and on the attribute he called 'genteelness'. The prevailing notion, he said, had 'led many to a total neglect of decency'; whereas 'true politeness consists in being easy oneself and making everybody about one as easy as one can. But the mis-taking brutality for freedom (for which so many of our young people of quality in particular have made themselves remarkable of late) has just the contrary effect.' For Pope, politeness and taste formed part of the same moral system; he felt, like Shaftesbury, that a truly civilized man would also be a moralist and, simultaneously, an aesthete; and Pope, the Augustan Man of Taste, frequently reappears in Spence's record. Now he discusses his theories of gardening and the judicious management of 'grove work'; now touches upon the other arts, and praises the Neapolitan artist Carlo Maratta, whom 'I really think . . . as good a painter as any of them'; now, while he and Spence are walking along a Thames-side path, illustrates his 'Idea of the Picturesque' by pointing to 'a swan just gilded with the sun amidst the shade of a tree over the water. . . .'

If he spoke of his contemporaries and older men he had known, Pope's description of their personalities was almost always fair and kind. To his friends Peterborough and Bolingbroke he paid enthusiastic tributes:

Lord Peterborough could dictate letters to nine amanuenses together, as I was assured by a gentleman who saw him do it when ambassador at Turin. . . .

One perhaps was a letter to the Emperor, another to an old friend, a third to a mistress, and a fourth to a statesman. . . . And yet he carried so many and so different connexions in his head all the same time.

Peterborough, however, was 'not near so great a genius' as Bolingbroke:

Lord Peterborough . . . in the case just mentioned, would say pretty and lively things in his letters, but they would be rather too gay and wandering. Whereas was Lord Bolingbroke to write to the Emperor or to the statesman, he would fix on that point which was the most material, would set it in the strongest and finest light. . . .

There is one thing in Lord Bolingbroke [he added elsewhere] which seems peculiar to himself. He has so great a memory as well as judgment, that if he is alone and without books, he can set down by himself . . . and refer to the books, or such a particular subject in them, in his own mind . . . He sits like an Intelligence, and recollects all the question within himself.

Nor was he usually malicious in his comments on his fellow men of letters. Gay, for example, was 'quite a natural man, wholly without art or design, and spoke just what he thought, and as he thought it'. But he was 'negligent and a bad manager', and, having 'dangled for twenty years about a court', was eventually offered a very small reward. Only Addison, though Pope admitted his extraordinary charm, received some rather rough handling; and here he told the one scandalous story that figures in Spence's reminiscences. Addison and Steele, he announced, had been 'a couple of H—s', adding: 'I am sorry to say so, and there are not twelve people in the world that I would say it to at all.' This passage, suppressed in the nineteenth-century edition of the *Anecdotes*, has been replaced by Spence's modern editor, who suggests that 'H—s' must stand for 'hermaphrodites', which implies that both his old associates had had a homosexual tendency.*

Altogether, his disciple's portrait of the poet was that of a man essentially good and wise and generous, a man who had 'too great a soul' to harbour base or vulgar passions. In fact, when Spence arrived at Twickenham, Pope was preparing to enter the most violent period of his whole existence, and about to launch against the contemporary book world a particularly savage and ungenerous satire. There were also some indications, during the

* See *Observations, Anecdotes and Characters*, edited by James M. Osborn, who reminds us that the word 'homosexual' was introduced by Havelock Ellis in 1897, but that 'hermaphrodite', which had the same sense, was on several occasions applied by Pope to the notorious Lord Hervey.

years 1726 and 1727, that Pope, the literary strategist, was threatening to prevail over Pope, the *honnête homme*. His treatment of his Homeric collaborators seems not to have been entirely straightforward. Both Broome and Fenton had once been delighted to assist the great man in his labours; but the terms on which they were to assist him had conveniently been left rather vague; and, as the work progressed, they began to suspect that they had made a bad bargain. 'I fear,' wrote Broome to his collaborator in December 1725, 'we have hunted with the lion, who like his predecessor in Phaedrus, will take the first share merely because he is a lion; the second because he is more brave; the third because he is of most importance; and if either of us shall presume to touch the fourth, woe be to us. This perhaps may not be the case with respect to the lucrative part, but I have strong apprehensions it will happen with regard to our reputations. Be assured Mr Pope will not let us divide – I fear not give us our due share of honour. He is Caesar in Poetry, and will bear no equal.'

Broome's apprehensions were well-founded. Pope had come to regard the whole work as his own achievement; indeed, he may originally have intended to foist it as such upon his gullible subscribers; and he had been greatly annoyed when the talkative Broome betrayed the secret 'to so many people, that it would be dishonourable and unjust (he admitted) for me to seem . . . to take to myself what does not belong to me'. Even then, he was determined to minimize the extent of his assistants' help; and by some strange feat he managed to persuade Broome to sign a statement, which was printed at the conclusion of his learned notes upon the *Odyssey*, asserting that he, Broome, had been responsible for the sixth, eleventh and eighteenth Books alone, whereas he had really translated eight; and that Fenton, who had handled four, had rendered only the fourth and the twentieth.* If his performance had merit, declared Broome, either in his notes, 'or in my part of the translation . . . it is but just to attribute it to the judgement and care of Mr Pope, by whose hand every sheet was corrected'. There, no doubt, he told the truth; Pope, indeed, must have considered and revised every section of the manuscript; and the work was certainly his own in so far as it bore the imprint of his mind and style. But, not unnaturally, his good-natured aides felt that they deserved less grudging notice.

As to their financial reward, Pope was neither an unnecessarily prompt nor an over-generous paymaster. According to the poet, as reported by

* Fenton was taken aback by Broome's statement, but concluded, in a letter of 17 December 1726, that, unless Broome were resolved to break with Pope, 'I think the best way for you is to let it rest as it does'.

Spence, 'I had twelve hundred pounds for my translation of the Iliad, and six hundred for the Odyssey; and all the books for my subscribers. . . .' But here again he was not completely candid; and a modern authority calculates that he himself must have received for the *Odyssey* more than five thousand pounds; while for his collaborators, who had done half the work, he set aside some eight hundred. In Pope's defence, it may, of course, be argued that Broome and Fenton were almost unknown writers until he raised them on his wings. They were not poor men; Broome occupied a comfortable benefice, and was married to a rich widow. Both benefited from their association with Pope; but each left him, nursing a sense of injury; and Pope retaliated by a spiteful reference to his more prolific aide, first in his essay *Peri Bathous*, then in the Third Book of *The Dunciad*, where he described the hard fate of modern men of genius:

> Hibernian Politicks, O Swift, thy doom,
> And Pope's, translating three whole years with Broome.

In a 'critical postscript' to the *Odyssey*,* however, he endeavoured to make slight amends. If he were to be 'punctually just', he wrote, he must concede that, besides the portions listed at the end of the Notes, Broome and Fenton had also undertaken 'some part of the tenth and fifteenth books'; and, as time went by, he seemed ready to admit that they had contributed an even larger share.

It was a sorry episode. But then, Pope never appeared at his best with men whom he could not love or reverence. The spectacle of mediocrity always irritated him; and Broome and Fenton were clearly 'middling poets'. Apart from men and women who aroused his protective instincts, his consideration was mostly reserved for those he could regard as equals. In this attitude he was often encouraged by his friends; both Swift and Bolingbroke shared his sense of intellectual superiority; and, on 1 June 1728, Swift remarked to Pope that 'I look upon my Lord Bolingbroke and us two, as a peculiar Triumvirate, who have nothing to expect, or to fear; and so far fittest to converse with one another.' But he added that, whereas everything he did himself was the product of 'perfect rage and resentment, and the mortifying sight of slavery, folly, and baseness about me, among which I am forced to live', Pope hated 'the vices of mankind, without the least effect on your temper. . . .' Swift's masterpiece, the greatest proof of his rage and resentment, was by this time nearly two years old; for *Gulliver's Travels* had finally appeared towards the end of October 1726, and had at once aroused a 'vast demand'. Even supporters

* Attached to the edition of 1726.

of the government conceded that it was 'a pleasant humorous book'; and 'some folks', reported Dr Arbuthnot, 'went immediately to their maps to look for Lillypot', and were surprised and annoyed that they could not find the place. In mid-November, Pope wrote to the author to congratulate him 'upon what you call your Cousin's wonderful book,* which . . . I prophesy will be in future the admiration of all men. That countenance with which it is received by some statesmen is delightful; I wish I could tell you how every single man looks upon it, to observe which has been my whole diversion this fortnight.'

If we except *Robinson Crusoe*, a book that he also admired,† no other English work of such originality was issued during Pope's lifetime; and he would have appreciated not only the many contemporary allusions with which the satirist had barbed his narrative and, on another plane, the tremendous impact of the last book, with its picture of brutish mankind enslaved by wise and noble horses, but the storyteller's exquisite fantasy and his vein of delicate poetic feeling. Pope must have felt particularly at home amid the miniature amusements of the Lilliputian court, where, relates Gulliver, 'I have been much pleased with a cook pulling a lark, which was not so large as a common fly; and a young girl threading an invisible needle with an invisible silk.' Soon afterwards he wrote five long occasional poems, based on Gulliverian themes, *A Lilliputian Ode*, addressed to the Man Mountain: *The Lamentation of Glumdalclitch, for the Loss of Grildrig: The Grateful Address of the Unhappy Houyhnhms, now in slavery and Bondage in England*, to the hero of the *Travels: Mary Gulliver to Captain Lemuel Gulliver:* and *The Words of the King of Brobdingnag, as he held Captain Gulliver between his Finger and Thumb* . . . which he despatched to Swift for his approval in March 1727, and which were eventually printed in a later edition of the *Travels*.

Meanwhile Swift was planning his return; 'we all rejoice,' wrote Gay during the winter of 1726, 'that you have fixed the precise time of your coming to be *cum hirundine prima* . . . To us your friends, the coming of such a black swallow as you will make a summer in the worst of seasons.' But Swift himself, as the moment approached, began to hesitate and draw back; 'going to England,' he lamented, 'is a very good thing, if it were not attended with an ugly circumstance of returning to Ireland. It is a shame you do not persuade your ministers to keep me on that side, if it were but by a court expedient of keeping me in prison for a plotter; but

* The supposed publisher of the *Travels* was Gulliver's cousin Richard Sympson.

† 'The first part of Robinson Crusoe, good. Defoe wrote a vast many things, and none bad, though none excellent. There's something good in all he has writ.' Spence, op. cit.

at the same time I must tell you, that such journeys very much shorten my life, for a month here is longer than six at Twickenham.' Late in April, 1727, however, he duly re-appeared among his English friends. It was his last visit, and certainly the saddest. Soon after he arrived, a letter from Ireland informed him that Stella's life was once again threatened; and his observations of the current political scene did not help to raise his spirits. During the last few months, his own health had steadily grown worse and worse; and, further to darken the atmosphere, Mrs Pope, that fragile, but apparently almost indestructible old woman, fell sick with 'an inter-mitting fever', which grievously alarmed her son.

He had no companion, reported Pope in May, except 'the Dean of St Patrick's, who would hardly be here if he was not the best natured and [most] indulgent man I know. . . .' They took practical steps to amuse themselves by working on a new Miscellany; but, as Pope was later to remark, 'two sick friends never did well together'; and Swift's increasing deafness, and the attacks of vertigo and nausea that accompanied it, often made communication difficult. Neither friend found the other's society quite as inspiriting as he had hoped. Alone at Twickenham, they went their separate ways; and Swift described their plight in verse:

> Pope has the talent well to speak,
> But not to reach the ear;
> His loudest voice is low and weak,
> The dean too deaf to hear.
>
> Awhile they on each other look,
> Then different studies choose;
> The dean sits plodding o'er a book,
> Pope walks and courts the muse.

Nor did Swift's occasional visits to London afford him any lasting solace. In May he twice obeyed a command from the Princess of Wales to attend her drawing-room at Leicester House. 'She retains her old civility,' he told Sheridan, 'and I my old freedom; she charges me without ceremony to be the author of a bad book . . . but she assures me that she and the Prince were very well pleased with every prticular. . . .' Alas, her courtiers failed to follow suit; none of the politicians whom he encountered at Leicester House paid him the attention he expected. Evidently, they now considered him beneath their notice; 'and there hath not been one of them to see me'.

Then, in June, the prospect suddenly changed. On the 11th, the sexagenarian King, who had recently crossed the Channel to enjoy his usual German holiday, collapsed in his carriage while travelling to Osnabrück, where his brother, the Duke of York, had his residence as Prince Bishop, and died in the episcopal palace without recovering consciousness. On 14 June, Walpole received the news. It had been thought that the King's death would produce an immediate change of ministers; but, although George II, who had personally detested Walpole, made an abrupt and clumsy attempt to discharge his father's old servant, he was soon obliged to give way, when his own choice, a foolish, officious courtier named Sir Spencer Compton, proved quite unequal to handling even the simplest tasks of office. Thus, after a brief crisis, Walpole, First Lord of the Treasury and Chancellor of the Exchequer since 1721, reassumed his former powers. He would retain his post as Prime Minister – the pejorative title coined by his critics to define the extraordinary position that he occupied – until the year 1742, for a longer and more successful term than any other minister in English history; and under his guidance England entered the great age of the *Pax Walpoliana*, a period of immense prosperity at home and of uninterrupted tranquillity abroad. During the previous reign, neither Pope nor Swift had refused to dine and talk with Walpole, among his many other private virtues an immensely jovial and good-humoured person; and, early in August, Pope told Fortescue that he had recently 'waited on Sir R. W.'. But henceforward he and his fellow triumvirs began to cast Walpole in the rôle of arch-enemy – 'Bob the poet's foe', a triumphant gambler who had 'held the longest hand at hazard that ever fell to any sharper's share . . .' To Boling-broke the restoration of the Walpolian order was a particularly grievous blow. From Dawley he had been conducting a fierce campaign against the abuses of the Whig government, and had organized an Opposition newspaper, *The Craftsman*, in which, 'week after week, Walpole and his ministry were subjected to an endless stream of vilification and criticism' that delighted all Europe. Nothing availed him; the accession of the new sovereign saw him still a cultured farmer. Every plot he hatched, every effort he made, appeared to reach the same conclusion. His fortune invariably 'turned rotten at the very moment it grew ripe'.

Bolingbroke himself received the blow with his usual haughty stoicism – in his native soil, he wrote next year, 'I shoot strong and tenacious roots . . . and neither my enemies nor my friends will find it an easy matter to transplant me again'; while Pope could always escape into the happy world of the imagination. Swift's nature was far less philosophic. He had been in London, planning a journey to France, when he heard news of the King's death, and had duly visited the Court – though not, he explained, 'till the third day' – to kiss the King's and Queen's hands; but he admitted that none of the 'millions of schemes' in which he and his friends were engaged was very likely to materialize, and that the best they could now expect was some relief from persecution.* No doubt, it was nervous strain that brought on a fresh attack of his familiar malady. Hitherto his stomach had been 'pretty good'; but for the last few days, he wrote during the latter part of June, 'my head has not been right'; and shortly afterwards he succumbed to his 'old disease of giddiness', which left him weary and 'a little tottering'. He attributed the attack to a surfeit of 'cyder and champagne and fruit'. Neither a strict diet nor regular hours much improved his nerves and stomach; and by the beginning of August he was deafer, he informed Sheridan, 'than ever you knew me'. His kind host had a wonderfully well-stocked garden; but 'in the midst of peaches, figs, nectarines, and mulberries, I touch not a bit'.

Despite all Pope's warm-hearted care, the life that he led at Twickenham rapidly became intolerable. Illness bred a desperate sense of loneliness and restlessness. 'I am very uneasy here,' he complained, 'because so many of our acquaintance come to see us, and I cannot be seen; besides Mr Pope is too sickly and complaisant; therefore I resolve to go somewhere else.' On 31 August he fled to London, and took refuge at the house of his cousins, Lancelot and Patty Rolt. As he prepared to leave, he had had further reports from Ireland; Sheridan informed him that Stella, having caught a severe cold, was once more very gravely ill; and he had kept the letter an hour in his pocket before he dared to read its message, suffering 'all the suspense of a man who expected to hear the worst news that Fortune could give him; and at the same time was not able to hold up my head'. Again his courage deserted him; he could face the prospect of Stella's extinction; he could not bear to see her die. Had he better health, he assured Sheridan, 'I would go this moment to Ireland; yet I think I would not, considering the news I daily expect to hear from you. . . . The last act of life is always a tragedy at best; but it is a bitter aggravation to have one's best friend go before one. I desired in my last, that you would not enlarge upon that event; but tell me the bare fact.'

Evidently he was still reluctant to open his heart to Pope. Sheridan, however, otherwise so discreet, felt that, if Swift himself would not move, Pope must be called upon to use his influence, and sent him a letter, which has not survived, explaining Stella's situation. Pope, to whom Swift

* 'We have now done with repining, if we shall be used well, and not baited as formerly.' Swift to Sheridan, 24 June 1727.

seems never to have spoken of his most private relationship, was equally surprised and shocked. 'What you mention of a particular friend of the Dean's being upon the brink of another world,' he replied, 'gives me great pain; for it makes me, in tenderness, wish him with you; and at the same time I fear he is not in a condition to make the journey. . . .' Swift, he explained, had already left for London, 'where I see him as often as he will let me. I was extremely concerned at his opiniatrety in leaving me; but he shall not get rid of the friend, though he may of his house. . . . I will not leave him a day, till I see him better.'

Pope's solicitude for the unhappy Dean was shared by all the members of his English circle – by Bolingbroke, who counselled resolution; Arbuthnot, who gave him medical advice, and recommended a wholesome regimen that included copious draughts of asses' milk; and Mrs Howard, amusing and charming as ever, with whom, even in the worst stages of his malady, he kept up a lively correspondence. Now that her titular lover had succeeded to the throne, she felt her servitude no less keenly than in the days when he was still Prince; 'I have been a slave twenty years,' she wrote to Swift, 'without ever receiving a reason for any one thing I was ever obliged to do.'* Yet she retained her customary *sang-froid*, and reminded Swift that she, too, had always suffered both from deafness and from tiresome headaches. Yet, unlike him, she patiently endured her lot. Had she more philosophy, she enquired; 'or am I so stupid that I don't feel the evil? Swift refused to accept this rather specious mode of consolation – perhaps it tended to confirm his view that, under all the charm and urbanity, she hid a cool, self-centred spirit, and during September he wrote to bid her good-bye, explaining that he meant to return to Dublin 'before my health and the weather grow worse. It is one comfort that I shall rid you of a worthless companion . . . I am infinitely obliged to you for all your civilities'; of which he would 'preserve a remembrance' as long as his recollection lasted.

On 18 September, after a fortnight's agonized delay, Swift finally took the road to Ireland; and, having spent a wretched week at Holyhead, where the packet was detained by contrary winds, in a smoky tavern-room, he reached Dublin during the first week of October, to find Esther Johnson still alive. Almost as soon as he gained the Deanery, he had yet another proof of Pope's attachment. What especially grieved Pope was a poignant sense of helplessness; nothing he did or said could break through into his friend's solitude:

* Apart from the persecution she endured at Court, Mrs Howard was also troubled by her unruly husband's conduct.

It is a perfect trouble to me to write to you, and your kind letter left for me at Mr Gay's affected me so much, that it made me like a girl. I can't tell what to say to you; I only feel that I wish you well in every circumstance of life: that 'tis almost as good to be hated, as to be loved, considering the pain it is to minds of any tender turn, to find themselves so utterly impotent to do any good, or give any ease to those who deserve most from us. . . . I was sorry to find you could think yourself easier in any house than in mine. . . . To your bad health I fear there was added some disagreeable news from Ireland, which might occasion your so sudden departure. . . . I have given your remembrances to those you mention in yours: we are quite sorry for you, I mean for ourselves. I hope, as you do, that we shall meet in a more durable and satisfactory state . . .

Pope and Swift would never meet again. True, Swift clung to life with growing desperation another eighteen weary years; but, although he continued to indulge his spleen in savage verse and caustic prose, as time passed he became more and more a self-sentenced, self-imprisoned captive. Stella died, at the age of forty-six, on 28 January 1728; and, according to one story, related by the son of his good friend Thomas Sheridan, who cannot be regarded as a hostile witness, shortly before her death she begged Swift, in Sheridan's presence, 'to let her have the satisfaction of dying at least . . . his acknowledged wife. Swift made no reply, but . . . walked silently out of the room, nor ever saw her afterwards during the few days she lived. This behaviour threw Mrs Johnson into unspeakable agonies. . . .' When he was told that Stella's life had concluded, Swift was entertaining guests; and he stayed on among them, quiet and impassive, until his company had said good-bye, and he could sit down alone in his room to frame a secret valediction. Pleading sickness, he did not attend her obsequies. They took place after night had fallen; and he had 'removed', he wrote, 'into another apartment, that I may not see the light in the church, which is just over against the window of my bedchamber'. The tribute that he then composed to Stella included a mention of her heroic virtues: 'with all the softness of temper that became a lady, she had the personal courage of a hero. . . .' Yet his regard for Stella seemed merely to strengthen his abhorrence of her sex in general; and his later attacks on Woman have a particularly ferocious and salacious colouring.

No one who studies Pope's relations with Swift could claim that he was an insensitive, cold-hearted man. 'I really feel for my friends,' he assured Mrs Howard, whose own 'uneasy, tormenting situation' he wished that he could somehow remedy; and, earlier that year, besides taking a charitable interest in the welfare of poor Mrs Cope, he was endeavouring to arrange a pension for Thomas Deane, his old schoolmaster. In both plans he was assisted by John Caryll. He and Caryll had supported Mrs Cope ever since she left England; and, now that she was suffering from a cancer of the breast, 'the little I yearly send her cannot suffice', and he hoped that Caryll, being the richer of the two, could perhaps increase his contribution. As for Wright, the proprietor of the 'seminary' near Hyde Park Corner from which Pope had made his memorable expedition to see Dryden holding court at Will's, after a life-time of religious persecution he had become a conceited and vexatious dotard. But Pope was sure that he genuinely deserved assistance, and believed, he told Caryll, that 'giving him a small yearly pension among us and others . . . would keep him out of harm's way: which writing and publishing of books may bring him into'. Meanwhile he observed that personal vanity was to the philosopher what a good conscience was to a religious man, and noted that the retired pedagogue, however infirm in body, was still 'happy in the highest self-opinion'.

That year, another familiar name reappears among Pope's correspondents. 'Honest Cromwell' had once been foolish enough to hand over to his favourite, Mrs Thomas, a collection of the poet's early letters; and Mrs Thomas, having been plunged, as she said, 'into unforeseen, and unavoidable ruin', had sold them off to Edmund Curll, who had seized the opportunity of printing them in a volume of *Miscellanea*.* Cromwell was deeply contrite; he had not 'seen this Sappho . . .', he protested, 'these seven years', and was 'extremely concerned that my former indiscretion . . . should have given you so much disturbance'. He longed to see Pope; but we cannot tell whether Pope decided to forgive his old friend. When the book came out, he had been naturally much annoyed – no one enjoys seeing his youthful letters resurrected; and they appeared at a particularly awkward moment, while he was preparing to enter the field under the guise of literary judge and censor. His proposed campaign against the monstrous legion of Dunces, which had occupied his thoughts since 1725, was nowadays his chief interest; and, before he launched a massive frontal blow, he was doing his best to confuse his opponents by engaging them in minor skirmishes. It has been suggested, indeed, that he meant to draw their fire, and hoped to provoke a series of insulting returns, which would provide him with a *casus belli*. His major attack could then be represented as, above all else, a war of self-defence.

For this purpose he employed the *Miscellanies* that he and Swift and their fellow-Scriblerians had begun to plan in 1726. Pope's original idea had been to compose a private anthology, where the chief contributors would

* Published during the summer of 1726, but post-dated 1727.

'look like friends, side by side, serious and merry by turns ... walking down hand in hand to posterity; not in the stiff forms of learned authors, flattering each other, and setting the rest of mankind at nought: but in a free, unimportant, natural, easy manner; diverting others just as we diverted ourselves'. The contents of the third, or 'last', volume were extremely various; alongside his delightful Gulliverian poems, Pope found room for a number of flimsier pieces that did not merit resurrection, including *The Capon's Tale*, *A Receipt to make a Cuckold* and *On a Lady who P—st at the Tragedy of Cato*; while Swift provided *On Dreams*, *Stella's Birthday* and *Cadenus and Vanessa*. This volume was to have consisted of verse alone; but, although Pope informed Swift, in March 1727, that 'our Miscellany is now quite printed', it did not finally emerge for another twelve months; and during the interval Pope had completed, using material on which he had already worked with Arbuthnot, the elaborate essay he called *Peri Bathous*. Once it had appeared, there could be no drawing back; the wretched Dunces would immediately show their hand, and masked batteries of *The Dunciad* proceed to sweep them from the field of battle.

Pope's warlike intentions did not long remain a secret; as early as the beginning of February, 1728, Edward Young, future author of *Night Thoughts*, told Thomas Tickell that 'Mr Pope is finishing a Burlesque Heroic on writers, and the modern diversions of the town. ... 'Tis near done, and what is done is very correct.' Pope himself, however, though he knew the risks he was running, gave no sign that he felt strained or anxious. He had been ill in October, with his 'old complaints of the stomach', which, having 'turned into an inveterate colic', seldom left him with 'any lively sensation of life for two days together'. But, as a rule, his spirits were good; and that autumn he received a particularly flattering message. Pope's imagination had always been stirred by the ideas of distant romantic lands such as Persia and America; and in *Windsor-Forest* he had written of the 'feather'd people', their 'naked youths and painted chiefs', who might one day admire the riches of commercial London.* Meanwhile his own fame had spread across the seas. On 7 October, Mather Byles,†

* In 1710, three years before the appearance of *Windsor-Forest*, a deputation of Indian chiefs had visited London, clad in scarlet mantles edged with gold, and had been received at Court. Their arrival, which 'made a great bruit thro' the whole kingdom', evidently inspired Pope. See 'The Four Indian Kings' by John G. Garratt, *History Today*. February 1968.

† Mather Byles (1707–88) who inherited his uncle's library, afterwards distinguished himself as minister at Boston's Hollis Street Congregational Church; from which he was eventually dismissed for his pro-English sympathies. His *Poems on Several Occasions* appeared in 1744.

a twenty-year-old Bostonian poet, nephew of the celebrated Cotton Mather, scholar, witch-hunter and pillar of American faith, sent him a delightful tribute. Here was the authentic voice of the New World:

Sir, You are doubtless wondering at the novelty of an epistle from the remote shores where this dates its origin; as well as from so obscure a hand as that which subscribes it. But what corner of the earth so secret, as not to have heard the fame of Mr Pope? . . . To let you see a little of the reputation which you bear in these unknown climates, and the improvements we are making, I transmit to you the enclosed poems, assuring myself, though not of the approbation of your judgement, yet of the excess and lenity of that candour which is forever inseparable from a great genius. . . . How often have I been soothed and charmed with the ever-blooming landscapes of your *Windsor Forest*? And how does my very soul melt away, at the soft complaints of your languishing *Eloisa*? How frequently has the *Rape of the Lock* commanded the various passions of my mind? . . . And how have I been raised, and borne away by the resistless fire of the *Iliad*, as it glows in your immortal translation?

Pope's correspondence with Mather Byles continued into 1728. He offered the young man a collection of his works – a 'most valuable present', which Byles promised that he would donate to 'our public library', adding that likenesses of Pope were well-known in the New World, and that 'most of our genteel rooms are embellished with your large mezzotinto', an engraved version of Sir Godfrey Kneller's portrait. The year 1727 ended on an equally agreeable note. By way of Christmas gift, his old friend's son, the second Lord Oxford, presented the poet with a golden cup and salver – a token as splendid as it was unexpected; for 'till this day', he remarked, 'it was never known that poets received the same prize as horse-racers, or that Pegasus ever won the golden plate even in ancient times, in any of the Olympian, Pythian, Isthmian or Nemean games'. The cup was uninscribed; and Pope proposed to affix the words: '*This is the least thing Alex. Pope owed to Edw. E. of Oxford*'. Meanwhile he had drunk the Harleian family's health, 'separately, and in divors liquors' - a celebration 'whereof Mr Gay may probably give your Lordship an account not greatly to my advantage, for it ended in Sal Volatile'.

No less hopeful and interesting were the early months of 1728. He had now nearly finished *The Dunciad*; and John Gay had just completed the ballad-opera that was to bring him fame and fortune. A soft, slack, greedy, good-humoured man, with round cheeks, a cupid's-bow mouth and a flaccid, comfortable body, Gay was loved and spoiled by all his friends; but, as they admitted, he had one obvious weakness; besides being idle and self-indulgent, he often showed a somewhat pettish nature. Gay believed that the world owed him a good living; and, if for a moment it failed to realize his hopes, he would lapse into a mood of deep despondency. From the new Court he had expected much. Had he not dedicated a volume of *Fables* to the sovereign's younger son? In October 1727, however, when the royal household was reorganized, he had been offered the derisory position of Gentleman Usher to the two-year-old Princess Louisa. This post he had at once refused; but, although both Pope and Swift wrote to congratulate him, he felt the disappointment keenly; and in his new work he took up his stand as the poetic foe of Court and government.

On 29 January 1728, 'Mr Gay's new English opera' was presented for the first time at the playhouse in Lincoln's Inn Fields, where it was received with immense applause by 'a prodigious concourse of the Nobility and Gentry'. This distinguished audience included Sir Robert Walpole, who, despite the fact that the highwayman Macheath was thought to represent himself, and Peachum his associate Lord Townshend, sat smiling and clapping in a side-box. The opera's topical references ensured its success; but the novelty of the dramatist's conception also helped to charm his critics. Swift had once suggested to Gay that he should compose 'a Newgate Pastoral' and, having heard that the work was under way, had advised him to visit the ancient prison, and study its inmates, 'to finish his scenes the more correctly'. Whether or not Gay accepted his advice, the great attraction of the opera was its air of vivid realism. For some years, German and Italian operas, under the direction of the old King's favourite, Handel, and Lord Burlington's protégé, Buononcini, had dominated the English stage; and, after those splendid but slow-moving productions, in which portly, bejewelled eunuchs often sang the male parts, Gay's ballad-opera, with its catches and country dances, its grim background and picturesque glimpses of London low life, appeared extraordinarily fresh and bold.★

'Mr Gay's opera,' reported Pope to Swift on 23 March, 'has acted forty days running, and will certainly continue the whole season.' Swift did not begrudge his friend's success; 'The Beggar's Opera,' he observed on the 28th, 'hath knocked down Gulliver'; and he hoped 'to see Pope's Dullness knock down the Beggar's Opera, but not till it hath fully done its job'. By now, the third volume of the *Miscellanies* had already reached

★ Gay himself had not intended that his play should have a musical accompaniment. But Rich, the actor-manager, decided otherwise, and instructed his musical director, the Prussian Dr Pepusch, to provide a score. Meanwhile Rich had engaged Lavinia Fenton, an inexperienced nineteen-year-old girl, to take the part of Polly Peachum.

the booksellers, and Pope had warned Swift that into its pages he had inserted 'the Treatise *Peri Bathous*', which he had 'entirely methodized' and re-written, since his former collaborator, Dr Arbuthnot, had become 'quite indolent' about the project. For Pope, on the other hand, it was the volume's most important feature. Few of Pope's prose-works seem to have been more carefully written; and, although the humour may be a little long-drawn, few are livelier or more amusing. Among the grotesque inventions of the Scriblerus Club was the elderly pedant from whom they took their name. Martin Scriblerus stood for everything that was particularly absurd in the modern world of learning; and Pope shows him turning his sinister gaze upon the present condition of the art of poetry. But Scriblerus is not merely a purblind scholar; he is a literary Evil Spirit, who has convinced himself that bad writing has some positive, intrinsic value. The tendency of modern writers, he declares, is inevitably towards the depths; and he undertakes 'the arduous but necessary task of leading them as it were by the hand . . . the gentle downhill way to the bathos; the bottom, the end, the central point, the *non plus ultra* of true modern poetry!' In his *Essay on Criticism*, Pope had asserted that Nature itself was the ultimate source of intellectual beauty; Scriblerus announces that 'the taste of the bathos is implanted by Nature in the soul of man; till, perverted by custom or example, he is taught, or rather compelled, to relish the sublime. Accordingly, we see the unprejudiced minds of children delight only in such productions and such images, as our true modern writers set before them.'

Bad writing, moreover, is a wholesome form of natural exercise, poetry being 'a morbid secretion of the brain', which must be evacuated, just as we seek to evacuate other purulent and peccant humours. 'We find by experience, that the same humours which vent themselves in summer in ballads and sonnets, are condensed by the winter's cold into pamphlets and speeches'; and 'it is therefore manifest, that mediocrity ought to be allowed, yea indulged, to the good subjects of England'. The art of sinking in verse, he concludes, has its own aesthetic rules; 'many there are that can fall, but few can arrive at the felicity of falling gracefully. . . . For a man, who is among the lowest of the creation, at the very bottom of the atmosphere, to descend beneath himself, is not so easy a task, unless he calls in art to his assistance.' Scriblerus then attempts to illustrate 'the art of the bathos' with a series of examples drawn from the work of well-known modern poetasters – Dennis, Tickell, Theobald, Ambrose Philips, Thomas Cooke and, best of all, Sir Robert Blackmore, an elderly author frequently published by Curll, who had criticized Dryden, denounced Swift as an 'impious buffoon' and made abusive references to Pope. The selection is excellent; 'no mortal whatever,' Scriblerus suggests, 'following the mere ideas of nature, and unassisted with an habitual, nay laborious, peculiarity of thinking, could arrive at images so wonderfully low and unaccountable'. Next, Scriblerus seeks to distinguish between the various types of modern versifier, likens their habits to those of certain animals – flying fishes, swallows, ostriches, parrots, didappers, porpoises, frogs, eels and tortoises – with a lively note on each, and lists the different methods by which they explore the lowest and darkest depths of idiocy.

Altogether *Peri Bathous* consists of sixteen short chapters; and, although, towards the end of the treatise, the argument begins to lose direction, it shows Pope as a critical pamphleteer at his savagest and most effective. Many of his victims certainly deserved their punishment; but in the penultimate paragraph of Chapter VII he committed a needless act of personal cruelty. He had no real quarrel with William Broome, except that the poor man sometimes talked too much and clearly lacked poetic genius. Yet now he pounced on one of his more awkward couplets –

> Thus Phoebus through the Zodiac takes his way,
> And amidst monsters rises into day.

and held it up to public ridicule. This stroke of gratuitous malice alienated both Broome and Fenton; they had already formed an unpleasing picture of their 'good friend Mr Pope'; and next year, writing to Fenton, the patient Broome at last exploded:

You ask me if I correspond with Mr Pope. I do not. He has used me ill, he is ungrateful. He has now raised a spirit against him which he will not easily conjure down. He now keeps his muse as wizards are said to keep tame devils, only to send them abroad to plague their neighbours. I often resemble him to an hedgehog; he ... lies snug and warm, and sets his bristles out against all mankind. Sure he is fond of being hated. I wonder he is not thrashed: but his littleness is his protection; no man shoots a wren. He should rather be whipped; and it was pleasant enough in Mr Ambrose Philips to hand up a rod at Button's *in terrorem*, which scared away the little bard.

In the latest volume of the *Miscellanies*, Pope had also raised a dangerous spirit. Lady Mary was still established at Twickenham, where she kept a large, expensive household; and reports of her doings and sayings must have come regularly to the poet's ears. Since they parted, she had led an anxious life; for, although she was now reconciled with her proud and quarrelsome father, who had recently achieved a dukedom, she was on increasingly difficult terms with her frigid, self-sufficient husband; and her schoolboy son – once a beloved companion – was fast developing into 'the most ungovernable little rake that ever played truant'. She had always dreaded the approach of old age – she would be happy enough, she told her sister, 'but for the damn'd damn'd quality of growing older and older every day'; and in 1728, when the *Miscellanies* appeared, she was nearly thirty-nine. She, too, had often had news of her neighbour, and had been amused to learn that either she or Pope was popularly credited with the authorship of a diverting new political ballad. But she had not expected to hear from Pope himself, even in the form of an occasional satire; and she was no doubt astonished to find that the *Miscellanies* included an opprobrious mention of her name. Some ten years earlier, Lady Mary, Pope and Gay had frequently exchanged verses; and about this time she may have received the draft of a lampoon, which she had preserved among her papers, warning her in a jocose and friendly style that she must not allow her own random productions to be attributed to more distinguished poets. That lampoon – with important changes – was the ballad that she now read.

Neither as it was first written, nor as it was afterwards revised, is *The Capon's Tale: To a Lady who father'd her Lampoons upon her Acquaintance* a particularly agreeable production. Pope relates the foolish tale of how a crafty Welsh countrywoman, whose hen, the favourite of the barnyard, 'hatched more chicks than she could rear', had chosen a capon to become their foster-mother, made him drunk, plucked his rump, stung it with nettles, and then put him down to do the hen's duty. The draft that Pope had sent Lady Mary had reached a trite and innocent conclusion. By 1728 the Welsh farmer's wife had become a Yorkshirewoman, presumably because Lady Mary had passed so much of her early youth in Yorkshire; while the last four lines of *The Capon's Tale* had received an unpleasantly improper twist:

> Such, Lady *Mary*, are your tricks;
> But since you hatch, pray own your chicks:
> You should be better skill'd in Nocks,
> Nor like your Capons, serve your Cocks.

When he edited the works of Swift, in which he included the contents of the third *Miscellany*, Sir Walter Scott felt obliged to reprove Pope for 'addressing unmanly ribaldry to a female of rank and genius'. Today, it is not Pope's ribaldry that shocks us, so much as the spirit of motiveless malice that we distinguish through the lines. All Pope's previous attacks had had a fairly well-defined object. It was with good reason that he had libelled Dennis and Curll, just as he had had some excuse for teasing Ambrose Philips. Addison, he could claim, had treated him shabbily; and the portrait he had drawn of the famous journalist was itself a splendid literary monument. From Lady Mary, on the other hand, he had parted more than four years earlier; and during the interval, so far as we know, she had always done her best to keep the peace. Why Pope should have decided to begin hostilities – and launch them in so vulgar a form – remains a baffling psychological problem. But then, he was a man who never forgot an injury; and some small incident – a word repeated, an unkind story told – may have brought back all his earlier sufferings. He loved and respected Martha Blount; Lady Mary was the only woman for whom he had felt a deep, unruly passion; and that passion, under the distorting influence of memory, had now developed into violent hatred.

12

Pope's features were recorded more often, and, on the whole, by more gifted artists, than those of any other English poet. During the eleven years that divided the appearance of his *Works* from the publication of *The Dunciad*, he was portrayed by Jonathan Richardson, Godfrey Kneller, and the Swedish artist Michael Dahl; and Charles Jervas's canvas, which shows him seated in his leather armchair, while a female companion – either his Muse or Martha Blount – hovers serviceably just behind him, may have been produced about the same period. Sir Godfrey alone was responsible for three portraits; and the last was commissioned by Lord Harcourt to decorate his library wall.* It depicts Pope, at the age of thirty-four, in a fashionable pink night-cap and a dressing-gown of lustrous green silk. His right hand supports his heavy head; a volume of *Homer* rests beneath his elbow. His air is languid; and Kneller has softened the effect of the face by erasing every line and wrinkle. Richardson's portrait, though executed some four years earlier, tells a very different story. Here, too, he rests his head on his hand – no doubt it was a customary pose; but we can distinguish the contracted look of the brows that afterwards impressed Roubiliac, the heavy lines encircling the eyes, and the deep-etched furrow that joins mouth and chin. Pope, who wears a purple coat, without a waistcoat, over a linen shirt unbuttoned at the neck, sits brooding in a romantic crepuscular landscape and gazes fixedly towards the painter. Two versions of this portrait exist, and in one of them Richardson has included a large dog – Bounce, we know, was its name – lifting its devoted muzzle from the bottom of the canvas.

Since Pope was a painter himself, he must have scrutinized and passed each work. On another plane, he was equally concerned with the preservation of his own image. As long ago as 1712, he had begun calling in his

* See Pope to Harcourt, 22 August 1723. This picture still hangs in the library at Stanton Harcourt.

private letters; and John Caryll had resigned his entire collection, which, once they had passed into the poet's archives, he was never allowed to see again. At the time, Pope had said he needed them merely because they might provide some useful 'thoughts'; but when, in 1737, he eventually put forth an authorized edition of his correspondence, his real design was made clear. The letters he had recovered had been thoroughly pruned and revised; often he had changed the names of his correspondents, or had pieced together separate items to form a single, more impressive text. Thus the self-portrait he drew as a letter-writer may occasionally be misleading. Like Byron, Pope believed that his letters were bound to interest posterity; and, even in his least studied messages, he clearly had a double purpose: besides communicating with the friends he loved, he was establishing a link between himself and unborn readers. But he had none of Byron's reckless indiscretion; and, as soon as he took up his pen, he assumed the vigilant attitude of the true creative artist. His sense of style, which was immediately brought into play, affected both his use of language and his general handling of his theme. Wherever he felt that the record needed improvement, he hastened to apply the proper touches.

This process of editing was apt to involve deception. But then, Pope's moral faults were closely connected with his high regard for virtue; and what he sought to impose on the world was less an intentionally fictitious portrait than an accurate representation of the man that he had always wished to be – the man he knew he might have been, in happier circumstances of mind and body. Though he was not yet the nearly crippled invalid, needing constant care and attendance, that he would become in later years, his life was still a 'long disease'; and during the early months of 1728 he had had yet another painful illness. Pope survived by a deliberate effort of will; and it was the struggle to exist, and simultaneously realize his lofty conception of how an *honnête homme* should live, that sometimes revealed him in his most unpleasing aspect. Together with the legitimate pride of genius, he had a sick man's suspicious and irritable moods; and, as youth receded and his feeling of helplessness increased, he had been growing more and more belligerent. By 1728 he had reached the point where a suspicion, once it has entered the mind, immediately hardens into an accepted fact; and, if he suspected that his genius were challenged or his personal integrity called in question, no counter-stroke was too violent, no strategem too dark or devious. Those who threatened his private peace and dignity were also attacking, he managed to convince himself, the general interests of mankind.

The word 'paranoiac' has now and then been employed to describe the state of spirit that led up to, and succeeded, Pope's publication of *The Dunciad*; and, in so far as it implies a disturbance of the entire mental pattern, it is evidently mis-used. On the level of ordinary living, he had a sober and well-balanced character; his conduct of his private affairs was shrewd; and, if he were not actually confined to bed, he worked and 'rambled' with the same zest. Many of his friends – Spence, for example – were inclined to take him at his own value. They saw a courteous, generous, dignified poet – all the more dignified and imposing because he was so small and frail – who loved the quietude of his gardens and plantations, but, being in every sense a 'polite' man, was not averse from fashionable society, where he was received and made much of by the haughtiest English grandees. He liked to dine out; and, towards the end of his life, Johnson informs us, 'his dress of ceremony was black, with a tye-wig and a little sword'. As for his table-talk, it was grave and ceremonious; he rarely smiled, never laughed, and seldom indulged in conversational wit.*

The adult Pope was certainly no ascetic. Among his faults, writes Johnson, was one 'easily incident to those who, suffering much pain, think themselves entitled to whatever pleasure they can snatch. He was too indulgent to his appetite: he loved meat highly seasoned and of strong taste; and, at the intervals of the table, amused himself with biscuits and dry conserves. If he sat down to a variety of dishes, he would oppress his stomach with repletion; and, though he seemed angry when a dram was offered him, did not forbear to drink it. His friends, who knew the avenues to his heart, pampered him with presents of luxury, which he did not suffer to stand neglected.' At Twickenham, his diet was often abstemious; and, Spence having mentioned 'a friend of mine who used to eat apples to give him spirits, he said they were the best things in the world for it, and that they were his constant supper'. But he seems never to have lost his taste either for liqueurs or for more elaborate food; and he was particularly attached to a dish of potted lampreys, which he was fond of heating in a silver saucepan.

It is obvious, both from his private letters and from contemporary references, that Pope was always a fairly heavy drinker, and that, after a night of claret and champagne, he frequently required a draught of Sal Volatile.† Nor was he indifferent to other worldly pastimes. We know that, during his London apprenticeship, he had done his best to become

---

* 'He may be said to have resembled Dryden, as being not one that was distinguished by vivacity in company. It is remarkable, that so near his time, so much should be known of what he has written, and so little of what he has said. . . .' Samuel Johnson, *Lives of the Poets*.

† See p. 229

a man of pleasure, and that, in a poetic epistle addressed to Martha Blount, he had spoken of paying gallant visits to the famous brothel kept by Mrs Needham. How literally should we accept his protestations that his conduct was sometimes as wild and rakish as that of any London libertine? The only detailed evidence that has come down must be treated with considerable reserve. In 1742, the actor-dramatist Colley Cibber, Poet Laureate since 1730, infuriated by the succession of poisoned barbs with which, for several years, Pope had been goading him, produced a brisk retaliatory pamphlet.

Here he recounted an episode, said to have occurred 'when Button's Coffee-house was in vogue' and Mr Pope had 'not translated above two or three Books of Homer' – that is to say, about 1715 or 1716. At the outset, *A Letter from Mr Cibber to Mr Pope, inquiring into the motives that might induce him in his Satyrical Works to be so frequently fond of Mr Cibber's name* takes a line that is humble, almost plaintive. Cibber acknowledges the poet's splendid gifts, owns that he himself has always written 'more to be fed than to be famous', and admits that he is still 'so contented a Dunce, that I would not have even your merited fame in poetry, if it were to be attended with half the fretful solicitude you seem to have lain under to maintain it. . . .' Why did Pope, then, refuse to let him alone? 'That Cibber ever murmured at your fame . . . or that he was not always, to the best of his judgment, as warm an admirer of your writings as any of your nearest friends could be, is what you cannot, by one fact or instance, disprove.'

Pope, however, in a comparatively recent satire, had mentioned Cibber's acquaintance both with the great world and with the demi-monde:

And has not Colley still his lord, and whore?

– which prompted Cibber to reply that 'I believe I know more of *your* whoring than you do of *mine*', and thereupon fall to the relation of an absurd and unbecoming incident. The villain of the piece was Addison's step-son, the eighteen-year-old Lord Warwick, 'a late young nobleman*
. . . who had a good deal of wicked humour, and who, though he was fond of having wits in his company, was not so restrained by his conscience, but that he loved to laugh at any merry mischief he could do them'. Warwick seems to have been a natural mischief-maker; for it was he who had helped to increase the 'unkindness' between his step-father and Pope; and on the present occasion he exhibited all his malice:

This noble wag, I say . . . with another gentleman . . . one evening slyly seduced the celebrated Mr Pope as a wit, and myself as a laugher, to a certain

* Lord Warwick, after a misspent life, had died while still a very young man.

house of carnal recreation, near the Hay-Market; where his Lordship's frolic proposed was to slip his little *Homer*, as he called him, at a Girl of the Game, that he might see what figure a man of his size, sobriety, and vigour (in verse) would make, when the frail fit of love got into him; in which he so far succeeded, that the smirking damsel who served us with tea, happened to have charms sufficient to tempt the little-tiny manhood of Mr Pope into the next room with her.... But I ... observing he had stayed as long as without hazard to his health he might ... without ceremony, threw open the door upon him, where I found this little hasty hero, like a terrible Tom Tit, pertly perching upon the Mount of Love! ... Such was my surprise, that I fairly laid hold of his heels, and actually drew him down safe and sound from his danger.

This story, told by Cibber more than twenty-five years after the alleged event, may have been partly, or very largely fiction; but it provoked the victim to an interesting rejoinder. He did not deny that he had ever visited brothels, and merely remarked that, if such an incident had occurred, he was unlikely to have forgotten it:

The story published by Cibber, as to the main point, is an absolute lie. I do remember that I was invited by Lord Warwick to pass an evening with him. He carried me and Cibber in his coach to a bawdy house. There was a woman there, but I had nothing to do with her of the kind that Cibber mentions, to the best of my memory – and I had so few things of that kind ever on my hands that I could scarce have forgot, especially so circumstanced as he pretends.

Here Spence slips in a note supplied by the famous surgeon Dr William Cheselden, designed to refute another damaging report: 'I could give a more particular account of his health than perhaps any man. Cibber's slander of a carnosity is false. He had been gay, but had left it upon his acquaintance with Mrs B.' Cheselden added that Pope 'had been in fear of a clap, but even that without grounds'.

It seems clear, therefore, that, although Pope did not lack sexual experience, any adventures he may have engaged in were of a mercenary and transient kind, and that the rakish principles he held as a young man had seldom been put into very strenuous practice. Far worse than the thwarting of his senses was the slow starvation of his heart. In Pope the desire to love was strong; he had not only a keenly physical but a passionately romantic nature; and, since the loss of Lady Mary, no single beloved face had haunted his imagination. True, Martha Blount remained a devoted friend. But both Pope and Swift had now agreed to regard their dear Patty as a golden-hearted simpleton, always busy, eager, disturbed, and always floundering in and out of trouble. 'Mrs Patty,' Pope informed

Swift during the early months of 1728, 'is very grateful for your memory of her, but not a jot the wiser for another winter. It's hard Time should wrinkle faces, and not ripen heads. But she is a very honest woman, and deserves to be whipt. To make her wise is more than you can do, but 'tis in your power by writing to her once in your life to make her proud. . . .' Swift consented. 'Dear Patty,' he wrote on 29 February, 'I am told you have a mind to receive a letter from me, which is a very undecent declaration in a young lady. . . . I am told likewise you grow every day younger and more a fool', and then proceeded to tease her at length about the modish and expensive life she led, concluding that 'if Teresa beats you . . . I will buy her a fine whip for the purpose'.

No doubt Patty's helplessness and air of vulnerable innocence were among her most disarming qualities; but by 1728 she had evidently ceased to play a romantic part in Pope's existence. She aroused nowadays, not his passions, but an affectionate solicitude. He was a man who 'really felt for his friends', as he had once reminded Mrs Howard; and any demand on his sympathy or tenderness was sure to bring out all his latent virtues. At Twickenham, his mother's failing health was still the middle-aged poet's chief concern; and, unlike Swift, he never groaned beneath the tyranny of long affections. Not until March that year, when old Mrs Pope was supposed once again to be very near her end, did he first allow himself some mild complaints. His mother's life now appeared to hang by a thread; and 'I am many years the older,' he wrote to Swift, 'for living so much with one so old; much the more helpless, for having been so long helped and tended by her; much the more considerate and tender, for a daily commerce with one who required me justly to be both to her; and consequently . . . the less fit for others. . . . I am as much in the decline at forty as you at sixty.'

May it not at times have occurred to Pope that his mother's longevity had been perhaps a somewhat mixed blessing; and, although she had helped to save him from an early death, her gentle but inescapable presence had overcast his youth and manhood? In such relationships, protracted year after year, there are always hidden strains and crises. It is possible that Pope's devotion to his mother may ultimately have had an embittering effect upon his attitude towards mankind at large; and that, having done his duty by loving Mrs Pope, which now and then required a conscious effort, he was apt to take his revenge, and exorcize the spirit of revolt, by antagonizing and tormenting others. Love and loyalty he kept for his intimates; and, even among his friends, Johnson records, he showed a 'great delight in artifice, and endeavoured to attain all his purposes by indirect and unsuspected methods'. Among strangers his natural relish of artifice had consequences that were very much more dangerous. The time came when he deceived for the sake of deception and, as every campaign brought him fresh enemies, indulged his hatred from sheer love of loathing.

Hatred was among the dominant passions that inspired him to produce *The Dunciad*; and nowhere else has the poet's divided nature left so strong a mark upon his style and subject. But before considering the qualities of the poem itself, something should be said about the position it occupies in the history of his poetic progress. When Pope completed *The Dunciad*, he had a further sixteen years to live; and during the next decade he would bring into being some of his most splendid and successful works – poems in which he achieved a triumphant synthesis of his various contradictory attributes. But, meanwhile, he had already established his authority over the modern English world of letters and, just as definitely as Dryden, had become the poetic spokesman of his age.*

If Pope spoke for his age, he had also helped to mould it. From a literary standpoint, the first decade of the eighteenth century had been an exceptionally sterile period; and, although nowadays we are apt to assume that the whole century formed a continuous and coherent pattern, the subjects of George III were to look back on the Age of Anne as a remote and semi-barbarous epoch, during which manners were crude, speech was coarse and aesthetic standards were still unrefined. Nor were Pope's contemporaries by any means unaware of their own intellectual shortcomings. Since Dryden's death, both prose and poetry, they felt, had descended to a very low level; and the language itself was in a state of flux. Such was the opinion, for example, of Swift and Bolingbroke; and, while Swift had talked of founding an academy to reform and regularize our native tongue, Bolingbroke had insisted that Pope must on no account abandon poetry; for by writing original verse he would 'contribute to fix' the language, and raise it to the classical dignity of Greek and Latin.

Thus Bolingbroke had been particularly insistent that Pope should not become 'a mere translator'. But, in the event, his superb translation of the *Iliad*, which showed that a modern Englishman could establish a harmonious correspondence with the noblest of the Greeks, had done almost as much as his original poems to raise the literary standards of his day. Like his fellow reformer Burlington, he was an intellectual theorist;

---

* 'Pope's first and most important claim to greatness is the fact that he was pre-eminently the poet of his age'. Norman Callan, 'Alexander Pope', in *From Dryden to Johnson*, edited by Boris Ford.

but none of his theories would have carried very much weight, had he not been, at the same time, an exquisitely accomplished artist. His reforming influence on English language and literature was exerted primarily through the use of words, which he handled more boldly, yet more delicately and sensitively, with a finer appreciation of their lightest shades of meaning, than almost any other English poet. Whereas our first reading of a passage by Dryden is usually sufficient to display his genius, Pope, whenever we re-read him, is apt to reveal some unexpected subtlety. Dryden's virtues lie on the surface; in Pope's verse, several layers of significance are compressed into a single image; and his imagery has a protean charm that constantly changes and grows beneath the reader's eye. To satisfy Pope, the meaning of a line must be closely associated with its verbal music. A slow worker, he would endlessly repeat a passage until it had achieved its final shape; and Swift describes him walking in his garden with a sheaf of nearly indecipherable notes,* often scrawled across the backs of old letters, out of which, little by little, he evolved the image or cadence that he needed.

So decisive was Pope's influence, and so strong, even tyrannous, his hold upon succeeding writers, that the Romantics came to regard him as the type of arch-reactionary, who had twisted and tortured English poetic diction into a series of dead, unmeaning arabesques. Hazlitt summed up the case for the prosecution.† Pope's mind, he declared, was 'the antithesis of strength and grandeur. . . . He was in poetry what the sceptic is in religion.' He was 'the poet of personality and polished life. . . . The fashion of the day bore sway in his mind over the immutable laws of nature. He preferred the artificial to the natural in passion, because the involuntary and uncalculating impulses of the one hurried him away with a force with which he could not grapple; while he could trifle with the conventional and superficial modifications of sentiment at will, laugh at or admire, put them on or off like a masquerade dress. . . .' Yet even Hazlitt felt obliged to concede that 'the question, whether Pope was a poet, has hardly yet been settled, and is hardly worth settling; for if he was not a great poet, he must have been a great prose-writer; that is, he was a great writer of some sort. . . . The capacious soul of Shakespeare had an intuitive and mighty sympathy with whatever could enter into the soul of man. . . .

* 'Now backs of letters, though design'd
For those who more will need 'em,
Are fill'd with hints, and interlin'd,
Himself can hardly read 'em.'
                Dr Swift to Mr Pope, 1727.
† Byron appeared for the defence. See Byron to Thomas Moore, 3 May 1821.

Pope had an exact knowledge of all that he himself loved or hated, wished or wanted. . . .'

Seen through Hazlitt's eyes, Pope's chief offence was that he had been pre-eminently a social man and a 'poet of personality and polished life'. In the Romantic view, every poet is at heart a born rebel; and Pope's intellect was perfectly attuned to the conditions of the existing social system. When Lord Chesterfield remarked that 'the present age has . . . the honour and pleasure of being extremely well with me', he was voicing the mood of a far more self-complacent epoch; but Pope, too, despite the evils of his day – religious persecution, political strife, the rise of Sir Robert Walpole and 'the moneyed interest' – did not undervalue the society in which he had been born and bred; and his 'exact knowledge' of that society was among his greatest literary assets. He was qualified to speak to his contemporaries in the terms they understood. Unlike the hard-pressed, neglected Romantics, he could rely on a receptive audience – no small group of rebellious sympathizers, but the consensus of educated men and women. 'Any man who wears a powdered wig and a sword,' wrote Johnson, extolling the civilization of a slightly later age, 'is ashamed to be illiterate'; and Pope's readers would have felt equally ashamed, had they failed to recognize one of the classical references with which he winged his modern satires.

The poet's attitude towards his audience – friendly, easy, sympathetic – had an important effect upon his literary style. Pope addresses his poems to the *whole* man – not only to a man in his desperate, rapturous, elegiac moments, but to the more prosaic aspects of his personality, to his worldly wisdom, his sense of humour, his social tastes and intellectual leanings. Another result of this happy relation was his splendid self-confidence – 'the first requisite', decided Johnson, 'to great undertakings; he, indeed, who forms his opinion of himself in solitude . . . is very liable to error, but it was the felicity of Pope to rate himself at his real value'. Pope's spirit had always been proud; and, by 1728, whatever doubts may have occasionally troubled him must have long ago subsided. Nevertheless, he was about to publish a work that would show him at his least Olympian. In *The Dunciad* his proud self-confidence seems to have degenerated into furious arrogance, and we observe the grosser manifestations of the personal struggle that had absorbed him since his boyhood.

Although we cannot hope to lay bare the origins of genius or, indeed, define its nature – is it a characteristic entirely unique, or simply an exalted form of talent? – we can distinguish some of the outward circumstances that frequently accompany its birth and growth. Every masterpiece appears to be the record of a conflict, of the artist's struggle against an unkind universe and of his efforts, no less passionate and prolonged, to harmonize his own character. Pope's youth might have been especially calm and cheerful, had he not been attacked on the verge of adolescence by a crippling and disfiguring disease. Thenceforward, between his mind and his body, there had existed a perpetual state of civil strife; and from his bodily reverses and from a more general sense of frustration – the feeling that he was weak where others were powerful, and powerful where the 'tall fellows' who surrounded him were insignificant and ineffective – sprang the agonized life-long conflict that he endeavoured to resolve through poetry. Pope's efforts to reconcile art and life included, as we have already seen, the composition of a eulogistic self-portrait; but meanwhile, with very much greater success, he was building up in his poetic creations a world of order, grace and dignity, an imaginative system in which the discordant materials of life were reduced to forms of classic elegance.

When we are considering *The Dunciad*, such a description of the poet's method may seem curiously ill-applied. His warmest admirers are bound to admit that it is a mis-begotten masterpiece, which occupies the same position in the work of Pope as *Bouvard et Pécuchet* among Flaubert's novels. Vulgarity, stupidity, futility are not themselves enlivening subjects; and the poet who devotes over a thousand lines to depicting Dullness and evoking its atmosphere, evidently runs a grave risk. But Pope was delighted by his offspring, which, he said, not only included his most beautiful couplet, but had cost him 'as much pains as anything I ever wrote'. It was 'my chef d'oeuvre', he assured Swift in January 1728; and 'after I am dead and gone', it would be 'printed with a large commentary'. Nor did his affection wane; and, lest his successors should forget to supply the critical apparatus that his work demanded, no sooner had the poem appeared than he began to furnish it with learned notes – lengthy footnotes, *The Prolegomena of Scriblerus*, *Testimonies of Authors* and an elaborate *Dunciad Variorum* – until all three books of the original poem were firmly embedded in a solid mass of prose.

On 21 May 1728, Pope celebrated his fortieth birthday; on the 18th, the earlier version of *The Dunciad*, *An Heroic Poem*, accompanied by an address from the publisher to the reader and, at that stage, only nineteen footnotes, all comparatively brief, appeared without the author's name. Even the title-page that Pope had drawn up revealed his natural 'love of artifice', the imprint, 'DUBLIN, Printed, LONDON Reprinted for A. DODD, 1728', being deliberately planned to mislead. No Irish edition had ever existed; and Mrs Dodd, an industrious saleswoman of pamphlets and news-sheets, was almost certainly not the real publisher, but seems to have been acting on behalf of the printer James Bettenham, who subsequently claimed the copyright. Quite apart from his relish of mystification, Pope had had a sound prudential motive; if the work should happen to run into trouble, he could point to the strange circumstances in which it had entered the world, and assert that Mrs Dodd's action had been totally unauthorized. Another ingenious move was to attach to the first edition an advertisement that announced the forthcoming publication of *The Progress of Dulness*, a non-existent poem on the same theme, thus suggesting that *The Dunciad* was not the heroic burlesque by the famous translator of the *Iliad*, of which reports had already gone round London. Pope's stratagem had a somewhat absurd result. His advertisement caught the eye of Edmund Curll, who immediately dashed into print with just the kind of work that the reading public now expected.*

From these inky clouds emerged one of the most remarkable productions in the history of English verse. Pope, however, was not breaking new ground. The subject of literary dullness had long attracted English satirists; and they had often pontificated, more or less effectively, against the pretensions of contemporary poetasters and the faults of modern taste.† Pope's greatest example was Dryden's *Mac Flecknoe*, the satire of 217 lines with which, in 1682, he had belaboured the ambitious versifier Thomas Shadwell, who, after the accession of a Protestant sovereign, was to succeed him as Historiographer Royal and Poet Laureate.‡ *The Dunciad's* readers were, of course, expected to recognize its origins; and, having enjoyed Pope's magnificent preliminary picture of the Goddess Dulness and her Kingdom:

> Here she beholds the Chaos dark and deep,
> Where nameless somethings in their causes sleep ...
> How Hints, like spawn, scarce quick in embryo lie,
> How new-born Nonsense first is taught to cry,
> Maggots half-form'd, in rhyme exactly meet,
> And learn to crawl upon poetic feet.
> Here one poor Word a hundred clenches§ makes,
> And ductile dulness new meanders takes. ...

* For a much more detailed account of the problems involved, see the Introduction to *The Dunciad*, edited by James Sutherland, Twickenham Edition. Vol. V.

† 'The good work had been carried on by many of Pope's dunces themselves', *The Dunciad*, edited by James Sutherland. Introduction.

‡ Thomas Shadwell (1642?–92), a true-blue Protestant, had himself attacked Dryden and the pro-Catholic court party earlier the same year. In 1689, after the fall of James II, Shadwell obtained the posts of which Dryden had been stripped.

§ Puns.

– they would naturally turn back to Dryden's account of a similar forcing-house of current nonsense:

> Where their vast Courts the Mother-Strumpets keep,
> And, undisturb'd by Watch, in silence sleep.
> Near these a Nursery erects its head,
> Where Queens are form'd, and future Hero's bred;
> Where unfledg'd Actors learn to laugh and cry,
> Where infant Punks their tender voices try,
> And little *Maximins* the Gods defy.

Between Dryden's method and Pope's, however, they might have noticed one important difference. The justification of poetic satire is that it should enlarge its theme. In his masterpiece, *Absalom and Achitophel*, Dryden's eloquent dislike magnifies every personage he introduces; so that, on the bad eminence to which he has raised them, Achitophel and Zimri – Shaftesbury and Buckingham – become enormously impressive figures; while in *Mac Flecknoe*, even the tun-bellied Shadwell is invested with a kind of burlesque dignity. The satirist, before he indulges his hatred, must be sure that he has a worthy object; but Pope's hatred provided its own excuse – it was a greedily self-centred passion; and, although he was fascinated by the idea of destroying the Dunces, none of the opponents who had excited his contempt and disgust was capable of arousing any nobler feelings. As a rule, they were nonentities, 'nameless names', nowadays only remembered because they happen to have exasperated Pope. This was a danger that Swift had foreseen. 'Take care,' he had written on 26 November 1725, 'the bad poets do not outwit you, as they have served the good ones in every age, whom they have provoked to transmit their names to posterity. . . . Gildon will be as well known as you if his name gets into your verses. . . .' Such, indeed, was the Dunces' good fortune. 'Could you have let them alone,' protested Cibber in 1742, 'by this time, poor souls, they had been all peacefully buried in oblivion! But the very lines you have so sharply pointed to destroy them will now remain but so many of their epitaphs. . . .'

That Pope's inquisitorial campaign had no very serious moral motive is demonstrated by the thorough-going revision of his poem that he undertook in later years, when, besides adding a new Book, he produced a completely new hero, dethroning the insignificant Theobald and boldly substituting Colley Cibber, who now presented a more engaging target. Among the most obvious weaknesses of the original version was that Theobald himself had failed to take shape. Perhaps 'Tibbald' was a somewhat colourless man. Certainly Pope found it impossible to endow him with any genuinely distinctive features. He remains a type of the bad poet, as the satirist had already established it in *Peri Bathous*, a blank personification of the various qualities that he had inherited from his great primaeval parent:

> In each she marks her image full exprest,
> But chief, in Tibbald's monster-breeding breast*. . .
>   She ey'd the Bard, where supperless he sate,
> And pin'd, unconscious of his rising fate;
> Studious he sate, with all his books around,
> Sinking from thought to thought, a vast profound!
> Plung'd for his sense, but found no bottom there;
> Then writ, and flounder'd on, in mere despair.

Thus *The Dunciad* is a poem that lacks a hero; and its charm consists in the imposing periphery that Pope constructs around a central void. But, if he did not sufficiently detest Theobald, he had many other attractive private foes. For example, there was his neighbour Lady Mary, whom, since the appearance of *The Capon's Tale* had whetted his appetite, he regarded with more and more impassioned loathing, and whose memory he proceeded to attack in a peculiarly offensive couplet. How he should launch his attack demanded careful thought. And, having at first contemplated ridiculing her as a dishevelled literary maenad –

> See Pix and slip-shod W— traipse along,
> With heads unpinn'd and meditating song.†

– he decided to adopt an entirely different line. Lady Mary had never been allowed to forget her disastrous friendship with her French admirer; and Pope revived the story that she had swindled Rémond out of his hardearned South Sea winnings. The stroke was oblique; he reminds his reader of a practice common in the London brothels, whose inmates often went by the names of fashionable modern beauties:

> As the sage dame, experienc'd in her trade,
> By names of Toasts retails each batter'd jade,
> (Whence hapless Monsieur much complains at Paris
> Of wrongs from Duchesses and Lady Marys). . . .

Should an objection be raised, Pope could reply that the critic had

---

* A reference to the mythological pantomimes that Theobald composed for John Rich.
    † A variant of this couplet was inserted, without Lady Mary's name. Mrs Mary Pix was a struggling dramatist, who belonged to a far less distinguished social milieu.

evidently missed his point – he referred, not to the real Lady Mary, but to a mercenary imposter for whom the mistress of the brothel had borrowed Lady Mary's name – knowing, of course, that the use of her name alone would be enough to revive the old scandal. In 1735, moreover, he added a footnote: 'This passage,' he explained, 'was thought to allude to a famous lady who cheated a French wit of 5000 pounds in the South-Sea year. But the author meant it in general of all bragging travellers, and of all whores and cheats under the name of ladies.'*

Otherwise the victims at whom he struck were usually his fellow-writers, some of them already dead, but many still alive and scribbling. Not infrequently he could claim a solid grievance; in an appendix, Pope printed *A List of Books, Papers, and Verses, in which our Author was abused, printed before the Publication of the DUNCIAD*, including thirty-four items, from Dennis's early pamphlet attacking the *Essay on Criticism* to the most recent diatribes against himself and Swift. The eighteenth century was an age of paper warfare; and both Pope's fame and his own aggressive instincts had made him a particularly easy target. No doubt he had suffered; but, although the journalists had hurt and annoyed him, few, with the exception of John Dennis, had done him any lasting damage. Indeed, he seems to have enjoyed the excitement of a hard-fought battle; and, besides engaging his real antagonists, he also directed his shafts at completely inoffensive characters. When Topham Beauclerk enquired of Johnson why, he supposed, Pope had devoted a satirical couplet to the harmless clergyman he called 'modest Foster', 'Sir', replied Johnson, 'he hoped it would vex somebody'. That Pope often vexed merely for the sake of vexing is obvious throughout *The Dunciad*. His resentment appears to extend far beyond the immediate field of action; and again and again a terrible distaste for life, and for the squalor of man's physical existence – a distaste no less pronounced than Swift's – bursts forth in a repellent image.

> In ev'ry loom our labours shall be seen,
> And the fresh vomit run for ever green!

proves to be a daring parody of the 'late noble author', Lord Halifax. But

> Like the vile straw that's blown about the streets
> The needy Poet sticks to all he meets. . . .

was an entirely original product of the satirist's imagination. Here, as through a cavernous archway, we glimpse a perspective of melancholy

---

* This footnote was omitted from subsequent editions of *The Dunciad*.

London streets, where a cold east wind is scourging the house-fronts, and driving dirt and dust across the cobbles.

Pope's ridicule of the Dunces, writes a perceptive critic, 'occupies a mere corner in the universal illumination of the ludicrous and the sordid'. But Pope is constantly returning to particular instances of human folly; and the fact that we cannot appreciate *The Dunciad* without referring to the notes and index – who were Bond, Foxton, Jacob, Durgen, Duckett, Welsted, Concanen, Mears and Brown? – makes it an exceedingly difficult poem from the uninstructed reader's point of view. Pope had forgotten nothing, and forgiven no one. Well over a hundred personages are called up to receive their punishment; and, besides branding them as stupid and trivial, the Grand Inquisitor goes on to insist that they are poor and mean and ugly, half-starved citizens of Grub Street, glad to turn out a pamphlet or play for a few much-needed shillings. It must be admitted, however, that he does not spare the more powerful. His first publisher, Jacob Tonson, and 'lofty Lintot', who had published his *Iliad*, were both important businessmen; but Pope associated them with Curll in a singularly grotesque episode, when the tree, at the Goddess's behest, run an awkward race along the Strand, and Curll slips on the nauseous puddle left that morning by his own 'Corinna'.*

For Pope's contemporaries, part of the poem's attraction was its mock-heroic framework; each book parodies the epic mode, and is full of Homeric and Virgilian echoes. Although the opening scenes are staged in contemporary London, the time is not the current year, but Lord Mayor's Day, 1719; and why Pope should have chosen this comparatively remote period is a question that still requires an answer. Perhaps the early draft that Swift had snatched from the fire concerned the election of a City Poet – a servile office, which naturally involved a steady output of mediocre verses. That year, the writer selected had been Dryden's adversary Elkanah Settle,† and the Lord Mayor was Sir George Thorold; and Pope recalls their joint triumph in his stateliest mock-majestic vein:

> 'Twas on the day, when Thorold, rich and grave,
> Like Cimon triumph'd, both on land and wave:‡
> (Pomps without guilt, of bloodless swords and maces,
> Glad chains, warm furs, broad banners, and broad faces).

* In a note, 'Curll's Corinna' is identified with Mrs Thomas, who had sold him Pope's early letters to Cromwell.

† Elkanah Settle (1648–1724), playwright and versifier, immortalized by Dryden as Doeg in the second part of *Absalom and Achitophel*.

‡ Cimon, the fifth-century Athenian soldier who obtained a double victory over the barbarians.

Now Night descending, the proud scene was o'er,
But liv'd in Settle's numbers, one day more.
Now Mayr's and Shrieves all hush'd and satiate lay,
Yet eat in dreams the custard of the day;
While pensive Poets painful vigils keep,
Sleepless themselves to give their readers sleep.

Among these sleepless writers was the indefatigable Theobald; and, as the poem gets into its epic stride, he is shown building a pyramid of books from which he invokes the tutelary goddess. Having granted him the beatific vision he seeks and crowned him as her favourite son, Dullness next proclaims a day of rejoicing, to be celebrated in the Homeric style with 'high, heroic Games', and held on the site of the Strand's ancient Maypole. Pope gives all these contests an elaborately fantastic or indecent turn. After the foot-race, a competition is organized to determine which of the Dunces can relieve himself most manfully – the first prize is the novelist Mrs Haywood: the consolation-prize, a chamber-pot. Then they display their skill at tickling a noble patron – here the ingenious youth who prevails is a homosexual interloper; at cat-calling; at swimming and diving in the filthy Fleet Ditch; and at exerting their soporific powers over the assembled crowd.

Meanwhile we have had a glimpse of the Roman goddess of the sewers attending Jove upon his heavenly close-stool, and have followed Jonathan Smedley, the Dean of Clogher and an old enemy of Swift's, into the region of the Mud-nymphs:

... Young Lutetia, softer than the down,
Nigrina black and Merdamante brown

from which he rises again, 'clad in majesty of mud', accompanied by a clap of thunder –

Shaking the horrors of his ample brows,
And each ferocious feature grim with ooze.

In Book II, the Goddess's challenge to her worshippers:

'Here strip my children! here at once leap in!
Here prove who best can dash thro' thick and thin,
And who the most in love of dirt excel,
Or dark dexterity of groping well.'

seems to have been taken up by Pope himself. The early eighteenth century was not a squeamish age; but Pope certainly outdid his competitors in their love of scatalogical pleasantries; and, like Swift, he reveals a morbid affection for any aspect of human existence that he found unnerving and revolting. May he not perhaps, while he ducked and befouled the Dunces, have sought a method of symbolic revenge against his own defective flesh-and-blood? It was a horror of life that had helped to produce *The Dunciad*, just as much as the hatred he professed for 'the common enemies of mankind'.

Many great writers, from Shakespeare to Tolstoy, have experienced the same emotions – a fear and horror of life, powerfully counterbalanced by the love of beauty and the joy of living. In *The Dunciad* Pope displays both his destructive and his creative genius; and, although Cloacina and the Mud-nymphs overshadow Book II, the grimmest passages are enlightened with noble passages of poetic fancy. When the 'three Cambridge sophs' and the trio of 'pert Templars' engage in their sleep-giving contest, Pope compares them to pine-trees that sway and nod beneath a summer gale:

> Then mount the clerks; and in one lazy tone,
> Thro' the long, heavy, painful page, drawl on;
> Soft, creeping, words on words, the sense compose,
> At ev'ry line, they stretch, they yawn, they doze.
> As to soft gales top-heavy pines bow low
> Their heads, and lift them as they cease to blow,
> Thus oft they rear, and often the head decline,
> As breathe, or pause, by fits, the airs divine:
> And now to this side, now to that, they nod,
> As verse, or prose, infuse the drowzy God.

A succession of commentators, old and new, have credited *The Dunciad* with a moral tendency. 'One cannot fully appreciate the poem,' declares a modern critic, 'until one recognises the genuine moral indignation behind it.' Well, Pope himself always believed that he wrote in the spirit of a high-minded moralist; but the indignation that excited him sprang ultimately from a somewhat turbid source. Others, less sure of the poem's morality, have been content to dwell on its astounding vigour. Warton, for example, although he deprecated its 'excessive vehemence', added that the poem 'has been compared to the geysers propelling a vast column of boiling water by the force of subterranean fire'. But neither its dubious morality nor its indubitable energy lends *The Dunciad* its true distinction. At its worst, a rogues' gallery of indifferent writers, at its best, like the *Essay on Criticism*, it is a poem about the art of writing; which Pope illustrates, not only by negative means, but through his own magnificent example. Style, and the uses and abuses of language, inspire him to his highest flights of eloquence; and the faults of bad poets prove a far more rewarding subject than their repellent personalities, whether he is satirizing pedestrian scribblers who take refuge beneath a load of scholarship:

> Here to her Chosen all her works she shows;
> Prose swell'd to verse, Verse loitring into prose;
> How random Thoughts now meaning chance to find,
> Now leave all memory of sense behind:
> How Prologue into Prefaces decay,
> And these to Notes are fritter'd quite away.

or derides their fondness for the mixed metaphor:

> She sees a Mob of Metaphors advance,
> Pleas'd with the Madness of the mazy dance. . . .
> How Time himself stands still at her command,
> Realms shift their place, and Ocean turns to land.
> Here gay Description Ægypt glads with showers;
> Or gives to Zembla fruits, to Barca flowers. . . .
> On cold December fragrant chaplets blow,
> And heavy harvest nod beneath the snow.

By the time he reached Book III, even Pope had had almost enough of the squalor of the modern literary world; and we are translated to an imaginary universe, bathed in the romantic light of prophecies and visions. Slumbering with his head on the Goddess's lap, Theobald dreams that he beholds his worthy predecessor Elkanah Settle; and Settle predicts the rapid decay of learning destined to overtake contemporary Europe. At this point, Book III reaches its tremendous climax; and what has hitherto been a profession of personal dislikes becomes a general trump of doom. Augustan Englishmen believed their civilization to be directly descended from that of the Roman Empire in the first and second centuries. But they had also heard of the Chinese Empire, its wise rulers and law-giving sages; and Pope therefore describes how an early Chinese emperor had ordained a solemn Burning of the Books:

> 'Far Eastward cast thine eye, from whence the Sun
> And orient Science at a birth begun.
> One man immortal all that pride confounds,
> He, whose long Wall the wand'ring Tartar bounds.
> Heav'ns! what a pyle! whole ages perish there:
> And one bright blaze turns Learning into air.'

The civilization of the Roman Empire itself had at length declined and perished; and it was with the first couplet of the passage transcribed below that Pope once 'declared his own ear to be most gratified':*

> 'Lo where Mœotis sleeps, and hardly flows
> The freezing Tanais thro' a waste of Snows,
> The North by myriads pours her mighty sons,
> Great nurse of Goths, of Alans, and of Huns. . . .
> See, where the Morning gilds the palmy shore,
> (The soil that arts and infant letters bore)
> His conqu'ring tribes th'Arabian prophet draws,
> And saving Ignorance enthrones by Laws.
> See Christians, Jews, one heavy sabbath keep;
> And all the Western World believe and sleep.
>
>   'Lo Rome herself, proud mistress now no more
> Of arts, but thund'ring against Heathen lore. . . .
> See, the Cirque falls! th'unpillar'd Temple nods!
> Streets pav'd with Heroes, Tyber choak'd with Gods!
> Till Peter's Keys some christen'd Jove adorn,
> And Pan to Moses lends his Pagan horn;
> See graceless Venus to a Virgin turn'd,
> Or Phidias broken, and Apelles burn'd.'

It is interesting that Pope, brought up as a devout Catholic, should, like Gibbon, have identified the progress of Christianity with the decline of art and science. No doubt, he would have objected that he was merely speaking for Elkanah Settle. But, once Settle eventually falls silent after 222 resounding lines, it is the poet who rounds off *The Dunciad* in a gigantic burst of lamentation. Chaos is eternal; Order temporal. Human intelligence is a transitory gleam, soon submerged by everlasting darkness. Poetry, the prime exponent of Order, must submit at last to blind inanity:

> She comes! she comes! the sable Throne behold
> Of *Night* primaeval, and of *Chaos* old!
> Before her, *Fancy's* gilded clouds decay,
> And all its varying Rain-bows die away.
> *Wit* shoots in vain its momentary fires,
> The meteor drops, and in a flash expires.
> As one by one, at dread Medea's strain,
> The sick'ning stars fade off th'ethereal plain;
> As Argus' eyes by Hermes' wand opprest,
> Clos'd one by one to everlasting rest;
> Thus, at her felt approach, and secret might,
> *Art* after *Art* goes out, and all is night. . . .

* Johnson admitted, however, when he told this story, that he could not understand the poet's choice.

Lo! thy dread Empire, CHAOS! is restor'd;
Light dies before thy uncreating word:
Thy hand, great Anarch! lets the curtain fall;
And Universal Darkness buries all.*

On the Dunces, whose triumph he thus predicted, the effect of Pope's poem was everything he hoped for. They were astonished, confounded, maddened, torn between bitter resentment and involuntary admiration; and, when the alarming volume was about to appear, 'a crowd of authors besieged the shop; entreaties, advices, threats of law and battery, nay, cries of treason, were all employed to hinder the coming out of *The Dunciad*'; while 'the booksellers and hawkers made as great efforts to procure it. . . .' Meetings were held, 'to consult of hostilities against the author'. One Dunce appealed to Sir Robert Walpole, 'assuring him Mr Pope was the greatest enemy the government had; and another bought his image in clay, to execute him in effigy; with which sad sort of satisfaction the gentlemen were a little comforted.'

Pope himself was unperturbed. 'My brother,' Mrs Rackett told Spence, 'does not seem to know what fear is. When some of the people that he had put into his *Dunciad* were so much enraged against him and threatened him so highly, he loved to walk alone,' and continued to visit his old friend Fortescue two miles away beyond the Thames. On these solitary walks, his only companion was his 'great faithful Danish dog', Bounce;† but at the time, his half-sister added, he always carried pistols in his pocket, remarking that, 'with pistols the least man in England was above a match for the largest'. Although both daily journalists and a scurrilous pamphleteer assured their readers that, since the publication of his book, he had been severely chastised, no assailant ever crossed his path; and, on 17 June, he wrote to Lord Oxford, who had recently expressed his 'kind concern', to inform him that his person was so far 'as unhurt (I thank God) as my temper. . . .' The harm that he suffered was of a much more subtle kind. In the past, he had often looked forward to reaching some secure haven, where he could enjoy the dignified status of an *honnête homme* and perhaps a measure of ordinary human happiness; and those hopes he had finally destroyed by publishing the first *Dunciad*. Henceforward he must devote his energies to a life of incessant work and warfare.

---

* Whereas all previous quotations are taken from the 1728 edition of *The Dunciad*, this passage appears in the much improved and enlarged version printed in *The Dunciad* of 1743.

† Pope, a life-long dog-lover, owned in succession several Great Danes, each of whom he named Bounce.

Appendix A

Having recorded Father Mannock's statement that Pope 'was a child of a particularly sweet temper and had a great deal of sweetness in his look when he was a boy', Spence continues: 'This is very evident in the picture drawn for him when he was about ten years old, in which his face is round, plump, and pretty, and of a fresh complexion. I have often heard Mrs Pope say that he was then exactly like that picture. . . . The laurel branch in that picture was not inserted originally, but was added long afterwards by Jervas.' Professor William Kurtz Wimsatt, author of *The Portraits of Alexander Pope*, identifies the picture to which Spence refers with a portrait of a boy, bearing the painted inscription '*A.Pope/Anno Aetatis/7*', that came up for sale at Christie's in October 1960, as a 'Van Loo Portrait of a Boy, said to be Alexander Pope . . .', and was acquired by Mr and Mrs James M. Osborn of New Haven, Connecticut, in whose collection it now hangs. Mr Osborn, of course, is the distinguished editor of Spence's *Observations*.

It would be pleasant to agree with Professor Wimsatt that this is indeed a portrait of the young Pope; but the provenance of the picture cannot be traced back beyond 1960; Professor Wimsatt admits that 'the style of the painting, the chevalier bearing of the child, the costume, and the coiffure, have an air that seems French'; and he points out that the portrait has a considerable resemblance to the portrait of the Old Pretender and his sister as children, executed by Nicholas de Largillière in 1695, now at the National Portrait Gallery. Certainly the so-called portrait of Pope has an extremely French look; and particularly French is the red bow tie – a fashion popular among the courtiers of Louis XIV – that the young sitter wears beneath his chin. Professor Wimsatt suggests that the artist may have been, not Van Loo, but possibly the *émigré* portraitist Simon Dubois, described by Vertue, who reached England in 1685.

It is, however, somewhat difficult to understand why Pope's father, a retired merchant, living in the country, and always anxious to avoid notice, should have commissioned so stylish a painter to portray his only son; or why the future poet should have been represented in the costume and attitude of an aristocratic young Frenchman. One possible theory remains, which I present with due deference. As devout Catholics, may not the Popes have owned a picture of their rightful sovereign's heir, adapted from Largillière's canvas, and, for the benefit of their Protestant neighbours, have passed it off as young Alexander's portrait? Later, when the sprig of laurel was painted in, this may have become a family tradition, accepted even by old Mrs Pope, whose memory – in 1726, when Spence made her acquaintance, she was already eighty-four – had, no doubt, become a little hazy.

Appendix B

Throughout the eighteenth century, publishing by the subscription method, though it led to many disputes between authors and publishers, often produced extremely good results. Having first advertised his 'Proposals', the writer, with his friends' help, proceeded to enlist a body of important subscribers, whose names appeared in a preliminary section of the book, and thus excited public interest. Pope had obtained particularly generous terms. Besides paying him £200 for each of the six volumes of his translations of the *Iliad*, Lintot gave him free of charge 650 subscription copies, valued at £900; while the poet was allowed to retain all the subscriptions that he had collected. It was by the sale of later editions that the publisher expected to recoup himself. But here Lintot was apparently disappointed, when a pirated Dutch edition reached the English book-market. He was less generous towards Pope over the translation of the *Odyssey*; and they failed to agree about the subscription copies that Pope expected he would provide for Broome. This difference may have inspired Pope's satirical description of Lintot in Book II of *The Dunciad*.

Bibliography

All books cited in the Bibliography were published in London.

Ault, Norman, (ed.) *The Prose Works of Alexander Pope*, 1936.
Ault, Norman, *New Light on Pope*, 1949.
Ayre, William, *Memoirs of the Life and Writings of Alexander Pope, Esq.*, 1745.

Brower, R. A., *Alexander Pope: The Poetry of Allusion*, 1959.

Callan, Norman, 'Alexander Pope', in *From Dryden to Johnson*, Pelican Guide to English Literature, 1957.
Cibber, Colley, *A Letter from Mr Cibber to Mr Pope*, 1742.
Collins, John Churton, *Bolingbroke; and Voltaire in England*, 1886.
Courthope, William John, *The Life of Alexander Pope*; with *The Works of Alexander Pope*, edited by Whitwell Elwin and W. J. Courthope, 1889.
Cowper, Mary Countess, *Diary*, 1864.

Dennis, Nigel, *Jonathan Swift*, 1965.
Dilke, Charles Wentworth, *The Papers of a Critic*, 1875.
Dobrée, Bonamy, *Alexander Pope*, 1951.

Eliot, T. S., *Homage to John Dryden*, 1924.

Ford, Boris (ed.), *From Dryden to Johnson*, 1957.
Fussell, Paul, *The Rhetorical World of Augustan Humanism*, 1965.

Gay, John, *Letters*, edited by C. F. Burgess, 1966.
Gay, John, *Trivia, or the Art of Walking the Streets of London*, with introduction and notes by W. H. Williams, 1922.
Gildon, Charles, *Memoirs of William Wycherley*, 1718.
Griffith, Reginald Harvey, *Alexander Pope: A Bibliography*, 1922.

Halsband, Robert, *The Life of Lady Mary Wortley Montagu*, 1956.

Hart, Jeffrey, *Viscount Bolingbroke: Tory Humanist*, 1965.

Hazlitt, William, *Lectures on the English Poets*, 1818.

Hervey, Lord, *Memoirs*, edited by Romney Sedgwick, 1931.

Honour, Hugh, *Chinoiserie; The Vision of Cathay*, 1961.

Hopkinson, M. R., *Married to Mercury: A Sketch of Lord Bolingbroke and his Wives*, 1936.

Hussey, Christopher, *English Gardens and Landscapes*, 1967.

Jack, Ian, *Augustan Satire*, 1952.

Knight, D., *Pope and the Heroic Tradition*, 1951.

Leavis, F. R., *Revaluations: Tradition and Development in English Poetry*, 1936.

Lees-Milne, James, *Earls of Creation*, 1962.

Malins, Edward, *English Landscaping and Literature*, 1966.

Mumby, Frank Arthur, *Publishing and Bookselling: A History*, 1956.

Murry, John Middleton, *Jonathan Swift*, 1954.

Plumb, J. A., *Sir Robert Walpole*, 1956.

Plumb, J. A., *The Growth of Political Stability in England, 1675–1725*, 1967.

Roscoe, William, *Works of Alexander Pope, with a Life of the Author*, 1824.

Ruffhead, Owen, *The Life of Alexander Pope, Esq.*, 1769.

Sherburn, George, *The Early Career of Alexander Pope*, 1934.

Sherburn, George (ed.), *The Correspondence of Alexander Pope*, 1956.

Sichel, Walter, *Bolingbroke and his Times*, 1901.

Sitwell, Edith, *Alexander Pope*, 1930.

Smithers, Peter, *The Life of Joseph Addison*, 1954.

Spence, Joseph, *Observations, Anecdotes and Characters of Books and Men*, edited by James M. Osborn, 1966.

Stephen, Leslie, *Alexander Pope*, 1880.

Sundon, Viscountess, *Memoirs*, edited by A. J. Thomson, 1847.

Swift, Jonathan, *Correspondence*, edited by Harold Williams, 1963.

Tillotson, Geoffrey, *On the Poetry of Pope*, 1938.

Tillotson, Geoffrey, *Pope and Human Nature*, 1958.

Vereker, Charles, *Eighteenth-Century Optimism*, 1967.

Walpole, Horace, *Letters*, edited by Mrs Paget Toynbee, 1903.

Warburton, William, *A Vindication of the Essay on Man*, 1739.

Ward, Charles E., *The Life of John Dryden*, 1961.

Warton, Joseph, *Essay on the Genius and Writings of Pope*, 1782.

Wentworth Papers, The, 1705–1739, edited by James J. Cartwright, 1883.

Wimsatt, William Kurtz, *The Portraits of Alexander Pope*, 1965.

Wortley Montagu, Lady Mary, *Letters and Works*, edited by Lord Wharncliffe 1837.

Wortley Montagu, Lady Mary, *The Complete Letters of Lady Mary Wortley Montagu*, edited by Robert Halsband, 1967.

Young, Edward, *Poetical Works*, 1864.

Source Notes

All books cited in these notes were published in London.

Page

2   This story, recorded by Joseph Warton in his *Essay on the Genius and Writings* of Pope, 1782, is unsupported by any documentary evidence. See George Sherburn, *The Early Career of Alexander Pope*, 1934.

3   Joseph Spence, *Observations, Anecdotes and Characters of Books and Men*, edited by James M. Osborn.

4   *Ibid.*

6, line 4   See J. A. C. Brown, *Pear's Medical Encyclopedia*, 1963. The disease is named after an English surgeon, P. Pott (1713–88).

6, line 33   Spence, op. cit.

7, line 16   *Ibid.*

7, line 19   *Ibid.*

8   *Ibid.*

10   *Ibid.*

11   Charles Gildon, *Memoirs of William Wycherley*, 1718.

12, line 6   *'An Epistle to Mr Dryden, occasion'd by his desiring the author to join with him in writing a comedy'.*

12, line 19   Wycherley to Pope, 22 March 1706.

12, line 27   Pope to Wycherley, 10 April 1706.

13   Spence, op. cit.

14, line 4   *Ibid.*

14, line 17   Walsh to Pope, 9 September 1706.

17   'An Epistle to Dr Arbuthnot', 1735.

20, line 8   Edith Sitwell, *Alexander Pope*, 1930.

20, line 34   Dryden, *Faction Displayed*, 1704.

24   Joseph Spence, *Observations, Anecdotes and Characters of Books and Men*, edited by James M. Osborn.

25   Pope to Cromwell, 28 April 1708.

28, line 5   *Ibid.*, 29 August 1709

28, line 34   *Ibid.*, 10 April 1710.

30   Pope to Martha Blount, 24 November 1714.

36   See also Pope to Walsh, 22 October 1706.

38, line 19   A notice of a popular epic poem, which appeared in 1696. See Edmund Gosse, *English Literature: An Illustrated Record*, 1926.

38, line 31   Edmund Gosse, op. cit.

42   Spence, op. cit.

43   Pope to Cromwell, 21 December 1711.

47   Pope to Caryll, 28 May 1712.

48, line 25   *Ibid.*, 12 November 1711.

48, line 38   See *Pastoral Poetry and an Essay on Criticism*, edited by E. Auda and Aubrey Williams, Introduction to *Windsor-Forest*, 1961

55   Joseph Warton, *An Essay on the Genius and Writings of Pope*, 1756.

57   Pope to Caryll, 30 April 1713.

58, line 25   *Ibid.*, February 1713.

58, line 36   Ellis Waterhouse, *Painting in Britain*, 1530–1790, 1953.

65   First published by John Dennis in his *Remarks on Several Passages in the Preliminaries to the Dunciad*, 1729.

67   *The Analysis of Beauty*, 1753.

68, line 7   Joseph Spence, *Observations, Anecdotes and Characters of Books and Men*, edited by James M. Osborn.

68, line 20   *The Celebrated Beauties*, 1709.

69, line 2   A. Mary Sharp, *The History of Ufton Court*, quoted by Geoffrey Tillotson, *The Poems of Alexander Pope*, vol. ii, 1962.

69, line 17   Bedingfield's letter is dated by George Sherburn, *The Correspondence of Alexander Pope*, 1956, as 16 May. Lintot's *Miscellaneous Poems* appeared four days later.

72   Philip Ayres's translation, 1680; for the French text, see *Le Comte de Gabalis, ou Entretiens sur les Sciences Secrètes*, edited by René-Louis Dôyon, Paris, 1921. Anatole France made free use of Villars's book in *La Rotisserie de la Reine Pédauque*.

76, line 3   Pope to Walsh, 2 July 1706.

76, line 9   For a detailed account of Pope's borrowings and parodies, see Geoffrey Tillotson, *On the Poetry of Pope*, 1938.

77, line 22   William Hazlitt, *Lectures on the English Poets*, 1818.

77, line 39   Geoffrey Tillotson, op. cit.

78   Spence, op. cit.

79   Geoffrey Tillotson, op. cit.

81   Belinda's game has often been replayed. For a careful analysis, see *The Rape of the Lock*, edited by Geoffrey Tillotson, Twickenham Edition, 1950, Appendix C.

85   A. Mary Sharp, op. cit.

86   *Journal to Stella*, 31 July 1711.

87, line 3   G. M. Trevelyan, *The Peace and the Protestant Succession*, 1936.

87, line 31   Pope to Caryll, 25 February 1714.

88   *Ibid.*, 1 May 1714.

90, line 3   Pope to Arbuthnot, 11 July 1714.

90, line 35   Joseph Spence, *Observations, Anecdotes and Characters of Books and Men*, edited by James M. Osborn.

90, line 40   *Ibid.*

92   *Ibid.*

93, line 25   Winston S. Churchill, quoting from an unidentified source, *Marlborough, his Life and Times*, 1934.

93, line 28   Spence, op. cit.

94   Peter Wentworth to his brother, 29 June 1714. *The Wentworth Papers*, edited by J. J. Cartwright, 1883.

95   G. M. Trevelyan, op. cit.

96, line 5   *The Wentworth Papers.*

96, line 27   Pope to Caryll, 13 July 1714.

96, line 38   *Ibid.*, 25 July 1714.

97   *Ibid.*, 16 August 1714.

98   Spence, op. cit.

99, line 13   *Ibid.*

99, line 40   Pope to Caryll, 25 September 1715.

100   Pope to Martha Blount, 6 October 1714.

101, line 16   Pope to Martha and Teresa Blount, [September?] 1714.

101, line 36   Pope to Teresa Blount, September 1714.

102   *Ibid.*, late October 1714.

103   See *Minor Poems*, edited by Norman Ault and John Butt, Twickenham Edition, 1964.

104   *Ibid.*

105   Pope to Martha Blount, 24 November 1714.

110, line 33   Joseph Spence, *Observations, Anecdotes and Characters of Books and Men*, edited by James M. Osborn.

110, line 35   Lintot to Pope, 10 June 1715.

111, line 32   Spence, op. cit.

112, line 1   *Ibid.*

112 line 17   For a detailed discussion of the problems involved, see Norman Ault, *New Light on Pope*, 1949.

119   Pope to Teresa and Martha Blount, 23 July 1715.

120, line 27   Lady Louisa Stuart, *Introductory Anecdotes*, attached to her grandmother Lady Mary's *Letters and Works*, 1861.

120, line 36   See Robert Halsband, *The Life of Lady Mary Wortley Montagu*, 1956, not only the latest, but by far the best and most authoritative biography.

124, line 3   For the authorship of these 'town eclogues', see Robert Halsband, op. cit.

124, line 27   Pope to Martha Blount, 19 August 1715.

125, line 5   Pope to Caryll, 11 October 1715.

125, line 22   *Ibid.*, December 1715.

126   Pope to Edward Blount, 21 January 1715.

127   Swift to Pope, 28 June 1715.

128, line 4   Pope to Martha Blount, March 1716.

128, line 18   See James Lees-Milne, *Earls of Creation*, 1962.

129   Joseph Spence to his mother, 1741. Quoted by Robert Halsband, *The Life of Lady Mary Wortley Montagu*.

130, line 13   *Weekly Journal, or Saturday Post*, 5 April 1718.

130, line 15   'The Life of John Buncle', 1770.

130, line 39   For a less gallant interpretation of Pope's behaviour, see Robert Halsband, op. cit.

132   For a discussion of this pamphlet's date – probably late in 1716 – see Norman Ault, *New Light on Pope*, 1949.

133   '*A Strange but True Relation how Edmund Curll . . . out of an extraordinary Desire of Lucre . . . was converted by certain Eminent Jews . . .*', April 1720.

136, line 11   Pope to Swift, 20 June 1716.

136, line 31   Pope to Lady Mary Wortley Montagu, 'Tuesday morning' [July 1716].

137   Robert Halsband, op. cit.

140   Pope to Lady Mary Wortley Montagu, 10 November 1716.

145, line 8   *Satyre* II, 1594–5.

145, line 36   See Charles Wentworth Dilke, *The Papers of a Critic*, 1875.

146   Pope to Martha Blount, [March 1716?).

150   Pope to Lady Mary Wortley Montagu, autumn 1717.

151   *Ibid.*, autumn 1717.

152, line 7   Pope to Caryll, 6 August 1717.

152, line 28   Pope to Teresa and Martha Blount, 13 September 1717.

152, line 39   Pope to Lady Mary Wortley Montagu, 1718.

153, line 14   Pope to Teresa and Martha Blount, September 1717.

153, line 25   Pope to Martha Blount?, September 1717?.

153, line 37   Pope to Gay, 8 November 1717.

156   Pope to Lady Mary Wortley Montagu, 1718.

157   Walter Sichel, *Bolingbroke and his Times*, 1901.

159   Pope to the Duke of Buckingham, 1718.

163, line 21   Pope to Broome, December 1719.

163, line 33   Pope to Lady Mary Wortley Montagu, 1720.

170, line 15   Lady Mary Wortley Montagu to Lady Mar, March 1721.

170, line 26   *Ibid.*, December 1721.

171 *To Mr Gay, who wrote him a congratulatory Letter on the finishing his House.*

173 Lady Louisa Stuart, *Introductory Anecdotes*, attached to her grandmother Lady Mary's *Letters and Works*, 1861.

175 Pope to Atterbury, 20 November 1717.

176, line 1 Joseph Spence, *Observations, Anecdotes and Characters of Books and Men*, edited by James M. Osborn.

176, line 14 Pope to Harcourt, 20 February 1723.

182 Spence, op. cit.

184, line 15 Pope to Edward Blount, 2 June 1725.

184, line 21 See Edward Malins, *English Landscaping and Literature*, 1966.

185 Pope to Edward Blount, 2 June 1725.

188 Lord Hervey, *Memoirs*.

190 See James Lees-Milne, *Earls of Creation*, 1962.

191, line 8 *Miscellanies. The Third Volume*, 1732.

191, line 10 Otherwise entitled *Of the Characters of Women*, 1735.

193, line 9 Pope to Tonson, May 1722 [?].

193, line 13 *Proposals for Printing the Dramatic Works of William Shakespeare.*

194 Leslie Stephen, *Alexander Pope*, 1880.

196, line 20 Pope to Caryll, 25 December 1725.

196, line 32 Pope to Broome, 29 June 1725.

198 See M. R. Hopkinson, *Married to Mercury*, 1936.

200 Pope to Swift, 28 June 1728.

201 Pope to the Earl of Strafford, June 1725.

203, line 5 George Sherburn, *The Early Career of Alexander Pope*, 1934.

203, line 37 Quoted by George Sherburn, op. cit.

204 *Memoirs of a certain Island adjacent to the Kingdom of Utopia.* See George Sherburn, op. cit.

205 Swift to Pope, 29 September 1725.

206 Swift and Pope to Lord Oxford, 3 July 1725.

207 Swift to the Rev. John Worrall, 15 July 1726.

208, line 3 Swift to the Rev. James Stopford, 20 July 1726.

208, line 18 Pope and Bolingbroke to Swift, 14 December 1725.

208, line 31 Pope to Lord Oxford, 7 November 1725.

209, line 6 Pope to Fortescue, 2 April 1726.

209, line 19 Additional note to *The Dunciad*, edition of 1729.

209, line 36 Swift to Pope, 4 August 1726.

210 *Ibid.*, August 1726.

212, line 13 *Life of Voltaire*, Miscellaneous Works.

212, line 34 Owen Ruffhead, *The Life of Alexander Pope, Esq.*, 1769.

213 Pope to Aaron Hill, September 1726.

214, line 6 Pope to Broome, 4 June 1726.

Page

214, line 24   Quoted by James M. Osborn in his introduction to Joseph Spence, *Observations, Anecdotes and Characters of Books and Men*, 1966, from Joseph Warton's notebook, now at Trinity College, Oxford.

220   George Sherburn, *The Early Career of Alexander Pope*, 1934.

221, line 9   Pope to Swift, 16 November 1726.

221, line 32   Gay to Swift, 17 November 1726.

222, line 13   Pope to Fortescue, 16 May 1727.

222, line 27   'Dr Swift to Mr Pope, while he was writing the Dunciad', 1727.

223, line 25   Swift to Gay, 26 February 1728.

223, line 31   J. H. Plumb, *Sir Robert Walpole*, 1960.

223, line 34   Bolingbroke to Swift, headed 'at Pope's', 17 June 1727.

224, line 20   Swift to Sheridan, 12 August 1727.

224, line 34   *Ibid.*, 2 September 1727.

225, line 9   Pope to Sheridan, 6 September 1727.

225, line 23   Mrs Howard to Swift, 16 August 1727.

226   Pope to Swift, 2 October 1727.

227, line 4   Pope to Caryll, 10 May 1727.

227, line 12   *Ibid.*, 28 March 1727.

228, line 5   Pope to Swift, 8 March 1727.

228, line 27   Pope to Caryll, 5 October 1727.

229   Pope to Oxford, 26 December 1727.

230   Gay and Pope to Swift, 22 October 1727.

232, line 19   *Epistle to Fenton*.

232, line 32   Broome to Fenton, 3 May 1728.

235   William Kurtz Wimsatt, *The Portraits of Alexander Pope*, 1965.

237   Samuel Johnson, *Lives of the Poets*.

238   'An Epistle to Dr Arbuthnot', 1735.

239   Joseph Spence, *Observations, Anecdotes and Characters of Books and Men*, edited by James M. Osborn.

240   Pope to Swift, 23 March 1728.

241   See Mrs Thrale's remarks on *The Spectator. Thraliana*, 4 November 1728.

243, line 2   William Hazlitt, *Lectures on the English Poets*, 1818.

243, line 8   *The Rambler*, no. 97, February 1751.

244   Spence, op. cit.

246   Colley Cibber, *A Letter from Mr Cibber to Mr Pope*, 1742.

249   Geoffrey Tillotson, *On the Poetry of Pope*, 1938.

251, line 29   Norman Callan, 'Alexander Pope', in *From Dryden to Johnson*, 1957

251, line 35   Joseph Warton, *Essay on the Genius and Writings of Pope*, 1782.

254, line 16   *A Collection in Pieces in Verse and Prose . . .*, by Richard Savage, 1732.

254, line 25   *A Popp upon Pope. Or, a true and faithful Account of a late horrid and barbarous Whipping committed on the body of Sawney Pope . . .*, 1728.

Index

Loiret river, 198 & n.
London, 106, 125–6; bawdy-houses, 104; coffee houses, *see* coffee houses; taverns, 88 (*see also* Swan Tavern); *see also under individual place-names*
London Journal, 196
Longinus, 64
Longleat, 100
Lorrain, 181
Louis XIV, 73, 197, 255
Louisa, Princess, 230
Lovelace (in Richardson's *Clarissa Harlowe*), 202
Lucan, Pope's assessment of, 115; Rowe's translation of, 31
Lull, Ramon, 72 & n.
Lumley, Lord, 30
Le Lutrin, *see* Boileau
Lyons, 161
Lytton, Mr, 30

Madan, Captain Martin, 178
Maddison, G., 143 n.
Mandeville, Bernard, 111
Mann, Sir Horace, Horace Walpole's letters to, 186–7 & n.
Mannock, Father William, 3 n., 10, 255
Mapledurham, home of Blount sisters, 43, 102, 104, 119, 124, 126, 156
Mar, Earl of, 124
Mar, Lady, 170–1, 233
Maratta, Carlo, 128, 217
Marble Hill, Mrs Howard's house at, 187–90
Marlborough, Sarah, Duchess of, 86, 135, 153–6
Marlborough, 1st Duke of, 38, 129 n., 153
Marriot, Betty, 105 & n., 106
Masham, Lady, 95
Mather, Cotton, 229
Mawson's New Buildings, 127, 163; *see also* Chiswick
Menelaus, 142
Middlesex, Lord, 215
Mignard, Nicolas, 129 n.
Millamant, 121
Milton, John, 7, 48, 115, 140, 194, 198, 216; *Paradise Lost*, 1, 20 & n.
Miscellanea, 227
Miscellanies (eds. Pope and Swift), 209 & n., 222, 227–8, 230–3
Miscellanies, Poetical, (ed. Tonson), 1, 21, 68
Montaigne, Michel de, 13, 59
Montgaillard, Paul de Ferrovil de, 71–2
Mordaunt, Charles, *see* Peterborough
Morley, Mrs, 67
Morris, Professor Ivan, 181 n.
Morris, Roger, 188–9 & n.

Murray, Mrs Griselda, 165 & n.; mother of, 172
Mycenaean Age, 114

Needham, Mother, 104 & n., 238
Nelson, Mrs (Cromwell's Sappho), 25, 47
Newcastle, Duke of, 215
Nichols, John, 215
'nobleman look', 174 n.
Non-conformists, 94 n.
Northchurch, 205 n.
Nuneham, house of Lord Harcourt, 158; *see also* Stanton Harcourt

Oldfield, Mrs, 57
Oldmixon, Mr, 131, 134
Orléans, 198 & n.
Orléans, Regent duc d', 175
Ormond, Duke of, 95, 119, 127
Orrery, Lord, 90
Osborn, James M., ed. Spence's *Observations, Anecdotes and Characters*, 218 n., 255, 261–6
Osnabrück, 223
Otway, Thomas, *Don Carlos*, 20
Ovid, 4, 7, 14, 28, 31; *Epistles*, 148; Dryden's translation of, 115; *Epistles*, Henry Cromwell's translation of, 25; *Heroides*, Dryden's translation of, 148; *see also* Pope, Works: Ovid translations
Oxford, City of, 99, 124, 153; University of, 119, 138, 215
Oxford, Lord, Robert Harley, 1st Earl of, 86–7, 89, 93–5, 97, 127, 135, 204; death of, 204 n.; imprisoned in Tower, 119, 164; South Sea Company of, *see* South Sea Company
Oxford, 2nd Lord, Edward, 204 n., 205–6, 229, 254

Palladian, Bridge at Wilton, 188 n.; coterie, 23, 182; style, 179; style, at Marble Hill, 189; villa of Lord Burlington, 127–8
Palladio, Andrea, 178, 189; *see also* G. Leoni
'Palladio, Dame', 180 n.
Pannini, G. P., 107
Pantheon, Roman, 107
Paracelsus, 73 n.
Paradise Lost (Milton), 1, 20 & n.
Paris, 161, 170
Parnell, Thomas, 89 & n., 91–2, 99–100, 127; death of, 168; Pope's correspondence with, 143; *Life of Zoilus*, 151; *Poems on Several Occasions*, 168; *Works*, ed. Pope, 168
Pascal, Blaise, 71